POPULAR ENTERTAINMENT RESEARCH

how to do it
and how to use it

by

BARBARA J. PRUETT

The Scarecrow Press, Inc.
Metuchen, N.J., & London
1992

British Library Cataloguing-in-Publication data available

Library of Congress Cataloging-in-Publication Data

Pruett, Barbara J., 1942–
    Popular entertainment research : how to do it and how to use
it / by Barbara J. Pruett.
        p.   cm.
    Includes index.
    ISBN 0-8108-2501-5 (alk. paper)
    1. Performing arts—Research.   I. Title.
PN1576.P78   1992
791'.072—dc20   92-3800

CONTENTS

DEDICATION

I owe heartfelt thanks to a number of people in two different professions who gave me their time, advice, and the benefit of their minds over the past two years. One of the major points I have tried to make in this book is that good research is largely the result of the people involved; it is not just the product of meticulous detective work, analysis of published literature, or the willingness of the researcher to put in countless hours of effort. It is frequently the assistance of others that puts the "spark" in your work. That assistance may come in many different forms: pointing out mistakes, teaching you something you don't know, checking your facts or verifying information, sharing a difference of opinion or perspective they may have, taking the time to give praise when it's honestly warranted, or providing encouragement when it is needed. Despite all of the professional skills that must be in place to do effective research, it is still the magic of interpersonal relationships and the juices of emotional involvement that are the core foundation upon which one builds the determination to keep going. The words, "You're on the right track, keep at it!" are worth more than anything.

First of all, several librarians have taken the time to provide professional support in their respective fields and I would like to acknowledge their help. Katharine Loughney, Reference Librarian in the Motion Picture, Broadcasting, and Recorded Sound Division of the Library of Congress, has been most helpful throughout the whole project. She's also working on a book (*Film, Television, and Video Periodicals;* a comprehensive annotated list) and we have been able to share new learning experiences and perplexing frustrations in a collegial fashion. Dorothy Swerdlove, Curator of the Billy Rose Theatre Collection in New York, has been a significant resource person with the theater portion of this work and has been most accommodating in helping me make additional contacts.

In England, Claire Hudson, Librarian at the Theatre Museum Library, spent considerable time acting as coordinator with other people on my behalf and provided professional expertise. Enid Foster, The Librarian at the British Theatre Association, also gave me the benefit of her years of theatre research knowledge and assisted with background material. Barrie MacDonald, the head of the Independent Broadcasting Authority Library, provided support in helping sort out and explain Great Britain's broadcasting system. And Gillian Hartnoll, Director of Library Services at the British Film Institute, introduced me to the resources of the BFI and suggested other contacts. She was the first person I met on my initial research trip to England, and her courtesy made all of the difference in the world.

Secondly, I would like to acknowledge the contributions that associates and friends in the entertainment business have made toward this book. When I started getting involved in entertainment research and writing in 1982, I was pretty much of a novice. Fifteen years of experience as a library director, researcher, and academic writer had developed my basic skills, but I still lacked an understanding of what daily life was like in the entertainment business. I've learned a lot from the performers, agents, venue owners, public relations people, disc jockeys, radio managers, writers, and technicians I've met. Nashville comedy and script writer Pat Galvin, agent and country music entrepreneur Jim Halsey, publicist Kathy Gangwisch, Sherrill and J.J. Jackson from the radio business, and singer George Hamilton IV all went out of their way to help me learn about the entertainment business at a time when I was still a stranger. In addition, there are several people who deserve special recognition for the part they have played in my life the past several years. For many years (long before we both settled into our respective entertainment industry niches), attorney Bennett Lincoff has been a most supportive friend and always willing to give me his honest opinion. Judy Massa, the music director of the Voice of America, has shared her professional knowledge and acted as the intermediary on several occasions when I needed to contact performers. She is most helpful, unselfish, and generous in ways that few people are willing to be. And I'm grateful to Patrick McGoohan for his kindness in sharing his ideas about writing and for the encouragement he has given me on my own writing. He is a decent man who, had he not become an actor, could have been a perceptive and thoughtful educator in the finest sense of the word.

People in show business have a very practical attitude toward their work, while people outside of it tend to see it in more academic and theoretical terms. Probably the most important thing I've learned over the past seven years is to distinguish between these frames of mind. One can write hundreds of academic articles about film theory, the philosophy that goes into the making of videos, or the reasons songs become hits, but the people on the front lines are most influenced by time, money, and the immediate problems they face on the set, the stage, or in the studio. Most of the people involved in trying to get something accomplished within the next few hours don't sit around analyzing their motivations. There's considerably less philosophy and symbolism in the real world. Consequently, this book reflects a more practical approach toward research and the reference resources I've selected for the book than it otherwise might have had before I became aware of the kinds of research needed by people who work in the entertainment industry.

I'm indebted to the performers who have given me interviews over the past seven years and their staffs who have spent time with me. The honest comments from some of the artists about the unique world in which they live and work have put the human element in it all and affected the direction of my work, the critical way I now evaluate the printed background information I read, and my attitude toward the industry itself. Although I never perceived that it would be this way when I started, I think that the interviews, more than anything else, have been the main source of the self-confidence I needed to develop in order to grow and survive. Nothing in the world will motivate you to work harder (and get better) than receiving the respect or trust from someone you hold in esteem.

I am lucky in that I have been able to meet or interview the people in the entertainment business I've admired and respected the most. Unexpectedly, several of these people have gone out of their way to help me, thereby giving much more to me than I ever could return to them through my writing or research skills. One or two have become friends. None of this was planned, nor could it have been.

Lastly, I would like to recognize the help editor Hank Johnson has given me. He has acted as my teacher, editor, mentor, and devil's advocate over the past ten years. He occasionally took the meaning of "constructive criticism" to new heights, but he *always* justified his comments with the reasons why he made them.

I've been influenced by the personal attitudes and ideas of many of the people I've met the past seven years. I think you should look for influences; you want to find those people who are better at it than you are, or whose ideas and logic differ from yours, and learn from them. I was lucky enough to meet people in both professions who helped me do that.

Barbara Pruett
Washington, DC

INTRODUCTION

I have two pieces of advice for entertainment researchers:

First: Make friends with a librarian. It's the best advice I can give you.

Second: There is no substitute for hard work.

This book won't contain shortcuts; rather, it will try to tell you how to do a thorough job and perhaps how to make your work better. If it achieves its goal, this book will give you ideas about how to do more work, not less.

The ability to do successful research is a learned skill, but it helps if you naturally love solving a good mystery. To do entertainment research, you need a detective's mind. This is essential because one has to look at the question at hand with an investigative attitude and not prejudge or assume the answer will be found automatically through a predetermined process or in a certain location. Good librarians are masters at the art of discovery and, as with all detectives, it's their job to know *how to find* the answers; it is not their job to *know* the answers. Once you make this distinction, you will begin to understand why librarians should be part of your research detective team.

A team? What team? In the entertainment field, it takes the cooperation of a number of players to create a successful project, whether it's a stage play, feature film, record album, or magazine article. It is the people involved who often make the difference. In the same way, although not often thought of as such, successful research is in part the result of interactions between people. It is the communication between people who have questions and those who either have the answers or are in a position to help find the answers. Is it out of line to suggest then that a good researcher should pay some attention to developing an ability to work effectively with people? I don't mean that you need to develop a sparkling personality (although a positive attitude does help), but I do mean that you should approach those from whom you hope to gain assistance in a friendly manner and be able to talk clearly and intelligently about your needs. As you get deeper into your research project, you will find that each step of the way you have acquired the name and phone number of people who have supplied you with assistance and/or information. You will meet some of them only once, while you may return to others over and over again. These are members of your team.

When I write of the ability to speak with clarity, I don't mean that you must always be able to state in precise detail exactly what you want to find out. That's not the point. If you did know exactly what you wanted (and how to find it), the chances are that you wouldn't be on the phone or sitting in a library trying to find information about your topic. The point to be made here is that you should learn to ask questions firmly and clearly (and nicely). For example, you don't have to say, "I don't know anything about this . . ." Don't put yourself down; it creates an immediate negative image and rudely places an unfair burden on the person (whose help you are seeking) to respond in some manner. Likewise, approaching a reference librarian with "I don't know if you can help me but . . ." is not the most positive way to start. Instead, why not try a more affirmative opening, "I need to know about . . ." or "I need to develop some knowledge about . . ." Try to be clear and concise but state your problem in enough detail that the person trying to help you can understand what you are talking about. Keep personal weaknesses out of it. Don't mumble, talk in incomplete sentences, include totally extraneous comments, apologize for being dumb or having to ask the question, or be embarrassed. You wouldn't write that way, would you? Why talk that way? All people in libraries, museums, and archives are at their jobs in order to provide information to a clientele that has an interest in receiving it. You're the client. It's as simple as that. As you read this book, keep these things in the back of your mind. It may be the paper, the documents, the visuals . . . the facts . . . you are seeking, but it's the people you meet who help keep the process moving.

This book is the direct product of all I have been talking about. I got into entertainment research and writing because I wanted to become involved in country music and my initial education was through the viewpoint of the people and events of this business. During this time I found the special niches where I could merge my skills with my interests. But because no one part of show business is isolated from the others, it wasn't too long before I was branching out from the complexity of the music industry (songwriting, recording, live performance) into the fringes of film, television, and script research. Following this, I then took on a long period of research about a performer whose successful career spanned several decades in different countries and crossed through film, television, and the theater in equally strong doses. The project demanded an in-depth knowledge of film and television research beyond what I had acquired previously. On top of that, I had to develop a detailed knowledge of theater research (heretofore ignored) and the ability to use the British resources in all of these same fields. This led to simultaneous, but shorter, research projects on other actors, writers, and related subjects in each industry. Once I completed that project and sent the finished articles off to the publishers, I stared at the huge stacks of different types of material I had accumulated from years of work and thought, "There's a book here waiting to be written." And being a librarian, it seemed clear to me that the book should be about all of the different types of research materials that are available and how to do the research itself.

In refining the idea for this book, I once again went back to colleagues in both professions. The most frequent question from library and research associates was "What I want to know is how do you get to meet the people you've met and how do you get a foot in the door of the entertainment business?" Conversely, the prevalent question from entertainment professionals was "How do you go about finding the information and how do you do the research?" Each side was asking, from its own perspective, "How do you do what you have been doing?" I have combined these two perspectives and written something that discusses: (1) how to do research that would meet the needs of researchers in both the academic and entertainment professions; and (2) the ways one can use research skills throughout the entertainment industry, if you are so inclined. This book is the product of the interests and needs of two different professions. The people in each of these professions have made special contributions to this endeavor.

1 THE MYSTERY OF THE RESEARCH PROCESS

Research is really a two-part process:

(1) *Finding and collecting the information you need; and,*

(2) *the study and analysis of that information.*

The major focus of this book is on the process of finding information. The intent is to provide an introduction to the basics, to give some fresh ideas and practical advice about how to do the work, where to go to get started, and acquaint you with some of the literature from each field. The information contained within these pages is designed to help researchers and writers master the elementary forms of entertainment research. As such, this book does not try to provide a complete listing of the publications that are available for each field. It would take volumes more to list every reference book, periodical, or useful research tool for each area of the entertainment world if we wanted to do that.

Why compile this information? For what reason? In some ways this is really a resource book for use in the development of another project. Research does not function in a vacuum and therefore is rarely an end in itself. Usually it is conducted for a purpose. For example, information collected during the research process may be used as the foundation for books and magazine articles, to create publicity releases, to conduct interviews, to build historically accurate stage settings, or to verify facts for a script. Additionally, it is often necessary to conduct research in more than one part of the entertainment industry when covering a subject. Research about the career of a popular singer or actor may take you through the fields of the recording industry, stage, television, and films. You may have to do research about the artist's work in other countries. You may want to incorporate facts about the artist's hobbies or other interests, such as auto racing or writing. (You will then have to learn a little about these subjects too.) These facts provide a valuable insight into the private personality of your subject and give your readers an emotional feeling for the artist as a real person for whom they can care about, rather than someone who is distant from them. Because this book emphasizes a woven net of interrelationships, it provides a wide variety of ideas for the use of research in the entertainment industry. Therefore, it is for those researchers who need direction in finding information for writing books, articles, background information for TV productions, or other projects that require an in-depth knowledge about a person or subject.

When one thinks about doing research, the first picture that comes to mind is of a high school or college student half-hidden behind a pile of old books in the corner of a library (preferably an ancient one). But the truth is that not all research is done by students writing term papers or dissertations, even though it seems that way when you look for books about how to develop research skills. The fact of the matter is that the ability to do research is a practical job skill that is used every day by people working in the entertainment industry or related fields. This book presents the notion that a researcher ought to be able to make good use of those skills in what is a stimulating and exciting work setting—and get paid for the pleasure.

WHAT MAKES A GOOD RESEARCHER?

What skills should one develop in order to be a good researcher?

(1) *As already noted, an inquisitive mind is essential;*

(2) *Objectivity (an open mind) and a concept of what is*

valid evidence and what isn't; the ability to analyze and interpret;

(3) *The ability to work with a considerable amount of detail and organize it in a logical pattern; and,*

(4) *Perseverance and follow-through—the willingness to stick with tedious work over a long period of time with something close to the same intensity you had when you started.*

The first two skills call for developing the mind; the last two require developing logic and determination. Despite popular perceptions, these skills are not innate abilities you are born with (or without) and all of these skills can be learned. Just as writers are advised to learn to write by writing as much as possible, researchers can master the above skills through practice and experience.

When I started work on this project, I decided to leave out comments about writing skills and techniques under the assumption that this book is largely for people who are already writers or otherwise skilled entertainment industry professionals. But I find that research skills are best explained in terms similar to those used to discuss effective writing. There isn't much difference in the way the material is organized and presented. A good writer defines the topic, knows the audience for the work, provides focus for the content and then rewrites, rewrites, and rewrites. Similarly, a competent researcher clearly identifies the project, articulates the end goal, and repeatedly checks and rechecks facts, organizes and reorganizes the research in order to analyze it from new perspectives. Most people seem to think that if you're good, you should be able to organize information "correctly" the first time and go from there. But it's the experienced researcher who keeps reorganizing the facts and looking for that new relationship or idea that went undiscovered in the previously assembled structure. Therefore, you will find comments about writing techniques in various places throughout the book. And it may speed things along if you read this book with your own writing habits in mind.

Planning The Work

Start out well-organized and stay that way. It's worth the time and trouble involved. Plan your time realistically—set goals for various points in your project (*e.g.,* when to get letters out, how much research to do, when to input on a computer terminal, when to secure "permissions" if they are needed, etc.). Unless you actually have a deadline, don't predetermine one for the completion of your work; it's a mental barrier that will work against you. Be prepared to answer the well-known "W" questions:

Why?   Why are you doing this?

What?   What do you want to do to accomplish your goals? What resources will you need? What are the procedures or techniques by which you will conduct the work? How much time do you want to spend? How much material do you want to collect?

Who?   Who is your audience? Also, who are the people you will need in order to get the work done?

Where? Where will you have to go to get the job done (institutions and geographical locations)?

When?   When do you need to get things done? Do you have a time schedule for completing the various phases of the work?

Defining The Project

A scriptwriter I know always makes the point: in all cases, your first obligation is to tell the story. This is a good rule to remember when you are trying to define your project. And just as each story has its own plot, each research project will require its own strategy. *Try to state in brief and simple terms what you want to accomplish and then build all of your plans around that statement.* Following that, it will be easier to determine the amount of work needed to be done and the techniques required to do it.

Set the general parameters of your research before you start any work. The eternal show business question also needs to be defined at this stage: who is your audience? (Who are you working for? Who will benefit from the research? What will they want to know?) Conversely, also keep your options open. Don't define things too rigidly because you can't tell at the beginning of a project the exact direction your research will take as the work progresses. Projects are better defined in broad terms rather than narrow ones. It's much easier to eliminate information you have collected if you decide to narrow the topic at a later date than it is to try to go back through the sources to find additional information if you decide to expand the scope after you have completed most of the work. There is, of course, a "catch 22" here: you can more quickly find what you need to know about your subject if you know something about it before you start.

The way a project is defined will determine the resources you need and even the geographical location of your research. If you define a project in narrow terms of a specific field, such as films made in the 1950s, it will be apparent immediately that you will need to use specialized film literature resources and perhaps travel to another city to use a special library. If you have included Great Britain or Europe (or other parts of the world) in your study, additional travel may be required. In addition, each field of popular entertainment today depends more intimately on interaction between the fields than was true in the past and it may be necessary to conduct research in several fields.

No person, profession, or performing art operates independently of the culture and society in which it is located. In fact, the performing arts are largely controlled by these surrounding forces and often reflect their influences. Geographic and time factors are important to any in-depth study because they explain the development of the field. Indeed, it's important to realize that a popular entertainment field in one country can differ considerably from the same field in another country, even during the same time period (a particular decade, for example). The differences are especially evident today in the way television and radio is programmed and managed in Europe as opposed to the United States.

If a decision is made to explore the influences of cultural and societal events during a particular time period, the first thing to do is decide which influences you need to research and understand. Generally speaking, these will be the political, economic, historical, social, religious, scientific, and educational trends in each country. People's values, beliefs, customs, social concerns, and fashion (dress and hair style) play an important part and so does the work of other artists during the same period. The life and image of the modern woman of today is not the same as it was in 1930, and the differences are clearly demonstrated in every field of entertainment. But to be able to explain this effectively, one must be able to describe the lifestyles of each decade. Another example is the way smoking is presented on the screen. It's a small matter, but until recently men and women smoked in films and on television shows. As a sign of the times, it was considered normal and acceptable, even desirable. Smoking was a visual method available to a film director for creating an image of sophistication; it denoted strength in men and independence in women. Smoking was part of the script. This began to change by the mid-1980s and today smoking is not routine on the screen. Today's practice is a direct result of current beliefs and practices in our society. But so was the past, and it is important that the researcher know this, because it is the obligation of researchers or writers to assure that their subject is understood in the proper context.

TYPES OF RESEARCH

What type of research will you need to do to find out the information you need?

(1) *Historical research.* This type of research can be characterized as conducting a review of the literature

that has already been published or using material that has already been compiled and is located in a special collection. This type of research can make use of both *primary source material* (manuscripts, original letters, interview tapes, or other materials of direct relationship to the subject) and/or *secondary sources* (indirect sources, such as critical reviews, published letters, or bibliographies). Having the letter in hand is "primary"; reading a description of the letter is "secondary"; or,

(2) *Original research.* The need to do fresh research, collect facts that do not currently exist, or talk to people, for example, by conducting interviews or initiating correspondence; or,

(3) *A combination of the above two techniques.*

THE WORK PROCESS

Taking Notes

When you are reading books, periodicals, or newspapers, take the time to make clear and detailed notes you'll be able to read and understand months later when the citation will look completely unfamiliar to you because your mind has absorbed information from hundreds of other sources and you can no longer recall what was written where, and by whom. Remember, your goal is to make information available to others (often through the bibliographic form), not retain it in your own mind. If you are creating a bibliography, your job is to find the information and explain it in such a way that is usable to an audience who has not seen the actual document.

Be systematic. Keep detailed records of the references you have searched. Keep the same bibliographic information for each source, and keep it in the same order. Keep a record of the volumes, years, and issue numbers of each periodical title searched.

Keep similar records of volumes or issues **NOT** found on

the shelf at the time; those can be checked later if time allows. The main reason to keep these records is to avoid duplication of work when handling large amounts of material over a long period of time. Once into the project, it's easy to forget which journal or reference source you've reviewed. And, it's common to go through many issues of a journal without finding a citation. Maintaining a list of what you *have* found is *not* to be confused with keeping track of the work you have completed.

My personal preference for recording citations for journal articles is the old-fashioned 3 x 5 index card. Even though I go home and put the information on the computer, I start out this way. Another thing I do, especially for books, is photocopy the title page of the publication, write down all the additional bibliographic information I need, and take that with me. This, in turn, gets filed in a loose-leaf binder.

When you create a citation for an article you have read (or a film you have viewed), you are simply writing down information in enough detail that others can easily find it. Because research materials come in many different physical forms, the information needed for each citation will be determined by the format of the material. Here are some guidelines for information that should be included in citations for the most common types of research materials:

For Journal Articles: author; title; paging; name of journal; date of publication; volume and issue numbers; and a note regarding any illustrations.

For a Book: author; title; edition; publisher; place of publication; date of publication; number of pages; and note about illustrations.

For a Newspaper: newspaper title; author and title of the article; date; volume and issue number; page number; column number; and a note about any accompanying visuals (photo or graphic illustration).

For a Photo: title; description of the picture or location; photographer; date; identification number, if one is assigned; size; and the publisher where appropriate.

For an Audio Recording (Music or Spoken Word): title of the work; titles of the songs or other materials included in the main work, if it is an album or collection; the artist; date of release; and the company which released the product. Depending on your need, it also might be advisable to include the names of the technicians (if they are prominent in the industry); recording ID numbers; the time for each cut; the writers; and the photographers who may have done the cover photos.

For a Film, Radio, or Television Program: title; cast credits; production credits and company; running time; format (16mm, 35mm, etc.); date of release or broadcast; and distributor.

It helps to get into the habit of putting all of this information down in the *same order* on each card every time. It will make your work much quicker and easier when you want to use it or reorganize it for other uses. The order I like to use might not be the one you would like; create a sequence that is comfortable for you and the way you work. The important thing is to do it the same way each time so that when you are working with the material at a later date, you won't be slowed down by having to look all over each card for the information you know is there. In addition to the standard bibliographic information, I either write a brief summary of the article or make a point of noting the subjects covered in the article at the bottom of the card. If I need more than the front of the card, I use a second card and staple them together. I never use the back of a card or a sheet of paper. What you might save in pennies for the cost of additional cards, you more than lose in time and efficiency as you are using your notes later. And because I use so many different libraries, I indicate which library I found the book in, and the call number, in the corner of each card.

Make thorough notes of each "find" while you have it in hand. If you think you might want to make additional use of the information later, make a photocopy. Avoid the temptation to speed up the research process by leaving the abstract for some other time . . . with the intention of coming back to add the details later. It doesn't work. First, however well-intentioned, one rarely has the time to return to any but the most important sources. Second, the item sometimes isn't available at a later date and you may never see it again. And if I assign subject headings (index terms) on my own, I try to make a heading for each of the following: names of people; places; dates; events; titles of works (films, TV shows, etc.); awards; appearances; critical reviews; interviews; or any other term that may identify something unique to my subject that is included in the article I'm indexing.

Organizing Your Research

Again, the same basic principles you would use in organizing your writing apply to organizing the information that you have collected: *think about how you want to use the information and what the end product should look like.*

I am particularly fond of arranging the basic research materials I have collected in chronological order even though I may not actually use the information that way in the final product. This is strictly a personal habit, but one I feel is very helpful in analyzing the large amount of information I usually collect for even the smallest of projects. The chronological organization of material provides a picture of a developing story. Chronologies help show the relationship of specific activities and special events during each time period and the effects they may have on each other. These relationships can sometimes be overlooked if your material is arranged in a different order. And you can more easily spot conflicting facts and identify inaccurate information when your research is arranged by date.

Sometimes, however, it's also worthwhile to be able to organize your research by type of material: photos, films, biographical information, interviews, by geographical area, or other topics. Much of this will depend on the subject of your research and what you intend to do with the information you have collected. It is very easy to do this if you have a computer at home and can use one of the many bibliographic software programs that are available. There are several software programs on the market that will create sophisticated bibliographies for you; the programs automatically supply various forms on the screen for different types of citations (separate forms for books, newspapers, audiovisual materials, etc.); the user only has to fill in the blanks. Once the information has been entered for each citation, the user can add as many index terms as desired, and the program does the rest. All of the programs are designed to let the user search, organize, and retrieve the complete body of information in whatever order the user wants. In this way, the researcher creates both a useful bibliography and a specialized database of research information that can be easily searched in a number of ways in order to analyze what has been collected. It's worth the time and money to invest in one of these systems if you constantly deal with large amounts of research materials.

The Role of Computers

Commercial databases which index magazines and newspapers are discussed in Chapter 3. The comments here pertain to the use of home PCs in the research and writing process. Computers can be of help in some ways, but not in others. As discussed in the previous paragraph, computers can be a substantial help in keeping track of information once it is found and identified. You can improve your ability to work efficiently by placing all of the information you have collected online and indexing it. In this way, it is possible to create your own database that should be able to survive independently of the problems we previously discussed. This can reduce the necessity of actually owning and storing copies of all the articles you found during your research, particularly the ones considered to be of minor importance. If you cite each piece of research material separately in the database and include a detailed annotation of each item, the database can be used to identify everything you have found during your work (and the location where you found it). Then, if you decide that you need to see a complete copy of an article at a later date, it can be obtained from a library or another source. If the citations are annotated in a thorough manner (*i.e.,* the contents of the article described in great detail) it usually won't be necessary. The more detailed the description, the more useful the database will be on an immediate basis.

TARGETING YOUR RESEARCH RESOURCES

Now that you've defined your research project and decided how to handle different types of information as you collect it, the next question is where to go to find the information you need. Keep an open mind, the end goal is to find the information; the resources you will be using are the means to the end. What you want might be found in a library, a museum, at a professional association, or as a result of a phone call to an agent. Your answer might be found in a single reference book, a quick search on a database, or in a museum file. Take a look at all of the possibilities you have before you and start to develop your game plan.

Libraries and Other Research Centers

Libraries have always been the traditional source of information in this country. But unless you use a particular library on a regular basis, you may not be aware of what services are offered or what is in the collection. This is an age-old problem that has never been solved; there is no easy way to find out what is in various libraries in distant locations or how to use them.

In addition, there has always been a gap between the services that libraries offer and what researchers want to receive. This is a basic truism found throughout all types of research, not just in entertainment research. You can't walk into any library and expect to be handed everything you want to know about a subject in one neat package. Nor can you expect the library staff to do the research for you. Regardless of the expertise of the professional staff, researchers must do their own work. Librarians are there to provide assistance and guidance.

It's impossible for the library to organize different physical types of information in such a way that all the possibilities of user needs are conveniently satisfied. You will always have to identify the separate pieces of information you want to use through the library's card catalog and then collect them from different parts of the library. Film stills need to be housed together; the same holds true for books, periodicals, recordings, audio tapes, and so forth. There is simply no way around the problem.

Another problem that libraries have to deal with is the fact that many people today lack even a minimal training in research skills. While librarians are generally supportive and patient with the individual who simply doesn't know how to do the work but is willing to learn and make the effort, they are less sympathetic to patrons who are unwilling to commit themselves to the time and effort it takes to do the work.

Research doesn't have to be complicated and beyond the abilities of the average person. In fact, no one has yet improved on the most basic research technique of all: going to the area of the library that has books about your subject and taking a book off the shelf and looking in the index to see if it contains the information you are seeking. If it appears that I'm advocating something as unscientific as walking among the shelves and looking in the indexes of books one-by-one, well, I am. It's old fashioned, and it's physical labor, but it's a way to get started when you have no other way. In fact, that's the way I started two of my biggest research projects. It works.

The Reference Interview

Librarians frequently conduct what is called a "reference interview" when patrons come in to their library with large research projects. This process is designed to clarify what the patron wants and to help the librarian gauge how knowledgeable the person is about the topic being researched as well as the patron's familiarity with library resources and research methods. The librarian can then start to plan how best to help the patron find the needed information. This is usually accomplished by devising a search strategy for the patron to use in working with the library collection. The end strategy will identify the most likely resources to have the information the patron is after and prioritize the order in which they should be searched, an estimate of the amount of material that may exist, the library services available to assist the patron, the amount of time and work involved, the costs involved, location of the material, and any other factors that can help the patron get started.

Any librarian knows that when patrons walk up and announce they "want everything" on a given topic, that is most likely what they do not want. The following questions are the basis for a standard reference interview. In fact, this list can be useful in many ways and you might consider leading yourself through a hypothetical interview as a first step to planning your project. It's one more aid in providing a focus for your work.

Reference Interview Questions

Topic Limitations: Try to define what you are looking for as precisely as you can. Work backward from the universal to the specific. For example, you may start out saying you want films about World War I, then narrow your request to Arabic films of the war, but what you are really after is film of T. E. Lawrence's part in the campaign.

Date Limitations: Do you want current material only? Do you want historical material? If so, how far back?

Types of Resources: Are you looking for "primary" resources (original materials, such as interview tapes, radio broadcasts, correspondence, photographs, or real objects). Or, are you looking for "secondary" resources (indirect material, such as books, articles, opinions about your subject, translations, or copies).

Literary Formats: All formats? Books? Periodicals? Audiovisual resources? Microfiche or microfilm? Reports? Archive materials? Real objects?

Language Limitations: English only? Foreign languages or publications?

Geographic Limitations: Materials from the U.S. only? Other specific countries? International?

Time Limitations: Do you have a deadline? How much time are you willing to spend to find the information you want?

Financial Limitations: Do you have budget? Have you planned your expenditures? How much money are you willing to spend on the project? What are your spending priorities?

Even though commercial information search services are widely available and attractive options for research (as discussed later in this chapter), don't discount the traditional library sources of research. Not only have libraries kept pace with modern technology, they have often been on the cutting edge of new developments and services. Today virtually all reference librarians have been trained in automated search techniques and the libraries in which they work probably have at least a few of the more popular databases available. After all of these years, it's still their job to know how to find the answers to your questions; only the methods have changed.

As a result of modern technology, modern libraries are "information centers" and offer the ability to provide a wide selection of information resources for their patrons that reach well beyond the walls of their buildings. Let's look at some of the services that might be available in your local community:

(1) *Many local libraries offer database services at little or no cost to their patrons.* These are the same databases that are discussed in Chapter 3. Not every library will have all of them, but it will be worth your time to ask what is available.

(2) *Phone reference service is common now and many large urban libraries maintain a 24-hour schedule.* This is usually intended as a quick answer service and the staff will not be able to handle long, involved research

questions. They will be able to give you correct spellings of names, birth dates, and answer short reference questions that take only a few minutes to research.

(3) *If a library doesn't have the book or article you need it will usually try to borrow the information through its Interlibrary Loan (ILL) program.* This is a reciprocal agreement between libraries that provides for the temporary lending of materials or the photocopying of an article or a few pages of a book. A fee may or may not be charged, depending on the library's policies and the nature of your request.

(4) *Your library may belong to a consortium or a regional library network.* If so, you may have online access to the collections and/or services of the other libraries who are members of the group. The reason the libraries have joined together is to share resources and therefore make a much larger collection of materials available for the use of their patrons. This modern concept was developed with the idea of making more information available while at the same time reducing or stabilizing operating costs for each library.

(5) *Your library may be a member of a national bibliographic online network such as OCLC (Online Computer Library Center) or RLN (Research Libraries Network).* These networks were originally developed as shared cataloging records for member libraries. Consequently, thousands of libraries now have millions of records of their cataloging online. Each time a member library uses or creates an online record of a title they add to their own collection, that addition is recorded online. The value to researchers is tremendous:

(a) As a bibliographic tool to verify author, title, paging, date of publication, etc., of many rare items;

(b) As a way of locating material your local library doesn't have;

      (c) As a means of access to finding new information you didn't know existed; and/or,

      (d) As an expanded source of ILL material. Nearly every library collection in the country is at your fingertips.

(6) *Book catalogs of many special library collections have been published and may be available in the library you use.* For example, the card catalogs of the various divisions of the Performing Arts Research Center of the New York Public Library are available in book form, as is the catalog of the UCLA Film Archive. These catalogs are useful in and of themselves even if you don't get to the library they describe. They are an excellent source to verify the correct spelling of names and titles, and they document the existence of rare materials.

It is important to recognize that libraries, archives, and museums are different types of institutions and therefore each type has its own operating procedures and unique way of arranging the material in its special collections so that it can be used effectively. Different research skills are required in each type of institution in order to use the collection successfully.

In addition to the public libraries that are found in every town, many libraries are identified as "special libraries" because they cover one or two subject areas in great depth. The world of special libraries is a large one and should not be ignored. All colleges and universities, most professional associations, and many large private businesses have their own libraries. The resources of tax-supported college and university libraries are often available to the public under special circumstances, but private educational institutions may limit visiting researchers because of space or financial reasons. And although private business or association librar- ies are not normally open to the general public, researchers can occasionally receive special permission to use the collections if they can show that they have a need for the information that can not easily be fulfilled by other means. In each case, you are quite literally a guest in the house of your host, and should act as such.

It's more than good manners to call ahead to any facility you plan to visit and inquire about their operating procedures, it's to your advantage. Make an appointment with a staff subject specialist before your trip; you will receive much better assistance if the specialist has time to prepare for the meeting. And in order to plan the best use of your time, ask about the days and times the library is open to visitors, rules for use of the collection, equipment availability (photocopy machine, phone, electrical plugs, etc.), and any other information you need to know to make your visit an efficient one.

How do you find the libraries or research centers that are most likely to have good collections in your area of interest? Start with research guides about your subject if there are any. Or, look at the *American Library Directory, Directory of Special Libraries and Information Centers, Subject Collections* (edited by Ash and Miller), or the *Research Centers Directory*. The full citation for these books and several similar titles can be found in Chapter 4. Most libraries will have copies of these directories in their reference collections.

New Sources of Information

Today's researcher has more information available to work with than ever before and a range of options that has expanded far beyond the walls of the local library; modern technology has truly made many worldwide collections accessible to everyone, for a price of course. Although access to many of these resources was undreamed of just a few short years ago, the same technology has also created a major problem: today's researcher must be more highly educated and be knowledgeable about computer technology in order to take advantage of this full range of choices. Regrettably, these developments leave a lot of people behind in the name of progress. So, if keeping current with all of the computer companies and their latest programs is not your interest, you can still have the latest research technology at your service. How?

Two new business services have developed which provide access to this expanding world of information : (1) "information brokers" and (2) "document delivery services."

Information Brokers

Information brokers are professional researchers who offer what is frequently called "information on demand" or "information retrieval" services. Spawned from the development of the computer industry and the insatiable demand for huge amounts of information, largely by U.S. business, these commercial reference/research services are now easily available in most larger cities. For a fee, they will do the research for you, collect the information or data from various sources, and present you with a complete package by the deadline you have requested. They will compile bibliographies, write abstracts, locate rare publications or other materials (photos, films, or real objects), provide a clipping service for special subjects, deal with document delivery services, and purchase research materials, verify facts, and do database searches or traditional library research. These businesses can be either large offices with staffs of fifty people or small one or two person operations which are run much in the same manner as consultant services.

The people are skilled information specialists who use a combination of database services, libraries, or other resources to acquire information for their clients. Many are specialists in particular areas. The people usually go by the titles of "Information brokers" or "Information specialists." To find specialists in the field of entertainment research, look for ads in the industry magazines, such as *Variety, American Film,* or *Billboard.* In addition, ASIS (American Society for Information Science), the Special Libraries Association, the Information Industry Association, and the Association of Independent Information Professionals (newly founded in 1987) are four organizations which include many firms and individuals as members. The following publications will provide more in-depth coverage about information brokers:

Dialog (DIALORDER SUPPLIERS).
This is a commercial database, not a reference book. It is possible to communicate with many of he major information brokers listed in the reference books below and document delivery services described ahead through one of the files on *Dialog*. See Chapter 3 for further information about *Dialog*.

Directory of Fee Based Information Services. Edited by Helen P. Burwell. Annual, 1977-   . Burwell Enterprises, 5106 F.M. 1960 W., Suite 349, Houston, TX 77069.
A worldwide listing of over 600 commercial information services, including libraries and professional associations which offer some of these services. Each entry includes a summary of the services the firm or individual offers, areas of expertise, and staff personnel. The same publisher offers a bimonthly journal, *Information Broker* (previous title: *Journal of Fee Based Information Services*) for anyone interested in the information services business. Each newsletter reports on new services and developments, reviews new literature in the field, discusses how to market services, and evaluates new products.

Directory of Library & Information Professionals. 2 Vols. (3000 p.). Detroit, MI: Gale. 1988. ISBN 089235-125-X.
Provides directory information for over 43,000 library and information specialists. Each entry includes a brief biography and career data, address, and area of expertise. Access is by a detailed subject index; there are supplementary indexes by geographical area, employer, and freelance workers.

The Electronic Business Information Sourcebook, by John F. Wasik. New York: John Wiley & Sons. 208 p., 1987. LC 87-8289, ISBN: 0-471-62464-0.
The book provides a general overview of the information services industry and includes specific coverage of a number of databases relevant for business research. An appendix provides a useful, but brief directory of information brokers (names, addresses, and phones) and a summary of the services they offer.

Information Sources. Annual, 1977-   . Washington, DC: Information Industry Association. Previous title: *The Membership Directory of the Information Industry Association.*
   Annual directory of IIA members, companies of all sizes which provide information services. Heavily weighted to database companies and software producers rather than the information service vendors themselves.

Online Database Search Services Directory. Edited by Doris Morris Maxfield. Detroit, MI: Gale. 2d ed. 1,268 p., 1988. ISBN 0-8103-2114-9.
   The directory provides information about nearly 2,000 libraries, information brokers and firms, and other organizations that provide computerized information services. Arranged geographically, each entry identifies the library or organization, the key staff, and the database services that are available.

Document Delivery Services

The second offshoot of the booming high technology industry is the growth of "document delivery services." The cost of storing back issues of periodicals and older books is so high that many libraries now retain back runs of magazines only of the titles most essential to meet their patrons' needs. And it has always been the case that no library can afford to subscribe to every periodical or buy every book in any field of interest.
   Until recently, the only way patrons had to acquire information not located in their library was through the library's interlibrary loan service (referred to by the letters, ILL). This service still exists in most libraries and works in the following manner: If a library doesn't have the book or periodical the patron wants, the library will arrange to borrow the book for the patron or acquire a photocopy of the periodical article. Sometimes there is a cost involved to cover postage or the cost of staff work by the lending library. Often there is no cost, with libraries on both ends of the transaction bearing the expense as a "trade" in services to the benefit of their patrons.
   Document delivery firms offer a similar service for a fee.

They will provide a photocopy of hard-to-find articles and/or some excerpts from books upon request. Large organizations, such as University Microfilms (UMI Article Clearinghouse) and the British Library Document Supply Center (discussed in Chapter 11, p. 454), can supply virtually anything; more specialized vendors like Predicasts (which provides business information) and ERIC (an education index) aim for a specific market. Even the BBC in London has gotten into the act and provides a combination research/document delivery service via their *BBC Data Enquiry Service* (see also Chapter 11, p. 519). It's one of the better services because they use their own exclusive library system, long acknowledged to be one of the best in the world. Copyright clearances and royalties are usually taken care of by the service. The costs vary, but at this writing, I'd say that a good guideline for figuring costs would be at least $10 an item of normal length of perhaps ten pages or less. Suffice to say that the researcher's ability to acquire information has been expanded considerably in recent years, but so has the cost.

Deciding on The Use of Commercial Research Services

The important decision to be made in this confusing mass of new services is when to use these services and under what circumstances. As always, the best decision can be made through knowledge and understanding. There is obviously an overlap between what you can get from libraries for free and what you will pay to obtain from information services. Only you can decide which approach is worth the most to you for a particular project.

An agreement with an information broker should be approached as a standard business deal. Some of the reasons to contract with a broker are:

(1) the firm may have a wider range of research resources available to work with than you do (libraries across the country, a number of databases, access to experts in the field);

(2) the staff may be trained in research skills you lack;

(3) because of their special resources and skills they may be able to work in a much more cost-effective manner than you can.

Database searching is a special skill that requires continual training because most database companies frequently change their programs as they upgrade their systems, and because each individual database uses its own instructions for its system. In addition, databases can be expensive, with some online costs running several dollars a minute. Unless you have lots of money, searching databases is no place for a novice to practice! If you contact an information specialist to do research for you, be prepared to sit down and clearly define what information you need (and how much), what material you may want ordered and are willing to pay for, and any time limit you may have. Be sure to have a mutual understanding about how much the service will cost, even if it is only an estimate.

A comparative analysis can aid in your decision-making process. Your time is one of the important commodities to be considered. The quality and quantity of resources you will have access to if you decide to do the job yourself is another factor. If you are using the resources of your local community, are they comprehensive enough to do the job? If you must travel in order to use specialized collections, what is the cost of that travel? Does the information specialist you are considering have expertise in the field you need researched? How does the specialist propose collecting the information you want? Will that person or firm work in as detailed a way as you might want for a price that is agreeable to you? Are you prepared to pay a fee for a "negative result" search? There's always the chance that an information specialist can do days of work and find nothing, especially if the topic is fairly obscure. The cost of the work will be the same as if a large amount of material had been found. Most businesses approach these services to do complicated research projects for them because the requesting firm lacks the in-house expertise to do the job and the consultant has the knowledge, skills, and ability to do the work. Only you can make the decision.

SUSTAINING THE MOMENTUM

Research has something else in common with writing: An emotional involvement has to be there just as it does in any type of writing. This is the foundation for the energy needed to sustain the intensity for a long period of time. Call it a challenge, enthusiasm, stimulation, excitement, love, ambition, whatever you want. The creative process works best when some sort of emotion exists as the driving force, be it for poetry, drama, music, or research.

Because of the need to cover so much literature in order to find a relatively small number of citations, it helps to have a general interest in the broader topic (in my case, the country music industry). For example, if you are researching a performer, you need to realize that most artists are lucky to be mentioned in the literature a few times a year; even the most popular of performers will not be mentioned in every issue of every journal. For the average popular performer, there will be perhaps a half-dozen articles in the industry literature per year, plus articles in other sources. For most artists, there will be less attention. But because I have a strong interest in country music in general, one of the incidental benefits of years of research has been the opportunity to gain an in-depth history of country music and a wide knowledge of the literature of the field.

WORKING WITH ENTERTAINMENT LITERATURE

One of the most important things I've learned from experience is that if you're interested in a topic, no matter how obscure, something has been written about it, or some sort of record has been kept somewhere. However, finding it is another matter.

A number of problems exist in trying to conduct research in the entertainment field. The good news is that there is an immense body of literature covering popular entertainment. The bad news is that virtually none of it is indexed. That is to say, there is no easy access to most of the information contained in the thousands of journals that cover decades of film, music, and theater history.

There's a lack of understanding on the part of both industry professionals (including the artists) and the public, a mistaken belief that once something is in print, it is forever available for people to see and read. Regrettably, this is not true! For all practical purposes, information is "lost" if it can not be identified, found, and retrieved. Accessibility is the issue; if it can't be found, for all practical purposes, it does not exist.

Bibliographies and Guides to The Literature

Before doing any other work, try to find out if any bibliographies or guides have been published about your particular topic. Why reinvent the wheel? If someone has already compiled the literature, review it. Then decide what additional searching you need to do. You should look at bibliographies with an eye toward:

(1) *Insight they may provide for your topic.* This is especially helpful if you lack an in-depth background about your subject.

(2) *Type of literature and dates that they covered.* Did they cover only part of what you intend to search? Did they cover it well? If so, don't spend your time retracing their footsteps.

(3) *Whether they provide perspective about how others have treated the topic.*

(4) *The degree to which they develop relationships between your topic and other topics.*

Again, information in the entertainment field is available in an amazing range of publications. Be aware that there are bibliographies to direct you to other bibliographies: most libraries will have *Bibliographic Index; a cumulative bibliography of bibliographies,* a semiannual publication of the H. W. Wilson Company since 1938. This is a good place to once again reinforce the concept that libraries today can provide access to a great deal more information than they actually store within their walls. Because they can use databases, interlibrary lending programs, document delivery services, and other means of finding and obtaining information not immediately available in their own facility, your chances of getting what you need have greatly improved.

Newspaper Research

Newspapers are the most important source of immediate information, and eventually become one of the most valuable sources of historical information in all areas of popular entertainment. But indexing newspapers has always been a problem. While the larger newspapers may have their own index, thousands of papers from small and midsize towns don't maintain one; or if they do, it isn't available to anyone outside of their office. Even the large indexes are inadequate in that the level of indexing is usually stated in broad terms. For example, a performer's name may appear in the index if the newspaper publishes a performance review, but it may not appear if the article published is about a general industry topic (such as "cross-over" artists) and that performer's name is only one of several mentioned. Both articles may be important in documenting the history and persona of the artist, but only one can be found and retrieved by looking in the index under the artist's name. Of the printed indexes, probably the *New York Times* and *The Times* (London) are the most widely used and the index for each goes back to the start of the title. But if you want full-text indexing, only the automated database systems such as *Nexis,* can provide it (and coverage is only for recent years).

As might be expected, some of the writings which most clearly catch the uniqueness of an artist are the interviews and performance reviews from the newspapers across the United States over the period of their career. As also might be expected, these were the hardest to find. The majority of citations come from library clipping collections (frequently on microfiche). Probably the best service of this type is provided by *NewsBank,* which compiles and distributes articles about the arts from over a hundred newspapers from around the country. Its *Review of the Arts* monthly service is divided into two titles, *Film and Television* and *Performing Arts.* For a complete description, see pages 129-130.

Many special libraries maintain large clipping collections either compiled from the work of in-house staffs or purchased via subscriptions to commercial clipping services. Although you may find hundreds of newspaper articles in a single file, thousands more probably exist that are not part of any collection and can not be accessed by any indexing source.

There are a number of commercial clipping services available that work on a subscription or contract basis. For a fee, they will regularly search newspapers and/or periodicals for the subjects you request and send the information to you as they find it. You can expect to pay for a combination of the staff work involved and the number of items found. If the information you want is relatively obscure, the price per item will be higher than for broader subject areas about which a larger amount of material is written. Clipping services make the bulk of their money by dealing with large businesses who have a need for daily information, but most will provide their services to anyone who is willing to pay the cost and I know of several small performers' offices and individual agents who use these contracts. If you are interested in one of these services, the *Editor & Publisher International Yearbook* lists a number of them under the heading "Clipping Bureaus." How do you find out which service might do the best work in your area of interest? The best suggestion I can make is contact a library or organization which has a good collection in your subject area and ask which clipping service they use and to what degree they can recommend it.

Lastly, if you are researching a film or television show that was shot on location, you might consider contacting the local community newspapers and libraries to see if they have any files, photos, or other information about the event. If the town is small, such filming is usually considered an important event and covered in great detail by the local media.

Abstracts and Indexes

There are indexes to the literature of every field. They are not, perhaps, as comprehensive as we would like, but they do exist. Each section in this book will contain references to the best (and sometimes only) indexes in the field covered. But unless you live close to a university library or in a major city, most will not easily be available to you.

Indexes cover a large range of subjects, giving the basic bibliographic citation for literature about each subject. They tell you nothing about the contents of the article itself. Abstracts give the same information, but also include a brief summary of what the article is about.

As always, you can work from the general to the specific. If you are in a small town, *Readers' Guide to Periodical Literature* will cover film reviews and *Facts on File* will provide the opening dates of Broadway plays (see Chapter 3 on how to do research in small towns). But it's better to work with the *Film Literature Index* or the *Play Index* (see pages 188–189 and pages 302–303).

Tackling Problems of Indexing

Most periodicals in the entertainment field are not indexed, or indexed so superficially that only a small part of the information in the issue is actually included. As we have just discussed, a similar problem exists with newspapers.

When periodicals are indexed, the level of indexing is usually "primary", with such "secondary" levels of information as cover photos, items in news columns, photographs, and names within articles left out. Country music journals are not included in ANY index, so it's futile to even look.

HISTORICAL INFORMATION

The history of a performer's career is written everyday in reviews of their work in local or national newspapers, radio and television interviews, notes in news columns, and in the photographs that are taken constantly by professionals and fans alike. The interviews, particularly, are of tremendous value. I like to feel that a compilation of interviews make available performers' stories largely from their own perspectives, in their own words.

There is a wide variety of materials and formats that can be included. Periodicals (both fan and industry journals), news columns and/or monthly feature columns from journals, newspaper clippings of interviews and performance reviews, news releases, radio and TV programs (audio and video tape), photographs, films, recordings, album jacket notes, posters, movie and TV stills, sheet music, scripts, contracts, correspondence, Copyright records . . . the list can be endless. For example, there are a number of good country music journals from around the world: *Country Music People* from England, *Country Corner* from Germany, and *Kountry Korral* from the Netherlands. There are others from England, and from Sweden, Australia, Japan, etc.

Of particular note in the music field are the radio interviews done with disc jockeys around the country over the years, especially the all-night sessions.

To my knowledge, no one organization has a complete collection of everything in a particular subject area. The work on this book was done primarily in: The Library of Congress (The Music Division, the Film Division, and the Copyright Office); The Billy Rose Theatre Collection of the New York Public Library (Lincoln Center Branch); the Country Music Foundation Library and Media Center in Nashville; and three libraries in London (The British Theatre Association Library, The Theatre Museum Library, and The British Film Institute Library). These research centers contain major collections covering the fields of film, music, and the theater. Other research centers were visited during short trips; many more were contacted by letter or phone.

COMPILING BIBLIOGRAPHIES

A detailed bibliography, arranged in chronological order, will read very much like a biography, if a sufficient number of entries have been collected to provide the depth of reporting needed to accomplish this purpose.

The result? A research tool that broadly outlines the special qualities that make a successful performer a unique entertainer. It documents abilities, style, and personal interests. The citations chronicle professional accomplishments: record releases, performances, TV and film appearances, and awards. It also documents the personal life and thoughts and opinions of performers.

Arrangement of Material in Bibliographies

In the broader sense, it has been my experience in working with people in the entertainment industry that large amounts of information about the activities of performers is most helpful when arranged by date. Questions frequently arise about the various stages of a career and the facts that surrounded a particular event or events. There is a distinct relationship, for example, between record releases, concert tours, performance reviews, television appearances, awards, and personal activities.

Once many performers reach the point in their careers when they can afford to do so, they tend to be involved in business activities which are related to their careers: music publishing houses, film companies, recording studios, public relations firms, management agencies, and so forth. Actors become producers, directors, and scriptwriters. Many singers, particularly in country music, are successful songwriters. Fan clubs are formed, or newsletters are issued, from the performer's office for their fans. And for country music fans, there's Fan Fair, a week-long gathering between the performers and their fans usually held the first or second week of June in Nashville. It's a unique celebration, nothing like it exists anywhere else in the world! Often, the performers themselves spend considerable amounts of money and time on this event as a way of recognizing and thanking their fans for their support throughout the year.

In attempting to compile the historical record of a performer's career, include the things that accurately portray the picture to be presented. For example, where someone was featured on the cover of a issue of a periodical, this can be noted by use of the term "cover photo." It's important status in the entertainment business to be featured on the cover . . . it's recognition as the most important feature in the issue. In assuming the role of an archivist, one should also include such information as ads taken in the journals thanking the industry, fans, and others for their support; ads for new record releases; ads for products featuring performers; photographs; and tidbits and other items from news columns. The news columns especially serve to document the small everyday activities that happened in the life of a performer, but are not important enough to warrant a special article by themselves. Also, they tend to document the hobbies and other personal interests of performers—their special passions in life. Photographs that identify the events, people, and places in the life of a performer also belong in the archive and should be cited in the bibliography. Other items that should be cited in the bibliography include: stories about the awards the performer received because they chronicle a performer's success in the industry; the accolades, if any, a performer received for his or her writings; and finally, the tributes a performer received after death from the people who shared special moments in the performer's life.

An annotated bibliography provides names, places, events, facts, and other information needed for such activities. A bibliography is not an end in itself; it is designed to provide the basis for other works.

USES FOR RESEARCH IN THE ENTERTAINMENT FIELD

The most common use of research skills throughout the entertainment business is in market research and audience research. Market research is done to determine the best way to sell a product or a service. Many film and television companies have their own research departments whose job is to identify the best market areas for their company's productions and provide the background information used in sales campaigns and publicity releases. Research may be conducted by a film company trying to decide where to release a new film to the best effect; a network trying to decide whether or not to cancel a current show; a television company trying to sell a series rerun in a specific geographical area; a new radio station owner who wants to find out what type of music would bring in the biggest audience; a singing group interested in knowing which products their fans are most likely to purchase so that they can evaluate potential endorsement contracts; or a record company testing which cover to use on a new album. Regardless of the need, everyone wants to know what the audience thinks, what it's likely to think, and where it will most likely spend its money.

Following that, I think that the next most common use of research throughout the entertainment business is for publicity purposes. Information packets about performers must have accurate career histories; publicity releases about new films often include extensive historical information if the film is a period piece; and many offices of performers like to have information on hand about the awards that the artist has received. Additionally, considerable research can be required to track copyright ownership and rights holders for intellectual properties, such as scripts and music. One of the current trends today which bring several research skills into play is the use of deceased celebrities in advertising. James Dean, Marilyn Monroe, and Charlie Chaplin are three prominent examples. Not only must the legal heirs be located so that licensing agreements for the use of their images can be signed, but also historical information must be found for use in the advertising and publicity releases.

Another trend is the growing partnership of parts of the entertainment business with corporate businesses through the use of corporate sponsorship of touring artists. A complex interplay of research and marketing skills occur at all steps of this delicate, but elaborate, merging of financial interests in which an act receives a substantial amount of money to offset tour costs and the sponsoring company receives positive publicity for its corporate name and products. Pairing the right company with the right act is the key to a successful venture, and specialists in the field of corporate sponsorship are among the newest breed of independent business people. Depending on the particular deal, they may represent either the artist or the corporation. If an agent wants to approach a company as the representative of an artist he or she represents, the agent must have some understanding of the company and a perception of what the company will want out of the deal. The agent can then go to the company with a proposal that will, in effect, offer the company something of importance in return for their financial investment in the act. The agent may want to show the company the type of publicity it can receive (radio promotion, advertising exposure in newspapers, etc.) or demonstrate the potential for the growth of corporate name recognition by suggesting a program that spans several years. The common wisdom is to try to develop a "no lose" situation where everyone gains and nobody loses. How is this done? Through research. If the proposal is coming from the side of the agent and artist, the agent will have to research the company, its products, corporate strategy, past advertising styles, where and to whom it markets its products, the image it wants to project, and its financial goals. Conversely, if a company is approaching the artist, it will need to know the background of the artist, whether or not the artist will fit the image the corporation is seeking, the appeal the artist may have in the audience market the corporation has targeted, and statistics which indicate the success of the artist by audience size and geographical area.

A common research problem that crosses through all areas of show business is the need for information about people. It may be as simple as finding out how to contact a performer for a job or to set up an interview, or as complex as compiling complete career histories for the major stars of a film for use in publicity releases. This book contains a number of directories which list people, businesses, professional organizations, and services for each field. Most professional associations and labor unions have membership lists. Several publishers have stepped in and provided long-time directories for special areas of the entertainment business. But rather than using a book, this is one area of research where you are far better off to pick up the telephone and start making calls. If you don't find the person with the first phone call, keep on trying. Show business people don't work if they can't be found, and this is true for everyone from the lighting technician to the superstar. Consequently, someone somewhere knows how to reach the person you want to find.

The first place I'd call to contact a performer who has appeared in film, television, or on the stage is Screen Actors Guild (SAG). Even performers who are only remotely associated with acting belong to SAG, so this is your best bet on almost anyone. Many producers and directors also belong, as do some singers, musicians, and orchestra leaders. This organization maintains an Agent Referral Service, which is a computer database of actors and their agents that can be accessed from any SAG office. You can call their office, give them the name of the performer you are trying to contact, and they will give you the name of the agent and the agent's phone number. One of the most important factors is that the Referral Service is the only source that's completely up-to-date. Performers change agents so frequently (and vice versa) that no directory in the world can keep current regardless of how often it is published. It's a little harder to find the technicians in the industry, but directories exist for virtually every profession in the business.

If you are trying to contact a singer, call his or her record company and ask them to give you the name and phone number of the artist's record producer, booking agent, or management firm. In fact, a phone call may not be necessary because some of this information is usually included on the back of the artist's current record album. At any rate, record companies deal with artist representatives daily, and should be able to give you some help. Again, associations and unions are good places to call for information. Many music genres have professional associations, and they are usually willing to give you the name and phone number of any artist representative they can. All musicians belong to a union, and the union keeps updated files about how the members can be contacted. Musician unions have local branches that keep logs of each recording session that contain the names of the musicians who worked on the session, the songs that were recorded, and the time spent in recording songs.

If you need to contact photographers whose work you have seen and liked, call the place where you saw the work exhibited or a magazine you know has used the photographers' work and ask how to contact them. If you liked a record album cover, the photographer will be identified on the back. If you want to find a screenwriter, contact the Writers Guild. If that doesn't work, contact the production company that filmed the writer's last script.

Each part of the entertainment industry also has a need for the more familiar types of research. They are covered more thoroughly in their respective chapters. The needs of the film industry center around script research, the need to verify facts and historical information, and work done in support of each production (for example, finding the right location to shoot a film). Television research has the same demands as the film industry, with a few more nuances added. There is a considerable need for researchers in both local and national news departments, the talk shows hire researchers to compile background information for each interview that takes place, and quiz shows need researchers to develop questions and check facts. (Actually, questions are developed in reverse order; researchers find the facts and then make up the questions that require that fact as the answer.) The theater is hundreds of years of history ahead of the rest of the entertainment field and therefore has different research needs and interests. Costume design, stage design, and theater history in general are all big areas. The music industry researches everything from copyright rights to record cover information (known as liner notes).

USES OF RESEARCH IN A PERFORMER'S OFFICE

The practical application of historical information can be of great value to the career of a performer. The compilation of the public record can be provided to writers to use as background for articles, the presentation of introductions, and a way for new staff to gain a background quickly in order to serve the performer better, so he or she can make an effective presentation of facts when needed. Therefore, the two most valuable uses for such a collection of research are:

(1) *Promotion/publicity purposes.*

(2) *A reliable history of activity and accomplishments independent of management and staff changes.* When knowledge is lost, it affects the ability of an entertainer's staff to represent him/her in the best light (*i.e.,* the effective presentation of that artist's success, activities, and accomplishments). The loss of historical knowledge and institutional memory can severely impact the ability of an organization to support the efforts of the performer. The loss can momentarily hamper the forward movement of a career if one or two new members of a small staff have to take the time to learn about the performer's history, the things that are important to the image of that particular performer, and other information important to the functioning of that particular office. Such a transition period can be costly.

WORKING WITH ENTERTAINMENT ORGANIZATIONS

Prepare for the frustration of constant change that seems to be the norm in all areas of the entertainment business. Performers change agents, managers, record producers, and public relations firms at a stunning rate. Radio stations change DJs, station managers, and other personnel daily. (The average stay of a DJ at a station is less than a year.) About the time you settle into a working relationship with someone at a particular office or organization, the cast of characters begins a new cycle of change and you have to start all over again. If an actor leaves one representing agency for another, he or she immediately becomes a nonentity at the agency that lost out. It's been my experience that you will get absolutely no help from the old agency (or agent) in finding who the new representative is. It's quicker to call the Agent

Referral Office at the Screen Actors Guild than it is to argue about it.

One other thing: nothing is free. When an agent or office represents an artist, the phone calls, correspondence, staff time, publicity releases, photos, and transportation all cost something. The money has to come from some place, and that place is the performer's pocket.

WORKING WITH PERFORMERS' OFFICES

Performers rarely collect all of the material published about themselves. Few, if any, performers or their organizations maintain complete (or even good) in-depth collections/ histories of their careers . . . as strange as it may seem. The staff rarely has the time and the performers rarely worry about it. The day-to-day activity is aimed toward the immediate crisis . . . the hectic push for a successful career. Once a project has been completed, they move on to something new. Their mind is on creating the future, not remembering or preserving the past. Because of this, performers themselves are often the worst source of details about past events in their careers. There are a number of reasons for this:

(1) The publicity and booking of a performer is usually handled by a management firm and sometimes split among several agencies. These are the offices who retain the original contracts and signed agreements.

(2) Performers constantly change management; the publicity materials and/or contracts and other historically important documents do not follow the performer to the new firm.

(3) When a performer has his/her own organization and staff, that staff constantly changes. Because the offices are usually small, any staff member who leaves the organization for another job takes with them valuable

historical and institutional knowledge that is not easily replaced.

As a related problem, the individual staff members of a performer's organization look upon the files they use as their own personal property and frequently take them with them when they leave the organization . . . or feel free to destroy them (*i.e.,* throw them away) if they no longer need them for their own job.

(4) Life in the office of a performer is hectic. Usually, there is only enough time to handle the crises of the day. The emphasis is on providing the many services necessary to support the needs of the performer for the afternoon interview, the upcoming tour, or the next recording session.

(5) Most performers don't have anywhere near the amount of money people think they have. By the time a performer pays the band, road crew, office staff, publicity firm, agent, manager, and other obligations (such as tour bus expenses), there isn't much left . . . and paying someone to be sure the office has a complete set of published articles, tapes of TV or radio appearances, etc. isn't a priority. It takes a lot of time to provide the kind of follow-up needed to assure that writers send copies of their articles, TV production companies send film clips of the performances on a show, photographers provide proof sheets of photo sessions or publicity events, or that radio stations send audio tapes of interviews.

(6) The people surrounding a performer frequently lack the knowledge, skills, and abilities to create a workable file system that assures historical files will survive through the constant changes and pressures of the entertainment environment. Because of these problems, a system must be designed to be independent of other factors if files are to be effective.

(7) Lack of appreciation of the importance of historical information among performers and/or their staffs.

This type of information (interviews, performance reviews, etc.), integrated with other programs, (a public relations program for example) could be used to strongly support a number of areas of a performer's career.

RESEARCHING PERFORMERS

A major problem in researching a performer and his or her career is the need for an in-depth knowledge about your subject before you start. This is a *must* in order to set the parameters of your study and identify the areas to be included in your search. This is not a learn-as-you-go type of project.

You have to know what to look for before you start; names, events, dates, associates, businesses, and other facts relevant to the life and career of that performer. The headline of an article may feature one of these topics, not the name of the performer, even though the article may be about the performer himself or herself. For my project about Marty Robbins, I decided to include as much as could be found on every aspect of his life: friends, associates, business activities, career, auto racing. And, yes, I did have a fairly strong background in the areas mentioned before I started.

PROBLEMS TO ANTICIPATE

1. *Inaccurate information:* It's common in the entertainment industry to announce forthcoming projects and/or appearances. Publicity, photos, and a variety of announcements are released . . . and dates are set. Unfortunately, it's also common to change (*i.e.,* cancel) these plans for a variety of legitimate reasons. Often, no public announcement of these changes are made. Those involved simply move on to other projects. The consequence for bibliographers is a serious problem:

(a) You are left with "false" citations in the literature noting an event that never occurred. With any luck, you are familiar enough with the career of the artist to know that the announced event never happened. If this is not the case, and no additional citation exists to indicate the change, there is always the danger of creating false history!

(b) If a false citation can be identified, how should the bibliographer handle it? Keep it? Delete it? I always opt to keep these citations and add an editorial note explaining that the event never took place. This, I feel, is a service to future researchers. Otherwise, had I simply deleted the questioned citation, it might appear to others that it had never been found to begin with. And, in the end, the citing of inaccurate information is still providing accurate information. This too provides a service . . . and is information in its own right. Sometimes the false information is included in an interview or article that contains considerably more information of value.

2. *Bibliographic problems:* There are problems with title changes, name spellings, volume and issue number errors from the periodicals themselves. Even a small title change of one word can complicate things by moving the place the title is filed from one end of the alphabet to the other. Films constantly change titles from the time they go into production until they are released. The titles may continue to change during their release in different countries and even when they are broadcast on television.

The Copyright Office accepts filings exactly as they are submitted, including misspellings and various signatures for the same author or claimant. When I was doing research on Marty Robbins, I found a combination of 11 different variations of his name in the Copyright Office files, made up of his stage name (Marty Robbins), his personal name (Martin David Robinson) and a pseudonym (Lobo Rainey). To make matters worse, at times he gave away music he wrote to other people; and this music, if you knew about it, is copyrighted under the name of the person to whom he gave the song! These are the inconsistencies that make copyright research difficult to conduct.

Publicity photos that accompany an article are sometimes older than the date of the interview or article . . . sometimes by many years. For example, Marty Robbins had three different NASCAR racing numbers over the years and at times the racing photo used in an article was of a different car than the one covered in the story.

Titles of recordings sometimes are incorrectly cited in an article . . . and sometimes even on the single or album jacket.

There is still much to be done, however, to complete a thorough documentation of a performer's career. An extensive discography should be done, hundreds of radio shows should be indexed, and additional effort must be made to find and save such things as correspondence, film, interviews, and photographs.

Finally, after you've got all of your research completed, I've got one final friendly tip: keep it all. Keep the photocopies of articles, your research notes, the correspondence . . . everything. You've got a costly investment of time and money in it. You will be surprised how often the work you have put into one project can be used for another one. It's common knowledge that most professional writers harbor an unstated rule in the back of their minds: never write anything you can use only once. An article about a performer can be condensed for use in a biographical yearbook. A list of a performer's life work can be published separately in magazines that publish discographies or filmographies. You might even be able to get a good article out of explaining how you did the research for a large project. Journalists often break up a single interview with a performer into several parts and get more than one article out of it. Sometimes they have favorite questions they ask of all performers they interview and eventually compile the answers into a special article. My favorite along these lines was a writer who always asked performers if they ever fell off a stage during their career (most have) and what their reaction and the reaction of the audience was. The collection of stories made up one of my all-time favorite articles.

How To Use This Book

The citations in this book are pretty straightforward. I've supplied the authors, titles, publishers, and publication dates of books. I've also supplied the Library of Congress (LC) cataloging number, the International Standard Book Number (ISBN), and International Standard Serial Number (ISSN) whenever possible. These numbers are helpful to researchers because they identify a specific book (ISBN) or journal (ISSN). In theory, each title has its own number, and the system should work worldwide; that is why the numbers are "international." I'm sorry to say that reality does not match with theory. Once I had gotten into this project in some depth, it became evident that mistakes are common. It's not unusual to find several different titles with the same ISBN and ISSN numbers. For some reason a large number of foreign numbers don't appear on bibliographic databases that are supposed to include them. This omission made it difficult to verify a number of British publications. And some publishers apparently don't understand what an ISBN number is or the reason for its use . . . or simply don't care. I've found more than one publisher who has used the same ISBN number for separate yearbooks. Others have used less than the required ten digits. Worse still, I've occasionally found a publisher who has used the identification code of another publisher (the first digit in an ISBN number indicates the country, the following four are an assigned code for the publisher; the rest identify that specific book).

The Book Collection

The reference books selected are heavily weighted toward providing a basic educational understanding of each field, current facts, and directory information. I've tried to include research resources that will lead you to other sources of information, such as bibliographies that list books and articles about a particular subject. I haven't tried to cover particular genres within each field, hoping instead that the materials which are included will help you realize the immense body of literature that exists for each area and hone your research skills so that you can find it. Some reference sources have long been out of print, but are still listed because of their tremendous value to historical research. There are simply no replacements for *Poole's Index* or the *Dramatic Index*. So, I've included a mixed bag, but deliberately so.

One thing I've done, which is a departure from most book formats, is include a number of addresses and phone numbers of publishers, particularly if they are small publishers in the United States or Great Britain. It's a practical approach to a problem I thought would be common among readers of this book who are not academics or librarians. I did this on the assumption that most readers will not have easy access to publications that provide the names and addresses of publishers nor the experience to know which reference sources might contain the information. You should know, however, that you can call your local public library and usually get this type of question answered quickly and easily. There are a number of reference sources that publish the names, addresses, and phone numbers of publishers of books and periodicals worldwide. A number of these are listed in Chapter 4 (Small Town Research).

Periodicals

Each field of the entertainment industry has hundreds of periodical titles, sometimes thousands, which make up its unique body of literature. The brief list of periodicals I've compiled for each field was developed with the following goals in mind. First, I tried to put together a basic representative selection of titles which are available; often these are the most popular or most-used journals. Second, I've tried to combat the problem of availability by including only titles which are published in the United States or Canada and therefore most likely to be found in at least medium-size library collections around the country. The British titles are grouped together in their own chapter. Third, the majority of titles I've included were selected because they are indexed in one of the indexing publications.

One problem inherent in trying to correctly identify a large body of literature is that the same book (or film, or record album) may appear under different titles in different countries. I've tried my best to identify separate editions of the same book and cross-reference the different titles. But sometimes the publisher gives little or no indication that a book has been published previously in another country under a different title, especially if a different publisher was the source of the other edition. Similarly, publishers change the titles of their annuals, series, and periodicals at an alarming rate (or at least it seems so when one is trying to compile a book of this sort). Gale Research appears to be in the midst of changing the title of nearly every reference series they publish, and several film and television yearbooks change their titles ever-so-slightly with each edition. Periodicals often change names when they are purchased by a new publisher, when they want to "modernize" their image, or when they are absorbed by another publication. Technically, when one periodical title is "absorbed" or "incorporated" into another periodical this is not the same as going out of print, but the effect is the same from the reader's viewpoint.

Many periodicals come and go in a few short years. Only a handful last for decades. Journal volume numbers, issue numbers, or even the date of publication sometimes are printed out of sequence on the publication itself and have been known to continue in rare cases for several issues before being caught and corrected by the publisher. And some journals intentionally publish a cover date that bears little relationship to the actual date of publication. As a consequence, information appearing in the December issue of one journal may appear in the March issue of another; and both titles may be on the newsstand at the same time. While this problem is serious to the bibliographer who is trying to correctly identify a citation, little can be done beyond adding an editorial note explaining the inconsistency where it exists.

I've tried to track title changes for yearbooks and periodicals as much as possible so that you, as a researcher, will have accurate information about the historical coverage provided by each title. *The Stage and Television Today* assumed its title in 1960, but this is simply the current title for a wonderful theatrical weekly newspaper, *The Stage,* which actually began publication in 1880. Another publishing nuance which novice researchers should be aware of: the official date of publication may differ from the date on the cover of the publication or when it actually appears in the stores. That's why one can often find varying publication dates cited in bibliographies for the same title. A yearbook which was published in 1988 may be cited on the cover as "Volume 23, 1989/1990."

One of the frustrations with this type of book is the impossibility of ever being able to provide names, addresses, and phone numbers that are completely current. Even the directories that are published annually can't keep up with the changes and it's not unusual for their information to be two or three years behind the times. The reason for this is that the publisher of a directory has no way of knowing when a company has changed its address or phone number unless that company sends a notice about the change to them. I do have to give kudos to one publication, the two-volume annual, *Television & Cable Factbook* (Washington, DC: Warren Publishing). They are exceptional in their ability to provide current directory information and set a standard for others to follow. Every time I found a conflict between the information in their publication and another, they turned out to be right.

Unfortunately, you can't make the world stand still until your book is published and so, by default, some of this information will have changed by the time this book makes it to the bookshelves. In the two years since I have started work on this book, I've been awed at the speed and frequency with which journals have changed their titles or gone out of business completely, at the number of organizations which have changed addresses and phone numbers, and even at the libraries which have moved to new locations. We are truly a world on the move! Therefore, please be aware that the information included in this book is as accurate as I can make it up to the date of publication, but there is simply no way that it will ever be completely correct.

Lastly, there are simply a lot of errors around; every publication has its share. Some are the result of sloppy work, while others are simple typos. It's the human condition at work. Even publishers spell the names of their authors incorrectly on occasion. This is just one more reason to keep your inquisitive mind on guard and remember that there's more than one reason to believe "Not everything you read is true."

Source Listing of Abstracts And Indexes

I've included a number of abstracts and indexes throughout the book, and they are fully described in the chapter in which they appear. However, in order to help you draw a mental picture of the complete group, they are listed here in alphabetical order. I've indicated which ones are out of print and noted title changes. Some (but not all) of the indexes are cited throughout the book, especially in noting where a periodical title may be indexed. For those that are cited, I've used the abbreviations in the left-hand column.

Abbreviation or Status	Title
ABRG	*Abridged Readers' Guide to Periodical Literature*
Ceased	*Abstracts of Popular Culture*
Access	*Access:* the supplementary index to periodicals.
	Alternative Press Index
	America: History & Life
	American Humanities Index
	Applied Science and Technology Index
	Applied Social Sciences Index & Abstracts
	Arts & Humanities Citation Index
	Bibliographic Index
	Biography and Genealogy Master File Index
BI	*Biography Index*
	Book Review Digest
	Book Review Index
	British Education Index
BHI	*British Humanities Index*

	British Technology Index (Now: *Current Technology Index*)
	Bulletin of Bibliography
BPI	*Business Periodicals Index*
	Cable-Video Index
	Canadian Essay & Literature Index
	Canadian Literature Index
	Canadian Magazine Index
	Canadian Periodical Index
	Canadiana
	CD Review Digest
	Communications Abstracts
	Current Law Index
	Current Technology Index (Previous title: *British Technology Index*)
	Essay & General Literature Index (1900-1933, with supplements through 1947)
FLI	*Film Literature Index*
FRA	*Film Review Annual*
Ceased	*Guide to the Performing Arts*
HUM	*Humanities Index*
	Index to Book Reviews in the Humanities
ICFR	*Index to Critical Film Reviews*
	Index to Legal Periodicals
	International Bibliography of the Theatre
IIFP	*International Index to Film Periodicals*
IITP	*International Index to Television Periodicals*
	Jazz Index
LAN	*Landers Film Reviews*
	London Theatre Index
MAS	*Magazine Article Summaries*. Ebsco.
	Magazine Index
MRD	*Media Review Digest*
	Multi-Media Reviews Index (Now: *Media Review Digest*)
MLA	*MLA International Bibliography* (Modern Language Association)
MAG	*Music Article Guide*
MI	*Music Index*
Ceased	*New Periodicals Index*

	New York Theatre Drama Critics Reviews
NYT	*New York Times Index*
	New York Times Film Reviews
	Newsbank. Review of the Arts: Film and Television
	Newsbank. Review of the Arts: Performing Arts
	NICEM Index (National Information Center For Educational Media. Now under a new publisher and all indexes have new titles).
PAIS	*PAIS Bulletin*
	Performing Arts Biography Master Index
	Play Index
Ceased	*Poole's Index* (1802-1881, supplements for 1882-1907).
	Popular Magazine Review (Now: *Magazine Article Summaries*)
Ceased	*Popular Music Periodicals Index*
	Popular Periodicals Index
RG	*Readers' Guide To Periodical Literature*
RILM	*RILM Abstracts of Musical Literature*
	Social Sciences Citation Index
	Social Sciences Index
	Social Sciences and Humanities Index (Now divided into two titles: *Humanities Index* and *Social Sciences Index*)
Ceased	*Subject Index To Periodicals* (1915-1961). Continued by *British Humanities Index*.
	Theatre/Drama Abstracts
	Trade & Industry Index
UMI	*University Microfilms International*

2   THE ART OF INTERVIEWING

Let's cover the absolute rule first and then we can tackle the methodology of interviewing.

Above all else: *Do your homework.* If you learn only one thing from this chapter, this is it. Why? The main reason is that you will conduct a better interview and write a more perceptive article if you know what you are talking about and get your facts right. But more directly, it's a matter of showing respect to the artist. All artists want to know that the person they are talking to is working from at least a minimal understanding of who they are and what they have done. They want that assurance that if they say something (refer to a record title or mention an important event) you will understand what they are talking about. It is your best guarantee that an interview will start off right and stay that way. Nothing irritates an artist so quickly as realizing that the interviewer lacks knowledge about his or her career. They don't expect you to know everything, but they do have a right to expect you to know the highlights. And I'll tell you a secret, most artists are flattered when they talk to someone who knows a lot about their career. Do I need to tell you that this makes for a much friendlier interview? Ignorance always shows, and is embarrassing. I've had a sign up in my office for years that says: "Education expensive? Try ignorance." Think about it. Do your homework.

If you did your homework, you should have viewed the artist in several performances. In addition to being able to better understand the artist's work and career, you can pick up a lot of personal information about the person by analyzing these performances. The things you discover might help you put together a successful interview request. The real person is frequently like the entertainer you see. It's easy to watch singers in a live performance and tell what their private personality is like because they are not putting on an artificial act. But you can also watch actors in a film or a stage play and get some feeling about what they are like in person, even though actors are playing a role. The way they physically move around or how they speak their lines is largely their own personal style.

A second rule, almost as important as the first: *have a publisher before you start.* In other words, be able to say an end product will result. This is a necessary ingredient for getting the cooperation of any performer, regardless of which type of media you are working with (print, radio, TV, or film). Unless you are a well-known writer who is established in the artist's mind as someone who has the clout to get a publishing commitment after an article has been written, it will be necessary to prove up front that your work will see the light of day. Artists are busy people and many of them have more requests for their time than can be scheduled in a normal day. It's a practical matter and a good business decision for the artist to aim toward the writer who proves he or she can actually produce what has been promised. This does not mean that artists are going to refuse you if you are unknown or from a small publication. It simply means they want to know that they will get something in return for the time they spend on your project. You would be astonished at the number of people who write performers asking for interviews simply because they want to meet them. There are also the beginners who write saying "I know I could make it in the business if only I had the chance to write an interview (or book) about someone as important as you . . . " You get the idea. Don't be one of those.

TYPES OF INTERVIEW SITUATIONS

The press conference: This essentially is a situation which is a group activity and usually has a defined topic and time limit.

The purpose of the event is to introduce information that is considered to be "news." From an interview perspective, the situation is fairly restrictive. The subject matter to be covered is usually limited to the topic that is the center of attention, you will be one of many people, have no chance to establish a feeling of personal exclusivity, and you may or may not be selected to ask a question. On the other hand, you have the right to use any of the questions and comments that come out of the session, regardless of who made them.

The broadcast media interview (radio or television): This type of interview is frequently done live or taped shortly before broadcast. In radio language, it's called an "actuality," such as in "I only do actualities." A whole different set of rules and personal responses come into play here, many of which haven't the slightest bearing on providing good content for an interview. All artists know that the microphone or camera catches everything. Even small verbal mistakes or nervous physical habits that go unnoticed in normal conversation can appear to be glaring. If the interview is "live" there is no chance to go back and correct mistakes or change things and the artist may be far more worried about physical appearance, speech patterns, and avoiding embarrassing situations than in providing interesting comments. Conversely, interviewers who have worked in "live" situations also have experienced problems with artists who have misspoken themselves, acted in an unexpected manner, or have been less knowledgeable or articulate than anticipated. Interviews that can be recorded ahead of time often benefit from judicious editing.

The print media interview (newspapers and magazines): There is the chance to meet privately with the artist, put in the time that it takes to write an enlightening article, and get back to the artist if you need more information. Most of this chapter is written on the assumption that we are discussing this sort of environment.

So, regardless of whether your interview is long and introspective, quick and brief, public or private, know the strength and weaknesses of the different formats and the skills you need for each.

Winning The Interview

If I refer to the interview in contest terms, that's because it is a contest. The challenge is this: artists are busy people, they only have the same number of hours in their day as the rest of us. How, then, do you get a few minutes of that artist's day, instead of that time going to someone else? The following five rules may prove helpful:

Rule number 1: Find out how decisions are made by the artist or his/her organization. Some performers make all of their own decisions; others leave them to a staff member, usually their manager. Find out what kind of publicity they are looking for and what do they want? For example, one prime goal for all artists is to secure publicity for whatever current project they are working on. Even artists who rarely interview will be available at the point a new product is released.

Work through established channels. This is the way the artist has set it up and it's the way he or she wants it. Don't criticize a performer's staff if you don't get what you want. They're paid to take the heat.

Rule number 2: Try to understand the interview process from the viewpoint of the artist's publicist or management team. They're worried about all sorts of things that you're not concerned with. To them, an interview is only one part of what they see as a total publicity package to be coordinated as means for furthering the career of the artist. This month they may want to implement that part of the package; next month they may decide some other method of publicity is more advantageous for meeting their goals. Public relations people fret about such things as "overexposure," "burnout," and "image" of the artist and the artist's product. Simply stated, if the public sees or hears too much of a particular artist in one concentrated period of time, they get bored and lose interest. It's a perpetual and difficult balancing act from the public relations viewpoint to both inspire interest through interviews and other media appearances while at the same time not providing so much of it that you bore your audience and turn them off. It's true that "familiarity breeds contempt." And since interviewers generally tend to ask the same basic questions, answers provided by the artist are, by necessity, also repetitive. The end result, seen only too clearly by the artist's manager or publicist, is half a dozen articles or media interviews which all say the same thing in the same way. If these interviews were done at the local level where exposure is limited to an audience in a certain geographical area, there's no problem. In fact, such interviews are positive ventures because they create the feeling that a small group of people have received the time and personal attention of the performer. However, if multiple interviews are done in the national print or media arena, audience attention is likely to wane after hearing (or reading) an artist say the same thing in the same words over and over again. The common journalistic viewpoint is to promote interviews as avenues of opportunity; they're a way to let the world know an artist is an exciting person who has exceptional qualities. Certainly, as writers, that's the main point we are going to put forward when we request an interview. But the artist's representative may not see it that way. Therefore, it's important to realize that the interview structure itself is restrictive and, coupled with the limits of human nature and endurance, can become a negative force in the life of an artist. Part of your success in winning an interview will depend on the extent that you recognize this and are able to counterbalance it.

The more adept you can become at developing unique ideas or approaches which will break out of this mold, the better your chances become. What can you propose that will offer the artist a chance to give special information to your audience, something they haven't heard before? It's not easy, but it takes us back to our basic rule: do your homework. Look at the artist, his or her personality, beliefs, career history, personal strengths and weaknesses, and try to find that special approach that hasn't been done. Perhaps you can give the artist a chance to talk about a topic he or she finds interesting but hasn't been able to discuss simply because other interviewers haven't been interested in it.

Rule number 3: Present a professional proposal. You will usually be asked to put your interview request in writing, even if your initial contact was made by phone. Make it the best example of your capabilities that you can because it's your introduction to the artist or his/her representative; your professional skills will be judged by what you do with this proposal. Cover the following points:

(a) *The name of the publication*—perhaps give a little background about it.

(b) *The type of story you plan to write.* Do you have a special angle? Is it to be a straight interview? A historical piece? Will it cover just one part of the performer's life (hobbies, for example)? Will the artist be only one part of the whole article? Show where the work you want to do will fit into what the artist wants.

By the way, it's a myth that most performers are desperate for publicity and are eager to do interviews. The beginning performers who are working their way up may be glad to see you, but most of the established performers have more interview requests than they want and, in truth, don't much care for the process anyway. So if you can include something in your introduction which will make your project especially appealing to them or give them a unique reason to cooperate with you, by all means do so.

(c) *Give some information about yourself.* What is your interest in this? What is your background?

(d) *Say what you want from the artist.* What kind of information do you want, how much time do you need.

(e) *Discuss the mechanics of the meeting.* If you have special requests, now is the time to say so. Likewise, inquire about any demands or restrictions the performer may have. You usually don't have to ask; if a performer has special requirements, they will be made known at the point of agreement. But ask, just so there are no last minute surprises. What are the interview parameters? Are there any topics that can not be discussed? Where and when will the interview take place? How do you reconfirm the arrangement as the date nears? Who will be responsible for notifying you of any changes? How much time will you have? Can a current photo be provided for your use? Will there be other people present? Can you use a tape recorder? Can you bring a photographer with you?

The use of tape recorders can occasionally be a sticking point. Many performers are just as uncomfortable as the rest of us when faced with talking into a tape recorder. The second they see it going, their conversation becomes very stilted. One artist told me, "When I see that thing going, I feel like I have to keep talking to fill up the space. It makes me nervous and I can't talk naturally." Another performer was very conscious of the fact that a tape recorder picks up the voices of the participants but not the interpersonal relationships that were going on in the room at the time. It can't record the all-important visual accompaniments to the words: the facial expressions, the physical movements, or many of the real emotions, or words spoken in one way that were meant to convey a different meaning. For example, most of us at one time or another have expressed disgust at a rainy day by saying, "Great day, isn't it?" Our meaning is exactly the opposite of our spoken words, yet if those words were recorded, only the actual words and not the innuendo would be picked up. I have to admit the point is well-taken and I've been on the alert for this problem since then. It happens more often than I would have believed. I counter the effect by making notes about the circumstances of a statement when the physical setting is important to the accurate description of a particular conversation.

I need to use a tape recorder during interviews and am willing to fight for the privilege if I have to do so. In all honesty, I've never been refused the use of one, but if it did happen, here are the arguments I would put forward for its use: (1) a recorder can easily be kept out of the performer's sight if it makes him or her nervous; (2) note taking can be just as distracting and will slow things down; (3) an artist stands a better chance of being misquoted if an interviewer has to rely on incomplete notes or an inadequate memory; and (4) the personality and character of an artist is best illustrated by the use of his or her own words and speech patterns. If all else fails, I would plead for a little understanding and consideration of my position. Despite its shortcomings, the tape recorder is still the best aid in doing a good job. And the one thing you have in common with the artist is the fact that both of you want to see the best professional product possible come out of the interview.

Rule number 4: Be flexible. If you can agree to meet a busy artist at the time and place of his or her convenience, perhaps in a particular town when he or she is on a road tour, you improve your chances.

Rule number 5: Be prepared for the whole thing to fall through at the last second . . . for a hundred reasons that are not the fault of either you or the performer. There is one factor that will work in your favor and almost guarantee that the interview will take place despite the unanticipated problems that might arise: Most artists want publicity, or at least perceive they need it. Of course, there are counterbalancing factors that serve to work against you despite all of your hard work, chief among these that most performers find inter-viewing to be an unpleasant experience and you will always face a lot of solid competition from other interviewers.

Lastly, it's vital to realize the importance that professional contacts play in the interview process. Make the effort to attend industry meetings and events; it puts you in the position of getting to meet and know performers and their staffs. It's an investment of time, energy and money that will eventually pay off when people will start to recognize you as a member of the working community. This is one of the ways you make your own "luck" in an industry where timing is everything. Frequently, being in the right place at the right time is a consequence of patience, hard work, and the ability to see opportunities when they arise. If you have developed your contacts and proven yourself to be reliable and capable, you will find the saying to be true that "you're only three people away from the person you want to meet." This means that you know someone, who knows someone, who knows that person and can arrange the meeting you need.

Preparing For The Interview

Assume that you have observed the aforementioned rules and you have been successful in arranging an interview for a specific time and place. How do you prepare for the interview? The following steps are important:

(1) Call the performer's office the day before to be sure the arrangements you made are still valid.

(2) Review your questions and background material.

(3) Check your equipment to be sure it works. Have extra film, batteries, pens, paper, etc.

Conducting The Interview

Finally, you're there and about to meet the artist. What do you do? Start by realizing that each side plays a role and that each side has expectations they hope to accomplish from the time they spend together.

An interview is a business meeting in which each of the parties involved have agreed to provide certain services. Don't go into it with the expectation of making friends with the artist or talking about your own ideas and opinions. Keep a realistic perspective.

Because you've done your homework, you know a lot about the artist as a person; he or she is familiar to you. The reverse is not true. The artist has never met you, doesn't have a feeling for your personality, and will quite likely never see you again after the next hour. You could be one of three people he or she will interview with that day; one of ten that week. It doesn't matter how nice the performer is, these are the facts. Most performers are courteous enough to ask you a little about yourself so they can get a feeling about how to relate to you, but as a general rule, you should keep your response brief. Here are some guides for initiating and maintaining a smooth interview.

Introduce yourself: Polite manners and a friendly attitude are always great ways to start. Act just like you would act toward anyone else.

Be honest: Stick with the interview you arranged to do. If you want to do something totally different from your original proposal, get back to the artist before the interview date.

Be prepared to sit with the performer on an equal basis: Talk as one professional to another. Get rid of any fan adulation. Throw away mushy and overdone phrases of glory about the performer's abilities. Most artists don't want to hear it and it doesn't have a place in an interview. The tone of your voice and your knowledge of their career will tell them what they want to know about your attitude toward them. Performers make their living by being able to judge people and their emotions. Most of them take pride in being able to size up strangers in seconds. Any performer with even a little experience can spot a fan a mile off and no amount of professional veneer will cover it up. But keep it out of the interview. Left unstated, it can be an asset because the performer knows he/she has a friendly person to talk with. Brought out in the open, it can look childish and undercut the professional relationship you've worked so hard to establish.

Having said that, however, I'll also say that one of the things I like best about the country music field is the easy acceptance of the fan emotion; it shows up in the way many performers use the term to describe themselves. It's not un-usual to hear performers or other industry personnel openly state that they're "fans" or in awe of other artists. And most writers admit to being unabashed fans of their own favorites without feeling it affects their professional objectivity. That's not necessarily true in other areas of entertainment.

Give some attention to the physical setting: This is especially true if you are able to control it in some way. Try to develop a comfortable and relaxing, but professional, environment. Be sure the light won't be in the artist's eyes, that the temperature is appropriate for the day, that the room is reasonably attractive. Arrange furniture so that it is conducive for promoting conversation: chairs should face each other at a distance you judge to be right for conversation. Don't create artificial barriers such as sitting behind a desk, placing the chairs so closely together you're crowded, or so far apart that you're across the room. When possible, reduce the noise level. And if you can arrange it, have some food available (coffee and cookies). It doesn't have to be fancy.

Be aware that most artists will react to you as a person and this, in turn, can influence the way the interview goes: I wasn't prepared for that when I started interviewing people and hadn't given it any thought. The first time I realized a performer was listening to me and looking at me with an intense interest in what I was saying, I developed an immediate case of shyness. Be aware of body language . . . both the signals you're sending and those you are receiving. Try to maintain direct eye contact during the conversation; if you are using a tape recorder, you shouldn't have to have your head down taking notes. Your tone of voice (sincere), posture (relaxed, indicating a lack of nervousness), and facial expressions (interest, enthusiasm, etc.), all send signals to the artist . . . and he or she will in turn react to them. Your gestures can be supportive of an artist's attempt to think through unexpected or difficult questions. Conversely, distracting habits (such as hair twisting or playing with objects) can be damaging to the relaxed atmosphere you need to create. You want to appear confident . . . and create the feeling of confidence in the artist.

Try to develop verbal skills that are positive reinforcements: They should give the artist cause to have faith that you are paying attention and understand what is being said. Develop the ability to paraphrase accurately. It's important feedback to the artist. The ability to clearly explain the feelings of the artist as well as summarize ideas, concepts, and important comments succinctly as the interview progresses proves your capabilities to articulate the important points and illustrates that your memory is being used as an effective tool in the interview process. In addition, the ability to provide encouragement and emotional support to the artist through body language and verbal skills will improve your chances of coming away with interesting material.

Start out the interview with a clear, concise, brief, summary: It should state who you are, what types of questions you plan to ask, what you would like to get from the interview, and who your audience is. Give the artist the information he or she needs in order to organize his or her thoughts or make comments. The artist may or may not have been briefed by the staff person who set up your meeting. Most performers are willing to work with you and will make the effort to talk about the things you want to cover, but it's up to you to let them know what you want.

Be well organized: Make the best use of your time. It's been my experience that most interviews last about an hour. Some go longer; anything less than half an hour isn't worth the time it took to arrange.

Be prepared to direct the conversation: Take "prompts" if you think it will be necessary. Photos, old clippings, or other type of memorabilia connected with a performer's career. They're wonderful tools for stimulating the performer's memory and conversation as well as a crutch for you to lean on if the going gets rough. Prepare more questions than you think you will use. Be able to take the interview in several directions; if a performer isn't responding to the line of questions you're pursuing (*i.e.,* shows a total lack of interest), be prepared to switch to another subject with ease . . . and to still another if that line of questioning fails to hit pay dirt.

When I started conducting interviews I was surprised to discover that many performers are truly shy offstage. And some performers are more skilled and relaxed at interviewing than others. Length of time in the business doesn't seem to be a factor in explaining why this is so. Many artists can't think of much to say and are grateful for interviewers who come prepared to lead the conversation. In this kind of situation, patience, sympathy (and empathy), are valuable assets. One of my favorite people simply doesn't think in detail. Never has and never will. On top of that, he's also a slow talker. The man has a wealth of information and is willing to talk, but it takes hours of slow, mentally exhausting, hard work to help him tell what he knows. Another performer I know is so continually excited about what he's doing, it's all that can be done to keep him on track when talking with him. Both have been in the business over 30 years.

One young actress I talked with volunteered the information that she feared interviews. When asked why, her candid response was that she was afraid the interviewer would find out that she was really a very boring person. She spends all of her time either working or looking for work; consequently, she has no hobbies, reads nothing, and is unaware of current events. She admitted that other newcomers had the same secret fear. What she didn't see was that this story alone made her an interesting person. Her subsequent discussion about the amount of emotional energy and physical effort it takes to get work in New York and her problems of getting any publicity at all was fascinating. This is an excellent example of the power of the interviewer's attitude on the interviewee. Once she realized I was honestly interested in this story, she relaxed and talked articulately about her experiences. In this case, it was far more effective to center our discussion around her feelings and thoughts about her developing career rather than what she did during a normal day.

As the situation calls for it, be persistent: Perseverance can pay off if mixed properly with the right approach and demonstrated professional skills that appeal to a particular artist.

Most artists are more than willing to provide detailed, honest, and often candid answers to the questions they are asked; but when left on their own to provide the conversation, the sound in the room is likely to be deadly silence. It can happen anytime, even when you're working with the most popular of entertainers who have the most distinguished of careers. Go prepared.

Planning Your Questions

Put time and thought into your questions:

A. *Try to ask intelligent questions.* What's an intelligent question? Questions based on a knowledge of performers, their personalities, or their careers.

B. *Ask unbiased questions.* Questions that don't presuppose a particular response. Develop questions that will elicit open and honest responses that are that person's own thoughts and opinions. Be able and willing to recognize that there are valid reasons for different perspectives to the same event or philosophy.

C. *Try to be a little creative.* Use the information you have as a launching point rather than asking the artist to repeat familiar stories you know have already been published. It's not as easy as it sounds and sometimes can't be done. Entertainers frequently have their own agenda for what they want included in an interview, and stock answers they have recited verbatim to certain questions in a hundred recent sessions just like yours.

Ask for the story behind an event or a decision. For example, why did a singer decide to record a particular song or why did an actor decide to make a certain film. What was the inspiration behind the writing of a special song? When you're talking to an artist who has had a long career, questions about changes in the industry, performing styles, recording methods or personal goals, or beliefs over the years can bring forward interesting stories.

I like to look for influences in the lives of performers from two perspectives. First, it's always enlightening to find out who the performer credits with being an influence on his/her beliefs and actions. Second, because performers are in a position to influence their fans, it's revealing to discover how a particular performer perceives the way he/she influences the minds and attitudes of this audience. Although most of them deny they want to have this kind of impact, they will also admit that it takes place.

D. *Avoid questions or comments that can develop into adversarial situations.* You're not there to argue your point of view or give your opinions to the artist or make the artist defend his or her opinions. You want to ask an artist to explain his/her beliefs, not defend them. On occasion, that's a fine line that beginners fail to see.

E. *Look for the normal human emotions or reactions in the person or the situation.* Artists are normal people and often make decisions for human reasons rather than to achieve career or business goals. More than one entertainer has put his/her family's needs before financial gain or popular success.

Be ethical. If you agree not to print something that was discussed, keep your word. What often happens, if rapport is good, is that artists will say something as a way of explaining a situation or their beliefs that they don't want printed. This is especially true if trust has developed during the conversation. Sometimes, if the story is really good and you know it will enhance the interview, you can negotiate permission to use a modified version that is acceptable to both you and the artist.

Learn to listen. Make an effort to understand what the performer has to say and try to get it right. All performers hate being misquoted.

Remember who your audience is. The end article has to be written for your readers, not for you or the artist.

When you are finished, stop. You will know instinctively when you have the material you came for and any more time spent in the room will only generate repetition or empty effort. Thank the performer for giving you his or her time, promise to send a copy of the article, and leave.

An interviewer's responsibilities to the artist are: To show up on time, be prepared, and accept the performer's answers at face value.

The artist's responsibilities to the interviewer are: To show up, hopefully on time, and be willing to talk about the things he or she has agreed to talk about in enough depth that the writer gets the needed material.

Things that are *not* the performer's responsibility:

(1) *Stopping to explain his/her past history.*

(2) *Spelling the names of people or places for you unless there is an unusual reason.*

(3) *Having correct factual information at their fingertips.* This is your obligation as a writer, not that of the artist. It's not as outrageous a concept as it sounds. An interview is not a history test. Nor is it an interrogation. It's a conversation designed to bring out ideas and opinions. The artist has never met you before and usually hasn't a firm idea of the direction the conversation may take when he or she walks into the room to meet you. You can't expect anyone to be able to recite names, titles, dates, or statistics in detail under these circumstances. I've never met a performer in my life who could do this, no matter how cooperative they were or how hard they tried. The natural focus of any performer's career is on the future; that's where the time, attention, and all of the mental and physical effort is pushed. Past history is just that and many of the details are rapidly forgotten, with the exception of a few highlights. Most of them lead such busy lives that they *have* to learn to let go of the past and move on with their mind on the current business at hand. Plus, entertainers are only human and sometimes misspeak themselves. We all do. It's just that our mistakes aren't subject to finding their way into print for the public to read. It's fair game to ask them to provide general facts, but I always go back and check all details for accuracy at the office. And as a practical matter you want to keep the conversation flowing, keep the artist comfortable and talking, and you can't do that if you allow the rhythm of the conversation to be broken or become bogged down by shifting the train of thought to a date that nobody knows off the top of his or her head.

(4) *Spending time preparing for the interview.* For the same reasons we've just discussed. You've got their time and attention; it could have gone to someone else.

(5) *Thinking up things to say if the interviewer can't think of enough questions to ask.* It's your job to keep the conversation going. A smart journalist always has enough questions.

There's one basic truth about interviewing: The mystery ingredient of a really good interview is often the result of the "clicking" of the personalities of two human beings. Sometimes it's there; sometimes not. The interview was originally set up because each side had something the other wanted, but once the two of you are in the room together, the most important factor is how you get along. While it's usually the journalist who sets the initial tone of the interview, it's the performer who ultimately controls the session by the way he or she responds to your questions. He or she can give you fantastic material that thrills your creative senses . . . or send you away with nothing. And the performer can stop the interview at any point he or she perceives it's no longer in his or her interest to have it continue.

It's true that many performers in show business are temperamental and quick to show anger. There's a reason for it. If performers don't start out that way, it won't be long before they realize it's in their best interest to rapidly develop this personality trait. Why? Because if anything goes wrong it has to be fixed right then, on the spot. If artists want things done their way, they had better be forceful about presenting their ideas. The show business environment rarely allows the luxury of time for long arguments about which course of action to take. Lighting and sound systems have to be molded to fit the style of the performer by the time the curtain goes up; actors have to agree how a scene will be played at the time the cameras are ready to roll; and photographs have to be taken during a live event. There's no opportunity to go back and do it over again a different way. Nor is there any time to think in an orderly fashion about the problems that arise. It's not like the normal business world where meetings can be scheduled the next day to give everybody their say and systematically work through difficulties. Either you make the force of your demands felt that very second or someone else will make the decision and your chance will be lost. Life moves on very quickly in show business.

WHAT MAKES FOR GOOD AND BAD INTERVIEWS?

When an interview goes right, everyone is in a positive mood and enthusiastic; the personalities match and the people like each other. The artist is in a mood to talk, there are no outside disturbances to distract him or her, and you find out what you came to discover. When the interview goes wrong, it's the worse kind of misery. Why? Because you can't just walk out. Because you still have to write the story; you can't just go home and forget it.

From the Writer's Perspective: What can go wrong?—The artist shows up late or not at all. He/she is there only because his/her manager told him or her to come. He or she actually hates interviews . . . and *especially today,* because he or she is sick. You can't establish a rapport no matter how hard you try; the performer clearly has taken an immediate dislike to you. The artist thinks your questions are dumb. The performer doesn't have anything interesting (or original) to say and you know you won't even get a decent quote for a lead. There are three other people in the room and they all seem to be in perpetual motion. If you're doing the interview at the concert site, despite the fact that you've made careful arrangements the security guard won't let you backstage because your pass isn't the right color. And, no, the guard won't go look for someone who can vouch for you. Or, despite the fact that you've talked frequently with the performer's home office staff (in Nashville) arranging the interview, the performer's road manager hasn't the slightest intention of letting you anywhere near the artist (tonight in Charlotte).

From the Performer's Perspective: What makes a good interview? When the writer knows his/her stuff. When they have put some thought into the questions they ask and are actually interested in your response. People who have a sense of humor. When you can relax because that element of trust is there and you know if you don't have your grammar quite right, they'll clean it up a little. When someone asks that rare question that hasn't been asked before. When it comes out right in print for once.

The bad interviews? There are so many! So much of what ends up in print is wrong . . . it's nothing like what you meant or said. They didn't listen to you or understand . . . or didn't care. The interviewer didn't have the slightest idea who you are or what your latest record album (or book, or film, or TV appearance) is like. How can they discuss anything with you? Things can be misinterpreted so easily even under the best of circumstances! So often writers come with preconceived notions of what you are like or what they want the answers to their questions to be; and that's what they're going to put down regardless of what you have to say. When that happens enough, you end up feeling that it doesn't matter what you say, people will go back and write what they want anyway. And that doesn't even include the yellow journalism types that are just after dirt! Why bother? Because you need the publicity. You need that way of reaching the public. Your fans want it. What do you do about bad interviews? You do your best to forget them. Move on to the next one and hope for better. Stick with the writers that you know will try to do a decent job.

WRITING THE STORY

Once I have finished the actual interview, I try to make notes, record impressions of the performer, or think of approaches to use in the article, immediately after I leave the artist. I deliberately do this while I'm still under the emotional influence of the meeting, while that "high" still stimulates an uninhibited expression of my feelings. It's also the best time to make special notes about the interview that I may forget as time passes. If I'm in a hotel I go to the restaurant and have some coffee; or if I'm in a car I find a place to park where I won't be disturbed. I jot down physical descriptions, personality clues, moods, impressions, insights, and anything else I can remember. I'm more likely to have a heightened sense of descriptive ability at this point than at any other time. This is often when I am able to write my best insights about the artist. If the performer made physical movements that are important to the telling of a story I have on the tape, now is the time to recall them and their value in the telling of the tale. Later, the memory dims and plays tricks on you. And once the excitement has worn off, it's human nature to become coolly analytical. When this happens, the warmth, spontaneity, and emotion that made the interview so special is often lost. Get "the feeling" down on paper while you still have it.

The author has the right, once the interview has been completed, to write the article any way he or she sees fit. The writer may be under certain guidelines from an editor that define length or editorial direction, but the writer usually has control of the piece at this point. Any prior commitments to the artist should be honored, of course.

Before you start writing:

A. *Check all names for accuracy of use and spelling.*

B. *Check all dates, titles of an artist's work, and geographical locations.*

C. *Clean up the grammar, except where it helps the story.* Get rid of the excessive uses of "I", "Ah . . . ", "You know . . . " Many artists come from a poor background and started their careers at a young age, sometimes before they completed school. Few go back to pick up the missing education and occasionally this lack of formal schooling is apparent through the incorrect use of grammar.

D. *Feel free to combine statements, and otherwise restructure the interview so that it reads well within the context of your story.*

E. *Your obligation to the performer is to present an accurate, albeit colorful, picture of what he or she is like.* Straight facts alone don't often accomplish this purpose.

Indicative of the business, the public perception of what the people and the work is like, and the reality of the daily grind, are worlds apart. The fantasy that show business works so hard to create is put together with a lot of gritty work behind the scenes. The emotional and physical demands, the financial costs, and the exhausting hard work are constant daily requirements of a profession that may or may not bring success. All of the artists I've interviewed have worked hard for their success; and the ones with long careers have seen audience interest in their talents buffeted about by the frivolous cycle of changing popular trends over which they have no control. There's a wide gap between the theory of film production and making it through a day's shooting on the set. And the most carefully made plans and long rehearsals won't protect a performer from the glitches of a live stage performance. The best songs from the best writers still won't guarantee a singer a hit record.

Most of my interviews have gone well, but part of the reason for that is because I'm lucky enough to have the luxury of limiting my projects to the people or subjects I want to research and write about the most. That doesn't mean that I'll get an interview, of course, but it does mean that the only people I have reason to contact are those I can look forward to meeting. I'm also lucky in that I've been able to meet or interview the people in the entertainment business that I've admired and respected the most.

Interviewing has made me more aware of the part "chance" plays in shaping all of our lives. Nobody's life ever turns out quite like they thought it would or intended it to be. But what separates the rest of us from performers is that they live out their lives in the public light without the privacy that shields and protects the rest of us. Because of this, I'm more aware of the need to keep an open mind when I go into an interview and I've also become more sensitive to how I quote the people I've interviewed. Seasoned writers recognize the need to make ethical and value judgments now and then. It comes with experience and a few wounds of your own.

3 TOOLS OF THE INFORMATION AGE: COMPUTERS AND DATABASE SEARCHING

New technology has changed the way we do many things in our lives during the last ten years. Similarly, technology has changed the ways we can do research and has expanded our access to information that was only vaguely anticipated a few short years ago. Commercial databases such as *Nexis, Dialog,* or *Wilsonline* provide information (by either indexing other publications or providing their full text) have become big business.

But computers and database programs are not the answer to your prayers, even though some of them can be very helpful. You can not access any commercial information database service and instruct it to give you *everything* that exists about a particular subject. In addition, the scope of information on databases is largely limited to recent material; they really don't provide much historical coverage. Consequently, the services developed from the advent of computer technology should simply be seen as one of several tools available for your use in the research process. Database services are most effective when used along with other research methods.

Information technology has been slow to come to the entertainment field and where it has arrived, it is most often found in the market research business. Very few popular entertainment journals are included in online search services. In the age of automation, most research in the entertainment field has to be done by hand . . . and a page at a time at that. Information in the most general of sources are online, mostly the larger newspapers.

How Databases Operate

There are several different types of information retrieval systems. Some are simply online versions of printed indexes and provide the same bibliographic citations as their printed counterparts. Other databases provide citations along with additional information in the form of a summary, while still others provide the full text of any journal or newspaper in their files.

Commercial database services are designed to provide information, at a cost, to the consumer. They frequently operate as subscription services and charge a yearly membership fee plus an additional fee for actual time spent online; most will accept both personal and corporate subscribers, but a few restrict their services to the business community. Other charges may be made for the information received from the service. For example, you can have the results of your search printed out for you at the location of the database offices and mailed to you for a per-line cost and shipping charges.

The systems are generally indexed in one of two ways: full-text indexing or key-word indexing. The indexing is the method by which you gain access to the information in the system and the method each system uses will have to be mastered in order to initiate a request. "Full-text" indexing means the system can be searched by any word or combination of words in the database and is most often used by newspapers and magazines that have gone to electronic or desktop publishing where the complete text of their publication is fed into a computer at the time it is prepared to be printed. This allows for simultaneous placement on a database so that the information is available for use in electronic form by the public shortly after publication of the hard copy. *Nexis* is a prime example of the convenience of this type of service. The database includes the *New York Times,* the *Los Angeles Times, The Financial Times* (London), and a number of other newspapers and journals of prime interest to the financial community. The majority of newspapers are available online within minutes or a few short hours after each printed issue hits the streets.

"Key-word" indexing is similar to a library card catalog or
the printed indexes you have used all your life in that subject
headings are assigned from a standard list of terms. The
databases which use this method may or may not have the
complete text of the publication online, but the only way it
can be searched is by using key words. An indexer selects
what appears to be the key words used in the article and/or
major topics covered and assigns them terms that are then
entered in the database. In order to access the information
efficiently, you must have a working familiarity with the
language of the database. The limitations inherent in this
approach should be obvious. If the topic in which you are
interested isn't indexed by a specific term, it won't be
included in the database in such a way that makes it easy to
find. You may have to search under a much broader topic
and will end up receiving (and paying for) an additional
number of citations you do not need.

Benefits of Databases

There are a lot of compelling reasons to make database
searches a normal part of your research strategy; the best
reason is that they can do work you can't do. Databases do an
exceptional job as the following tasks:

(1) *They provide information quickly.* If you only have a
few minutes or hours to acquire the information you
need, this is the most expedient means.

(2) *Databases can provide timely information.* Most newspapers are online the day they are published and many
periodicals are online within a few days or weeks after
their publication date. This is in contrast with the time
lag of weeks and months (and sometimes years) for
printed indexes.

(3) *They expand your access to indexes* and will most likely
provide you with indexing services beyond the print
resources available in your library.

(4) *They can save you long distance phone calls, postage
bills, travel time, and other expenses* you might other-

wise have to spend to obtain the same information that can be found in a database.

Limitations of Databases

On the other hand, databases also have limitations peculiar to their own world. The researcher needs to exercise caution in the use of databases for several reasons. First, be aware of the distorted picture that database information can sometimes provide of a subject if it is used without the collaboration of any other type of research. For example, the newspaper databases can be useful in compiling some quick background about a performer, but be aware that they will leave out a lot. Newspapers may pick up recent performance reviews, awards, personal problems that have become news stories, and an occasional photo. But unless a performer has given extensive interviews in the sources indexed, the material you find will provide an incomplete picture. The stories that appear in the newspapers may, in fact, represent an inaccurate picture of the performer's life and career. The information retrieved from database searches can be a valuable contribution to your research when used in conjunction with other resources, but when used alone, it is like a puzzle with some of the pieces missing.

A second major limitation that must be recognized when using databases is the fact that their historical files don't go back very far in time. As a general rule, you can expect to get information from about the mid-1970s to date, but many publications only have current information online (perhaps a few months or a couple of years) and have made no attempt to provide retrospective text. Overall commercial coverage for the last ten years is good; beyond that it's chancy. As a result, if you need a combination of current and historical information, it will be necessary to search the printed indexes as well as the online systems. So, don't quit using those old printed volumes of abstracts and indexes quite yet!

A third problem, closely related to the second one, is that some databases have a small information base, often because they are new and still building their information bank. The number of records in each database can vary considerably and have an important impact on the quality and integrity of your research. Be sure to inquire about the size of the database before you decide to rely on the information it can provide; it won't do you much good to look for historical stage or film information if the database lists only several hundred plays or a few thousand film titles. If the database is small, you might find more information, and a more complete picture of your subject, if you searched the printed indexes.

Fourth, individual databases may treat the same information in a different manner. Where newspapers are concerned, the printed version and the online version is rarely the same. Keep the following in mind:

(a) *The same newspaper may be full-text on one service, but only abstracted on another.*

(b) *Full-text service may not actually include the complete text of the newspaper, and what is included may vary from service to service.* Two database companies can provide different "full-text" service of the same newspaper, with one company including a popular syndicated column and the daily want-ads section while another service leaves them out. Yet both companies will describe their service as "full-text." The following types of newspaper materials are occasionally left out of full-text databases: advertisements, side-bars and boxed text, comics, tabular data, sports scores, cross-word puzzles, obituaries, letters to the editor, editorials, and syndicated columns (if they are copyrighted and deny permission). And, of course, you will not be able to see or print the photos or graphics that may have accompanied the article. That's a long list and the only way to discover what may have been deleted from the full-text file is to ask the vendor.

(c) *Different editions of the same newspaper or journal may be used by individual databases. This can bring about the problem of being unable to find an article because it appeared in one edition, but not another.* And the citation you do find may refer to page numbers, column numbers, and titles that are unique to that edition. *The Wall Street Journal* and the *New York Times* both have several different editions and it pays to verify which one is on the database you are using.

(d) *The inclusive dates for a specific title may vary from database to database, with one system having a much larger historical file or more current text than another.* The text of a newspaper or wire service may be available the day of release on one service, but not for several days or weeks on another.

Another problem, especially with full-text searching, is that you will retrieve every combination of the words you input, whether or not there is a relationship to your topic. The broader the topic you have selected, the more likely this extraneous material will show up. And you pay just as much for the unwanted material as you do for the most useful of citations. Unless you limit your search by the right use of combined words, you're likely to find you have paid for information on more than one Kenny Rogers (or a whole bunch of Willie Nelsons) from the *Nexis* database. Another thing, even if you have properly communicated with the database, it will give you any article in which the words are included, not just the articles in which the subject is the major topic of the article. In fact, the computer program may retrieve articles with the words of your subject's name even if they do not appear in sequence. You may end up with articles that included the names of William P. *Rogers* and Arthur *Kenny*. Another example: it's almost impossible to search "The Prisoner" television series and retrieve only information on the series. The two words are too commonly used, even in articles about television programming, to isolate fully in a search.

Unless it is properly structured, the search of a popular name or topic could retrieve all articles in which the words are used, even if only in passing. Perhaps when they are mentioned by someone in order to illustrate an example in an interview. There's no way to screen out these citations and you pay for them.

PLANNING ONLINE SEARCHES

Once you have considered all of these things, you will be in a position to make your database search plans. The process is similar to the reference interview process discussed in Chapter 1. In this case, you will want to balance the benefits against the problems and decide if the searching is to be done by you or someone else, as well as the method of searching that has the potential for producing the best results.

If you are doing the searching, it will be necessary to learn about the system commands in order to formulate a search that is designed to clearly state what information you want in such a way that the database program will understand. It's a communications problem. You are, in effect, instructing a computer program to do the research searching for you. As before, you want to be as specific and as limiting as possible in order to exclude material in which you have no interest. The cost is well over $150 an hour for many services; at that price every second online counts. That's why all of the planning is done before the searcher turns on the computer.

If you decide to forego direct communication with a database, or if the database you need to access won't contract with private subscribers, you can turn to the libraries, information brokers, and information retrieval services mentioned in Chapter 1 (pages 13–15) and arrange for the searching to be done for you.

Once the search has been completed, you have a computer printout of information which may or may not satisfy your needs. Unless the database has provided a full text document, you have only completed the first step. You have a document (most likely a bibliography) that verifies the existence of articles and/or books; you do not have the publications themselves. If you have abstracts, you can read those and then decide which publications contain what you need, or at least appear promising enough, to acquire the complete document. If all you have are bibliographic citations, then you will have to find the actual text to the articles in order to tell if they contain what you want. To acquire the information, you are back to the first step again . . . that of using library services.

Locating Database Services

How can the researcher gain access to these services?

(1) *Subscribe to the services yourself.* Although the cost is not cheap, most database services are glad to accept personal subscriptions to their services.

(2) *Go to your local library. Most libraries subscribe to more than one online service.* The cost of the service may or may not be passed on to the library patron depending on the policy of the library.

(3) *Use one of the information search services described in the introduction to this book.*

If you do pay to have an expensive database search conducted for you, it might be possible to have the search copied onto a disk rather than printed out in hard copy form. If you have a computer at home, this might save you some time and money in the long run.

Several of the reference books mentioned in Chapter 1 list libraries, businesses, or information brokers which will do the searching for you. But if you are interested in finding out what databases exist, how to subscribe to them, and a brief explanation of what their files contain, the sources listed here will give you that information.

Computer-Readable Databases; a directory and data source-book. Edited by Kathleen Young Marcaccio. Detroit, MI: Gale

Research. 6th ed. 1379 p., 1990. ISBN 0-8103-2994-1, ISSN
0271-4477.

Directory of Online Databases. Quarterly, 1979-   . New York:
Cuadra/Elsevier. LC 85-648743, ISSN 0193-6840. Four issues a
year; two are directories, two are updates.

Although the above information is extremely useful, the
biggest fault the titles all have is that they only identify a
selected number of the journals or newspapers on each
database. Since this is one of the most important factors in
deciding which database to use, the researcher will find these
additional titles helpful. The following books reverse the
process and identify the journal titles that are included on
various databases:

Directory of Periodicals Online: indexed, abstracted, and full-
text. Washington, DC: Federal Document Retrieval. 3d ed.,
1987. Issued in three volumes and updated separately. Volume
1 is *News, Law, and Business;* Volume 2 is *Medicine and Social
Sciences;* and Volume 3 is *Science & Technology.*
   A most helpful listing of periodical titles that appear on
   databases. Alphabetically arranged by periodical title, with
   the database(s) which index them, the period of time included
   on the database, and format.

Fulltext Sources Online. Semiannual, 1988-   . Needham
Heights, MA: BiblioData. LC 88-8737, ISSN 1040-8258.
   A listing of periodicals and newspapers that are online, along
   with the names of the databases which carry them.

Selecting The Right Database For Your Needs

There are literally hundreds of commercial databases available today that index thousands of magazines, newspapers,
and books. Change is constant, with new titles being added
one day and others being deleted the next. Finding the ones
which might contain information relevant to your particular
need concerning entertainment research usually demands a

wider knowledge of the field than the average researcher has acquired. Consequently, the information contained in this chapter is accurate today, but some of it is bound to change before too long.

There are several entertainment databases in the early stages of development and the majority share one thing in common: they are geared toward supporting the daily information needs of industry professionals rather than research or academic interests. The people who subscribe to these systems are industry publicists, tour promoters, disc jockeys and other radio personnel, booking agents, artists' managers, and industry business executives.

As noted in Chapter 9 (Broadcast Research), the most-used industry research is market and audience analysis. The same companies which provide print studies also provide database services containing market and audience statistics. For the most part, they are marketed on magnetic tape and probably won't be easily located through a library or information broker. Arbitron has five files: the *Arbitron Network Program Analysis by ADI, Arbitron Radio County Coverage, Arbitron Radio Summary Data (ARB), Arbitron Television County Coverage,* and the *Arbitron Time Period Report.* Nielsen Media Research has two files: *Nielsen Station Index (NSI)* and the *Nielsen Television Index (NTI).* In addition, several smaller companies also offer audience statistics and market research. Among them are *Scarborough Reports* (New York), which provides audience data for television and radio stations, periodicals, and newspapers. *Simmons Study of Media and Markets* (New York) supplies information on viewing habits of audiences, product prefer-ence studies, and demographic profiles of U.S. age groups. It measures the viewing, listening, and reading habits of these groups. *Mediamark Research Data Base* (also in New York) provides audience and readership data of consumer maga-zines and users of broadcast services (television, cable, and radio). And in Washington, DC, the Market Research & Data Sales Division of Warren Publishing will conduct searches of the Warren cable and broadcast databases (used for its directory publications) for information for a fee.

ENTERTAINMENT DATABASE SERVICES

The following is an annotated list of the key database services for the entertainment industry. The list is by no means meant to be exhaustive.

A-V Online. Access Innovations. National Information Center For Educational Media (NICEM). P. O. Box 40130, Albuquerque, NM 87196. Phone: (505) 265-3591. Independent subscriptions accepted; also on *Dialog* (File 46).
   The database is the online version of the NICEM indexes and includes information about reviews and the availability on non-print materials useful for educators in all fields. It lists films, audio and video tapes, recordings, filmstrips, and other formats.

Baseline; information for the entertainment industry. 838 Broadway, New York, NY 10003. Phone: (212) 254-8235; California office: 8929 Wilshire Blvd., Beverly Hills, CA 90211.: (213) 659-3830. Service available by personal subscription. A number of publications are available on non-subscribers through a "Off-The-Shelf Reports" series.
   This is one of the few databases actively going after the entertainment research business. It's clearly still developing its database, but expansion is evident. Current files center around providing information of interest to film industry professionals. The database has production credits for nearly 100,000 international film and television productions; information about productions in development and in progress; information about the Academy Awards; box office grosses for the past two years; reports on literary rights and pre-publication reviews; the agents or representatives for over 10,000 actors and other celebrities; and corporate information/executives for the 500 top entertainment companies. Some film information can be provided from 1980 to date. An "Episodes" file was recently added which provides detailed information about approximately 5,000 TV programs. Each entry includes cast and crew credits, episode title, storyline, production company and running time. A monthly *Prepro Report* provides credits, casting, and contract information about hundreds of films and television shows in pre-production. The one big problem in working with the

database is that it's very slow and cumbersome to use, therefore making it a costly resource. One has to back out of files through a series of steps and/or follow complicated procedures for searching the files. Printing is also a slow process. Since one pays by the minute, most of the cost of a search is the result of technical clerical requirements of operating the system. While the information itself is good, this is by far the slowest system I've encountered.

BIN (Billboard Information Network). 1515 Broadway, New York, NY 10036. Phone: (212) 764-7300/7424.
   The database contains information from its *Billboard* and *Amusement Business* publications. This is available for corporations or individuals through its own in-house subscription service; *Billboard* is also indexed on the *Trade and Industry Database* and on *Dialog*. The system is also being marketed in Great Britain, Europe, and Japan. Emphasis is on practical information for industry professionals to use in their everyday work. For example, the "Touring Talent Database" has files of current weekly information which include the Artist Tour Report with details about particular artists' tours; the Artist Info Report provides details about artists and their staffs; the Artist Availability Report describes who's available for work and when; Artist Tour/City reports who's playing in what city; and Boxscores provides information about concert attendance and receipts. Other database services cover radio; record activity (both sales and airplay); audio and video sales and rentals; the *Billboard* and *Amusement Business* charts; and other information. Regretfully, BIN information is only "current" and no attempt has been made as of this date to build a historical file.

CineScan. Newsreel Access Systems, 885 Third Ave., 28th Floor, New York, NY 10022-4082. Phone: (212) 230-3250.
   This is a database of approximately 200,000 records which identifies and describes film and videotape collections on an international basis.

Hollywood Hotline. Publisher: Eliot Stein, P. O. Box 1945, Burbank, CA 91507. Phone: (818) 843-2837. Available on the following databases: *CompuServe, NewsNet,* and *QuantumLink* (QL).

Started in 1983 and updated daily, the service is the online version of the publication, *Hollywood Hotline,* and includes news of the film community, media reviews, soap opera summaries, weekly ratings for films and television, and performance reviews.

London Stage Information Bank (LSIB). Lawrence University, Appleton, WI 54911. Phone: (414) 739-3681. Available on tape by purchase agreement.
Contains information about London stage plays from 1660 to 1800.

Magill's Survey of Cinema. Salem Press, 150 S. Los Robles Avenue, Suite 720, Pasadena, CA 91101. Phone: (818) 584-0106. Online through: *Dialog* and the *Knowledge Index.*
This is the online version of the several *Magill's Survey of Cinema* series and includes reviews, production and cast credits, plot summaries, and other information about over 30,000 film titles. The file is updated regularly.

Movie Reviews Data Base. Cineman Syndicate. 7 Charles Court, Middletown, NY 10940. Phone: (914) 692-4572. Available online on: *Dow Jones News, The Source,* and others.
A small database which features reviews of current film releases, with brief summaries of their contents. Each film is rated for entertainment value.

Pollstar. 4838 N. Blackstone Ave., Suite A, Fresno, CA 93726. Phone: (800) 344-7383. Service is available to corporations or individuals.
This is an electronic version of their weekly news service which covers the concert industry. The service provides current news, tour schedules, box office results, directories of contact people, and current charts for ticket sales, album retail sales, and radio airplay in five formats. A special feature of Pollstar's database is that this service will, upon request, compile an "artist tour history" of individual performers which lists dates and locations of live performances, other acts of the bill, size of facility, name of promoter, ticket prices, number of tickets sold, and the concert gross.

GENERAL DATABASES USEFUL FOR ENTERTAINMENT RESEARCH

While the databases mentioned above will provide the most up-to-date information about the entertainment industry, none of them will supply significant amounts of historical data or a broad range of in-depth information about major entertainment subjects and issues. For that type of knowledge, you will need to go to automated services which index newspapers and magazines. Listed below are some of the services that are most appealing to entertainment researchers.

BRS. BRS Information Technologies, 1200 Route 7, Latham, NY 12110. Phone: 1-800-468-0908. Subscriptions to the complete service is available to individuals. A special subscription, *BRS After Dark,* provides access to many of the most popular files at reduced rates during special hours.

The following databases are some of the services which can be accessed through BRS: Arts & Humanities Search; Books In Print; Guide to Microforms in Print; Magazine Article Summaries; Magazine Index; National Newspaper Index; PAIS Bulletin; Popular Magazine Review; Social Sciences Citations Index; Sport Database; Ulrich's International Periodicals Directory; and Words on Tape.

CompuServe. CompuServe Information Services, Box 20212, Arlington Centre Blvd., Columbus, OH 43220. Phone: 1-800-848-8199.

A general-use service which includes *Hollywood Hotline* and *Soap Opera Summaries.* Current plans call for the addition of a rock music directory soon.

Courier Plus. Available on *Dialog* (File 484).

This is a relatively recent service started by UMI, with the articles for most titles available as photocopies through their UMI Article Clearinghouse Service. The database indexes and abstracts 25 regional and national newspapers as well as approximately 300 periodicals (mostly business-oriented journals), with coverage starting in 1988 for the journals and 1989 for the newspapers. Among the titles: *The Boston Globe, New York Times, USA Today,* and the *Wall Street Journal.*

DataTimes. 818 N.W. 63rd St., Oklahoma City, OK 73116. Phone 1-800-642-2525 or (405) 843-7323. Individual or corporate subscriptions.

This is a full-text database of nearly 20 daily newspapers from around the country, including *The Washington Post, The Dallas Morning News, San Francisco Chronicle,* and the *Chicago Sun Times.*

Dialog. Dialog Information Services, 3460 Hillview Ave., Palo Alto, CA 94304. Phone 1-800-334-2564.

Dialog is best described as an umbrella for over 250 databases covering every subject imaginable. Their *Knowledge Index* is a special service of 65 databases available on Dialog from 6:00 p.m until 6:a.m at a reduced price. The individual databases which make up the Dialog system are called "files" and each one is assigned a file number for searching purposes. Dialog includes the following indexes (files) of interest to entertainment researchers:

AP News (Files 258, 259) (Associated Press)

Arts & Humanities Search (File 439)

A-V Online (File 46) (previous title: NICEM)

Biography Master Index (Files 287, 288)

Book Review Index (File 137)

Books in Print (File 470)

British Books in Print (File 430)

Businesswire (File 610)

Canadian Business and Current Affairs (File 262)

Chicago Tribune (File 632)

Courier Plus (File 484)

Encyclopedia of Associations (File 114)

Facts on File (File 264)

Financial Times Abstracts (File 560)

Financial Times Fulltext (File 622)

ICC British Company Directory (File 561)

LC MARC (Files 426, 427) (Library of Congress MARC cataloging records)

Los Angeles Times (File 630)

Magazine ASAP (File 647)

Magazine Index (File 47)

Magill's Survey of Cinema (File 299)

Marquis Who's Who (File 234)

MLA Bibliography (File 71) (Modern Language Association)

National Newspaper Index (File 111)

Newsearch (File 211)

Newspaper Abstracts (File 603)

Newswire ASAP (File 649)

PAIS International (File 49) (Public Affairs Information Service)

Philadelphia Inquirer (File 633)

PR Newswire (File 613) (this is a file of news releases and publicity releases by companies and public relations firms)

Reuters (File 611)

RILM Abstracts (File 97) (*Repertoire International de Litterature Musicale*) 1971-   .

Social Scisearch (File 7)

Standard and Poor's

Trade & Industry ASAP (File 648)

Trade & Industry Index (File 148)

Trademarkscan (File 226)

Ulrich's International Periodicals Directory (File 480)

UPI News (Files 260, 261) (United Press International)

USA Today Decisionline (File 644)

Washington Post Online (Files 146, 147)

Washington Presstext (File 145)

IBT (International Bibliography of the Theatre). Theatre Research Data Center, Brooklyn College, Brooklyn, NY 11210. Phone: (718) 780-5998. Not a subscription service.
    The Center publishes the *International Bibliography of the Theatre* and will accept online research inquiries of their comprehensive database.

Magazine Index. 1976- . Information Access Company. 362 Lakeside Dr., Foster City, CA 94404. Phone: 1-800-227-8431.
    This company produces five databases that are available to libraries and corporations; no personal subscriptions. Unlike other databases, this one is designed to run on equipment provided by the company. All three magazine databases are extremely user-friendly and require no training to use. They are becoming increasingly popular in public and educational institution libraries, so you might be able to find them near you. The following is a more detailed description of the databases provided by Information Access:

> *General Periodicals Index*. An index to 1,100 periodicals. Titles relevant to entertainment research include: *American Film; American Record Guide; Amusement Business; Audio; Back Stage; Billboard; Broadcasting; Cinema Canada; Country Music; Dance Magazine; Down Beat; The Drama Review; Film Comment; Film Quarterly; Guitar Player; High Fidelity; Interview; Journal of Broadcasting & Electronic Media; The New York Times; Opera News; Premiere; Rolling Stone; Stereo Review; Television Digest; Television-Radio Age; Theatre Crafts; TV Guide; Variety; Video; Video Review; Writer;* and *Writer's Digest*.

Magazine Index Plus. A more limited index of 400 periodicals selected from the 1,100 titles of the main service.

Magazine Index Select. A very limited index of 200 periodical titles designed to meet the needs of smaller libraries. Even this limited edition manages to include a dozen titles from the journals I've noted above.

National Newspaper Index. An index to five major newspapers: *The New York Times, Wall Street Journal, Los Angeles Times, Washington Post,* and the *Christian Science Monitor.* Coverage is for the current year and the past three years.

Newsearch. This is a separate database service run by the Information Access Company which includes some of the other files named above as well as *Trade & Industry Index, ASAP,* and other files. This service is available on *BRS, BRS After Dark, Dialog,* and the *Knowledge Index.*

NewsNet. 945 Haverford Rd., Bryn Mawr, PA 19010. Phone: (215) 527-8030.

An index to a number of industry newsletters, the PR and UPI news services and *USA Today.* It also has *Hollywood Hotline, The Gold Sheet, Communications Daily* and files for the Federal Communications Commission (*FCC Daily Digest, FCC Daily Tariff Log,* and *FCC Week*), *Television Digest,* and three video files: *Video Marketing Newsletter, Video Week,* and *Videodisc Monitor.*

Nexis. Mead Data Central, 9443 Springboro Pike, P.O. Box 933, Dayton, OH 45401. Phone: (513) 865-6800. Subscriptions available to individuals and corporations.

Mead is another umbrella service for a series of individual files geared toward financial and business information. It was originally a newspaper indexing service, with the *New York Times* its flagship service. Listed below are some of the databases of interest to entertainment researchers, with the year the file information begins:

Newspapers:

The Christian Science Monitor (Jan., 1980-)

Financial Times (Jan., 1982-)

Los Angeles Times (Jan., 1985-)

Manchester Guardian (Jan., 1981-)

New York Times (June, 1980-)

Washington Post (Jan., 1977-)

Periodicals:

Back Stage (August, 1984-)

Broadcasting (Jan., 1983-)

Communications Daily (Jan., 1984-)

Facts on File World News Digest (Jan., 1975-)

Life (Jan., 1982-)

Newsweek (Jan., 1975-)

People (Dec., 1981-)

Saturday Evening Post (Jan., 1983-)

Sports Illustrated (Dec., 1981-)

Stereo Review (Jan., 1983-)

Time (Jan., 1981-)

Who's Who in Television & Cable (1983-)

News wires and services:

Associated Press (world, national, business & sports wires) (Jan., 1977-)

BBC Summary of World Broadcasts & Monitoring Reports (Jan., 1979-)

New York Times Biographical file (June, 1980-)

Reuters News Report (April, 1979-)

TASS (The Telegraph Agency of the Soviet Union) (Jan., 1987)

UPI (United Press International: (1) world, national, business and sports wires from September, 1980; and (2) state and regional wires from November, 1980 through December, 1987)

Universal News Service (October, 1986-)

QL Systems. 112 Kent St., Tower B, Suite 1210, Ottawa, Ontario, KIP 5P2 Canada. Phone: (613) 238-3499.
The system provides access to National Film Board of Canada files, *Film/Video Producers and Distributors* and *FORMAT* (a database of approximately 20,000 films and other audiovisual materials made in Canada). It also offers *Hollywood Hotline.*

UMI. University Microfilms International, 300 North Zeeb Rd., Ann Arbor, MI 48106. Phone: 1-800-521-3044. Subscriptions geared toward corporate use, but individuals wouldn't be refused.
As noted in other sections of this book, UMI has a number of services which utilizes its huge collection of periodicals, newspapers, and dissertations. In addition to offering the databases listed below, it offers the Article Clearinghouse, which is a document delivery service (see Chapter 1 for a description). UMI offers four main databases on CD-ROM:

ABI/INFORM. An index of several hundred business and management journals from around the world. The only entertainment information that would be found here would be in communications or a very narrowly-defined business area.

Dissertation Abstracts. An index to nearly one million doctoral dissertations and masters theses published since 1861 in over 500 universities worldwide. Most American and British schools are included. Approximately 35,000 titles are added annually. Each entry includes complete bibliographic information, and all newer records contain abstracts.

Newspaper Abstracts. A newspaper index (not full-text) for the following newspapers: *The Atlanta Constitution, The Boston Globe, The Chicago Tribune, The Christian Science Monitor, Los Angeles Times, New York Times, Wall Street Journal,* and the *Washington Post.* A weak point is that historical coverage only goes back to 1985 for several titles, and not even that far for two others.

Periodical Abstracts. An index of all periodicals listed in *Readers' Guide,* plus 100 other titles, make up a database of 300 titles. Among the titles of value for entertainment researchers: *American Film; Billboard; Dance Magazine; Down Beat; Film Comment; High Fidelity; Interview; Melody Maker; Musical America; People Weekly; Rolling Stone; Stereo Review; Theatre Crafts; TV Guide; Variety; Video; Video Review;* and *Writer.* Indexing is by subject terms. Each entry has complete bibliographic information and a brief abstract. The full-text reproduction of most articles can be ordered through their Article Clearinghouse service.

VU/TEXT. Information Services, Inc. 325 Chestnut St., Suite 1300, Virginia Beach, VA 19106. Phone: (804) 427-1555. Subscriptions available to individuals and corporations.

This service is a full-text database of 45 daily newspapers nationwide, 150 regional business journals, and six news wire services.

Wilsonline and *Wilsondisc.* The H. W. Wilson Company, 950 University Ave., Bronx, NY 10452. Phone: 1-800-367-6770. Subscriptions are available to individuals and corporations. All titles are offered on CD-ROM too.

Wilson provides online access to a number of indexes (many are their own titles), all of which are described in other chapters of this book. Indexes of interest to entertainment researchers include:

Applied Science and Technology Index (October, 1983-)

Art Index (September, 1984-)

Bibliographic Index (November, 1984-)

Biography Index (July, 1984-)

Book Review Digest (April, 1983-)

Business Periodicals Index (June, 1982-)

Cumulative Book Index (January, 1982-)

Essay and General Literature Index (January, 1985-)

Humanities Index (February, 1984-)

LC MARC File (January, 1977-)

MLA International Bibliography (1988-)

Readers' Guide Abstracts (1988-)

Readers' Guide to Periodical Literature (January, 1983-)

Social Sciences Index (April, 1983-)

Vertical File Index (December, 1985-)

The company has recently started publishing Readers' Guide to Periodical Literature with abstracts.

The following entertainment periodicals are indexed in select databases listed in this chapter. However, most are not indexed at the full-text level.

Amusement Business (*Dialog*)

Billboard (*Dialog*)

Broadcasting (*Dialog*)

Facts on File (*Dialog* File 264, *Mead Data*)

Film & Video Finder (*Dialog*)

Magill's Cinema Annual (*Dialog* File 299)

Manchester Guardian Weekly (*Mead Data*)

Monthly Index to the Financial Times (*Dialog* File 622)

New York Times Index (*Mead Data*)

Stereo Review (*Dialog*)

Variety (*Trade and Industry/Dialog*)

Video Week (*NewsNet*)

Videodisk Monitor (*NewsNet*)

FUTURE NEEDS OF RESEARCHERS AND LIBRARIES

Because the literature in the entertainment field so far has been bypassed by automation, it would be most helpful to researchers and writers if an assertive organized approach by the industry were made to solve the problem of information retrieval. The first step (information collection) is in large part solved with the development of the special libraries. Now, it is time to work toward providing "access" to the information in those collections. If this takes a joint industry effort, the industry would be better for the investment. The full-text indexing of periodicals and identification of special library collections could be achieved through a variety of ways: industry donations, special project funding, government grants, and gifts. Once in operation, it is likely that the indexing can realize a profit through user fees. The need and the market, is there . . . and no one is doing the work.

4 SMALL TOWN RESEARCH

Most residents of small towns are a long distance from large special entertainment library collections and a trip to a major research facility often requires considerable travel and expense. Any local library will provide the basics in two areas of research you may need; (1) biography, and (2) general research about U.S. and foreign societies and their histories. However, it is still possible to do some basic entertainment research in your local library. We discussed library services in Chapter 1 and computer databases in Chapter 3. If you combine the information in those two sections with that given in this Chapter, you should be able to fend for yourself in almost any geographical location. In this Chapter we'll highlight some of the common books and reference sources that are found in nearly every library. They're not usually thought of as entertainment research sources, but, in fact, they all contain a healthy amount of useful information from every field of entertainment. Again, it's just a matter of knowing how to look for it.

There's a great deal of entertainment information in the types of reading materials that every library collects: daily newspapers, popular magazines, and best-selling books. If you know how to go about finding what has been published over the years, you should be able to do minimal research on almost any topic. However, there's no way to get around the fact that if you want to do in-depth research, it will be almost impossible unless you go to the place that has the best collection. A friend of mine likes to make an analogy with a fledgling jazz musician in Visalia, California. You can get started there, and spend your vacations or days off in Los Angeles learning to play and meeting the contacts you need, but if you know you want to "make it bigtime," you have to go where the action is. There is only so much you can do in Visalia. The same is true of effective research; you can live in a small town and get some things done there, but there are only a limited number of magazines to read and only so many ways to compensate for the restrictions. If you want to do top-notch work over a long time period, you will eventually have to go where the best collections are located.

The reference sources listed in this Chapter are indexes and abstracts, directories, review sources, and other materials that will help you find information that has been published elsewhere. Most of these, such as *Readers' Guide to Periodical Literature,* are part of every library, regardless of size or location. Others, such as *Art Index* or the historical *Poole's Index to Periodical Literature* may be more difficult to locate. Some titles are used by the librarians themselves to order books and periodicals or verify bibliographic information (*Books in Print* and *the Directory of Directories* are two examples) and therefore may be in the office work area instead of on the shelves for public use. If you don't see them, ask for them. *Books In Print* (and the companion *British Books In Print*) are your best sources of current publisher addresses.

One of your best sources for information is, as always, the daily newspaper. If your library subscribes to any newspaper indexes at all, they will probably have the *New York Times,* and maybe the *Wall Street Journal.* With any luck, they may also have the *National Newspaper Index,* a computerized index of five major newspapers. Most newspapers and many periodicals (such as *TV Guide* and *Variety*) are available on microfiche or microfilm with a cost that is low enough to encourage many libraries to supplement their research collections with microform copies of newspapers and their indexes such as the *Los Angeles Times,* the *Chicago Tribune,* or the *Boston Globe.* Most major newspapers are on some online system now, but the catch is that their historical computerized files frequently go back only a few months or years. The print indexes, on the other hand, usually go all of the way back to the start of the newspaper. You will be able to find media reviews (film, television, radio, recordings); live performance reviews (stage, touring acts, comedy);

interviews (the famous, the unknowns, and the business people); industry financial information; broad historical perspectives or overviews of an industry; important industry-related events; and an unlimited amount of biographical information. Reviewing these general publications can give you valuable leads to additional areas of research by providing names, dates, descriptions of special events, and personal information.

The indexes to popular magazines are also extremely valuable, but the level of indexing may be less detailed than their newspaper counterparts. They tend toward broad subject terms rather than the specific. Whereas newspaper indexes only index one title (*that* newspaper), periodical indexes usually index from 50 to several hundred journals. They must, by necessity, use subject terms which will allow them to fit in the major articles from each magazine. But every major popular magazine that has ever been published is indexed somewhere, and that makes it worth your while to search the indexes.

You should be able to do quick, brief biographical research on almost any popular performer or prominent industry leader at your local library. There are a number of biographical reference books that will supply at least the basic life details of public figures. Some are better than others. Look for the ones that make every effort to collect their data from primary sources; *i.e.,* directly from the performers or their representatives. Many biographical reference sources such as *Who's Who in America* compile their entries by sending inquiry forms to the performers, executives, or their representatives asking for the relevant biographical and professional information. If the forms are not returned, that person is not included. I've been asked by more than one performer why he or she didn't appear in one or another reference book, and yet year after year that artist or the artist's staff member simply tossed out the publisher's inquiry because he or she didn't want to spend the time on it.

Other unconventional entertainment resources are the *Directories in Print* (which lists directories that are published by associations and other groups); *Dissertation Abstracts International* (for relatively obscure research that may have been done on your topic); *Facts on File* (for a quick fix on a date or notable event); *Encyclopedia of Associations* (just about every association is listed); and *Ulrich's International Periodicals Directory* (for a listing of the major periodicals in every field).

Many public libraries and smaller college libraries will rely heavily on a few main reference book publishers to supply the materials they need because they don't have the staff, time, or budget to seek out the smaller publishers or highly specialized materials. Therefore, you will notice that many of the titles listed here are by three main publishers: Gale Research, R.R. Bowker, and H.L. Wilson. Every library in the U.S. does some business with these publishers and, since the goal of this Chapter is to include materials most likely to be found in the "average" library throughout our country, many of their books have been included.

GENERAL REFERENCE RESOURCES

Abstracts of Popular Culture. Biannual, 1976-1982. No longer published. Bowling Green University Popular Press. LC 77-647685, ISSN 0147-2615.
    This index included film, television, popular entertainment, theater, and music as important elements of U.S. popular culture.

Access: the supplementary index to periodicals. Annual with two supplementary issues, 1975-   . Address: P.O. Box 1492, Evanston, IL 60204: John Gordon Burke, Publisher. ISSN 0095-5898.
    Indexes approximately 150 popular periodicals not included in other indexing sources. Strong enough to stand on its own, it does include some entertainment titles, mostly in the music field.

Almanac of Famous People. 4th ed., edited by Susan L. Stetler. Detroit, MI: Gale. 3 vols., 1989. ISBN (set): 0-8103-2784-8. Previous editions published as *Biography Almanac* (1981-1988).
    Coverage is from Biblical times to the present and includes brief

biographies for 25,000 worldwide. Some brief bibliographies refer the reader to additional biographical material about the subject. There are several indexes: the Chronological index lists the names by birth day from January 1 to December 31; the Geographic index lists the place of birth and death; and the Occupations index organizes the names by occupation.

Alternative Press Index. Quarterly, 1969-   . Northfield, MN: Radical Research Center. LC 76-24027, ISSN 0002-662X.
    Indexes about 200 radical and underground publications that are not indexed elsewhere. Includes some periodicals from other countries (Canada, Australia, England).

American Humanities Index. Quarterly, 1975-   . Annual cumulations. Troy, NY: Whitson. ISSN 0361-0144.
    Indexes approximately 225 scholarly and little known magazines not found in other sources.

American Library Resources: a bibliographical guide, by Robert B. Downs. Chicago, IL: American Library Association. 428 p., 1951. LC 51-11156. Updated to 1980 by five supplements.
    This set is a comprehensive bibliography of literature in print about library collections. It includes lists of printed library catalogs, descriptions of collections, lists of serials, and other published information about library collections. Even though it hasn't been updated recently, it is a valuable source for locating publications about the collection of a particular library.

American Reference Books Annual. Annual, 1970-   . Littleton, CO: Libraries Unlimited. ISSN 0065-9959.
    Found in virtually every library because it is used as a selection tool by librarians, the publication lists and evaluates new reference books that have been published during the past year. Indexed by author, title, and broad subject area. A convenient way to keep current with what is new in your field.

Art Index. Quarterly, 1929-   . Cumulated annual volumes. Bronx, NY: H.W. Wilson. LC 31-7513, ISSN 0004-3222. Available online: Wilsonline.

A comprehensive author and subject index of over 200 periodicals, yearbooks, and museum bulletins covering the field of art. International in scope. Entertainment researchers will find some information about film, television, video, and popular personalities.

Arts and Humanities Citation Index. 3 issues yearly with an annual cumulation, 1975- . Philadelphia, PA: Institute for Scientific Information. ISSN 0162-8445. *SEE ALSO:* Chapter 3, page 84, and Chapter 11, page 439, for information about their online service, Arts and Humanities Search.

A comprehensive index covering 1,300 journals of varying frequency and includes articles, letters, editorials, notes, and bibliographies. A good source to examine if you don't have one of the specialized sources available. Historical coverage limited to the year the series started. Includes plays, music scores, and filmographies. Indexes reviews of films, radio and television programs, theatrical performances, and recordings.

Association Periodicals. 1st ed. Edited by Denise M. Allard and Robert C. Thomas. Detroit, MI: Gale. 3 vols., 1987/88. ISBN (set) 0-8103-2082-7. ISSN 0894-3869. Volume 1: *Business, Finance, Industry and Trade* (494 p., 1987); Volume 2: *Science, Medicine, and Technology* (495 p., 1987); Volume 3: *Social Sciences, Education, and Humanities* (747 p., 1988).

Arranged by subject, the set lists thousands of newsletters, periodicals, and serials published by national associations throughout the United States. Each entry provides the address and phone of the association and some descriptive information about the publication listed.

Awards, Honors, and Prizes. 8th ed., edited by Gita Siegman. Detroit: Gale. 2 vols., plus suppl. Volume 1: *United States and Canada;* Volume 2: *International and Foreign.* The *Supplement* provides details about additional awards not covered in the main set. LC 85-070620, ISBN (set): 0-8103-5087-4.

Provides details about thousands of organizations that sponsor awards and describes details covering the awards themselves. SEE ALSO: *World of Winners.*

Ayer Directory. See: *Gale Directory of Publications and Broadcast Media.*

Bibliographic Index. Semiannual, 1937- . Annual cumulative volume. Bronx, NY: H.W. Wilson. LC 46-41034, ISSN 0006-1255.
   A subject index to bibliographies that have 50 or more citations and which appear separately or as parts of books, pamphlets, or periodicals. Emphasis is on English language publications, but some foreign language materials are included. Index by subject and personal name.

Biographical Dictionaries and Related Works. Edited by Robert B. Slocum. Detroit, MI: Gale. 2d ed., 2 vols., 1986. ISBN 0-8103-0243-8.
   A comprehensive listing of biographical dictionaries. The set is international in scope and divided into three sections: Universal biography; National or area biography; and Biography by vocation. Thousands of publications which cover biographies in each area are listed.

Biographical Dictionaries Master Index. Detroit, MI: Gale. 3 vols., 1975/1976. Continued by: *Biography and Genealogy Master Index* (1980- .)
   A personal name index to more than 50 biographical dictionaries and/or other reference sources containing biographical information about important people, including celebrities. Arranged alphabetically by the name of the person, with a listing of which dictionary or reference source has the biographical information.

Biography Almanac. See: *Almanac of Famous People.*

Biography and Genealogy Master Index. 1980- . Detroit: Gale. 8 vols., 1980. Annual supplements. LC 81-6160, ISSN 0730-1316. First edition published in 1975 as *Biographical Dictionaries Master Index.*
   The set indexes several hundred reference books and other sources of biographical information about people in all walks of life. The volumes are arranged in alphabetical order by personal

name, followed by a list of books and other materials that contain information about the person.

Biography Index. Quarterly, 1946-   . Cumulative annual indexes. Bronx, NY: H.W. Wilson. LC 47-6532, ISSN 0006-3053. Available online: Wilsonline.

This series is an index to English-language biographical information published worldwide. It is an ongoing and comprehensive bibliography of articles and books about notable people. Each issue arranges, in alphabetical order by the name of the subject, the most recent articles or other information published from a large number of periodicals, books, and other sources. Complete citations are provided for each work listed, be it journal article or pamphlet. Types of material included: biographies and memoirs, interviews, critical reviews, fiction, diaries, letters, drama, poetry, pictorial works, juvenile literature, and obituaries. Uniquely, the series also indexes the people it profiles by profession or occupation. It's therefore a handy place to go in order to find quick leads to who is currently prominent in a particular profession or occupation with which you are unfamiliar.

Book Review Digest. Monthly, 1905-   . Annual cumulative volume and special cumulated indexes: 1905-1974, 1975-1984. Bronx, NY: H.W. Wilson. LC 6-24490, ISSN 0006-7326. Supplementary titles issued: *Author-Title Index, 1905-1974* and *Author-Title Index, 1975-1984.*

The series indexes reviews of new books; the reviews themselves have recently been published in a variety of books, periodicals, and other sources. Entries are arranged alphabetically by author (and sometimes by title) of the publication that was the subject of the review, with the bibliography of reviews following. Citations include brief excerpts from the original reviews.

Book Review Index. Annual, 1965-   . Bimonthly supplements. Detroit: Gale. ISSN 0524-0581.

An index to new books and periodicals that were reviewed in more than 470 periodicals during the past year. The *Index* is international in scope and covers all fields. The current address is given for the publishers of periodical titles which were reviewed.

Books In Print. Annual, 1947- . Supplements. New York: R.R. Bowker. ISSN 0068-0214. *Subject Guide to Books in Print* (Annual, 1956- . ISSN 0000-0159).

The basic set is an author and title index of all current books published in the United States; the *Subject Guide* provides access by subject. Over 6,000 publishers and approximately half a million books are listed. Phone numbers and addresses for publishers are given. Similar information is provided for paperback books in the Bowker semiannual *Paperbound Books in Print.*

British Books in Print. Annual, 1874- . Distributed in the United States by R.R. Bowker. SEE ALSO: BRITISH GENERAL REFERENCE RESOURCES, Chapter 11, pp. 446-7.

British Humanities Index (1915-). SEE ALSO: BRITISH GENERAL REFERENCE RESOURCES, Chapter 11, p. 440.

Bulletin of Bibliography. Quarterly, 1897- . ISSN 0190-745X. Westport, CT: Meckler. Available on microform and document delivery service from University Microfilms International (UMI) of Ann Arbor, Michigan. Indexed in: Biography Index, MLA, Index to Book Reviews in the Humanities, and others. See: THEATER REFERENCE RESOURCES, p. 174, for a description.

Business Periodicals Index. Monthly, 1958- . Annual cumulative volume. Bronx, NY: H.W. Wilson. LC 58-12645, ISSN 0007-6961. Available online: Wilsonline, . . .

This serial indexes approximately 300 business periodicals by subject, with some corporate and personal names. It's a good place to start for economic information, international business developments, statistical information, and trends in the various fields of the entertainment industry. The business and financial aspects of motion pictures, television, broadcasting, and audio/video recordings are well covered. It's also a good place to go for information on copyright and intellectual property issues. Coverage of Great Britain and Europe is also current and detailed.

Canadian News Index. Monthly, 1977- . Annual cumulations. Toronto, Ont.: Micromedia. LC 85-643665, ISSN 0225-7459.

Previous title: *Canadian Newspaper Index.* Indexes approximately 30 Canadian newspapers and news magazines.

Canadian Periodical Index. Monthly, 1928- . Annual cumulative volume. Ottawa, Canada. Canadian Library Association/InfoGlobe. LC 49-2133, ISSN 0008-4719. Previous title: *Canadian Index to Periodicals and Documentary Films* (1948-1963), *Canadian Periodical Index* (1928-1947). Current title started in 1964. Beginning in 1964, the film section was continued in their National Library's *Canadiana.*

Indexes over 100 popular Canadian periodicals. Films have not been included since 1964 because they are indexed in *Canadiana,* a film index published by the National Library.

Canadian Serials Directory. Edited by Gordon Ripley. Toronto, Ont: Reference Press. 3d ed., 396 p., 1987. cn87-0938 72-XE, ISBN 0-919981-10-0.

An alphabetical list of Canadian periodicals. Each entry contains: addresses, previous titles, year started, and a brief abstract regarding the general contents and style of the publication. Only titles produced in Canada are included. A subject index of the titles is provided.

Canadiana; Canada's national bibliography. Monthly, 1951- . Annual cumulations. Ottawa, Canada: National Library of Canada. ISSN 0008-5391.

The series lists publications of Canadian origin or of Canadian interest that have been deposited in their National Library. Sound recordings are included. Films and video tapes were included until 1976. After 1976, they are listed in a separate publication, *Film Canadiana.*

Contemporary Newsmakers. See: *Newsmakers [year].*

Cumulative Book Index. Monthly, 1898- . Annual cumulations. Bronx, NY: H.W. Wilson. LC 86-655475, ISSN 0011-300X. Previous titles: *The Monthly Cumulative Book Index,* and *A Cumulated Index to the Books of. . . .* The current title started in 1908.

Frequently referred to as the "CBI." A listing of all books

published in the English language for the year by commercial publishers. Arrangement is by author, title, and broad subject area. It's one of the best sources for verifying information about older publications and for verifying the LC and ISBN numbers. If your local library doesn't have any other source for finding a broad range of publications, this is the place to go.

Current Biography. Monthly, 1940- . Bronx, NY: H.W. Wilson. LC 40-27432, ISSN 0011-3344. Annual yearbook cumulates the monthly issues under the title: *Current Biography Yearbook* (Annual, 1940- . ISSN 0084-9499). *Current Biography Cumulated Index, 1940-1985* (1986, 125p., LC 40-27432, ISBN 0-8242-0722-X). Online: Wilsonline.

Each monthly issue contains 16 to 18 profiles of men and women of note plus obituaries of recent deaths. A cumulative index in each issue lists all entries for the current year. Information about each subject includes: name, birth, address, profession, an overview of his or her life and career, information about the subject's views and opinions, comments by others about the subject, a recent photograph, and bibliographical references.

Current Law Index. Monthly, 1980- . Quarterly and Annual cumulations. Foster City, CA: Information Access. ISSN 0196-1780.

Directories in Print. 6th ed. Detroit: Gale. 2 vols. and suppl., 1989. ISSN 0899-353X. Previous title: *Directory of Directories.*

The set lists over 10,000 directories of associations, professional organizations, businesses, groups, and other types of directories. The "Arts and Entertainment" section lists directories for all areas of the performing arts. The directories for each section are listed in alphabetical order, with publisher, address, phone, and description given for each title. Monographs as well as serials are included. A number of other sections are also of interest to entertainment researchers, chief among them: "Specific Industries," "Biography," "Information Sciences," and "Hobbies." Indexed by subject, title, and key word. See Also: *International Directories in Print, 1989-90.*

Directory of British Associations and Associations in Ireland. 9th ed. Edited by G. P. Henderson. Published in London by CBD

Research; distributed in the United States by Gale Research (Detroit, MI). 548 p., 1988. ISBN 0-900246-49-9. See Also: page 442.

The latest edition covers approximately 7,000 national, regional, and local organizations and other membership groups based in England, Wales, Scotland, and Ireland. Indexing is by organizational title and subject.

Directory of Directories. See: *Directories in Print.*

Directory of Special Libraries and Information Centers. 1963- . Edited by Lee Ash and William G. Miller. Detroit: Gale. A companion set is *Subject Directory of Special Libraries and Information Centers* (irregular, 1975-).

The main set is arranged geographically and the subject directory is arranged by broad general topic. The entry for each library includes the address, phone, staff, collection emphasis and size, special collections of note, library policies (when known), and any other information the institution may have provided.

Dissertation Abstracts International (Monthly, 1938-), *Comprehensive Dissertation Index* (37 vols., 1861-1972, and suppls.), and *Master's Abstracts* (Quarterly, 1962-) are only three of a series of titles published by University Microfilms International (UMI) of Ann Arbor, Michigan.

The publications provide international subject access to dissertations, with a brief abstract for each title. With rare exceptions, the complete dissertation can be purchased from UMI.

Editor & Publisher International Yearbook. Annual, 1920/21- . New York: Editor & Publisher. LC 84-645309, ISSN 0424-4923, ISBN 9-993-7798-8-1.

A directory of all daily newspapers and weeklies published in the United States and Canada. Special interest newspapers are also listed. The major newspapers from foreign countries are also listed. Each entry includes address and phone, major staff, advertising rates, circulation, and technical information about the publishing of the paper. Syndicated services, news services, photo services, comic suppliers, and magazine sections are covered. In addition, the annual lists equipment, press organizations, suppliers, and services. For example, nearly half a page of newspaper clipping services are listed, and several pages of associations and organizations.

Encyclopedia of Associations. Annual, 1957- . Earlier editions were published irregularly. Detroit, MI: Gale. Each edition has multiple volumes with two supplements. LC 76-46129, ISSN 0071-0202. Currently issued in three volumes: Volume 1: *National Organizations of the U.S.* (in three parts); Volume 2: *Geographic and Executive Indexes;* and Volume 3: *New Associations and Projects.*

Provides full descriptions of over 22,000 associations, clubs, organizations, and other membership groups worldwide. Indexing is by organizational title, key word, and subject. Each entry provides the name, address, phone, titles of regular publications, and a description of the organization.

Encyclopedia of Southern Culture. Edited by Charles Wilson and William Ferris. Chapel Hill, NC: University of North Carolina Press. 1634 p., illus, 1989. LC 88-17084, ISBN 0-8078-1823-2.

The work covers the history of Southern culture in twenty-four main sections, each one covering a broad subject area. Entertainment researchers will find it to be of value because of its frequent identification of music, Southern performers, film and television portrayals of Southern life, and other events that relate to the performing arts. If you don't know what zydeco means, this is the place to find out.

Essay and General Literature Index. Semi-annual, 1934- . Annual cumulative volume. Cumulative five-year index. Bronx, NY: H.W. Wilson. LC 34-14581, ISSN 0014-083X. Available online: Wilsonline. First issue, 1934, but citations start for 1900.

Comprehensive index to English-language essay collections and anthologies from 1900 to the present. Includes drama and film criticism. Indexed by author and subject.

Facts on File. New York: Facts on File. Weekly, with semimonthly indexes, 1941- . *Yearbooks* cumulate all of the weeklies into one volume (ISSN 0014-6641). Multi-year cumulative indexes are available. Back years are available on microfiche from the publisher.

Weekly digest and index of national and international news. The information is culled from a number of leading newspapers and current evening journals worldwide. Includes information on play openings, film releases, and names in the news.

Gale Directory of Publications and Broadcast Media. Annual, 1869-   . Detroit, MI: Gale. Previous titles: *Gale Directory of Publications, IMS Directory of Publications* and *Ayer Directory of Publications* (1880-1982), *American Newspaper Directory* (1869-1908).
A directory of newspapers, periodicals, television and radio stations, and cable companies in the United States and Canada. Arranged geographically by state or province and then by city. Gives address, phone, and business information for each entry.

Gale International Directory of Publications. 1st ed. Edited by Kay Gill and Darren L. Smith. Detroit, MI: Gale. 573 p., 1989. ISBN 0-8103-4255-3.
Arranged geographically by country, the volume is a directory of important newspapers and general-interest periodicals for approximately 100 countries. There are some specialized periodicals noted, but these listings are not as complete. Information for each citation includes title, address, phone, and names of leading personnel, and production information (date started, frequency, editorial advertising staff contacts, subscription and advertising rates, and circulation statistics).

Handbook of American Popular Culture. Edited by M. Thomas Inge. Westport, CT: Greenwood Press. 2d ed., rev. and enl., 1989. 1613 p., 3 vols. LC 88-39092, ISBN: 0-313-25406-0.
A comprehensive overview of U.S. culture and life, both current and historical. The set includes a considerable amount of information about popular entertainment, with an emphasis on film, musical theater, music, radio, records, television, popular literature, religion, the media, games, and other similar subjects. A good place if you need to develop an understanding of what appeals to Americans now or in the past.

Humanities Index. Quarterly, 1907-   . Current series title started in 1974. Previously published under the titles *International Index* and *Social Sciences and Humanities Index* from 1907 to 1974 (LC

17-4969). Annual cumulative volume. Bronx, NY: H.W. Wilson. LC 75-648836, ISSN 0095-5981. SEE: *Social Sciences and Humanities Index* for full explanation.

The oldest and most easily found of the humanities indexes, it indexes nearly 350 periodicals by author and subject. Good coverage of theater and drama, film, music, and the performing arts in general. Original works are indexed, as are personal names and wide variety of subjects.

Index to Book Reviews in the Humanities. Annual, 1960- Detroit, MI: Phillip Thompson. LC 62-21757, ISSN 0073-5892.

Indexes hundreds of periodicals for the book reviews they contain. Thousands of book reviews are listed yearly; recent volumes include some reviews in foreign languages.

Index to Legal Periodicals. Monthly, 1908- . Quarterly and annual cumulations. Bronx, NY: H. W. Wilson. LC 41-21689, ISSN 0019-4077.

A comprehensive index to the major law journals, researchers can find information on copyright, corporate law, the film and broadcast industries, and other entertainment law subjects.

Information Please Almanac. Annual, 1947- . New York: Simon & Schuster. ISSN 0073-7860.

A general review of the events of the year covering the United States and the world, including new film releases, Broadway play openings, show business awards, and some news about entertainment figures.

International Directories in Print. 1st ed. (1989-1990). Edited by Julie E. Towell and Charles B. Montney. Detroit, MI: Gale. 1,125 p., 1988. ISBN 0-8103-2511-X.

Similar to Gale's *Directories in Print,* the book covers directories for associations, organizations, and other membership groups worldwide. Much of the information is duplicated in other Gale books, but if this is what you are looking for, it's nice to have the listings together on one source. Arranged first by subject area (The Arts is one), then by country, followed by title. Indexing is by country, specific fields and/or subject, and key word of the directory title.

International Index (1907-1965). This title became the *Social Sciences and Humanities Index*. The title is divided into two separate series; See: *Humanities Index* and/or *Social Sciences Index* depending on the subject matter.

International Literary Market Place (ILMP). Annual, 1965- . New York: R.R. Bowker. LC 65-28326, ISSN 0538-8562. Previous title: *European Literary Market Place*. See Also: *Literary Market Place*.

A directory of publishers, literary representatives, subsidiaries, and distributors.

International Organizations. Detroit, MI: Gale. Annual, 1983- . LC 89-645065, ISSN 0141-0023. Previously published as part of the *Encyclopedia of Associations* and retained the volume numbering sequence of that series when it started publishing separately in 1983.

A listing of approximately 9,000 organizations from virtually every country that have national or international members. The term is broadly defined to include everything from professional associations, to European marketing groups, to fan clubs. Arranged by subject, the set provides information about each organization and its interests and/or function.

International Research Centers Directory. Annual, 1982- . Detroit, MI: Gale. LC 82-641202, ISSN 0278-2731.

A comprehensive listing of research facilities in 145 countries, excluding the United States. Institutions covered include government, university, nonprofit, and private facilities. Emphasis is on libraries. Arranged by country, each entry contains a description of the facility, publications, its collection and staff size, and unique area of expertise. See Also: *Research Centers Directory* for United States and Canadian listings.

The International Who's Who. Annual, 1935- . London: Europa Publications. Distributed in the United States by Gale Research (Detroit). The 52d edition is 1988-1989 (ISBN: 0-813-0-946653-42-9, LC 35-10257), ISSN 0074-9613.

An international alphabetical listing of important people. Brief biographical sketches of a personal and professional nature are provided for each person.

International Who's Who in Music and Musicians' Directory. 11th ed., 1988. See: page 246.

Literary Market Place (LMP). Annual, 1940-   . New York: R. R. Bowker. LC 88-644926, ISSN 0000-1155.
The place to go for information about the publishing and writing industries. The names and addresses of people, publishing companies, and related services. See Also: *International Literary Market Place.*

Magazine Article Summaries. Weekly, 1984- . Leeds, AL: Ebsco. ISSN 0895-3376. Previous title: *Popular Magazine Review* (1984-1987).
Indexes approximately 200 magazine titles. Good descriptive annotations.

Magazine Index. See: pages 86-87.

Magazine Industry Market Place (MIMP). Annual, 1980-   . New York: R.R. Bowker. LC 80-648262, ISSN 0000-0434.
Information on nearly 4000 periodicals and related vendors and services of use to periodical publishers. Of special value is a section listing stock photo agencies which gives their name, address, phone, and subject coverage of their collection.

Magazines for Libraries. 6th ed. Edited by Bill Katz and Linda S. Katz. New York: R.R. Bowker. 1,159 p., 1989. LC 86-640971, ISBN 0835226328.
A subject listing of periodicals most likely to be found in public and school libraries. The titles selected and reviewed are considered to be the most appropriate for each subject area by a panel of specialists. A useful place to start if no specialized collections are available.

Marquis Who's Who. SEE *Who's Who in America.*

MLA International Bibliography of Books and Articles on the Modern Languages and Literatures. Annual (in a multi-volume set), 1921- . ISSN 0024-8215. Modern Language Association of America. Address: 10 Astor Place, New York, NY 10003. Available online on: Dialog, Wilsonline.

National Newspaper Index, 1979- . See: pages 87, 94.

New Periodicals Index. Semiannual, 1977- . Boulder, CO: Mediaworks. ISSN 0146-5716.
    Indexes alternative and new age magazines, newspapers, and newsletters. Each issue indexes approximately 70 titles.

New Serial Titles; a union list of serials commencing publication after December 31, 1949. Weekly, 1951- . Monthly, quarterly, and annual cumulations. Washington, DC: Library of Congress. LC 53-60021, ISSN 0028-6680.
    R. R. Bowker has published cumulative editions and now has the information on a database. A continuation of the third edition of: *Union List of Serials in Libraries of the United States and Canada.*

New York Times Biographical Service; a compilation of current biographical information of general interest. Monthly, 1969/70- . Annual cumulations. Ann Arbor, MI: University Microfilms International (UMI). LC 70-20206, ISSN 0161-2433. Previous title: *New York Times Biographical Edition.* Indexed in: BI.
    The publication provides actual reproductions of articles (many with photos) that were published in the *New York Times.* Articles which are reprinted include profiles, interviews, historical perspectives, and obituaries that are wholly, or in large part, about that person. No performance reviews are included. Entries cover people from all walks of life and are international in scope. The volumes are arranged chronologically by the date they were published in the *New York Times.*

New York Times Index. Semimonthly, 1851- . Quarterly and annual cumulations. Published by The New York Times Index (New York), distributed by University Microfilms International (Ann Arbor, MI). The *Index* has appeared in various formats and has had several publishers over the years. *See Also:* Nexis, pages 87-88.

This printed version of the *Index* is arranged alphabetically by personal names and broad subject areas. The more significant articles contain lengthy abstracts. It's not as comprehensive as the Nexis (Mead) online full-text version, but once you understand which terms to use and how to look for the information you need, it's a most helpful source. Keep in mind, however, that the indexing is broad and if the person or event was not the major focus of the article in which it appeared, it probably won't be included in the index.

New York Times Obituary Index, 1858-1968. New York, New York Times. 1,136 p., 1970. LC 72-113422. *Supplement:* 1969-1978 (131 p., 1980; ISBN 0-667-00598-6). Continued by the *New York Times Biographical Service* (1969-   .).

An alphabetical listing of deceased notables, followed by the date the obituary was published in the *New York Times.* Each citation notes the date, issue number, volume number, page number, and column.

Newsmakers [year]. Quarterly, 1985-   . Annual cumulations. Detroit: Gale. ISSN 0899-0417. Previous title: *Contemporary Newsmakers.* Indexed in: *BI, BGMI.*

A quarterly periodical which provides lengthy biographies of current newsmakers (including entertainment figures). Some interviews; photos accompany most articles. A brief bibliography of books and periodical articles about the subject follows each profile. Recent obituaries are also included.

Nineteenth Century Readers' Guide to Periodical Literature. Bronx, NY: H. W. Wilson. 2 vols., 1944. LC 44-5439, ISBN 0-8242-0584-7.

This set indexes 51 periodicals by author and subject for the period 1890-1899 and provides supplementary indexing for 14 of the titles from 1850 up through 1922. The index includes reviews, plays, and other entertainment information.

PAIS Bulletin. Monthly, 1914-   . Annual cumulations. New York: Public Affairs Information Service. LC 86-21739, ISSN 0898-2201.

112 Popular Entertainment Research

There is also a *Cumulative Subject Index to PAIS Bulletin, 1915-1974.*

This serial indexes an international selection of periodicals, reports, books, and pamphlets that are published in the English language from a number of countries. Subject emphasis is on business, economic, and social conditions. Although limited in coverage of the entertainment fields, it does provide some access to the business industries involved. Subjects recently indexed include: Cable television, Compact discs, Movies, Sound recordings, and Video recordings.

Poole's Index to Periodical Literature. 1802-1908. The main set of volumes were published from 1802 to 1881, with *Supplements* being published for the years 1887 to 1908. Boston: Houghton. No longer published. A revised edition was published in six volumes that included the original volumes and supplements. No LC or ISBN numbers.

While smaller public libraries may not have this, many medium-size or larger libraries will. Valuable for its extensive coverage of early American and British literature. As the major periodical index for the 19th Century, it indexed approximately 500 periodicals over a 100-year period. The organization of the index is difficult to use in that articles are indexed by subject only; articles with no clear subject are included under title of the article. Still, the complete set is considered important enough that several independent indexes to the set have been published. Of these, the most important is *Cumulative Author Index For Poole's Index to Periodical Literature, 1802-1906,* compiled and edited by C. Edward Wall (Ann Arbor, MI: Pierian Press; 488 p., 1971, LC 77-143237, ISBN 87650-006-8). Another useful aid is *Poole's Index: date and volume key* by Marion V. Bell and Jean C. Bacon (Chicago: American Library Association/ Association of College and Research Libraries; 61 p., 1957, LC 57-7157, reprinted by University Microfilms International, Ann Arbor, MI, in 1980).

Popular Periodical Index. Quarterly, 1973- . Annual cumulation. Address: P.O. Box 1156, Rosalyn, PA 19001: Popular Periodical Index. LC 74-640955, ISSN 0092-9727.

This publication regularly indexes about 40 periodicals by

subject, including *Emmy* and *TV Guide, Down Beat, Audio, American Record Guide, Film Quarterly, Rolling Stone,* and *Video Review.* This index specifically selects titles which are not in *Reader's Guide.*

Readers' Guide to Periodical Literature. 1900-   . 18 issues yearly, annual cumulative volume. Bronx, NY: H.W. Wilson. LC 6-8232, ISSN 0034-0464.

The best known and most used reference tool of all time; don't pass it by as a beginning aid to your research. And if you don't live near a large entertainment library collection, this is the place to start because it's available in virtually every library. It began indexing a broad range of popular-interest periodicals published in the United States in 1900 and is still going strong today.

The 200 periodicals selected for the service change constantly; therefore, many of the early titles are not in it today. This makes it a valuable historical resource as well a current one. Regarding material of interest to entertainment researchers, the *Index* to the *Readers' Guide* includes: interviews; performance reviews (for films, television, live shows, and stage plays); articles about performers in all areas; critical essays; and a large number of specific subject areas.

Like any other index, you have to get used to the unique terms that *Readers' Guide* uses and the way it arranges the material before you can find the information you want. Film reviews are indexed under "Motion picture reviews" rather than the film title. In addition, films are separately indexed by the name of the director, but *not* by their title or the names of the leading actors. Record reviews are grouped under the heading "Phonograph records." Reviews of radio programs are indexed together under "Radio program reviews." Videodisc and videotape reviews are found under those headings, but theatre reviews are indexed under the dramatist's name as well as "Theatre reviews." Therefore, it's important to realize that in many cases you won't find titles indexed separately; instead, a title may be located under one of the subject headings just mentioned.

Unlike many indexes that are locked into a rigid subject heading system that no longer reflects modern terms (for example, putting country music under "folk music"), the *Index* of *Readers' Guide* is willing to change with the times and adopt subject headings that are relevant to today's language. For example, a recent issue contained the following subject terms: 3-D television; American film market; Amusement parks; Cowboy poetry; Digital audio tape recorders and recordings; Jazz music; Motion picture actors and actresses; Radio broadcasting; "Star Trek"; Television performers; and Theatre buildings.

Because *Readers' Guide* has indexed such standard long-running titles as *Life, Time, Newsweek,* and *Business Week* from their first issue forward, there's a historical continuity available that is not found in similar reference sources. And even the smallest libraries will probably have the back issues you need. In fact, many libraries make it a point to subscribe to the periodicals included in the *Readers' Guide* before they purchase anything else simply because the *Index* provides their patrons with "access" to the information in the journal.

The following entertainment periodicals are currently indexed: *American Film; Dance Magazine; Down Beat; Film Comment; High Fidelity; Opera News; People; Rolling Stone; Stereo Review; Theatre Crafts; TV Guide; Video; World Press Review;* and *The Writer.*

Research Centers Directory. Irregular, 1960-   . Detroit, MI: Gale. LC 84-1050, ISSN 0080-1518. Supplement: *New Research Centers* (ISBN 0-8103-1803-2). ISSN 0028-65917.

Covers over 10,000 nonprofit research centers and collections in all subject fields. A number of libraries and special collections are listed for motion pictures, music, popular culture, television, and theater. Arrangement is by geographic area. Access is enhanced by a detailed subject index. See Also: *International Research Centers Directory.*

Research Services Directory. 1981-   . See also page 18 for related sources and information.

Social Sciences and Humanities Index. Bronx, NY: Wilson.

The series was published under this title from 1965 to 1974, and under the title *International Index* from 1907 to 1965, then separated into two titles in 1975: *Humanities Index* and *Social Sciences Index.* LC 17-4969. It indexed around 200 titles, mostly

American, with some British titles. Other foreign titles were included in earlier volumes, but dropped after World War II.

Social Sciences Index. Quarterly, 1907- . Annual cumulations, Current title started in 1974. Bronx, NY: Wilson. LC 75-649443, ISSN 0094-4920. Previous title: *Social Science and Humanities Index.*
   The series in an index to over 350 periodicals in the social sciences, including a number of subjects of interest to entertainment researchers.

Subject Collections; a guide to special book collections and subject emphasis as reported by university, college, public, and special libraries and museums in the United States and Canada. 6th ed. Edited by Lee Ash and William G. Miller. New York: R.R. Bowker. 2 vols., 1985. LC 85-126315, ISBN 0835219178.
   The set provides brief, but descriptive, profiles of over 11,000 library and museum collections. Once you have found collections that look promising for your research needs, the individual institutions can be contacted for more details.

Subject Collections in European Libraries. 2d ed. Compiled by Richard Lewanski. New York: R.R. Bowker. 495 p., 1978. LC 79-302719, ISBN 0859350118.
   One of the few guides available to the collections of European libraries, both public and academic. Directory information is provided for each institution as well as a profile of the collection. Hours of operation and internal library services are noted where known. A little outdated, but still useful.

Subject Directory of Special Libraries and Information Centers. 1975- . See: *Directory of Special Libraries and Information Centers.*

Tony, Grammy, Emmy, Country; a Broadway, television, and records awards reference. Compiled by Don Franks. Jefferson, NC: McFarland, 1986. (160 pp.). LC 85-43577, ISBN 0-89950-204-0.
   Complete awards data on the Emmy (Academy of Television Arts and Sciences); the Tony (American Theatre Wing); the

Grammy (National Academy of Recording Arts and Sciences); and the Country Music Awards given by the Country Music Association. A description and history of each award is given; index by names and titles of works and/or shows.

Ulrich's International Periodicals Directory. 1932- . Annual; 3 vols. New York: R. R. Bowker. Frequency has varied over the years. LC 32-16320, ISBN 0-8352-2563-1, ISSN 0000-0175. Now incorporates *Irregular Serials & Annuals.*
Worldwide listing of current periodicals, serials that are published irregularly, and annuals that are published once a year. Information about ceased titles covers a three-year period. Daily newspapers and membership directories of organizations are not included.

Bibliographic information for each entry includes: title of the publication; year first published; frequency of publication; country of origin; ISSN or CODEN; subscription price; publisher's address and phone number; name of the editor; any special features to be found in the publication; and the circulation statistics. Each entry also includes information about other formats (if back issues are available, if it is microform, or can be purchased through a document delivery service); if it is included in an indexing service; or if it is on a computer database. Lastly, a notice of title change or listing of previous titles is given if necessary. Some entries include a brief description of the contents of the publication.

One special feature is ABSTRACTING AND INDEXING SERVICES, which brings together in one file all of the special indexes and abstracting publications listed throughout the set. In addition, *Ulrich's* now includes separate sections for titles which can be found on automated databases. The SERIALS AVAILABLE ONLINE section lists, in alphabetical order, the titles of periodicals and the online services in which they are included. A separate section, VENDOR LISTING/SERIALS ONLINE, is an alphabetical listing of online vendors, with a list of periodicals included in their database below the vendor name.

While there is a comprehensive listing of all titles in alphabetical order, the major part of the three volumes is devoted to listing the titles in broad subject areas. Subjects of interest to entertainment researchers include: Clubs; Biography;

Communications—Radio and Television; Dance; Motion Pictures; Music; Photography; Sound Recording and Reproduction; and Theater. The treatment is uneven, however. For example, newsletters about performers or entertainment interests are inconsistently handled: a Sinatra newsletter is in BIOGRAPHY; The Beatles and Bing Crosby are in MUSIC; one title about Elvis is in CLUBS and another in MUSIC; James Bond is in FILMS; *Gone With The Wind* is in HOBBIES; Science Fiction is in both CLUBS and MOTION PICTURES; and newsletters about Henrik Ibsen are in LITERATURE. Unfortunately, it's not possible to look up a person by name and find out what is listed. And if the title itself does not clearly indicate that it is about a particular person, there is no way to find out. Nor are the other subjects detailed enough to be as useful as one would like. Nevertheless, this is a great basic resource that researchers can find in even the smallest library. It's a worthy place to start pulling together your research plans.

Union List of Serials in Libraries of the United States and Canada. Bronx, NY: H.W. Wilson. 3d edition. 5 vols., 1965. Continued by: *New Serial Titles.*
  Very old, but still a useful tool for tracking down the location of periodicals in libraries around the country. In fact, it's extremely helpful for finding which libraries once had (and may still have) periodicals which have long ago stopped publishing. It lists over 150,000 periodicals held in nearly 1,000 libraries at the time the set was published.

Whitaker's Almanack. 1869-   . Distributed in the United States by Gale (Detroit). See: Chapter 11, Research Resources in Great Britain, page 445.

Who Was Who in America. 11 vols. (1607-1989). Wilmette, IL: Marquis Who's Who. 1989. ISSN 0083-9345.
  Updates added approximately every four years. The set profiles over 100,000 notable Americans who are no longer living. With the exception of those in the earliest historical volume, most of the sketches appeared in earlier editions of *Who's Who in America* and have been updated for this publication with details about the biographee's date of death and place of interment.

Who's Who. See: Chapter 11, Research Resources in Great Britain, page 445.

Who's Who In America. Biennial, 1899-   . Issued with supplements. Wilmette, IL: Marquis Who's Who. ISSN 0083-9396.
A valuable source of brief biographical information about nearly anyone who is important because the information is acquired directly from the person (or a representative) listed. Back volumes are useful for historical research and should not be overlooked because people who appear in one issue will not necessarily appear in another. Each entry includes basic biographical information, professional accomplishments, and an address where he or she can be contacted.

Who's Who in Entertainment. 1989-   . Wilmette, IL: Marquis Who's Who. First ed. 800 p., 1989-1990. ISBN 0-8379-1850-2.
Extremely useful for entertainment researchers because it includes performers and industry personnel from all areas of entertainment. As with the other Marquis publications, each profile includes biographical information, major professional accomplishments and appearances, awards, organizational memberships, and current address (usually an agent). It's a good brief overview resource of documentary information for performers who have been active in more than one field. For example, the sketch for Johnny Cash identifies his films, television programs, and recordings. The publication doesn't claim to provide complete lists of works, of course, but there is enough there to cover the important elements of each career.
The Marquis regional series of *Who's Who* books also has regional volumes that might be helpful for finding people not included in the national volumes: *Who's Who in the East, Who's Who in the Midwest, Who's Who in the South and Southwest,* and *Who's Who in the West.*

The Working Press of the Nation. Annual, 1945-   . Chicago, IL: National Research Bureau. 5 vols. LC 46-7041, ISSN 0084-1323.
Each volume has a distinctive title and can stand alone. Volume 1 is the *Newspaper Directory* and lists daily and weekly newspapers, feature syndicates, news and photo services. Each entry includes production information, key personnel, and

market information. Volume 2 is *Magazine Directory,* which lists nearly 5,000 magazines in all subject areas. Volume 3 is *TV and Radio Directory* which lists nearly 10,000 radio and television stations. Each entry includes owner and network affiliation, address, phone, call letters, key personnel, power, format, population served, geographical area, and locally produced programs. Volume 4 is the *Feature Writer and Photographer Directory* which lists nearly 2,000 writers and photographers. Each entry has a contact address and phone number, the writer's area of interest, and publications who have used their work. A subject specialty index is provided. Volume 5 is an *Internal Publications Directory* listing internally produced publications of over 3,000 companies, government agencies, and other groups.

World Almanac and Book of Facts. Annual, 1868-   . New York: World Almanac. LC 78-1564, ISSN 0084-1382. Previous titles: *World Almanac* (1868-1893) and *World Almanac and Encyclopedia* (1894-1922).

A general review of the year's important events, with an emphasis on the United States. Sections containing information of interest to entertainment researchers include a listing of awards (for theater and broadcasting, Academy Awards, and the Grammies); an Arts and Media section which lists Broadway theatre openings for the season, motion picture releases for the year, and the top films of the year; the Recording Industry of America Gold and Platinum Awards for albums and singles (videos have recently been added); notable U.S. dance and opera companies; a number of television and viewer statistics; the names, place of birth, and birth dates of thousands of current and recent entertainment personalities; a listing of hundreds of entertainers of the past with their birth and death years; and a special listing of entertainers who have changed their names (arranged by their stage names followed by their original names).

World of Learning. 1947-   . London: Europa Publications, and Detroit, MI: Gale. 39th edition, 1,925 p., 1989. LC 47-30172, ISBN 0-946653-46-1.

A long-standing volume of educational, cultural, and scientific resources from around the world. A good listing of special libraries.

World of Winners. 1st ed. Edited by Gita Siegman. Detroit, MI: Gale. 977 p., 1989. ISBN 0-8103-0474-0.

While Gale's *Awards, Honors, and Prizes* provides information about the prizes themselves and the organizations that give them, this companion volume lists the winners of those prizes. Approximately 75,000 winners of over 2,000 awards are listed. Arrangement is by broad subject classification, with complete historical coverage listing all of the past winners. Various "Hall of Fame" awards are also included. Indexing is by award name, personal name, and sponsoring organization.

5 GENERAL ENTERTAINMENT REFERENCE RESOURCES

The fences between the different fields of the entertainment industry have largely been broken down the past twenty years due to changes in the ways entertainment is brought to the public and because researchers are smart enough to broaden their perspective beyond the research literature of a single field. Today it is common to see stage plays on television, motion picture and television actors making hit recordings, singers becoming actors, and fictional films based on real news events being produced and distributed. *Everyone* in the entertainment business appears on television and radio talk shows; and it is quite typical for the morning news programs to do show business publicity interviews.

`Because of the interrelationships between so many of the performing arts areas, many publications make a point in covering more than one field and can not easily be pigeon-holed into one subject area. Therefore, this chapter identifies the major books and periodicals that provide information about the entertainment industry in general. Even with this definition, some titles don't fit a mold. *Variety* and *Daily Variety* are so strongly identified with the film industry that they remain in Chapter 8 even though they provide current news and reviews from every field. *Billboard* is in Chapter 7 because of its relationship with the music industry even though I also find that it provides one of the most comprehensive lists of new video releases. Conversely, some of the video magazines are the best source for reviews of music videos. Probably the best current source of biographical profiles of actors, *Contemporary Theatre, Film and Television,* is in the theater chapter because it started out as a source of information about stage performers under its previous title (*Who's Who in the Theatre*) and the back volumes continue to be one of the most important sources of theatrical history. Gale Research has published research guides for specific fields of the performing arts in a series called *Performing Arts Information Guide Series;* these guides are listed in this book under their individual authors and titles.

This chapter contains as many sources for contacting people as I can find. But I'll repeat a point I've made before: there's no substitute for picking up the phone and making a well-placed call. The agent referral office at Screen Actors Guild is the best place to start; and many performers belong to the Guild even though they may not be considered actors in the eyes of the public. If you want to contact a recording artist, the artist's record company always has the name and phone of the performer's office, his or her current manager, public relations firm, or record producer at its fingertips because it deals with recording artists daily. If someone turns out to be incredibly hard to find, start by contacting a company that person has worked for, an organization or association in which that performer is likely to hold a membership for career reasons, or people whom you know the performer has worked with recently. If you stick with it, you will eventually find someone who knows how to reach the performer you want to contact.

As in the other chapters, I've also included some out-of-print books that have a historical value. I've also included law journals because they're interesting and can be useful to the layperson even though they are written for lawyers. They supply current important legal developments news and often give an insider's viewpoint of the mechanics of the industry that's not easily found elsewhere. If you want to improve your understanding of the financial workings of the industry, take the time to look at a few issues of *Entertainment Law & Finance.* And, frankly, I also find these journals a great source of ideas for stories. A lot of unusual things happen in the courtroom and not all of them make the daily newspapers or the weekly tabloids.

REFERENCE RESOURCES

American Theatrical Arts: A Guide to Manuscripts and Special Collections in the United States and Canada, by William C. Young. Chicago: American Library Association. 166 p., 1971, LC 78-161234, ISBN: 0-8389-0104-2.

Arranged geographically and then by institution, this volume describes the collections found in 138 libraries and/or archives throughout the United States and Canada.

Amusement Business (Box 24970, Nashville, TN 37202.)

This firm publishes a series of directories for use by people in the live entertainment industry. Their major publications are covered in detail in other parts of the book, but these smaller annuals are also worth a mention. *The Directory of Fairs, Festivals, & Expositions* lists over 6,000 state and county fairs, local and national expositions, and festivals in the United States and Canada; *Audarena Stadium Guide* lists over 6,000 arenas, auditoriums, and exhibit halls; and the *Funparks Directory* lists 2,000 amusement and theme parks, major tourist attractions, and zoos. Additionally, two of the firm's directories are buyers guides which list products and services for these industries: *Entertainment Facility Buyers Guide* and *Amusement Industry Buyer's Guide.*

Annotated Bibliography of New Publications in the Performing Arts. Quarterly, 1970- . New York: Drama Book Shop. LC 77-641702, ISSN 0360-6538.

Awards, Honors, and Prizes; a directory and sourcebook. Edited by Gita Siegman. Detroit, MI: Gale. 7th ed., 2 vols., 1988. Volume 1: *United States and Canada* (1,136 p., ISBN: 0-8103-0663-8); Volume 2: *International and Foreign* (673 p., ISBN: 0-8103-0664-6). A *Supplement* (251 p., ISBN: 0-8103-0665-4) updates the set by listing additional organizations and their awards.

The set lists, in alphabetical order, approximately 6,000 organizations worldwide that sponsor over 15,000 awards, including those in film, television, the stage, and radio.

Cavalcade of Acts & Attractions. See: Music Reference Resources in Chapter 7, pages 235-236.

The Celebrity Birthday Book, by Robert Brett Bronaugh. New York: Jonathan David Publishers. 492 p., 1981. LC 80-14221, ISBN: 0-8246-0253-6.
   The book provides the birth dates of famous people in the entertainment field as well as other professions. The information is arranged both by the name of the celebrity and chronologically.

The Celebrity Book of Lists: Fascinating Facts About Famous People, by Ed Lucaire. New York: Stein and Day. 256 p., 1984. LC 83-61721, ISBN: 0-8128-2935-2.
   This book provides a wide variety of facts about celebrities: where they were born, what they did before they were famous, levels of education, religion, famous quotes, and interesting stories or other facts that might be unusual.

Celebrity Bulletin. See: General Periodicals in this chapter, page 136.

Celebrity Register. 5th ed. Detroit, MI: Gale. 484 p., 1990. Data compiled by Celebrity Services International. ISSN: 0278-4556. Previously known as Earl Blackwell's *Celebrity Register* (1st ed., 1959). ISBN: 0-8103-6875-7. This edition has a cumulative index for all other editions.
   The approximately 1,800 celebrities selected for inclusion reflect current popularity and therefore many entries change with each edition. All of the performing arts are represented; and some of the best known figures in other professions are also included. A photo accompanies each profile.

Celebrity Resources: A Guide to Biographical Information About Famous People in Show Business and Sports Today, by Ronald Ziegler. New York: Garland. 578 p., 1990. LC 89-11762, ISBN: 0-8240-5946-8.
   The book has selected approximately 900 top celebrities and provides a listing of reference sources that contain biographical information about them. Some sources listed are common enough (like *Who's Who in America*) to be found in almost every

library collection, which should be a help to researchers who don't have access to large research centers. The addresses of some fan clubs are listed, which is always useful.

Chicorel Bibliography to the Performing Arts, by Marietta Chicorel. Chicorel Index Series. 498 p., 1972. LC 73-155102, ISBN: 0-87729-222-1.
Bibliography of books about the theater, with some entries for film and television. Arrangement is by broad subject listing.

Comedy on Record, by Ronald L. Smith. See: Chapter 7, page 237.

Contact Book; trade directory/entertainment industry. Annual, 1944- . Address: Celebrity Service International, 1780 Broadway, Suite 300, New York, NY 10019. Phone: (212) 757-7979. ISSN: 0069-1372.
One of the older and more reliable directories of agents and others representing celebrities and public figures in all areas of entertainment. International in scope with geographical coverage for major cities of the world. The book is organized by city and lists the following: agents, associations and organizations, production companies, distributors, technical services, publishers, and a variety of other phone numbers of use to entertainment people.
Celebrity Service International also offers an information subscription service which provides access to its huge collection of files on individual celebrities that have been gathered throughout the years. A subscription to the service includes their daily *Celebrity Bulletin* (see the periodicals section of this chapter).

Contemporary Theatre, Film, and Television. See: Chapter 6, page 176 and Chapter 8, page 291.

Daily Variety. See: Chapter 8, page 330.

Directory of Archives and Manuscript Repositories in the United States. Compiled by the National Historical Publications and Records Commission. 2d ed. Phoenix, AZ: Oryx Press. 853 p., 1988. LC 87-30157, ISBN 0897744756.

A comprehensive listing of archives which provides details about the holdings of each institution listed. Entertainment resources make up only a small part of the listings, but this Directory does include some collection information for film, photos, scripts, personal papers, and other special research materials.

Directory of Experts, Authorities & Spokespersons: An Encyclopedia of Sources. Annual, 1984-   . Broadcast Interview Source, 2233 Wisconsin Ave., N.W., Washington, DC 20007-4104. Phone: (202) 333-4904. The 6th edition was published in 1990. Previous title: *Talk Show Guest Directory of Experts, Authorities, and Spokespersons.* LC 88-659560.

A unique reference source marketed to radio and television stations, and independent program producers, as a resource tool in finding people who are available to be interviewed. The book is a listing of people who are experts on a wide variety of topics or organizations which represent special interest groups. The book is arranged by broad topic, with detailed subject, geographical, and alphabetical indexes also providing access. In addition to organizations and people who can provide expert commentary, it also includes a number of companies who can supply programming on special subjects.

The Directory of Free Programs, Performing Talent, and Attractions. Annual, 1983-   . Pageant Publishing Company, P.O. Box 240334, Memphis, TN 38124. ISSN: 0736-7759.

As the title indicates, this is a directory of acts that will perform free or for little cost.

Directory of Humor Magazines & Humor Organizations in America (and Canada). Triennial, 1985-   . Address: Wry-Bred Press, Box 1454, Madison Square Station, New York, NY 10159. Phone: (212) 689-5473. 2d ed., 192 p., 1988. ISBN: 0-9616190-7-0.

A detailed listing of more than 60 magazines, newsletters, and organizations concerned with humor. An appendix provides sales and market information for comedy writers.

Gadney's Guide to International Contests, Festivals & Grants in Film & Video, Photography, TV-Radio Broadcasting, Writing, Poetry, Playwriting & Journalism. Biennial, 1979-   . Address:

Festival Publications, Box 10180, Glendale, CA 91209. Phone: (818) 718-8494.

Guide to the Performing Arts. Published annually from 1958 to 1968; no longer published. Metuchen, NJ: Scarecrow. LC 60-7266, ISSN: 0072-873X.

Worthwhile as a research tool if you can find a set. The work indexed approximately fifty periodicals and covered all areas of the entertainment business. Access is by author, title, and subject.

How to Locate Reviews of Plays and Films: A Bibliography of Criticism From the Beginnings to the Present, by Gordon Samples. Metuchen, NJ: Scarecrow. 114 p., 1976. LC 76-3509, ISBN 0-8108-914-1.

If you don't have much experience at researching reviews, this slim volume offers good basic advice about how to do the work and provides an effective series of titles to use. It can be considered a little outdated by now because a number of new publications have been released since it was published, but it is still a useful tool.

Index to Characters in the Performing Arts. Compiled by Harold S. Sharp and Marjorie Z. Sharp. Metuchen, NJ: Scarecrow. 1966-1973, 4 vols. (in six books). LC 66-13744, ISBN: 0-1808-0486-7.

The set identifies fictional and real characters in all types of performing-arts productions, from plays to television. Volume 1 (in two actual volumes) lists characters in stage plays, excluding musicals; Volume 2 covers musicals and operas; Volume 3 covers ballets; and Volume 4 covers radio and television productions. Each volume has an alphabetical listing of characters, with information about the characters and the productions in which they appeared. I find this a great help in verifying characters and using the information as background for information in articles.

The Language of American Popular Entertainment: A Glossary of Argot, Slang, and Terminology, by Don B. Wilmeth. Westport, CT: Greenwood Press. 305 p., 1981. LC 80-14795, ISBN: 0-313-22497-8.

This is an absolutely fascinating dictionary which defines and explains the special languages of various forms of live entertainment. Some of the areas covered are medicine shows, popular theater, the circus, magic, outdoor amusement industry terms and pitchmen's slang. It's as chocked full of strange terms as anything I've encountered, and worth reading for its own entertainment value.

The Language of Show Biz: A Dictionary. Chicago: The Dramatic Publishing Company. 251 p., 1973.

The terms and phrases come mainly from the stage and live performing—that is, show biz in the old-fashioned sense. This Dictionary includes a lot of slang (it manages to define some risqué terms in an inoffensive way), some circus language, and a lot of Broadway language. If you want to know what "Boffo" or "Green Room" mean, this is the place. This Dictionary also has the clearest definition of "The Fourth Wall" that I've read. You can almost feel yourself sitting at Sardi's.

Lively Arts Information Directory: A Guide to the Fields of Music, Dance, Theater, Film, Radio, and Television in the United States and Canada. 2d ed. Edited by Steven R. Wasserman and Jacqueline Wasserman O'Brien. Detroit, MI: Gale, 1985. 1,040 pp. ISBN 0-8103-0321-3, LC 85-6949.

This volume includes information about performing arts (film, theater, television, and radio) organizations, libraries, and research collections in the United States and Canada. Some of the material duplicates information found in Gale's *Encyclopedia of Associations,* which is updated annually, but there is enough original material to make this a helpful reference source on its own.

Mass Media: A Chronological Encyclopedia of Television, Radio, Motion Pictures, Magazines, Newspapers, and Books in the United States, by Robert V. Hudson. New York: Garland. 435 p., 1986. LC 85-45153, ISBN: 0-8240-8695-3.

A chronological history of the mass media up to 1985, the book provides a detailed listing of dates, events, personalities, and technological developments.

Media Review Digest. See: FILM REFERENCE RESOURCES.

Motion Pictures, Television, and Radio: A Union Catalogue of Manuscript and Special Collections in the Western United States. Compiled and edited by Linda Mehr. Boston: G.K. Hall. 201 p., 1977. LC 77-13117, ISBN: 0-8161-8089.

Arranged alphabetically by institutions from eleven Western states; a detained description is provided for each collection. Includes film material collections and sources for photographs. It provides a good subject index to the collections.

The New Address Book: How to Reach Anyone Who's Anyone, by Michael Levine. New York: Perigee/Putnam. 285 p., 1988. LC 88-5860, ISBN: 0-399-51487-2. On verso (left side) of the title page are the words: "Completely revised and updated."

The book lists, in alphabetical order, the names, and address of famous people from all walks of life.

NewsBank. Review of the Arts: Film And Television. Monthly microfiche distribution service (with printed monthly, quarterly, and annual cumulative indexes), 1975-   . NewsBank, 58 Pine St., New Canaan, CT 06840. Phone: (203) 966-1100. ISSN: 0737-3988.

This NewsBank service, and its companion service listed below, is unique in that it reproduces complete articles from the daily newspapers of approximately 450 cities around the country on microfiche. Access to this huge fiche collection is provided via hard-copy printed indexes. This *Film and Television* section of the service reproduces articles about the film and television industries and includes interviews with personalities, film and television program reviews, news stories, and special events. The broadcast and cable industries are also covered. The articles are indexed in a variety of ways: name of performer, director, title, production company, genre, geographical area (country or nationality), and subject content.

This is an amazing collection. I don't know of any other place you can go to find so much current material about the entertainment business in one place; not even the database services can begin to compare. Although it is an invaluable source, it is a slow and difficult system to use. Each article which is selected for inclusion is assigned an identifying number, and it is this number which follows each term listed in the printed index; no other information is given. For example, the name of a performer may have rows of numbers following it; the only way you can find out what the article is about is go to the fiche and look at it. The fiche itself is complicated to find and pull. It is filed first by subject category, then year, and finally by the fiche number assigned to the article. That's a time-consuming process to follow if you want to view a large number of articles. The way the system is structured may keep down labor-intensive costs of producing the service, but it leaves no way for a researcher to make a preliminary decision about the relevance of an article to his or her work, and therefore whether or not it's worth the time to retrieve it. You can waste a lot of valuable time pulling material you wouldn't have bothered with if you had known what it was beforehand.

One enduring special value is the fact that all of the articles are cleared for permissions and can be reproduced on the spot if you so desire (and have access to a fiche printer).

NewsBank. Review of the Arts: Performing Arts. Monthly (with quarterly and annual cumulative indexes), 1975-   . NewsBank, 58 Pine St., New Canaan, CT 06840. Phone: (203) 966-1100. LC 88-13503, ISSN: 0737-3996.

This NewsBank service reproduces, on microfiche, reviews of recordings and live performances from the daily newspapers of approximately 450 cities around the country. Articles, interviews, news events, and reviews are also included for the following areas: record releases, the music industry, the theater, celebrities, and other areas of the performing arts. The fiche is indexed in great detail (with frequent updates) in hard copy. Access is by performer, title, and subject. This service is just as valuable and just as flawed as the companion service noted above.

Performing Arts Biography Master Index. See: pages 187 and 291.

Performing Arts Books, 1876-1981; including an international index of current serial publications. New York: R.R. Bowker. 1656 p., 1981. LC 81-187862, ISBN: 0-8352-1372-2.

The major part of the volume is a listing of over 50,000 books published in all areas of the performing arts (film, television, the theater, etc.) for the years noted. It's an especially valuable source of information for historical radio research. Indexed by author, title, and subject. A separate section lists serials in all areas of the performing arts and includes some useful information about titles that might be difficult to find elsewhere. Both sections have been compiled from databases, with the books coming from the American Book Publishing Record database and the serials extracted from the Bowker Serials Bibliography database.

Performing Arts Research, by Marion K. Whalon. Detroit, MI: Gale. 280 p., 1976. ISBN: 0-8103-1364-2. (Performing Arts Information Guide Series, Volume 1). LC 75-13828.

A book of annotated reference sources for performing arts research, with sections on guidebooks, abstracts and indexes, directories, bibliographies, sources for reviews, dictionaries and encyclopedias, and other research resources. Coverage is provided for film, television, the theater, many areas of the live performing arts, music, and related areas.

Power Media "Selects". Semiannual, 1989-   . Washington, DC: Broadcast Interview Source. 1st ed. LC 89-3729, ISBN: 0-934333-06-8.

A directory of approximately 500 important media and print contacts, giving the name, title, address, and phone for each person listed. It includes contacts for news wires, newspapers, magazines, television talk shows, radio stations, and public relations professionals for the entertainment world.

The Publicists Guild Directory. Annual, 1983-   . Sherman Oaks, CA: The Publicists Guild of America. ISSN 0742-4000. Alternate title: *Directory of Members.*

A directory of members, with phone numbers and addresses. The membership includes both firms and individuals.

The Recreation and Entertainment Industries: An Information Sourcebook, by Norman F. Clarke. Jefferson, NC: McFarland. 240 p., 1990. LC 89-43641, ISBN 0-89950-464-7.

The book takes thirty major areas of the entertainment and recreation industries and provides information about the research tools of each area, professional associations, and business information.

Review of the Arts: Film and Television. See: NewsBank.

Review of the Arts: Performing Arts. See: NewsBank.

Scholar's Guide to Washington, D.C. Film and Video Collections, by Bonnie Rowan. Washington, D.C.: Smithsonian Institution Press. 282 p., 1979. ISBN: 0-87474-818-6.

Identifies the major collections in the Washington, DC area, both private and public.

Sourcebook For the Performing Arts. Compiled by Anthony Slide, Patricia King Hanson, and Stephen L. Hanson. Westport, CT: Greenwood. 227 p., 1988. LC 87-23630, ISBN: 0-313-24872-9.

The book provides directory information for researchers in film, the theater, and television. The major section of the book lists, by state, the major libraries and archives along with a brief description of their collections. Another section is a "who's who" of scholars, librarians, and critics which gives brief professional credentials for each and an address where they can be reached. The other directory information can be found in current annuals for the various fields, but is conveniently located here in case you don't have easy access to specialized directories. The information consists of a listing of periodicals, associations and organizations, publishers, production companies, U.S. and international film commissions, television networks, and book shops.

Sponsorship Principles & Practices: A Practical Guide to Entertainment, Sport, Music and Event Marketing, by Ron Bergin. Nashville, TN: Amusement Business. Phone: (615) 321-4254. Rev. ed., 137 p., 1989. LC 89-674896.

The book defines itself as a "practical guide to entertainment, sports, music, and events marketing." It provides a detailed account of the practice of corporate sponsorship of live events, with an emphasis on musical events such as tours by popular performers. It's largely a business manual for putting together sponsored shows and contains a directory of over 250 corporations which sponsor shows of various types. Includes a list of corporate sponsors, case studies of agreements, and a sample contract.

Star Guide; how to reach movie, TV stars and other celebrities. Annual, 1984- . Address: Axiom Information Services, Box 8015, Ann Arbor, MI 48107. Phone: (313) 761-4842. Previously titled: *Celebrity Directory.*

The Stars of Stand-up Comedy: A Biographical Encyclopedia, by Ronald Lande Smith. New York: Garland. 227 p., 1985. LC 84-48408, ISBN: 0-8240-8803-4.
The book profiles comics from all parts of the field, briefly describing their lives and careers. Emphasis is on modern comics, but coverage goes back to vaudeville days. Entertaining examples of the comics' humor and a liberal use of photos make the book enjoyable to use.

Talk Show "Selects". Washington, DC: Broadcast Interview Source. 1989, ISBN: 0-934333-08-4.
A directory of talk show producers, hosts, and talent coordinators, with information about how to contact each one. It lists the people responsible for finding and selecting guests on radio and television talk shows, both national and local.

Theatrical Variety Guide. Annual, 1966- . Theatrical Variety Publications, 1400 Cahuenga Blvd., Los Angeles, CA 90028. Issued on behalf of the American Guild of Variety Artists.

Tony, Grammy, Emmy, Country: A Broadway, Television, and Records Awards Reference. Compiled by Don Franks. Jefferson, NC: McFarland 202 p., 1986. LC 85-43577, ISBN 0-89950-204-0.
Complete awards data on the Emmy (Academy of Television Arts and Sciences), the Tony (American Theatre Wing), the Grammy (National Academy of Recording Arts and Sciences)

and the Country Music Awards given by the Country Music Association. A description and history of each award is given; index by names and titles of works and/or shows.

Variety International Showbusiness Reference. Daily Variety. (Published and distributed by Garland) 1135 p., 1981. LC 81-2329, ISBN: 0-8240-9341-0.

The volume has a substantial biographical section for performers, a listing of film credits and television show credits for the years 1976-1980, Broadway and London play credits for 1976-1980, Platinum records for 1976-1980, and the top Nielsen-rated television shows. Especially useful are the lists of awards (The Oscars, Emmys, Tonys, Pulitzer Prize Plays, and Grammys). The section for each award lists, in yearly chronological order, all of the winners *and* the nominees.

Variety Obits. See: page 324.

Variety Who's Who in Show Business. Edited by Mike Kaplan. New York: Garland. Rev. ed. 412 p., 1989. LC 85-20578, ISBN: 0-8240-9806-4.

Brief biographies of approximately 6,500 people in all areas of show business. Prominent names in the technical areas are included as well as actors, producers, and directors. Some credits are given although the lists do not claim to be complete.

Variety's Directory of Major Show Business Awards. Edited by Mike Kaplan. New York: Bowker. 750 p., 1989. LC 89-186032, ISBN: 0-8352-2666-2. Previously published as: *Variety Presents: The Complete Book of Major U.S. Show Business Awards* (Edited by Mike Kaplan. New York: Garland. 564 p., 1985. ISBN 0-8240-8730-5, LC 84-18734).

Includes nominations and awards in all categories for the Oscars, Tonys, Emmys, Grammys, and Pulitzer Prize plays.

Variety's Show Business Annual. Annual, 1905- . New York: Variety. The Annual is part of the yearly subscription to the periodical and is usually published as the second issue each January.

The publication indexes all of the weekly *Variety* reviews of the previous year, including film reviews, live performances, stage shows, records, shows abroad, and new literature. It also provides industry statistics for the different media and reviews industry trends and events of the year in each industry. New developments are highlighted, such as the growth of the cable and satellite industries in Europe.

Who's Who in Entertainment. 1st ed., 1989-1990. Wilmette: Marquis Who's Who. 712 p., 1989.

Who's Who in Show Business: The National Directory of Show People. Annual, 1950-   . New York: Who's Who In Show Business.

World of Winners. Edited by Gita Siegman. Detroit: Gale. 1st ed., 977 p., 1989. ISBN: 0-8103-0474-0.
Designed as a companion to Gale's *Awards, Honors, and Prizes,* the volume lists award winners of such "popular" awards as best dressed and worst dressed lists, advertising awards, and show business awards. Some overlap with the other Gale book, but still original enough to be worthwhile.

GENERAL PERIODICALS

Amusement Business: International News Weekly for Sports and Mass Entertainment. Nashville, TN: Billboard Publications/ Amusement Business Division. Weekly, 1894-   . ISSN: 0003-2344. Address: Box 24970, Nashville, TN 37202. Phone: (615) 321-4250. Available on microform from UMI. Indexed in: Business Index, Trade & Industry Index. Available online: Dialog.
A current events paper covering performance activities, physical facility news, and financial developments of interest to fairs of all sizes, amusement parks, hotels, arenas, concert halls, and other forms of mass entertainment. Articles cover performers and successful business people, promotion and marketing programs, news of current tours, international news, and the changing European market of 1992. The publication regularly covers the top forms of entertainment as well as dance shows, ice capades, the circus and carnivals, various athletic events (*e.g.,*

baseball and water sports), and news of local and state fairs. Its "want ads" pages are a fascinating mix of people looking for work and an amazing array of equipment and services for sale.

Broadcasting. Washington, DC: Broadcasting Publications. Weekly.
A trade journal covering radio and television.

Celebrity Bulletin. Daily. New York: Celebrity Service International.
Tracks celebrity movements and news internationally with coverage for New York, Hollywood, London, Paris, and Rome. It makes every effort to keep current with celebrity changes in agents, phones, and addresses. It tells which celebrities are arriving in a particular city, the nature of their business, and where they will make a public appearance. Much of the information is supplied by agents, because Celebrity Service International is often used by other professionals and organizations as a means of locating performers. See Also: *Spotlight Contacts* in BRITISH REFERENCE RESOURCES for information about British contacts.

Columbia-VLA Journal of Law & the Arts. Quarterly, 1975- . New York: Columbia University Law School/Volunteer Lawyers for the Arts. LC 87-658525, ISSN 0888-4226.
An interesting newsletter with articles that provide practical advice and discuss current issues of interest to entertainment professionals. Recent articles covered issues dealing with the protection and licensing of intellectual property: photocopy rights, lending rights in the United Kingdom, and the copyright of software.

COMM-ENT: The Journal of Communications and Entertainment Law. Quarterly, 1977- . University of California at San Francisco, CA: The Hastings College of Law. ISSN: 0193-8398.

Contacts: The Media Pipeline for Public Relations People. Basic looseleaf volume with weekly updates. Larimi Communications, 5 West 37th St., New York, NY 10018. Phone: (212) 819-9310.

The Entertainment and Sports Lawyer. Quarterly, 1982- . Chicago: American Bar Association (Forum on the Entertainment and Sports Industries). ISSN: 0732-1880.

An ABA membership publication designed to provide an account of the latest legal developments; emphasis is on film and broadcast litigation. It's written for the experienced attorney and is formal and technical in nature. Each issue reports on court decisions, discusses legal methods and theories, and reviews new publications in the field.

Entertainment Law & Finance. Monthly, 1985- . Leader Publications, 111 Eighth Ave., Suite 900, New York, NY 10011. Phone: (212) 463-5709, or 1-(800) 888-8300. ISSN: 0883-2455.

Current news about legal activities and practices. The publication takes an easy-to-read, practical approach that is appealing to non-legal industry personnel as well as attorneys. The emphasis is on the music and recording industry although all areas receive some coverage. Articles offer practical advice and/or discuss such things as the way new technological developments affect the law. For example, recent articles have offered detailed advice about how to commission music scores for films, how to work out an effective deal between producers and actors in a series, and the impact new recording techniques (like DAT) have on copyright law. Worth reading for the insight it provides into the functioning of the entertainment business.

Entertainment Law Reporter. Monthly, 1978- . Entertainment Law Reporter Publishing Co., 2210 Wilshire Blvd., Suite 311, Santa Monica, CA 90403. ISSN 0270-3831.

The publication covers the latest legal news, court cases or decisions, and theory in entertainment law. Motion pictures, television, radio, music, publishing, the performing arts, and sports are represented. It publishes court decisions along with a synopsis of the case, discusses new laws or regulations that affect the industry, and reviews new literature of interest to entertainment attorneys.

Entertainment Legal News. Bimonthly, 1983- . Address: P.O. Box 2100, New York, NY 10185. Phone: (212) 429-6613. ISSN: 0747-8593.

Written in non-technical terminology with an emphasis on legal and court news of interest to the New York entertainment industry. Strong coverage of the theater, the recording industry, broadcasting, and film. Articles provide practical information about contracts, copyright, the collection fees and royalties, and other business practices in the entertainment industry. Successful attorneys and business executives are interviewed.

The Journal of Arts Management and Law. Quarterly, 1969- . Washington, DC: Journal of Arts Management and Law. LC 82-645237, ISSN 0733-5113. Previous title: *Performing Arts Review* (1969-1982). Indexed in: MI, Index to Legal Periodicals.
     The journal covers artists' and writers' rights, ethics issues, management problems of the performing arts (with an emphasis on the stage), financial and funding problems and ideas, and a wide variety of policy issues.

Journal of Popular Culture. 1967- . Bowling Green, OH: Popular Culture Association. Indexed in: FLI, ICFR, MI.

Mediasource; the total film and video magazine directory & review. Irregular, 1986- . Address: Fandom Unlimited Enterprises, Box 70868, Sunnyvale, CA 94086. Phone: (415) 960-1151.

Medical Problems of Performing Artists. Quarterly, 1986- . Hanley & Belfus, 210 South 13th St., Philadelphia, PA 19107. LC 85-6290, ISSN 0885-1158. Indexed in: Biological Abstracts.
     The periodical covers illnesses and injuries that are a consequence of work in all areas of the performing arts.

Performance. Weekly. See: Chapter 8, pages 276-277.

Performing Arts Review. Washington, DC: Helen Dwight Reid Educational Foundation. 1970- .

Show Business; the entertainment weekly. Weekly, 1941- . ISSN: 0037-4318. Address: Leo Shull Publications, 1501 Broadway, New York, NY 10036. Phone: (212) 354-7600.

PHOTO RESEARCH

Once you have completed your research and written your book or article, there are two factors that can enhance your work or sadly diminish it: physical design and photographs. The first, the physical design of the page (layout, typeface, etc.), is usually in the hands of the publisher and you may have only minimal input. The second factor, the use of photographs, is something over which you can exercise more control. Photos are important because they establish the visual perceptions your reader will have of your story. If they are of poor quality or an inappropriate match with the written word, you've become your own worst enemy by building an additional hurdle between the mind of your reader and the effectiveness of your writing. Therefore, if what you are writing calls for the use of photographs, it may be worth your time to hunt for them yourself rather than leave it up to the publisher to accentuate your piece with whatever pictures they may have in their office archives. Otherwise, your hard work may be illustrated with boring photos; worse, they might be accompanied by photos that are so outdated as to be embarrassing. Even though it's not your fault, you will pay the price.

Although this chapter centers on the finding of photographs, I also want to take a moment to discuss the legal and ethical issues involved in the use of photographs with your work. I've been lucky enough to have the cooperation of many photographers during the past ten years and their work has *always* enhanced my own. In several cases, they provided me with special assistance in a way that was unselfishly more beneficial to me than to them. I think I was able to establish this working relationship because I was honest about what I was doing, and I always kept my word. Photographers often have their work used without permission (and without pay or recognition), and therefore are cautious about who they deal with. If they learn from experience that you don't live up to the agreement you have with them, the chances are that you won't get anything from them in the future.

The proper (and legal) use of photos is often a confusing situation for beginners, but some solace can be found in the fact that they are not alone. For some reason, even experienced writers and professionals in the entertainment field have trouble understanding when they need to get permission to use photos, and when they do not. It's actually very simple: photographs receive the same legal copyright protection that books and other forms of intellectual property enjoy. The rights belong to the person who created the work. There are two exceptions to this: (1) the photographer may have sold the rights to someone else, and (2) the photo may have been a "work done for hire." Two examples of this are photos taken for use by a performer and film stills taken for use in publicizing motion pictures. Even then, the contract between the photographer and the purchaser of work may specifically limit ownership and use to certain circumstances.

Incidentally, I've found a strange misperception toward photos in that many people want to distinguish in their minds between photographs taken by "professionals" and those taken by amateurs. Their argument is that if a photo is taken by a professional, it is subject to the copyright law, while a photo taken by a fan or an ordinary citizen is not. This is not true. The law makes no such distinction, and all photographs are equally protected. The law doesn't care who you are, how good (or bad) your work is, what you do for a living, or anything else. This problem is a double-edged sword in that it's not just writers who think this way; more than one entertainer's office has been guilty of using photos without permission that have been sent to them by fans or amateurs because the office staff used the logic we've just discussed.

My own experience in this area points out how infuriating the situation can be. Several years ago a performer's office staff was responsible for using one of my photos on a successful commercial product without requesting my permission or offering payment, and I found out about it only because I saw the product unveiled on a national talk show! I didn't take legal action, but I did talk to a lawyer and found out that I had an unquestionable case. The reason I was given by the office staff as to why they used my photo without permission was the one noted above: they didn't believe that they needed to get permission to use photos that weren't taken by professional photographers. In fact, they were rather angry that I had this "attitude!" The underlying reason for their anger was the fact that my objection made them realize that they couldn't use hundreds of other photos received over the years just like mine. They could have used them, of course, because all they had to do was obtain permission from the people who took the pictures.

However, the office staff in this case didn't want to go to the trouble to obtain permission because their attitude was that "those amateur photographers are just fans" and they didn't want to give them the same accord they would a professional photographer. They had so locked their own thinking into this discourtesy toward "fans" and low esteem of their worth that they couldn't overcome these self-imposed restrictions. Their action was rude, unethical, and illegal. They hurt themselves more than anyone else because, as a consequence, they lost out on the potential use of a number of good photographs. Most of the "fans" would have been most willing to let them use their work free. This story should be taken for what it's worth, as a word of caution. For every performer's office who might do this, a hundred others will be most grateful to receive and use good photographs by anyone, and routinely go through a clearance and permission procedure for everyone without discrimination. You only have to look at beautifully produced tour books and some autobiographies to be aware of the contributions amateur photographers can make.

Although photographs can not be used without permission of the "rights" owner of the photo, who is usually (but not always) the photographer, a frequent exception to this rule is the use of standard publicity photos that are made available by film companies and performers offices for use in advertising a particular film, concert, play or appearance. Such photos have been "cleared" for mass use by the offices which issue them and frequently carry a small print statement indicating that the photo may be used, without permission, for publicity purposes. Even then, the photo may carry the name of the photographer and require that photo credit be given for that person.

Independent film studios, television networks, and production companies will usually provide photos for journalists writing about one of their productions or stars. Contact their publicity departments and/or public relations departments. Another source of photos are the photo departments of local newspapers and/or local newspaper internal libraries. Some will supply photos for a fee and others won't, but it never hurts to ask. Professional Associations can refer you to well-known photographers in their field. Some keep membership lists by categories and can provide lists of photographers via that method.

Stock photo and film houses are also helpful; many magazines and newspapers purchase from them. All rights clearances have been taken care of and the companies can provide photos for a large number of subjects. Many specialize in the entertainment field. They are generally expensive and many will only deal directly with magazine editors for legal and financial reasons. They will, however, usually meet with writers if they are assured that an article has been approved and the money budgeted for the purchase of photographs. From my point of view as a writer, I'd rather have as much control over the selection of photos as possible because I've learned by experience that it doesn't take much to ruin a good piece of writing by the use of inappropriate or outdated photos. Editors who don't know your subject as thoroughly as you do are often not the best judge of which photos should accompany the piece. For that reason, I'm willing to go to the extra work to find the photos myself.

Frequently, the simple direct approach is the easiest way to find photographers whose work you want to use. If you see photographs you like of a performer in a magazine, call the journal and ask how to contact the photographer. Most magazines will have their addresses and phone numbers readily available and can provide the information quickly. In addition, the names of the photographers who did the work for album covers are always on the back of the album; a quick call to the record company will net you their address and phone number.

Regarding costs, it's been my experience that photos

purchased from professional photographers and stock photo agencies can be expensive, but you have a chance of finding good quality and/or little-used materials. It is, after all, the way they make their living. Photos purchased from libraries and archives are in the moderate range and you will be paying for reproduction costs and occasionally for rights permission. Most likely, however, the institution will tell you that you are still responsible for obtaining rights permission from the copyright owner even though the institution has provided the photo. Film stills can be purchased for a relatively low cost from most of the memorabilia dealers listed in the chapter on collecting. In addition, it is possible to purchase good, current, concert photos from a number of photographers for reasonable prices. It's possible to find these people through professional and fan magazines for your particular area of interest. The end reality is that a single photo and rights permission may cost you anywhere from "free" to $500, depending on the source you use.

REFERENCE RESOURCES

Footage 89: North American Film and Video Sources.
   This book is probably the most comprehensive new source of information about stock footage, video, and newsreel collections. It lists over 1,600 library and commercial collections in North America. See: page 305 for a full description of the book.

International Museum of Photography at George Eastman House. *Index to American Photographic Collections.* Edited by Andrew Eskind and Greg Drake. 2d ed. Boston: G. K. Hall. Illus., 299 p., 1989.
   The volume lists over 500 photo collections in the United States, provides details about the collections. Arranged by city and state, with the name of the institution (and address and phone). There is also an extensive index of photographers whose works can be found in these collections.

Magazine Industry Market Place (MIMP); the directory of American Periodical Publishing. Annual. New York: R.R. Bowker. See: page 109.

The directory includes a chapter listing stock photo agencies. Each entry includes name of agency, address, phone, the approximate number of photos in the collection, subjects covered, and how to order. Some agencies act as an umbrella for a large number of individual photographers.

Motion Pictures, Television, and Radio: A Union Catalogue of Manuscript and Special Collections in the Western United States. Boston: G. K. Hall. 201 p., 1977.

The book provides in-depth details of special collections in eleven Western states, including which ones have photo collections and their policies regarding use and duplication.

Photographer's Market. Annual, 1974- . Cincinnati, OH: Writer's Digest Books. LC 78-643526, ISSN 0147-247X. Previous titles: *Artists and photographer's market* and *The Artist's market.* Updated by the monthly *Photographer's market newsletter.*

This publication provides information about how and where to market photo work, lists photographers, photo houses, and publishers. The same information is useful to researchers who are trying to find photos of a specific subject matter.

The Picture Researcher's Handbook; an international guide to picture sources - and how to use them. by Evans, Hilary, and others. London: Van Nostrand Reinhold. 4th ed. 480 p., 1989. gb89-28365, ISBN 0747600384.

This handbook has a comprehensive listing of libraries, special collections, and commercial sources of photographs. A good place to start any photo research.

Picture Sources, by Ernest H. Robl. New York: Special Libraries Association. 4th ed. 180 p., 1983. LC 83-625, ISBN 0871112744. (A revised edition of *Picture Sources; collections of prints and photographs in the United States and Canada,* edited by Ann Novotny.)

A joint project between SLA Picture Division and the American

Society of Picture Professionals. A listing of collections and commercial sources of photos.

Picture Sources UK. See: page 443.

Sources for Photographs in the Los Angeles Area. Compiled by Sally Dumaux. 3d ed. Los Angeles: Southern California Answering Network. 59 p., 1980.

More of a pamphlet than a book, this reference lists organizations and commercial sources of all types of photos. Some sources listed have changed addresses or are no longer in business, but this is still a useful source if you are looking for material around Los Angeles.

Stock Photo and Assignment Book: Where to Find Photographs Instantly. Edited by Fred W. Darrah. New York: The Photographic Arts Center. 2d ed. p., 1984. LC 84-232412, ISBN 9-93069-01-9.

An extremely useful handbook listing, by source type, places that supply photographs in the United States and Europe. Even though it's a little outdated by now where addresses and phone numbers are concerned, most of the places listed are still in existence and still provide photos. You may have to use a more current reference book to find the right address and phone, but this book is worth having for the variety of sources and ideas listed. Separate chapters are included for independent photographers and stock agencies; business sources (including publishers, record companies, and associations); historical sources (publishers, institutions and societies); official sources (government agencies); media sources (film libraries, television stations); newspaper sources (national, local, and foreign); reference sources (publications and researchers); photography associations; and technical matters (copyright, legal advice).

Ulrich's International Periodicals Directory. See: SMALL TOWN REFERENCE RESOURCES, Chapter 4, pp 116-117.

This publication lists photography directories useful in finding names and addresses of photographers as well as a long list of periodicals which cover the subject.

Periodicals

Photograph Collector; for collectors, curators, and dealers. Monthly, 1980-   . ISSN: 0271-0838. Address: Photographic Arts Center, 127 E. 59th St., New York, NY 10022. Phone: (212) 838-8460.

Archives and Libraries

The following archives and libraries will make copies from their photo and film stills collection for what they determine to be "legitimate use." Since these libraries are covered in some detail in other parts of this book, they are briefly listed here. In fact, most of the libraries listed in other chapters have large photo collections and will make copies of specific pictures available for approved use.

Academy of Motion Picture Arts and Sciences. Margaret Herrick Library. 333 S. LaCienega Blvd., Beverly Hills, CA 90211. Phone: (213) 247-3020. Another point of public contact as the same location is their **National Film Information Service,** which functions as their commercial stock photo outlet. 8949 Wilshire Blvd., Beverly Hills, CA 90211. Phone: (213) 278-4313.

> **The collection:** Production stills filed by film title; biographical stills (portraits, publicity photos, informal, etc.) filed by name of the performer; and general stills are filed by subject. Several special collections are available by permission only. Of particular note is the Academy's special collection of AMPAS or Academy Awards program stills. Authorization for use must be secured from AMPAS. Award stills are filed by year and award category.

> **Copy policy:** Copies of stills can be purchased on a per print basis. Copies from pages of bound volumes can be made for a slightly higher cost. Work is usually done by the library's own photo staff. Prepayment in full is required, a release must be signed, and the patron is responsible for finding the rights owner

and obtaining necessary publication permission when needed. Permission to use an outside photographer can be granted upon request, but a use fee is still required. Orders take about a week; large requests (over 20 photos) will take longer.

American Film Institute. Louis B. Mayer Library. 2021 N. Western Ave., Los Angeles, CA 90027. Phone: (213) 463-9784.

Bettmann Archive. 136 E. 57th St., New York, NY 10022. Phone: (212) 758-0362.

California. University of California at Los Angeles. Theater Arts Library, Los Angeles, CA 90024. Phone: (213) 825-4880.

California. University of Southern California at Los Angeles. Cinema Library, and its **Department of Special Collections.** Los Angeles, CA 90007. Phone: (213) 741-6058.

George Eastman House. International Museum of Photography. 900 East Ave., Rochester, NY 14607. Phone: (716) 271-3361. Publications: *Image* (quarterly).
Established in 1947, it now has one of the largest collection of photos and film stills in the world. Open to researchers by appointment.

Library of Congress. Prints and Photographs Division, Reference Section. Washington, DC 20540. Phone: (202) 707-6394.
Has some performing arts photos; few performers.

The Library of Congress. Motion Picture, Broadcasting, and Recorded Sound Division. Washington, DC. Phone: (202) 707-1000.
Will not make copies of any photos or film stills without signed release statement from the copyright owner (usually a film company). Even then, the Division reserves the right to approve the work.

Museum of Modern Art. Film Stills Archives. 11 W. 53d St., New York, NY 10019. Phone: (212) 708-9830.
Approximately four million film stills from productions world-

wide and photos of film celebrities and important people in the industry. Sales for professional use only; by appointment only.

Museum of the City of New York. 5th Ave. and 103d Street, New York, NY 10029. Phone: (212) 534-1672.

New York Public Library. Performing Arts Research Library has two collections which will provide copies of their photos: the **Billy Rose Theater Collection** and the **Music Division Dance Collection.** 111 Amsterdam Ave., New York, NY 10023. Phone: (212) 870-1639.

Upon approval, the library will make copies of their stills (on a per still basis) for research or publication purposes. Although the work is usually done by the library staff, the library will allow you the option of bringing in your own photographer to do the work. The Library does not provide rights permission, which must be obtained from the copyright owner.

Wisconsin. University of Wisconsin. Wisconsin Center for Film and Theater Research. 816 State Street, Madison, WI 53706. Phone: (608) 262-0585.

Stock Photo and Film Footage Agencies

After Image. 3807 Wilshire Blvd., Suite 250, Los Angeles, CA 90010. Phone: (213) 480-1105.

Archive Film Productions, Inc. Stock Footage Library. 530 West 25th St., New York, NY 10001. Phone: (212) 620-3955 and 1-800-876-5115.

Footage from silent films, feature films, newsreels, documentaries, industrial films, and other sources. Copyright clearance provided.

Authenticated News International. 29 Katonah Ave., Katonah, NY 10536. Phone: (914) 232-7726.

Collection includes news and personalities.

Bettmann Archive. 136 East 57 St., New York, NY 10022. Phone: (212) 758-0362.

Photos on all subjects. Includes United Press International photos and photos from Reuters.

Black Star. 450 Park Ave. South, New York, NY 10016. Phone: (212) 679-3288.

A major source of photos for newspapers. Includes photos of personalities. Good place to go for theater personalities and photos of stage play openings.

Compu/Pix/Rental. Box 4055, Woodland Hills, CA 91365. Phone: (818) 888-9270.

Provides a computerized service which matches clients and approximately 5000 freelance photographers on their database.

CONTACT Press Images. 135 Central Park West, New York, NY 10023. Phone: (212) 496-5300.

Photos on current cultural events and sports.

Culver Pictures. 150 West 22nd St., New York, NY. (212) 645-1672.

Photos of performing arts, film, television, and personalities.

Fred Fehl. 415 West 115 St., New York, NY 10025. Phone: (212) 662-2253.

Large collection of photos of Broadway and off-Broadway stage productions from 1940-1970, productions of the New York City Opera, and other performing arts events held in the city. Good place to search for dance, ballet, and classical music performances.

Fotos International. 130 West 42nd St., New York, NY 10036. Phone (212) 840-2026.

Entertainment industry photos covering all areas and locations.

Gamma-Liaison Photo News Agency. 150 East 58 St., New York, NY 10155. Phone: (212) 888-7272. The firm also has a sales branch in Los Angeles at 6606 Sunset Blvd., Los Angeles, CA 90028

Represents photographers worldwide; has photos on celebrities and performing events.

Globe Photos. 275 Seventh Ave., New York, NY 10001. Phone: (212) 689-1340. The firm also has a branch in Los Angeles at 8400 Sunset Blvd., Suite 2B, Los Angeles, CA 90069. Phone: (213) 654-3350.
Celebrity and entertainment industry photos.

G.D. Hackett Picture Library. 116-40 Park Lane S., Kew Gardens, NY 11418. Phone: (718) 441-2574.
American and European arts, music, and entertainment photos.

The Image Bank. 111 Fifth Ave., New York, NY 10003. Phone: (212) 529-6700. Has branches in several cities.
Photos on all subjects from over 300 photographers.

Image Photos. Main St., Stockbridge, MA 01262. Phone: (413) 298-5500.
Photos of personalities and the theater subjects.

Keystone Press Agency. 202 East 42nd St., 4th Floor, New York, NY 10017. Phone: (212) 924-8123.
News and cultural events, as well as personalities.

Life Picture Service. Time & Life Building, Room 28-58, Rockefeller Center, New York, NY 10020. Phone: (212) 841-4800.
Some rights restrictions on use of photos. Arts, performing, and celebrity photos included in a large collection of Time, Inc. collection.

Fred W. McDarrah. 505 LaGuardia Pl., New York, NY 10012. Phone: (212) 777-1236.
Celebrities, public personalities, some European photos.

Magnum Photos. 251 Park Avenue S., New York, NY 10010. Phone: (212) 475-7600.
Celebrities and public personalities.

NBC News Video Archive. 30 Rockefeller Plaza, New York, NY 10112. Phone: (212) 664-3797.
Footage from the NBC archives covers decades of news events,

people, and background footage from around the world. Research assistance provided.

NYT Pictures (A division of the *New York Times*). 229 W. 43d St., New York, NY 10036. Phone: (212) 556-1243, 7119.
The *New York Times* photo archives dating back to 1900. Photo research available.

Michael Ochs Archives. 520 Victoria Ave., Venice, CA 90291. Phone: (213) 306-6111.
Specializes in music events and performers.

People Weekly Syndication. Time & Life Building, Rockefeller Center, 38th Floor, New York, NY 10020. Phone: (212) 841-4145.
Photos for sale that have been taken for *People Magazine,* both those used in articles and unused frames.

Personality Photos. Box 50, Brooklyn, NY 11230. Phone: (718) 645-9181.
Film stills, television shows, and celebrities.

Photo Files. The Frank Driggs Collection. 1235 E. 40th St., Brooklyn, NY 11210. Phone: (718) 338-2245 or (212) 580-2800.
Entertainment photos, with an emphasis on jazz and popular music.

Photo Trends. Box 650, Freeport, NY 11520. Phone: (516) 379-1440.
Film and celebrities.

PhotoDataBank. (A subsidiary of PhotoSource International) Pine Lake Farm, Osceola, WI 54020. Phone: (715) 248-3800.
A database file of photographers and the subject areas they handle. Information available online through NewsNet subscription service.

Photonet. 250 West 57th St., New York, NY 10019. Phone: (212) 307-6999.
A national computer database of stock photo agencies which

includes information about the photographers they represent and the subjects covered in their photo collections.

Photoreporters. 875 Avenue of the Americas, New York, NY 10001. Phone: (212) 736-7602.
   News, celebrities, entertainment and performance photos going back to 1950. Some European photos.

PhotoSource International. Pine Lake Farm, Osceola, WI 54020. Phone: (715) 248-3800 or 800-242-FOTO.
   Referral service for all subjects for nearly 1500 photographers. Publishes newsletters: *Photobulletin, Photoletter,* and *Photomarket.* See also: PhotoDataBank listed above.

Pictorial Parade. 130 W. 42nd St., Suite 614, New York, NY 10036. Phone: (212) 840-2026.
   Celebrity and public figures.

H. Armstrong Roberts. 4203 Locust St., Philadelphia, PA 19104. Phone: (215) 386-6300.
   Represents over 200 photographers, some of whom deal in entertainment photography.

Shooting Star Photo Agency. Box 93368, Hollywood, CA 90093. Phone: (213) 876-2000. For news and educational use only.
   Film, television, and music personalities; candid and portrait photos.

Martha Swope Studio. 460 West 43rd St., New York, NY 10036 Phone: (212) 594-9431.
   Large selection of photos from Broadway theater productions. The Studio is the official photographer for many shows.

UNIPHOTO Picture Agency. Box 3678, 1071 Wisconsin Avenue, N.W., Washington, DC 20007. Phone: (202) 333-0500.
   Publishes a newsletter; represents approximately 150 photographers, some of whom have entertainment industry photos.

United Press International (UPI). See: Bettmann Archives.

Wide World Photos. 50 Rockefeller Plaza, New York, NY 10020. Phone: (212) 621-1930. Branches in several cities.
  Large file of photos dating from 1880 on all subjects.

SEE ALSO: Chapter 10 on Collectors and Collecting. This Chapter lists a number of dealers of film and television memorabilia, including photographs.

SCRIPTWRITING AND RESEARCHING

Scripts and songs have one thing in common: everyone under the sun either has one in the works or knows how to write a good one if only they had the time. In Nashville, everyone is an undiscovered songwriter; in Los Angeles, everyone is a budding scriptwriter.

  Script writing and script research are two very different procedures with two different purposes. The creative writing process, the development of a story line, is always the paramount concern; if you can't write a good story you won't sell a script. But it is the research which can occasionally stimulate ideas or give the feeling of authenticity.

  Two events govern the life of a writer: (1) the period of time and energy required to write a successful script, and (2) the effort it takes to sell it. Like most other areas of the entertainment business, what counts most is talent and hard work. It also helps to have an agent. In addition to creating the product and selling it, writers also have another worry that is unique to their business: the theft of their ideas. Anyone who has been around for a while has had one of their storylines stolen by someone else. In order to combat intellectual property theft, the Writers Guild of America has implemented a Register, where scriptwriters may register their story treatments or completed scripts.

  There are a number of good books out about scriptwriting style and form, and several regular newsletters which publish interviews with successful writers and generally provide listings of markets that are looking for finished scripts or listings of agents who represent writers.

Script research is, in reality, basic research on a specialized subject. Scripts require research when the writer wants to incorporate special facts or other information into a script. The research may be as simple as checking the date the first astronaut went into space or as complicated as understanding how a police investigation is handled. The scriptwriter may have the plot well in mind and just need to know enough facts to demonstrate credibility, or the writer may be looking for an in-depth explanation of the subject in order to develop a more detailed storyline. The researcher (who may or may not be the scriptwriter) checks to be sure that facts are correct and that explanations that may be used in dialogue are accurate. For historical scripts, the researcher may look for information regarding the manner of dress, transportation, way of speaking, and social events during the time period covered in the script. Have you ever tried to find the words to the "Pledge of Allegiance" as they were spoken in the 1950s?

Depending on the need of the writer and the complexity of the subject matter in the script, some scripts are researched before they are written in order to provide the writer with the proper atmosphere and stimulate story ideas; others are researched afterwards, just to be sure that minor details are accurate.

Television makes a wide variety of demands on script researchers. Drama and series programming have the same script and research requirements as the film industry. In addition, a number of other types of programs require what is essentially script research. Virtually every program on television is formally scripted, even though some of the conversation may be spontaneous. Scriptwriters are hired to create questions for game shows, put together the interview questions for talk shows, write the evening news shows, and prepare the presentations for award shows.

Game shows require a different type of script research; it's unique in that researchers must find interesting facts and then write challenging questions. These questions are part of scripts and script research even though they may not be perceived as such by the public. In addition, the dialogue spoken by presenters during award shows or the tributes made to fellow performers are scripted and often demand substantial research. Lastly, all television news departments have script writers and researchers whose job is to be sure facts are correct or find information about past events that are to be included in current programming. Both NBC and CBS have such large historical archives of film footage, photographs, and other information that they now sell copies of their collection on a commercial basis.

Scripts have rarely been best sellers at bookstores and, therefore, few publishers have actively sought to add them to their inventory. They are more difficult to read, editors believe, because the production and camera instructions tend to break into the rhythm of the reader's movement and always serve as a reminder that it isn't a real story. Whatever the reason, the general perception is that published scripts don't hold the reader's attention and emotions like regular novels do. Grove Press, St. Martin's Press, Crown Books, and a number of university presses have published selected screenplays over the years, and Applause Theater & Cinema publishes both stage plays and film scripts. Most publishers aim for scripts that have been written by big name writers or only publish screenplays of highly successful movies. Either way, the publication often relies more on this additional status for sales than its own merits. A variation of script publishing is the occasional published transcription of a film, in which the actual film dialogue is published rather than the working script. This can sometimes be more acceptable to readers because it repeats what they heard on the screen and are familiar with; few readers are sophisticated enough in the ways of filmmaking to realize that the working script and the finished movie are rarely an exact match.

Reference Resources

There are a large number of books about how to write scripts. A few basic ones are included here, but many more good titles are available. You might want to look up reviews in *Library Journal, Publishers Weekly,* or some other source before purchasing.

Books About Scriptwriting

The Art of Screenwriting, by William Packard. New York: Paragon House. 184p., 1987. ISBN: 0-913729-36-1.
  The book takes a practical approach and covers a wide variety of activities having to do with scripts: writing by collaboration, editing, copyrighting, and the mechanics of scriptwriting.

The Dramatist's Bible: Script Requirements & Submission Procedures of Theatres and Other Producing Organizations in the English-speaking World. Annual, 1984- . See: Chapter 6, pages 178 and 179.

Dramatists Sourcebook. Annual, 1982- . ISSN: 0733-1606. Address: Theatre Communications Group, 355 Lexington Avenue, New York, NY 10017. Phone: (212) 697-5230. See: Chapter 6, page 179.

The Elements of Screenwriting: A Guide for Film and Television Writers, by Irwin Blacker. New York: Macmillan. 116 p., 1987. ISBN: 0-02-511180-9, LC 86-16340.
  The book is based on lectures by the author. The book covers the structural elements of scriptwriting chapter by chapter. It also includes a list of agents and information about the Writer's Guild of America and its role in the business.

The Fiction Writer's Research Handbook, by Mona McCormick. New York: Plume/New American Library. 305 p., 1988. LC 88-5168, ISBN 0452261570.
  The book is not exclusively for writers, but is extremely useful because it approaches research from the needs of fiction writers. It is an interesting, well-written book that tries to guide fiction writers to the places and sources that will answer their most common questions.

Making A Good Script Great: A Guide to Writing and Rewriting, by Hollywood script consultant Linda Seger. New York: Dodd, Mead. 204 p., 1987. LC 87-19906, ISBN 0396089356.

The Screen Writer's Guide (almost everything you need to know to get your script produced), by Joseph Gillis. Second edition. New York: Baseline/N.Y. Zoetrope. 159 p., 1987.

 The major part of the book is a directory of film and producers (names, address, phones); brief sections include advice on submitting scripts, signing releases and other forms relevant to industry business, and a brief dictionary of terms. The book does not discuss the actual art of screenwriting.

Script into Performance: A Structural Approach, by Richard Hornby. New York: Paragon House. 215 p., 1987. ISBN: 0-913729-59-0.

 Script analysis for stage plays discusses the relationship between scripts and stage performance, and how each can affect the other.

Writer's Market. Annual, 1922- . Cincinnati, OH: Writer's Digest Books. LC 31-20772, ISSN 0084-2729.

 The book is both a directory and an information guide. It includes the names and addresses of publishers, agents, editors, and others important in a number of writing fields. In addition, it has overview articles on such topics as using photographs in your work and how to sell your scripts, articles, books, and other literary works. An appendix contains samples of contracts and other useful forms.

Books About Screenwriters and Scripts

American Screenwriters. Part of the series: *Dictionary of Literary Biography* (series). Detroit, MI: Gale. Volume 26: *American Screenwriters* (388 p., 1984, ISBN 0-8103-0917-3); Volume 44: *American Screenwriters* (second series, 464 p., 1986, ISBN 0-8103-1722-2).

 Each volume in this series profiles a particular field of writing, a special time era, writers of a specific nationality, or successful writers in a unique genre. The two volumes on screenwriters provide a comprehensive overview of each writer's life and career; supplementary materials such as bibliographies, filmographies, and photographs contribute to the understanding of each writer.

The Drama Scholars' Index to Plays and Filmscripts: A Guide to Plays and Filmscripts in Selected Anthologies, Series, and Periodicals, by Gordon Samples. Metuchen, NJ: Scarecrow. 1974, 1980, 1986. 3 vols. LC 73-22165, ISBN (for Vol. 3) 0-8108-1869-8.
   A comprehensive listing of scripts from the areas of film and theater. The reader will need to know, however, which medium the script was written for since it is not always easy to tell.

Film Writers Guide, by Ken Bales. Beverly Hills, CA: Lone Eagle. 126 p., 1988. ISBN 0-943728-3, ISSN 0894-864X.

A Guide to American Screenwriters: The Second Era, 1929-1982, by Larry Langman. 2 volumes, 1984. New York: Garland. LC 84-48018, ISBN 0-8240-8927-8.
   Volume 1 is arranged alphabetically by writer and contains biographical information and a chronological listing of films written by that person. Volume 2 is a title index to the films listed in volume 1, with the name of the writer.

Guide to Critical Reviews, Part IV: The Screenplay, by James M. Salem. See the *Guide* series in Reference Books in Chapter 6, page 181.

Play Index. See: Chapter 6, pages 188-9.

Published Radio, Television, and Film Scripts, by G. Howard Poteet. Troy, NY: Whitsun Publishing Company. 245 p., 1975.
   The book is divided into the three areas indicated. Citations include only those scripts which have appeared in print. It excludes scripts in their original form; *i.e.,* the bound copies used during the production work of a film. Radio and television scripts are listed under the name of the program or series on which they appeared. Production information and date of broadcast are given, along with the name of the writer. The publisher and/or the title of the collected work which includes script is provided. Film scripts are listed in alphabetical order by title, with the publishing information.

Published Screenplays: A Checklist, by Clifford McCarty. Kent, OH: Kent State University Press. 127 p., 1971. LC 73-138656, ISBN 0873381122.
A listing of nearly 400 screenplays that have been published commercially and the publication source. Some have been published as books, others are parts of collections.

Scriptwriters Market. Annual, 1979- . Filmmakers Publishing Co., 8033 Sunset Blvd., Suite 306, Hollywood, CA 90046. Phone: (818) 762-3726. ISSN: 0734-8592.

Who Wrote the Movie and What Else Did He Write? Subtitle: *An Index of Screen Writers and Their Film Works, 1936-1969.* The Academy of Motion Picture Arts and Sciences. Los Angeles: AMPAS. 491 p., 1970. LC 78-27347.
The book is divided into three sections of brief bibliographical information: (1) an alphabetical listing of writers and the screenplays they have written, (2) an alphabetical listing of approximately 13,000 film titles and the names of the writers, and (3) a chronologically arranged awards index of screenwriting awards from various film organizations.

Periodicals and Newsletters

Gene Perret's Round Table; a gathering place for comedy writers and humorists. Monthly, 1981- . Address: Perret Enterprises, Box 1415, South Pasadena, CA 91030. Phone: (818) 793-4716.

Globe: script opportunities for dramatists in all media. Monthly, 1984- . Address: International Society of Dramatists, Box 1310, Miami, FL 33153. Phone: (305) 756-8313.

Hollywood Scriptwriter. 1626 N. Wilcox, Suite # 385, Hollywood, CA 90028. Monthly, 1980- . Editor: Kerry Cox. Phone: (818) 991-3096.
Newsletter which covers the latest news in scriptwriting. Each issue includes a long interview with a writer about scriptwriting techniques and skills. Special issues update information regarding agents and the types of material they are seeking. Regular features include: "The Script Doctor"; and "Current Markets."

Ross Reports Television; New York casting-national script contacts. Monthly, 1949- . ISSN: 0035-8355. Address: Television
Index Inc., 40-29 27th St., Long Island City, NY 11101. Phone:
(718) 937-3990.

An industry newsletter listing new shows, production companies
planning work, and other information about projects under
consideration or in the works. A good place to find current key
personnel in all fields of film and television and the positions
they occupy.

The Writer. Monthly, 1887- . Boston, MA: The Writer. LC
17-19531, ISSN 0043-9517. Indexed in: RG. Available on microform from University Microfilms International (UMI) of Ann
Arbor, Michigan.

This is a writing journal with an emphasis on articles of interest
to fiction writers. Although most articles are not directly about
scriptwriting, much of what they publish is useful. They tend to
tackle such subjects as creating emotion, developing interesting
characters, how to create suspense, and how to write comic
dialogue.

Writer's Digest. Monthly, 1921- . Cincinnati, OH: F & W
Publications. LC 27-6282, ISSN 0043-9525.

Another general writing magazine with a lot of useful information for scriptwriters. It tends to contain more news and short
interest items, but also publishes longer articles on fiction
writing techniques.

Associations and Organizations

Authors' Guild, Inc. 234 W. 44th St., New York, NY 10036.
Phone: (212) 398-0838.

Authors League of America, Inc. Address: 234 W. 44th St., New
York, NY 10036. Phone: (212) 391-9198.

Dramatists Guild. See: THEATER ASSOCIATIONS, Chapter 6.

Writers Guild of America, East. 555 West 57th St., New York, NY
10019. Phone: (212) 245-6180.

Writers Guild of America, West. 8955 Beverly Blvd., Los Angeles, CA 90048. Phone: (213) 550-1000. Publications: *Writers Guild Directory*. Los Angeles: Writers Guild of America, West. 1974 to date. Published irregularly.

Lists address, agent, credits. Writers are encouraged to register their scripts with WGA.

Where to Buy Scripts

Larry Edmonds Bookstore. See: COLLECTING, Chapter 10.

Rick's Movie Graphics. See: COLLECTING, Chapter 10.

Scotland McFall. P.O. Box 2584, Sepulveda, CA 91343. (818) 344-5011. Scripts and other items.

Script City. 1765 N. Highland Ave., Suite 760, Hollywood, CA 90028. Phone (213) 871-0707. Catalog available.

Large selection of feature film and television scripts, U.S. and foreign. Includes television series scripts. Script City also sells a large selection of industry books: industry directories as well as publications about producing, screenwriting, directing, and acting.

Script Collectors Service. Address: 8033 Sunset Blvd., Suite #1105, Los Angeles, CA 90046. Phone: (213) 650-7883. Write for catalog.

This service sells scripts from the 1930s to the 1980s.

There is one major research archive devoted solely to television scripts:

The Annenberg School of Communications
Television Script Archive

University of Pennsylvania, The Annenberg School of Communications, Television Script Archive, 3620 Walnut St., Philadelphia, PA 19104. Access to the collection is by appointment only by written application to this address. A fee is charged to non-university researchers. Oryx Press has recently published two books about the collection: *Index to the Annenberg Television Script Archive* and *Thesaurus of Subject Headings For Television.* See the section in Chapter 8 on film and television libraries for more information about the collection and Chapter 9 on Broadcast Research for information about the books.

COPYRIGHT AND TRADEMARK RESEARCH

A lot has been said about protecting the intellectual property of people working in the entertainment field and anyone who does research or intends to publish or otherwise sell creative work should know the basics of how to protect your own work and when to seek the rights to use the work of others. One only has to look at the legal journals for the entertainment field to realize that the laws dealing with the control and use of images and intellectual property rights are complex and confusing. In fact, the law constantly changes and important entertainment art forms were not even included in the beginning. Although the first film was made in 1894, the first film was not copyrighted until 1912 and sound recordings were not copyrighted until 1972. But you owe it to yourself to develop a minimal understanding of the basics, if for no other reason than to keep yourself out of as much trouble as possible. An ounce of prevention is worth a pound of cure.

In most cases, securing the proper permission to reproduce copyrighted or trademarked materials is a fairly simple and straightforward process. But occasionally it can become a hectic and trying experience because identifying the proper owner of the copyright or trademark is not always a simple matter. Works do not have to be registered with the Copyright Office in order to receive the protection of the law. It's best if they are registered of course, because the registration strengthens the case if it goes to court, but it's not required.

Copyright forms clearly distinguish between the author of a work and the claimant of that work. The claimant, in official copyright terminology, is the owner of the copyright.

This person (or corporation) might not be the author of the work or even the current owner of the actual physical product, but the claimant is the one who owns the right to determine the use of the work and receive payment for this use. It gets even more confusing once the rights have been assigned or sold through several transactions. A songwriter may have sold the copyright of his or her song to an individual, who in turn sold or assigned the rights to a music publishing company, which in turn sold its catalog to another publisher. The songwriter remains the author, but the rights have passed through many hands. In fact, the music business is currently going through such a shakedown that determining current ownership of a song is more difficult than ever. There has been tremendous growth and change in music publishing in the past few years; it's become a lucrative business and companies have been bought and sold (some more than once in a short period of time) and international corporations now control the majority of rights to American music. In theory, copyright records are supposed to reflect all changes in ownership, but in truth many of these transactions have yet to be recorded by the new owners.

Sometimes rights are sold or assigned for a limited time period or for a specific project. A stage producer who has purchased the right to adapt a novel for a play may have a contract which limits this right to a specific time period, after which the rights revert back to the original holder. The contract could also include a clause which forbids or restricts other media productions of the novel during this time period. As a result, a film company which subsequently purchases the film rights may be in the unusual position being unable to use them at a time of their choosing. Similar ownership problems exist in the trademark field, where logos, symbols, and graphic images may be bought and sold in much the same manner.

If all of this sounds confusing, it is, even for the people who are responsible for keeping track of who owns what. That's why entertainment people occasionally find themselves in strange situations. Vocalists have been unable to sing tunes they wrote themselves (performance rights belong to the claimant); writers can not use characters in their current stories that they created in previous books (someone else owns the image now); and actors find their pictures on products without their approval (the film company owns the rights to sell images of the film or series). Sometimes rights ownership can be a two-way sword: performers can not use photos of themselves without permission (the rights belong to the photographer), but the photographer can not sell the photo which he or she took of the performer for use on a commercial product (the performer's image belongs to the performer).

OBTAINING COPYRIGHT AND TRADEMARK INFORMATION

Writers can acquire copyright and trademark information by writing for pamphlets from the agencies which are responsible for the programs. You can copyright your own work if you want and the Copyright Office will be glad to send you the proper forms. They also make available a series of free pamphlets which explain copyright procedures for the various types of material eligible to be copyrighted (books, music, films, audio, etc.). In addition, they publish brief booklets which explain what copyright is and how to do copyright research. Some of the most useful are *Copyright Basics* (Circular 1); *Copyright Registration Procedures* (Circular R1c); *How to Investigate the Copyright Status of a Work* (Circular R22); and *The Copyright Card Catalog and the Online Files of the Copyright Office*. To request copyright forms and booklets, write to the Copyright Office, Library of Congress, Madison Building, Washington, DC 20559.

The Patent and Trademark Office is part of the U. S. Department of Commerce and provides trademark registration and protection in much the same way as previously described for copyrights. A trademark as defined by law "includes any word, name, symbol, or device, or any combination thereof adopted and used by a manufacturer or merchant to identify his goods and distinguish them from those manufactured or sold by others." Trademarks can be distinctive name logos used by performers (The Oak Ridge

Boys and Alabama both have them) or images (The MGM lion, the RCA Records gramophone and dog, and the NBC peacock). For a detailed explanation of trademarks and how to register them, write for the booklet *General Information Concerning Trademarks.* The address is: U.S. Department of Commerce, Patent and Trademark Office, Washington, D.C. 20231. The booklet provides a brief introduction to trademarks, defines trademarks and their function, and tells applicants what they must do throughout the application process.

Both agencies provide research services for a fee and a number of private businesses also offer search services in each field. But you can expect to pay higher fees for this type of research than any other because the work is so complex and labor-intensive. Still, experienced researchers are worth their weight in gold if you are unable to do the work in person or decide you don't want to spend the time learning the techniques.

There is a trademark database, *Trademarkscan,* which is on the *Dialog* system (File 226). The file includes both registered trademarks and applications that are in the process of obtaining approval and can be searched by title, ownership, registration number, and description. Uniquely, users can retrieve and print both the text and the image of the registration.

6 THEATER RESEARCH

The stage is a fascinating area to research. It shares (along with music) the distinction of being the oldest of the entertainment professions. The theater has been around as long as mankind has possessed any sense of literary drama and it is generally considered to be the most prestigious of performing arenas; "great" actors are more frequently identified in terms of their stage success than for their film or television work. And yet, despite the long history and recognized status, the theater pays less than any other medium; consequently, actor after actor has left the stage for film and television in order to make the kind of money their name and reputation could command.

Theater research is difficult because it's a small industry with the most visible parts of it located either in New York or London even though thousands of small theater companies operate around the world. Since the medium centers around live performances, and modern technology didn't exist until the turn of the century, there is only sparse knowledge of theater history when one considers the hundreds of years and vast numbers of productions that occurred throughout the history of mankind. Even today, there's virtually no film or video tape of important recent performances, and precious few photographs, to document production details and/or inspire interest in those who haven't actually seen the production. You are left with the agility of your own imagination when trying to bring forth images of what historic great performances must have been like. Of course, the text of the plays themselves have survived, but since each production of a play was staged and acted with a unique personality of its own, the words alone do not suffice.

Although some photographs exist for stage plays and the stars of the late 1800s, the use of the camera didn't become commonplace until the 1900s. Sound recording technology followed a few years later. Before the camera and the tape recorder, a history of the stage could only be preserved by the hand of individuals who wrote about what they had seen. Consequently, paintings and line drawings, handbills, promptbooks, written reviews, commentaries, personal correspondence, costumes, and props take on added importance in the area of theater research.

There are some rare exceptions due to the early trend in television programming of broadcasting successful plays, although the cast of the successful theater production was not always used for the televised version (the practice continues today in both television and film). In Britain, the BBC can take credit with having preserved some critically acclaimed West End plays of the 1950s (with their original casts) because they televised many of the plays as special programs. For example, they televised *BRAND,* the top West End play of 1959, which in turn became the top television program of the year. The film still exists today as the only record of what critics consider to be the definitive production of that particular Ibsen play. But such film is indeed rare; even BBC failed to recognize the significance of the many plays it televised and routinely destroyed much of its video tape collection. But the climate is starting to improve (albeit, somewhat slowly) as industry people become more aware of preservation as an economic commodity. Just as the television industry has become aware of the financial value of its old programs and the record industry is moving to protect and restore old master recordings, the theater industry has started to realize the value of saving its own work and is looking for ways to save it. Some recent tapings have been done and it appears that the theater community is more willing to cooperate with organizations that have an interest in creating historical records of performances. For example, The Billy Rose Theatre Collection in New York has been able to gain special permission to make both video and audio tape of recent stage performances.

What are the most common types of research conducted about the theater? The most common type of research, of course, is the search for information about specific productions (dates, cast and technical credits, theater, reviews, photos). But researchers also want to know about costumes and props; the lives of particular actors; the credits for directors; business and management practices; legislation affecting the stage; the history of a particular theater or production company; copyright information for a play; stage design and theater architecture; the history of various types of live entertainment (music halls, the circus, pantomime); symbolism and allegory; the lives and styles of playwrights; and how to write a play.

Books and journals are hard to find in library collections outside of theater libraries or college drama schools. Photographs are next to impossible to locate. The only easily available materials are published editions of the plays themselves and biographical information about the playwrights. So, unless you are resigned to making the effort to spend time at a large theater library collection, you will find rough going with your research.

Some information can be found in sources not normally thought of as theater research tools. You can often find the opening dates of Broadway plays in *Facts on File*. If you have problems finding the cast credits and opening dates of the lesser known plays, don't forget to search *Variety* and *Plays and Players* as two additional sources that often review minor productions that are passed over by the major sources. For London shows, earlier years of *The Stage* included full cast credits of most productions.

REFERENCE BOOKS

American Actors and Actresses: A Guide, by Stephen M. Archer. See: Chapter 8, page 295.

American Actors, 1861-1910: An Annotated Bibliography of Books Published in the United States in English from 1961 through 1976, by Ronald L. Moyer. Troy, NY: Whitston. 268 p., 1979. LC 79-64229, ISBN 087875167X.

A listing of books which contain information about American actors for the period noted. Approximately 350 books are evaluated.

American and British Theatrical Biography: A Directory, by J. P. Wearing. Metuchen, NJ: Scarecrow. 1007 p., 1979. LC 78-31162, ISBN 0-8108-1201-0.

Arranged in alphabetical order by name of performer; following each name is the individual's birth date and brief citations referring the reader to one or two biographical resources. The emphasis is on theater yearbooks, biographical dictionaries and encyclopedias, and other reference sources.

American and English Popular Entertainment, by Don B. Wilmeth. Detroit, MI: Gale. 465 p., 1980. [Vol. 7 of the Gale Research *Performing Arts Information Guide Series.*] LC 79-22869, ISBN 0-8103-1454-1.

A guidebook to general sources about popular entertainment. Chapters include general reference sources as well as information on such subject areas as the circus, magic, popular theater, puppets, and other subjects. An appendix includes lists of periodicals, museums and special collections, organizations.

American Drama, 1909-1982, by James M. Salem. Third edition. Metuchen, NJ: Scarecrow. 657 p., 1984. LC 84-1370, ISBN 0-8108-1690-3. (The second edition, 1973, was identified as a new edition of Salem's *A Guide to Critical Reviews*)

The book lists reviews and articles about nearly 300 playwrights and their plays.

American Drama Criticism, Interpretations, 1890-1977 Inclusive, of American Drama Since the First Play Produced in America. Edited by Floyd Eugene Eddleman. Hamden, CT: Shoe String. 2d ed. 488 p., 1979. LC 78-31346. *Supplement 1* (255 p., 1984). *Supplement 2* (LC 88-37507).

Arranged alphabetically by playwright, and then by the works of that author, the volumes list reviews and commentaries that have appeared about that specific work. The literature cited has been culled from several hundred books and over 400 periodicals

and offers an extensive collection of writings about early
American theater and playwrights.

✗ *American Musical Theatre;* a chronicle. New York: Oxford
University Press, by Gerald Bordman. 787 p., 1986. The first
edition was published in 1978. LC 86-8385, ISBN 0-19-504045-7.
A chronology (by theater season) of the American musical
theater from early times to shortly before the book was
published. Details are sketchy until the mid-1800s, then the
records become fuller. Boston, Chicago, and Philadelphia
receive coverage along with New York until about 1920, then the
book centers on the New York stage. Complete production
information is given for each play listed, plot summary, and an
evaluation of the play and its merits. Indexing for song titles and
personal names.

*American Song: The Complete Musical Theatre Companion,
1900-1984,* by Ken Bloom. New York: Facts on File, 1985. (2 vols).
LC 84-24728, ISBN 0-87196-961-0.
Contains information for over 5,000 American theatre productions.

American Theatre Annual. Annual, 1976-   . Detroit: Gale.
Incorporates: *New York Theatre Annual* (ISSN 0162-7333).
Only 2 volumes were published: 1978/79 and 1979/80.

✗ *American Theatre Companies.* 3 volumes published separately.
Edited by Weldon B. Durham. Westport, CT: Greenwood.
Volume 1: 1749-1887 (1986, 598 pp., ISBN 0-313-20886-7, LC
84-27947); *Volume 2:* 1888-1930 (1987, 541 p., ISBN 0-313-20886-
7, LC 85-30213). *Volume 3:* 1931-1986 (608 p., 1989, LC 88-32039,
ISBN 0313253609).
The set offers a detailed history of American theater companies,
regional repertory groups, experimental and children's theaters,
and other types of theaters of all sizes. As far as possible, it
supplies information about personnel, the physical facility itself,
and programs presented by the companies. Volume 1 covers 81
of the earliest companies. Volume 2 covers 105 regional and art
groups, providing as much historical and biographical informa-

tion as possible. Volume 3 covers 78 theatre companies, including the Federal Theatre Project.

X *American Theatrical Arts;* a guide to manuscripts and special collections in the United States and Canada. See: Chapter 5, page 123.

X *American Theatrical Periodicals, 1789-1967: A Bibliographical Guide* by Carl J. Stratman. Durham, NC: Duke University Press. 133 p., 1970. LC 72-110577, ISBN 0822302284. Reprinted in 1986 by University Microfilms International (Ann Arbor, MI).

A union listing of approximately 700 theater periodicals and serials located in 137 library collections around the United States. An unequaled resource for locating rare periodicals in the performing arts. The only drawback which makes it slow to use is the fact that the arrangement is chronological by date of first publication. That's a minor inconvenience, however, when weighed against the value of the information. One only wishes for an updated edition. SEE ALSO: Stratman, Carl J. *Britain's Theatrical Periodicals, 1720-1967.*

Annals of the New York Stage, by George Odell. New York: Columbia University Press. 15 vols., 1927-1949. LC 27-5965. Reprinted in 1970 by AMS Press (New York): LC 77-116018, ISBN 0404078303.

Arrangement is chronological by years. Covers plays, actors, published reviews and criticism, and other theater history for the period from 1699 to 1894. The most comprehensive work about early American theater. See Also: *Index to the Portraits in Odell's Annals of the New York Stage.*

The Back Stage Handbook for Performing Artists. Edited by Sherry Eaker. New York: Back Stage Books/Watson Guptill. 247 p., 1989. LC 88-34446, ISBN 0-8230-7508-7.

Published by the weekly trade paper *Back Stage,* this is an insightful guidebook containing everything a beginner should know about how to survive in the New York theater community. In addition to explaining how the industry functions and providing some directory information, the book also provides advice regarding auditions, publicity photos, writing resumes, and many other topics. This is a useful tool for researchers who need some understanding about the inner workings of the entertainment industry.

Best Plays of [year]. Annual, 1899-   . New York: Dodd, Mead. Subtitle: *The Burns Mantle Yearbook of the Theater.* LC 79-5600, ISSN 0276-2625.
Each volume contains summarized versions of the ten best plays on Broadway for the year. Full cast and credits are given for each play. In addition, the volume contains information and news of the theater world for the year. It includes theater awards, obituaries, and some biographical information about theater people.

Bibliographic Guide to Theater Arts. Annual, 1975-   . Boston: G.K. Hall. LC 76-647338, ISSN 0360-2788.
Covers the theater, film, TV, and radio. Annual listing of new items cataloged by The Research Libraries of the New York Public Library; intended as a supplement to their *Catalog.* Additional citations taken from the Library of Congress MARC tapes. The majority of publications listed are available in the library system. Arrangement is like a library card catalog: in alphabetical order by author, title, and subject. See Also: *Catalog of the Theatre and Drama Collections* (New York Public Library).

X *Bibliography of the American Theatre, excluding New York City,* by Carl Joseph Stratman. Chicago, IL: Loyola University Press. 397 p., 1965. LC 65-3359.
Arrangement is geographical, by state and then by city. A bibliography covering the theater in each area includes books, periodical articles, and other materials both of a historical and current nature up to the early 1960s.

Bibliography of Costume: A Dictionary Catalog of About Eight Thousand Books and Periodicals. Compiled by Hilaire Hilier and Meyer Hilier. New York: H.W. Wilson. 911 p., 1939. Reprinted in 1967 by B. Blom (New York). LC 66-12285.

A comprehensive guide to the historical literature about costumes.

A Biographical Dictionary of Actors, Actresses, Musicians, Dancers, Managers & Other Stage Personnel In London, 1660-1800, by Philip H. Highfill, Kalmin A. Burnim, and Edward A. Langhans. See: THEATRE REFERENCE RESOURCES in Chapter 11, page 469.

✓ *Biographical Encyclopedia and Who's Who of the American Theatre*. Edited by Walter Rigdon. Published by James H. Heinman, 475 Park Avenue, New York, NY 10022. 1,101 p., 1966. LC 65-19390. Superseded by *Notable Names in the American Theatre*.

Britain's Theatrical Periodicals, 1720-1967: A Bibliography, by Carl J. Stratman. 2d ed. New York: New York Public Library. 160 p., 1972. LC 72-134260, ISBN 0871040344. First published in 1962 under the title *A Bibliography of British Dramatic Periodicals, 1720-1960* (58 p., 1962, LC 62-14880).

An absolutely invaluable listing of British theatre periodicals and related performing arts. The arrangement by chronological date of first issue makes it a little difficult to use, but the publishing information it provides for each title makes the effort worthwhile. A unified listing indicating the libraries in both England and the United States which hold back issues in their collections follows each title.

British Musical Theatre, by Kurt Ganzl. New York: Oxford University Press. See: THEATRE REFERENCE RESOURCES in Chapter 11, page 470.

British Theatre Yearbook. Annual, 1989- . Edited by David Lemmon. New York: St. Martin's. 352 p., 1989. ISBN 0-312-03198-X. First edition was published in 1989. See: THEATRE REFERENCE RESOURCES in Chapter 11, page 470.

Broadway in the West End: An Index of Reviews of American Theatre in London, 1950-1975, by William T. Stanley. Westport,

CT: Greenwood Press. 206 p., 1978. LC 77-89108, ISBN 037198526.

An informative book about American productions that have been presented on the London stage. Each play is listed, along with the theater in which it appeared, the dates of the run, and a listing of critical reviews culled from approximately 17 of the most noted review sources (newspapers, periodicals, etc.).

Bulletin of Bibliography. Quarterly, 1897-1978. No longer published. Boston: Faxon. Title varied over the years. The title was *Bulletin of Bibliography and Magazine Subject-index* from 1907 to 1912; *Bulletin of Bibliography and Dramatic Index* from 1912 to 1953; and *Bulletin of Bibliography and Magazine Notes* from 1956 to 1978. Even though the hard copy can no longer be purchased, the set is available on microform from UMI (Ann Arbor, MI). See also two other titles: *Cumulative Index to the Bulletin of Bibliography and Magazine Notes,* compiled by Eleanor C. Jones and Margaret L. Pollard (vols. 1-32, 1897-1975, 1977) and *The Cumulated Dramatic Index.*

The series started with short reading lists and notes about particular subjects, but soon grew to a style of providing long bibliographies of considerable research about topics and prominent people in the social sciences and humanities.

The Burns Mantle Yearbook of the Theater. See: *Best Plays of [year].*

The Cambridge Guide to World Theatre. Edited by Martin Banham. New York: Cambridge University Press. 1,104 p., 1988. ISBN 0-521-26595-9, LC 88-25804.

A comprehensive quick guide to modern theater and people in it. Entries are alphabetical and include actors, playwrights, history, theaters, plays, and a variety of other topics.

Canada On Stage: the National Theatre Yearbook. Annual, 1974- . Toronto, Ont., Canada: PACT Communications Centre. LC 77-31521, ISSN 0380-9455. Previous titles: *Canadian Theatre Review, Canadian Theatre Review Yearbook.* Indexed in: Canadian Literature Index.

✗ *Catalog of the Library of the Museum of Modern Art.* New York: (City) Museum of Modern Art Library. Boston, MA: G.K. Hall. 14 vols., 1976. (Originally published in 1967 in 21 volumes). LC 76-383620, ISBN 0816100152.

The set contains an alphabetical listing by author, subject, and title of all of the plays, the books and periodicals, scripts, and cataloged files in the collection.

Catalog of the Theatre and Drama Collections. Authorship by New York Public Library; The Research Libraries. 51 vols. Published 1967-1976, Boston, MA: G.K. Hall. Part I: *Drama Collection* (12 vols., 1967); Part II: *Theatre Collection* (9 vols., 1967). Part III: *Non-book Collection* (30 vols., 1975). Supplements update the set to 1973. Annual supplements for Parts I & II are published under the title *Bibliographic Guide to Theatre Arts* (Annual, 1976-   .).

The basic set is a dictionary catalog of the New York Public Library Drama Collection from 1931 to 1973. It reproduces the card catalog entries for authors, titles, and subjects of the books in the collection. Includes theater, film, and television. Part I is a listing of published plays in many forms. Part II is the catalog for research materials about the theatre. Part III indexes the Library's huge collection of theater programs from around the world, photos and film stills, newspaper clipping files, and other special collections.

Chicorel Theater Index to Plays in Anthologies, Periodicals, Discs, and Tapes. Edited by Marietta Chicorel and Veronica Hall. New York: Chicorel Library Publishing. Vol. 1, 1970; Vol. 2, 1971. LC 71-106198, ISSN 0590-983X.

A listing of plays in print; indexed by author, title, editor, and subject.

Complete Catalogue of Plays [year]. Annual, 1936-   . New York: Dramatists Play Service. LC 63-289, ISSN 0419-7178.

Each edition cumulates and supercedes earlier editions.

Contemporary American Theater Critics: A Directory and Anthology of Their Works, by M.E. Comtois and Lynn F. Miller. Metuchen, NJ: Scarecrow. 1,017 p., 1977. LC 77-23063, ISBN 0-8108-1057-3.

✕ *Contemporary Theatre, Film, and Television.* Detroit, MI: Gale. Basic volumes plus yearly updates. Volumes 1-7 published as of 1989. Illus. LC 84-649371, ISSN 0749-064X. Cumulative indexes in each volume. Maintains continuity with *Who's Who in the Theatre* by providing revisions of entries from the last published edition.

A biographical guide featuring performers, directors, writers, producers, designers, managers, choreographers, technicians, composers, executives, dancers, and critics in the United States and Great Britain. Each volume has about 700 profiles and photos are provided for many of the entries. A good source for the famous and beginner alike. Articles vary from several pages to just a few brief paragraphs. The information is documented, when possible, from primary sources. Quotes used from printed sources are credited.

Cumulated Dramatic Index, 1909-1949; a cumulation of the F.W. Faxon Company's *Dramatic Index.* Boston: G.K. Hall. 2 vols., 1965.

A great source of historical information about the theater. This is a cumulated edition of the 41-volume *Dramatic Index* noted under the title: *Bulletin of Bibliography and Dramatic Index.* An index of British and American theater periodicals arranged by subjects, including personal names.

The Dictionary of Costume. by Ruth Turner Wilcox. New York: Scribner, 406 p., 1969. LC 68-12503. Reprinted in 1986 by Macmillan (New York, LC 86-18121).

Describes all types of costumes and defines different parts of clothing. Also discusses costume design, styles, fads, fashion, fabrics, and noted people in the profession. Good line drawings are used throughout the work.

Dictionary of the Theater. Edited by David Pickering. London: Sphere Books. 556 p., 1988. LC 88-69046, ISBN 0747400199.

An alphabetical listing of performers, writers, plays, theatrical terms, theater houses, touring companies, and other subjects. Not all-encompassing, but still a good, quick reference work.

Directors Directory: A National Guide to American Stage Directors. Edited by James W. Thomas. New York: American Directors Institute and Broadway Press. 1st ed., 79 p., 1988. ISBN 0-911747-11-7.
The volume is arranged in alphabetical order by name of the director. Each entry contains an address and phone number where the person can be reached, membership in professional associations, and a list of stage credits (play titles, opening dates).

Directory of Theatre Training Programs, II. Edited by Jill Charles. New York: Theatre Directories. 163 p., 1989. ISBN: 0-933919-13-1.
This directory provides a listing of approximately 250 theater training programs throughout the United States. While most of the listings are of college and university programs, it also includes private commercial teaching programs. Each entry lists degrees or credits offered, a list of courses (if available), fee structure, personnel, production facilities, and a general description of the program.

X *Documents of American Theater History: Famous American Playhouses,* by William C. Young. Out of Print. Chicago: American Library Association. 2 vols., 1973. Volume 1: *Famous American Playhouses, 1716-1899* and Volume 2: *Famous American Playhouses, 1900-1971.* ISBN 0838901360. Photocopy reprint available from UMI (Ann Arbor, MI), 1986.
Arranged in general chronological order, the set documents the histories of over 200 historical buildings from around the country using information from books, periodicals, correspondence, publicity materials, and other sources.

The Drama Dictionary, by Terry Hodgson. New York: New Amsterdam Books. 432 p., 1988. LC 89-179185, ISBN: 0-0941533-40-9.
A good basic dictionary of theater terms covering all aspects of the theater. Some illustrations are used.

Dramatic Criticism Index: A Bibliography of Commentaries on Playwrights from Ibsen to the Avant-garde. Compiled by Paul F. Breed and Florence M. Sniderman. Detroit, MI: Gale. 1,022 p., 1972. LC 79-127598.

Worldwide coverage, with emphasis on American and British playwrights of the 20th Century. The volume contains approximately 12,000 brief critical commentaries from books and periodicals about the playwrights and their plays.

Dramatic Index. Annual, 1909-1949 (41 v.). No longer published. Boston: Faxon [1910-1952]. LC 88-645157.

Despite the fact that the set has long been out of print, it remains one of the more important tools for historical theater research. These were cumulated editions of the quarterly *Dramatic Index* (published by the *Bulletin of Bibliography*). The Annuals were published both as separate titles and as one part of the *Annual Magazine Subject Index.* The set indexed articles about actors (film and stage), plays, the theater in general, reviews, and other topics. This complete set has been cumulated and reprinted as two volumes in the *Cumulated Dramatic Index, 1909-1949.* See also: *Bulletin of Bibliography and Dramatic Index.*

The Dramatists Bible: Script Requirements & Submission Procedures of Theatres and Other Producing Organizations in the English-speaking World. Annual, 1984-   . Fort Pierce, FL: International Society of Dramatists. Address: ISD Fulfillment Center, Box 1310, Miami, FL 33153. Phone: (305) 756-8313. LC 87-37045. Supplemented and updated by a monthly newsletter, *Globe* (Fort Pierce, FL).

This is a combination directory and guide for the marketing of scripts. Although the emphasis is on the stage, there is a significant amount of information about film and television scripts too. Introductory articles discuss the needs and interests of different parts of the theater world (Broadway, off-Broadway, regional theater); how to market different types of scripts; registration and copyright procedures; and the most effective ways to submit scripts. The *Bible* provides the names and addresses of agents, publishers, production companies, and theaters throughout the United States and several foreign countries (Canada, England, and New Zealand). It also prints the details about subject interest, script requirements, and submission procedures of the theaters and production companies listed.

Dramatists Sourcebook: Complete Opportunities for Playwrights, Translators, Composers, Lyricists, and Librettists. Annual, 1982-   . New York: Theatre Communications Group. LC 82-644562, ISSN 0733-1606. Alternate title: *TCG Dramatists Sourcebook.* Previous title: *Information for Playwrights.*
   A directory of organizations and societies, theaters, and information of use to playwrights. It emphasizes script opportunities (and lists production companies, contests and prizes) and career development (associations, agents, funds, and professional publications).

Drury's Guide to Best Plays. Edited by James M. Salem. Metuchen, NJ: Scarecrow Press. 4th ed. 480 p., 1987. LC 87-380, ISBN 0810819805.
   This book lists nearly 2,000 plays considered to be the best from ancient times to the present. Each entry provides author, title, date of publication or first production (if known), publisher, and technical requirements for staging the play.

The Encyclopedia of the American Theatre, 1900-1975, by Edwin Bronner. San Diego, CA: A.S. Barnes. 659 p., 1980. LC 75-2439, ISBN 0498012190.
   An extremely useful listing of plays performed both on and off-Broadway, excluding musicals. Arranged alphabetically by play title, each entry gives cast and technical credits, opening date, the theater, and a brief plot summary. Appendices provide some statistics and historical information about awards, longest running plays. and other compilations of note.

Encyclopaedia of the Musical Theatre, by Stanley Green. New York: Dodd, Mead. 488p., 1976. LC 76-21069, ISBN 0396072216. A new edition was published by Da Capo Press in 1980 under the title: *Encyclopedia of the Musical Theatre: An Updated Reference Guide to Over 2000 Performers, Writers, Directors, Productions, and Songs of the Musical Stage, Both in New York and London* (New York: Da Capo, 492 p., 1980, LC 79-27168, ISBN 0306801132).

The book has compiled the most prominent people, productions, and songs of the musical theater in New York and London up to 1976. Special bibliography and discography sections are helpful, but not comprehensive.

The Encyclopedia of the New York Stage, 1920-1930. Edited by Samuel L. Leiter and Holly Hill. (2 vols., 1985, LC 84-6558, ISBN 0-313-23615-1) and *The Encyclopedia of the New York Stage, 1930-1940* (1,310 p., 1989, LC 88-5668, ISBN: 0-313-25509-1) Westport, CT: Greenwood.
A fairly thorough attempt to cover all on and off-Broadway productions in the New York City area during the years indicated in the titles. Each entry includes performance dates, cast and production credits, plot synopsis, and additional information when available. Each book reviews the theater world during the decade and provides interesting appendices about the era.

European Drama Criticism, 1900-1975. Compiled by Helen H. Palmer. Hamden, CT: Shoe String. 2nd ed. 653 p., 1977. LC 77-171, ISBN 0208015892.
Arranged alphabetically by playwright, the volumes list criticism and articles about each author and his or her work. Emphasis is on British authors from historical times to the 1950s, but other European writers are included. Shakespeare is excluded because of the huge volume of writing about him and the availability of this material through other resources.

The Facts on File Dictionary of the Theater. Edited by William Packard. 576 p., illus., 1988. LC 88-28379, ISBN 0-8160-1841-3.
Arranged alphabetically like a dictionary, the book provides concise entries for actors, playwrights, plays, awards, and other topics.

Famous Actors and Actresses on the American Stage, by William C. Young. New York: R.R. Bowker. 2 vols. (1298 sequentially numbered pages), 1975. Also on title page: "Documents of American Theatre History." LC 75-8741, ISBN(set): 0-8352-0821-4.
An excellent source of information for early stage performers

with profiles often running several pages. Portrait illustrations and photos are of high quality and sometimes show the person in costume. A good place to conduct research about some performers who are not easily found in other sources.

The Great Stage Stars: Distinguished Theatrical Careers of the Past & Present, by Sheridan Morley. New York: Facts on File. 484 p., illus., 1986. LC 85-27548, ISBN 0-8160-1401-9.

Short biographies of over 200 stars of the American, British and Australian stage, taken from a broad time span of four centuries. Photographs accompany some profiles. Not very comprehensive, but still useful, particularly because of the Australian material.

A Guide to Critical Reviews, by James M. Salem. Metuchen, NJ: Scarecrow. Part 1: *American Drama, 1909-1982* (3d ed., 657 p., 1984, LC 84-1370, ISBN 0-8108-1690-3); Part 2: *The Musical, 1909-1974* (2d ed., 611 p., 1976, ISBN 0-8108-0959-1); Part 3: *Foreign Drama, 1909-1977* (2d edition, 420 p., 1979, 73-3120, ISBN 0-8108-1226-6); Part 4: *The Screenplay: From "The Jazz Singer" to "Dr. Strangelove"* (2 vols., 1971, LC 66-13733, ISBN 0-8108-0367-4); Part 4, Supplement 1: *The Screenplay, 1963-1980.* 698 p., 1982, LC 82-5933, ISBN 0-8108-1553-2.

An excellent source of historical reviews for the genres indicated in each volume. SEE ALSO: Salem, James. *American Drama, 1909-1969,* 2d edition.

Guide to the Performing Arts (1957-1968). See: Chapter 5, page 127.

A Guide to Reference and Bibliography for Theatre Research, by Claudia Jean Bailey. 2d edition, revised and enl. Columbus, OH: Ohio State University Library. Publications Committee. 149 p., 1983. LC 83-61581, ISBN 0882150499.

The first part of the book is a listing of general reference resources useful to the theater researcher and college students, including books, periodicals, newspapers, and catalogs. The second part lists reference resources that specifically cover the theater and related fields, with an emphasis on American and British theater.

Handel's National Directory for the Performing Arts. 4th ed., 2 vols., 1988. Distributed by Wiley/Interscience (New York). LC 73-646635, ISBN 0-913766-02-X. Volume 1: *Organizations and Facilities* (1,136 p.); Volume 2: *Educational Institutions* (585 p.). Alternate title: *National Directory for the Performing Arts.*

Arrangement of the directory information is alphabetically by state, then city, followed by subject/arts area. Subject indexes by major arts area.

The Historical Encyclopedia of Costumes, by Albert Racinet. Facts on File. 320 p., 1988. ISBN 0-8160-1976-2, LC 88-11186.

A quick illustrated guide to what historical dress looked like around the world, from the poor to the rich.

History of the Theatre, by Oscar Gross Brockett. 5th ed. Boston: Allyn and Bacon. 779 p., 1987. LC 86-26535, ISBN 0205104878.

A concise but thorough international history of the theater up to 1985, with emphasis on European theater. A good source for historical information.

How to Locate Reviews of Plays and Films: A Bibliography of Criticism From the Beginnings to the Present, by Gordon Samples. Metuchen, NJ: Scarecrow Press. 114 p., 1976. LC 76-3509, ISBN 0810809141.

Index to Plays in Periodicals, by Dean H. Keller. Rev and enl. ed. Metuchen, NJ: Scarecrow. 824 p., 1979. LC 79-962, ISBN 0-8108-1208-8. Supplement: *Index to Plays in Periodicals, 1977-1987,* by Dean H. Keller. 1990, 391 p. Scarecrow Press. ISBN 0-8108-2288-1.

A brief, but useful, collection of publications which include reviews of plays and films.

Index to the Portraits in Odell's Annals of the New York Stage. Transcribed from the file in the Theatre Collection at Princeton University. New York: American Society for Theatre Research. 179 p., 1963.

This indexes the photographs and portraits of actors which appeared in the *Annals of the New York Stage* from 1927 to 1949. A rare source of photos of many early actors.

A comprehensive listing of plays published in theater and general periodicals. Includes one-act plays as well as longer ones.

International Bibliography of Theatre (IBT). Brooklyn, NY: Theatre Research Data Center. Two volumes in the series published to date: *IBT: 1982* (1985), *IBT: 1983* (ISBN: 089062-219-1, 384 p., 1987), and *IBT: 1984* (852 p., 1987, ISBN 0-89062-225-6). LC 86-640942, ISSN 0882-9446. Order from: Publishing Centre for Cultural Resources, Department 86, 625 Broadway, New York, NY 10012-2662. Address for the Theatre Research Data Center: Brooklyn College, Bedford Avenue and Avenue H, Brooklyn, NY 11210. Phone: (718) 780-5998. The Center has an online research service. Inquiries can be made in writing or by phone.
A subject index of an international selection of theater journals with entries for performers, writers, plays, directors, theaters, geographical areas, and many other topics.

An International Dictionary of Theatre Language. Edited by Joel Trapido and others. Westport, CT: Greenwood. 1032 p., 1985. LC 83-22756, ISBN 0313229805.
An excellent basic dictionary of over 15,000 terms; international in scope, but with heavy emphasis on the English language. Entries date from the earliest theater history to modern day usage.

International Theatre Directory: A World Directory of the Theatre and Performing Arts. Edited and compiled by Leo B. Pride. New York: Simon & Schuster. 577 p., 1973.
This is an international directory, arranged alphabetically by country, of theaters, acting and opera companies, and leading ballet and dance troups. The name and address is given for each group, and some historical information is provided whenever possible.

The Lively Arts Information Directory. Edited by Steven R. Wasserman. Detroit, MI: Gale. SEE: page 128.

The London Stage, 1660-1800; a calendar of plays, entertainments and afterpieces, together with casts, box-receipts and contemporary comment; compiled from the playbills, newspapers, and theatrical diaries of the period. Carbondale, IL: Southern Illinois University Press. 5 parts in 11 vols., 1960-1968. SEE: Chapter 11, page 473.

The London Stage series, by J.P. Wearing. Metuchen, NJ: Scarecrow Press. See: Chapter 11, page 473.

McGraw-Hill Encyclopedia of World Drama. New York: McGraw-Hill. Edited by Stanley Hochman and others. 2d ed. 5 vols., 1984. Illustrated. LC 83-9919, ISBN 0070791694.
Arranged alphabetically by personal names, titles of plays and other writings, theater terms, theater companies, theater in various countries, and subject areas. Some bibliographies and biographies included for major works, playwrights, and actors. Clear synopsis of play plots.

Modern Drama: A Checklist of Critical Literature on Twentieth Century Plays, by Irving Adelman and Rita Dworkin. Metuchen, NJ: Scarecrow. 370 p., 1967. LC 67-10189.
A bibliography of over 800 books and magazine articles containing reviews and comments about the more popular modern plays. Some brief bibliographies for playwrights. A useful source for finding older theater literature.

Modern World Theater: A Guide to Productions in Europe and the United States since 1945, by Siegfried Kienzle. New York: Ungar. 509 p., 1970. LC 73-98342, ISBN 0804431299.
Arranged by name of the playwright, the volume contains reviews for 578 major plays, along with cast credits, plot summaries, and date of performance.

National Directory for the Performing Arts. See: *Handel's National Directory for the Performing Arts.*

New York Casting & Survival Guide; and Datebook. Annual, 1980-   . New York: Peter Glenn Publications. LC 85-2191, ISSN 0730-9945.
An all-around handbook for theatre people working in New

York. In addition to useful names and addresses, it also provides advice on how to obtain success in the market.

New York Theatre Critics Reviews. Biweekly, 1940-   . New York: Critics Theatre Reviews. LC 42-1744, ISSN 0028-7784. Previous title: *Critics' Theatre Reviews* (1940-1942).

Reprints reviews from New York and selected East Coast newspapers. No photos are reproduced. The index to each issue lists all current New York plays and cites the issue in which reviews for the play appeared.

The New York Theatrical Sourcebook. Annual, 1984-   . Compiled by the Association of Theatrical Artists and Craftspeople. New York: Broadway Press. LC 86-25818, ISBN 0911747125 (1989 ed.). 1990 ed. by Chuck Lawliss and published by Fireside. ISBN 0671688707.

A directory of people, associations and organizations, production companies, services, and businesses involved in the theater and entertainment industry in the New York geographical area. It lists more than 300 theaters and gives their phone numbers and addresses.

The New York Times Directory of the Theatre. New York: Arno Press. 1009 p., 1973. LC 73-3054, ISBN 0812903641.

This is actually an index to the theater reviews which were published in the *New York Times* from 1920 to 1970. Each play title is accompanied by the date and page of the newspaper issue in which the review appeared. Indexing is by play title and personal name. An appendix lists theater awards and cites the newspaper articles (and date) that covered the awards.

New York Times Theatre Reviews. Biennial, 1870-   . Published in a set and biennially, first by the *New York Times* and currently by Garland (New York):

New York Times Theater Reviews, 1870-1988. 25 vols, 1989. New York: Garland. (The original set of 10 volumes was published by the New York Times in 1971.)

Reproductions in full of the *New York Times* theater reviews. Arranged chronologically. Indexed by individuals, play title, and production company. Cast credits, dates, and other vital information accompany each review.

New York Times Theater Reviews, 1920-1970. 10 vols. New York: New York Times. 1971. LC 76-378290, ISSN 0160-0583.

Play reviews and related background articles about the theater and the people involved with it (playwrights, actors, and directors). Published to accompany the set: *New York Times Theatre Reviews Index* (New York: New York Times and Arno Press).

NewsBank. *Review of the Arts: Performing Arts.* Monthly, 1972- . Quarterly and annual cumulations. New Canaan, CT: Newsbank. LC 88-13503, ISSN 0737-3996. See: Chapter 5, pages 129-30.

Nineteenth Century Theatre. Semiannual, 1973- . Amherst, MA: University of Massachusetts, Department of English. Current title started in 1987 with volume 15. LC 88-659834, ISSN 0893-3766. Previous title: *Nineteenth Century Theatre Research* (vols. 1-14, 1973-1986, ISSN 0316-5329).

Available on microform and through document delivery service from UMI. Indexed in: MLA, American Humanities Index, Arts & Humanities Citation Index, Literary Criticism Register.

Notable Names in the American Theatre. Clifton, NJ: James T. White, 1,250 p, 1976. LC 76-27356, ISBN 088371-018-8. An earlier edition published in 1966 was titled: *The Biographical Encyclopaedia and Who's Who of the American Theatre.*

Actually more extensive than the title indicates, the work covers stage productions, theatre buildings, and other theatre facts. Most of the book, however, covers biographies, which are in alphabetical order by name. Entries cover personal information and career details of American performers or prominent people, including credits from other areas of the entertainment industry when appropriate. This is a good place to look for early career stage credits of film and television stars.

On Performing: A Handbook for Actors, Singers, Dancers on the Musical Stage, by David Craig. New York: McGraw-Hill. 298 p., 1987, 1989. LC 86-21010, ISBN 0-07-013343--3.

A career guide from a teacher at the American Musical Theater includes chapters on performance techniques and interviews with successful performers.

Ottemiller's Index to Plays in Collections: An Author and Title Index to Plays in Collections Published between 1900 and 1985. 7th ed. Revised and enlarged by Billie M. Connor and Helene Mochedlover. Metuchen, NJ: Scarecrow. 564 p., 1988. LC 87-34160, ISBN 0-8108-2081-1.
The scope has been expanded in this edition to include collections throughout the English-speaking world.

The Oxford Companion to American Theatre, by Gerald Bordman. New York: Oxford University Press. 734 p., 1984. LC 83-26812, ISBN 0-19-503443-0.
Coverage includes biographical information about important figures involved in the theater, plays (and plot summaries), individual productions, early history, theater buildings, theater companies, and other broad subjects.

The Oxford Companion to the Theatre. See: Chapter 11, pages 474-475.

Performing Arts Biography Master Index. Irregular, 1979-   . 2d ed. Edited by Barbara McNeil and Miranda Herbert. Detroit, MI: Gale, 1982. 701 pp. LC 81-20145, ISBN 0-8103-1097-X. Previous title: *Theatre, Film, and Television Biographies Master Index.*
Contains over 260,000 citations to biographical articles and other information about people involved in all of the performing arts. Arrangement is alphabetical by the name of the person, with a list of reference books and other sources (encyclopedias, biographies, yearbooks, filmographies, etc.) that contain biographical information about that person.

Performing Arts Books 1876-1981; including an international index of current serial publications. New York: R.R. Bowker. 1,656 p., 1981. LC 83-17105, ISBN 0-8352-1372-2.
Compiled as a retrospective bibliography of Library of Congress cataloged entries for the performing arts back to 1876. The work lists approximately 50,000 books and journals in motion pic-

tures, music, theater, dance, and other subjects. Indexing is by author, title, and subject.

Performing Arts Libraries and Museums of the World/ Bibliotheques et musees des arts du spectacle dans le monde. 3d ed. Published under the direction of Andre Veinstein and Alfred S. Golding in cooperation with the International Federation of Library Associations. Paris: National Center for Scientific Research. 1,181 p., 1984. ISBN 2222032652.

A listing, by country, of the major libraries and museums holding theater collections. Each description notes the size of the collection, and special collections, library operating procedures, and other information of importance. The text is duplicated on alternating pages in English and French.

Performing Arts Research, by Marion K. Whalon. Detroit, MI: Gale. See entry in Chapter 5.

Performing Arts Resources. Annual, 1974- . New York: Theatre Library Association. Published by Drama Book Specialists (NY) for the TLA. LC 75-646287, ISSN 0360-3814. Indexed in: MLA.

Each volume contains a collection of articles on theater research, libraries, and special collections within libraries and archives.

The Periodical Press of London, Theatrical and Literary (Excluding the Daily Newspaper), 1800-1830, by Felix Sper. Boston: Faxon. 58 p., 1937. LC 37-10990. Also issued as a thesis (Ph.D), New York University.

A listing of what can only be considered very rare citations and journals. The journals covered are weeklies and scholarly publications.

Play Index. 1949- . Published irregularly (about every 4+ years). To date, seven volumes include indexing of plays from 1949; the latest edition covers 1983-1988. Bronx, NY: H.W. Wilson, [1953-1987]. LC 64-1054, ISBN 0554-3037.

A guide to English-language plays published during the time period noted on the volume and where to find them. The major part of each volume pertains to stage plays, but television and radio plays are also included. Each entry includes author, title, brief plot synopsis, cast size needed, and set notations. A brief bibliography indicates publication data for each title, including where collected works may be found. Indexed by author, title, subject, and dramatic style. Lists publishers and distributors of indexed works. This is a useful work for compiling lists of plays by a particular author.

Player's Guide; the annual pictorial directory for stage, screen, radio, and television. Annual, 1944-   . New York: Player's Guide. Address: 165 W. 46th Street, Suite 1305, New York, NY 10036. Phone: (212) 869-3570. The 1987-1988 edition was published in 1987 and is 1439 p. No LC or ISBN numbers.

This is a one-volume listing of actors and actresses who are available for work. There are three main sections: (1) women (leading women, ingenues, character/comediennes, and girls); (2) men (with a similar breakdown); and (3) musical, commercials, stage managers, and directors/choreographers. The entry for each person includes a photo, professional memberships (AEA, AFTRA, SAG), and the representing agent. Similar to the *Academy Players Directory,* but not as extensive or published as regularly. It started as a guide to theater actors and later expanded to include television and film players. It still provides the best coverage of stage personalities.

Plot Summary Index. Compiled by Carol L. Koehmstedt. Metuchen, NJ: Scarecrow. Out of Print. 312 p., 1983.

Well worth using if you can find a copy in your library. This book indexes a dozen reference books or sets of books (such as Magill's *Masterplots*) that provide plot summaries. Title and author lists refer to the reference sources that contain the plot summary needed.

Producing Theatre: a Comprehensive Legal and Business Guide, by Donald C. Farber. Revised and updated edition. Limelight Editions, distributed by Harper & Row (New York). 472 p., 1987. LC 86-27312, ISBN 0-87910-074-5.

An interesting book that provides a lot of practical details about how the theatre industry functions. A great source of inside information.

Restoration and Eighteenth Century Theatre Research: A Bibliographical Guide, 1900-1968, by Carl Joseph Stratman, David G. Spencer, and Mary Elizabeth Devine. Carbondale, IL: Southern Illinois University Press. 811 p., 1971. LC 71-112394.

An annotated bibliography of over 6,500 books, periodicals, and other materials on the Restoration and research during that time period.

Review of the Arts. See: GENERAL ENTERTAINMENT RESOURCES.

Selected Theatre Criticism. Edited by Anthony Slide. Three volumes. Metuchen, NJ: Scarecrow. *Volume 1:* 1900-1919 (1985, 383p., ISBN 0-8108-1811-6, LC 85-2266); *Volume 2:* 1920-1930 (1985, 270p., ISBN 0-8108-1844-2, LC 85-2266); *Volume 3:* 1931-1950 (1985, 289p., ISBN 0-8108-1846-9, LC 85-2266).

Provides the complete text of original reviews, reprinted in their entirety from a wide variety of periodicals, of New York stage productions up through 1950. Arrangement in each volume is alphabetical by title of the works included. Cast and production credits are also included along with the reviews. Indexed by play name and name of critic. See also: *Selected Radio and Television Criticism.* Edited by Anthony Slide. Metuchen, NJ: Scarecrow Press. 213 pps., 1987. LC 86-27891; *Selected Vaudeville Criticism.* Edited by Anthony Slide. Metuchen, NJ: Scarecrow Press. 318 pps., 1988. LC 87-28553.

A Selective Index to 'Theatre Magazine', by Stan Cornyn. Metuchen, NJ: Scarecrow. 289 p., 1964. LC 64-11778.

The book is an index to *Theatre Magazine* (1900-1931). The magazine covered both stage plays and films. The book indexes articles, reviews, and some subjects. It's a good source for historical literature, but can probably be found only in special libraries.

Songs of the Theatre: A Definitive Index to the Songs of the Musical Stage, by Richard Lewine and Alfred Simon. Bronx, NY: H. W. Wilson. 916 p., 1984. LC 84-13068, ISBN 0-8242-0706-8. This title supersedes two previous works by the same author (and containing the same information): *Encyclopedia of Theater Music* and *Songs of the American Theater.*

Provides information about songs (both published and unpub-

lished) of 1,200 Broadway and off-Broadway shows produced
between 1891 and 1983. Lists the early shows considered to be
the most important and music from them, including vaudeville
and some operettas. From the early 1920s on, it lists all
Broadway shows and their music, as well as off-Broadway shows
that ran for over 15 performances and/or are considered to merit
inclusion. Indexed by song title, author/songwriter, and show.
Films and television shows of the plays are also listed.

X *Sourcebook for the Performing Arts.* Compiled by Anthony Slide,
Patricia King Hanson, and Stephen L. Hanson. Westport, CT:
Greenwood. 211 p., 1988. LC 87-23630, ISBN 0-313-24872-9.
An annotated directory of research collections throughout much
of the United States for the fields of the theater, film, television,
and radio. Not every state is covered and the collections are only
briefly discussed, but it is still a useful tool for quick information.
The book also contains shorter directories for bookstores,
publishers, professional associations and organizations, and
related services.

Stage Managers Directory. Annual, 1983- . Broadway Press, 120
Duane St., New York, NY 10007. (1987 ed., 174 p., LC
86-646929). Previous title: *Stage Managers' Association Directory.*
A directory of stage managers and the address and phone
numbers where they may be contacted.

*Stage Scenery, Machinery, and Lighting: A Guide to Information
Sources,* by Richard Stoddard. Detroit, MI: Gale. 274 p., 1977. LC
76-13574, ISBN 081031374X. (Gale Performing Arts Information
Guide Series, Vol. 2)
Lists books, periodical articles, and other materials about the
mechanics of running a stage.

Stagecraft: The Complete Guide to Theatrical Practice. Edited by
Trevor R. Griffiths. Published in Oxford, England in 1982 by
Phaidon; distributed in the United States by Drama Books (New
York). 192 p., 1982. LC 83-210034, ISBN 0890095302.
A handbook of theatre production written for the nonprofes-
sional. Covers every aspect of the artistic, technical, and
business details one needs to know.

✗ *Theater Collections in Libraries and Museums: An International Handbook,* by Rosamond Gilder and George Freedley. Published under the auspices of the New York Public Library and the National Theatre Conference, with the cooperation of the American Library Association. New York: Theater Arts. 182 p., 1936. Reprinted in 1970 by the Johnson Reprint Corp. (New York). LC 78-314679.

The Theater Props Handbook: A Comprehensive Guide to Theater Properties, Materials, and Construction, by James Thurston. Betterway Publications. 288 p., 1988. LC 87-15924, ISBN 0-932620-88-4.
  A well-illustrated guide to theater props suitable for both the beginner and professional. A good source for clear explanations about backstage theater work.

Theatre: Stage to Screen to Television, by William T. Leonard. Metuchen, NJ: Scarecrow. 2 vols (1,812 p.), 1981. LC 80-22987, ISBN: 0-8108-1374-2.

Theatre and Allied Arts: A Guide to Books Dealing With the History, Criticism, and Technic of the Drama and Theatre and Related Arts and Crafts, by Blanch M. Baker. New York: H.W. Wilson. 536 p., 1952. Reprinted in 1967 by B. Blom (New York). LC 66-12284.
  An annotated bibliography of books published from 1885 to 1948 covering all areas of the theater and related areas such as music and dance. International in scope.

✗ *Theatre and Performing Arts Collections.* Edited by Louis A. Rachow. New York: Haworth Press. (Their series, *Special Collections,* Vol. 1, No. 1, Fall 1981) 166 pp., 1981. Out of print. LC 81-6567, ISBN 091772447X.
  Ten articles about theatre libraries in America, with a directory of performing arts libraries.

Theatre Annual. Annual, 1942- . Akron, OH: University of Akron, Department of Music, Theatre and Dance. LC 43-10722,

ISSN 0082-3821. Back issues available from publisher. Indexed in MLA, Abst. of English Studies.

Scholarly articles and research on the history of the theater. Although this Annual is international in scope, its emphasis is on American theater history. The 1988 edition is a tribute to Eugene O'Neill.

Theatre Arts Publications Available in the United States, 1953-1957; a five year bibliography. Edited by Roger M. Busfield. Evanston, IL: American Educational Theatre Association. 188 p., 1964. LC 65-3361. A continuation of the W. W. Melnitz book, *Theatre Arts Publications in the United States, 1947-1952.*

A bibliography, without abstracts or annotations, of books and articles about the performing arts (mostly theater) for the years cited. Despite what the title implies, the bibliography is international in scope as the materials were actually published in the United States, Canada, and Great Britain. A worthwhile collection of information for that time period.

Theatre Backstage from A to Z, by Warren C. Lounsbury. Seattle, WA: University of Washington Press. 3d ed., 1989. LC 89-14715, ISBN 029596829X. The first edition (1959) was published under the title *Backstage From A to Z.*

This is considered a standard in the field and does an excellent job at defining and explaining the physical/technical aspects of stage management. It's the place to start for anyone who wants to know the names of terms and how things function in the backstage area.

Theatre Collections in Libraries and Museums: An International Handbook, by Rosamond Gilder and George Freedley. New York: Theatre Arts. 182 pp., 1936. LC 36-21492. Reprinted in 1970 by Johnson Reprint (New York, LC 78-314679).

A little outdated, but still useful for finding special theater collections worldwide.

Theatre Companies of the World. 2 vols. Edited by Colby H. Kullman and William C. Young. Westport, CT: Greenwood, 1986.

2 vols, 1979. LC 84-539, ISBN 0-313-21456-5. Volume 1: *Africa, Asia, Australia and New Zealand, Canada, Eastern Europe, Latin America, Middle East, Scandinavia;* Volume 2: *United States, Western Europe.*

   This set provides detailed information and the history of more than 300 of the great theater companies of the world.

Theatre Dictionary: British and American Terms in the Drama, Opera, and Ballet, by Wilfred Granville. New York: Philosophical Library. 227 p., 1952. Reprinted by Greenwood Press in 1970. LC 76-110046, ISBN 0837144280.

   British emphasis. Good for historical research and finding the meaning to words and terms that are not currently in use.

Theatre Directory: the Annual Contact Resource of Theatres and Related Organizations. Annual, 1972-   . New York: Theatre Communications Group. LC 80-644683, ISSN 0271-3136.

   The title says it all. It lists just about any person, theater company, professional organization, association, or business of interest to the theater community.

Theatre Documentation. New York: Theatre Library Association. Volumes 1-4, 1968-1972. Volume 1 (no. 2) includes a listing of the current theater periodicals received by the New York Public Library.

Theatre, Film, and Television Biographical Master Index. See: *Performing Arts Biography Master Index.*

Theatre Language: a Dictionary of Terms in English of the Drama and Stage from Medieval to Modern Times. Edited by Walter P. Bowman and Robert H. Ball. New York: Theatre Arts. 428 p., 1961. LC 60-10495.

   It covers over 3,000 terms and phrases, both technical and literary.

Theatre Resources In Canadian Collections, by Heather McCallum. Ottawa: National Library of Canada. 113 p., 1973. No LC or ISBN.

   A brief, but valuable survey of over one hundred Canadian

collections which contain theatre books and other resources. A little old, but still useful since most of the collections are in libraries or archives which still exist.

Theatre World. Annual, 1944/45-   . Edited by John Wills. Frequent publisher changes have occurred over the years. Current publisher is Crown (New York). LC 46-13321, ISSN 0082-3856. Previous titles: *Daniel Blumn's Theatre World* and *John Wills' Theatre World,* so named for their editors.

An annual review of the New York theater season for both Broadway and Off-Broadway. Although the emphasis is on New York, it does devote one section to theater productions and companies around the country. Theater awards, obituaries and some special events for the year are also listed.

Theatre World Annual (London). See: page 476.

Theatrical Costume: A Guide to Information Sources, by Jackson Kesler. Detroit, MI: Gale. 308 p., 1979. LC 79-22881, ISBN 081031455X. (Gale Performing Arts Information Guide Series, vol. 6)

A subject arrangement of books and other reference sources about costume and costume design.

Touring Artists Directory of the Performing Arts in Canada. Biennial (irregular), 1975-. Ottawa, Canada: Canada Council, Touring Office. LC 89-70096, ISSN 0715-755X. 7th ed. is 1986. Previous title: *Touring Directory of the Performing Arts in Canada.*

List of performers and other personnel available to tour in the theatre, musicals, and other live performances.

Twentieth Century Theatre, by Glenn Loney. New York: Facts on File. 2 vols (521 p.), 1983. LC 81-19587, ISBN 0-87196-463-5.

A chronological history of theater (by year) in Great Britain and the United States from 1900 to 1975. An extremely useful source for finding dates, events, and people.

Who Was Who in the Theatre, 1912-1976; a biographical dictionary of actors, actresses, directors, playwrights, and producers of the English-speaking theatre. Detroit, MI: Gale, 1978. 4 vols. Compiled from *Who's Who in the Theatre,* volumes 1-15 (1912-1972). (Gale Composite Biographical Dictionary Series, number 3) LC 78-9634, ISBN 0-8103-0406-6.

Coverage is international in scope and includes both living players (who have not been active in the theater for many years) and deceased players. This is a good source of accurate historical documentation and an excellent place to find relatively obscure stage credits of film and TV performers who have appeared in the theater. Players who are currently active in stage careers are listed in *Who's Who in the Theatre.*

Who's Who in the Theatre. Biannual, 1912-1981 (Volumes 1-17). No longer published. The 17th edition (2 vols.) is the final one of the series. Detroit, MI: Gale, 1981. LC 81-6636, ISSN 0083-9833. The series is superceded by *Contemporary Theatre, Film, and Television,* which profiles actors and other professionals in the performing arts.

The set includes two types of information: biographies of prominent actors and other professionals in the theater world (with each edition containing new or revised biographical sketches), and theater playbills for both Broadway and London for 1976-1979 as well as other information dating back many years (principal theaters, longest running plays, opening dates). The Playbill section of this reference tool (London playbills first appeared in 1921; Broadway bills were added in 1972) made this a most important and valuable source for documentation about opening dates, cast credits, and other information for specific productions over the years. The set originally specialized in British performers, with only the most important Americans included. It gradually reversed its emphasis and included mostly Americans and more international performers.

THEATER PERIODICALS

ASTR Newsletter. Semiannual, 1957-   . (N.S. started in 1972) Greenvale, NY: American Society for Theatre Research. ISSN 0044-7927.

American Theatre; the monthly forum for news, features, and opinions. Monthly, 1979- . New York: Theatre Communications Group. LC 86-647441, ISSN 8750-3255. Previous title: *Theatre Communications* (1979-1984).

Arts Management. 5 issues/year, 1962- . New York: Radius Group. LC 80-120, ISSN 0004-4067. Available through UMI microform and document delivery.

Artsearch; the national employment service bulletin for the performing arts.

Back Stage; the complete service weekly for the communications and entertainment industry. Weekly, 1960- . Address: Backstage Publications, 330 W. 42nd St., New York, NY 10036. LC 78-1204, ISSN: 0005-3635. Microfiche and document delivery service available from UMI. Incorporates *Business & Home TV* into a supplement, *Business Screen* (ISSN: 0160-7294), which in turn was incorporated into the publication in 1977.

A newspaper format weekly which includes information about the companies and people in the news for the entertainment industry. It provides a substantial amount of theater news and reviews. It also provides casting information for productions on stage and in film and television. Regularly reviews film and theater releases. A supplement is also issued, *Back Stage Magazine Supplement/ Business Screen* (1979- . ISSN: 0734-1911), which covers equipment and technical information, and production techniques for the industry. Most of the advertising in the publication are for services directly related to entertainment needs. In early 1990, the publication announced it would expand its operations by splitting into two separate periodicals, with weekly news of the film and video industry in *Back Stage/SHOOT* and theater news continuing to be provided in *Back Stage.* Plans were also announced for separate editions of *Back Stage* to be published for Los Angeles and Chicago in the near future.

Broadside. Quarterly, 1940- . (N S started in 1973- .) New York: Theatre Library Association. LC 82-1429, ISSN 0068-2748. Indexed in: Library Literature.

The newsletter of the Theatre Library Association.

Canadian Drama/Dramatique Canadien. Semiannual, 1975-   .
Guelph, Ontario, Canada: University of Guelph. cnLC 75-33505,
LC 87-649991, ISSN 0317-9044. Indexed in: Canadian Literature
Index, Canadian Review of Comparative Literature.

Canadian Theatre Review. Quarterly, 1974-   . Toronto, Ont.,
Canada: University of Toronto Press. 79-644805, ISSN 0315-0836.
Includes: *Canadian Newsletter* (1978-   .) Available on microfilm
from Micromedia (Toronto, Canada). Indexed in: MLA, Arts &
Humanities Citation Index, Canadian Periodicals Index, Index to
Book Reviews in the Humanities.

Critical Digest, NYC & London Theatre. Semimonthly, 1947-   .
New York: Critical Digest. LC 85-10810, ISSN 0049-9090. Previ-
ous title: *Critical Digest.* Available on microfilm from UMI (Ann
Arbor, MI).

Drama Review. See: *TDR.*

D.G. Newsletter. Monthly, 1977-   . Dramatists Guild, 234 West
44th St., New York, NY 10036. LC 84-11527. Previous title:
Dramatists Guild Newsletter.

The Dramatists Guild Quarterly. Quarterly, 1964-   . New York:
The Dramatists Guild. Address: 234 West 44th St., New York, NY
10036. Free to members. LC 64-9425, ISSN 0012-6004. Previous
title: *Dramatists Bulletin.*
   Each issue includes listings of agents, Broadway and Off-
   Broadway producers, sources of financial support, play contests,
   and a year-in-review section of theater activity.

Equity News. Monthly, 1915- . New York: Actors Equity
Association. LC 73-646820, ISSN 0092-4520. Previous title: *Equity.*

The Globe. 15 issues yearly. International Society of Dramatists,
P.O. Box 1310, Miami, FL 33153.
   A companion to *The Dramatist's Bible* annual, this newsletter
   regularly updates information for playwrights, screenwriters,
   and lyricists. It provides current information about the markets

and what production companies are looking for in the way of scripts and provides suggestions and ideas for selling your work.

Horizon; the magazine of the arts. Monthly, 1958-   . Horizon Publishers, 1305 Greensboro Ave., Tuscaloosa, AL 35401. LC 58-4110, ISSN 0018-4977. Indexed in: Magazine Index, Readers' Guide to Periodical Literature, America History & Life, Historical Abstracts A & B, Popular Magazine Review.

Journal of Arts Management and Law. Quarterly, 1969-   . Washington, DC: Heldref Publications. LC 82-645237, ISSN 0733-5113. Previous title: *Performing Arts Review: the Journal of Management & Law of the Arts* (1970-1981). Indexed in: Index to Legal Periodicals. Available on microfilm from UMI.
   The journal combines special theme issues with a concern about arts management and legal issues. A recent issue was built around the theme of social responsibility in the arts.

Latin American Theatre Review. Semiannual, 1967-   . Lawrence, KS: University of Kansas, Center for Latin American Studies. LC 78-369, ISSN 0023-8813. Indexed in: MLA, Index to Book Reviews.

Live. Quarterly, 1979-   . New York: Performing Arts Journal, Inc. LC 82-22133. Previous title: *Performance Art Magazine.*

Marquee; the journal of the Theatre Historical Society. Quarterly, 1969-   . Springfield, PA: Theatre Historical Society of America. LC 82-3578, ISSN 0025-3928. Available on microform from UMI. Indexed in: Avery Index to Architectural Periodicals.

Modern Drama. Quarterly, 1958-   . Downsview, Ont., Canada: University of Toronto Press. LC 76-308880, cnISSN 0026-7694. Back issues available on microform from UMI (Ann Arbor, MI) and Micromedia (Toronto, Canada). Indexed in: Social Sciences & Humanities Index, Humanities Index, MLA, Abstracts of English Studies, FLI, Index to Book Reviews in Humanities.

Modern International Drama; magazine for contemporary international drama in translation. Semiannual, 1967-   . LC 73-13445,

ISSN 0026-7856. Binghamton, NY: State University of New York at Binghamton. Indexed in: Arts & Humanities Citation Index. Available on microform from UMI.

New Theatre Quarterly (NTQ). Quarterly, 1985- . Cambridge, England and New York: Cambridge University Press. LC 85-643629, ISSN 0266-464X. Continues: *Theatre Quarterly* (1971-1981). Indexed in: Humanities Index.
  Internationally noted for critical studies about modern drama and classical repertory. Includes news about the theater, theatrical theory and practice, and educational programs.

New York Theatre Critics' Reviews. Biweekly, 1940- . Critics' Theatre Reviews, Four Park Ave., Suite 21D, New York, NY 10016. LC 42-1744, ISSN 0028-7784. Looseleaf format. Indexes are available for 1940 through 1986; complete years can be purchased on microform. Previous title: *Critics' Theatre Reviews* (1940-1942). Indexed in: Arts & Humanities Citation Index.

New York Theatre Review; America's national theatre magazine. Monthly, 1977- . New York: New York Theatre Review. LC 78-1635, ISSN 0164-8098.

On Stage. See: American Theatre Association, page 214.

Performing Arts in Canada. Quarterly, 1961- . Toronto, Ont., Canada: Canadian Stage and Arts Publications. LC 80-1303, ISSN 0031-5230. Available on microform from UMI. Indexed in: MI, Magazine Index, Canadian Periodicals Index, Arts & Humanities Citation Index, Music Index, Canadian Magazine Index.
  Provides coverage of film, theater and music in Canada.

Performing Arts Journal. 3 issues yearly, 1976- . New York: Performing Arts Journal. LC 83-641813, ISSN 0735-8393. Indexed in: Humanities Index, American Humanities Index, Book Review Index, Arts & Humanities Index.

Performing Arts Review. See: *Journal of Arts Management and Law.*

Playbill; the magazine for theatre goers. Monthly, 1884- . New York: American Theatre Press. ISSN 0032-146X.

Playboard; professional stage magazine. Monthly, 1966- . Burnaby, B.C., Canada: Arch-way Publishers. LC 76-302395, ISSN 0048-4415.

Players; the magazine of American theatre. Bimonthly, 1924- . Dekalb, IL: National Collegiate Players, University Theatre, Northern Illinois University, Dekalb, IL 60015. LC 80-1492, ISSN 0032-1486. Previous title: *Players Magazine* (1924-1966). Indexed in: Humanities Index.

Plays and Players. See: page 479.

Plays and Playwrights. Biennial, 1985- . Miami, FL: International Society of Dramatists. LC 86-38061.

Show Business. Weekly. See: GENERAL ENTERTAINMENT PERIODICALS, Chapter 5.

Sightlines: USITT Newsletter. Monthly, 1965- . ISSN: 0565-6311. New York: Published for the members of the U.S. Institute for Theatre Technology. Incorporates: *Administrative Supplement* to the newsletter (81-1029, ISSN 0730-1340). See Also: THEATER ORGANIZATIONS.

Southern Theatre. Quarterly, 1956- . Greensboro, NC: Southeastern Theatre Conference, University of North Carolina. LC 83-8463, ISSN 0584-4738. Previous title: *Southern Theatre News* (1956-1962).

Stages; the national theatre magazine. Monthly, 1984- . Address: Seymour Isenbery, Publisher, 8 Frasco Lane, Norwood, NJ 07648. Phone: (201) 836-8940. LC 85-11835, ISSN 1041-6048.

TD&T (Theatre Design and Technology). Quarterly (to membership), 1965 - . New York: U.S. Institute for Theatre Technology, Inc. OCLC 16582078, ISSN 0040-5477. Address: 330 West 42nd

St., Suite 1702, New York, NY 10036-6978. Previous title: *Theatre Design and Technology.*
Includes news on the construction of theaters; new technical developments; costume design; engineering; stage design; lighting; sound; health and safety; administration; and education. Available on microform and through document delivery service of UMI. Indexed in: Current Technology Index (British Technology Index).

TDR. Quarterly, 1955- . Cambridge, MA: MIT Press. LC 88-21803, ISSN 0012-5962. Previous titles: *The Drama Review, Tulane Drama Review,* and the *Carleton Drama Review.* Available on microform and document delivery service from UMI. Indexed in: MLA, Humanities Index, Arts & Humanities Citation Index, Book Review Index, Magazine Index, others.
Covers new trends in contemporary, avant-garde, original, and experimental theater, performance, dance, and film.

Theater. 1968- . New Haven, CT: Yale School of Drama. LC 78-642332, ISSN 0161-0775. Previous title: *Yale/theatre* (1968-1977).

Theater Three; a journal of theater and drama of the modern world. Semiannual, 1986- . Carnegie-Mellon University, Department of Drama, Pittsburgh, PA 15213. Phone: (412) 268-2404. LC 88-640091.
Original essays and reviews about modern drama. Also reviews the classics.

Theatre Crafts. Monthly, 1967- . Holmes, PA: Theatre Crafts Associates . LC 70-2567, ISSN 0040-5469. The June/July issue is: *Theatre Craft Directory.* Subscriptions to: Theatre Crafts, P.O. Box 630, Holmes, PA 19043-0630. Editorial offices: 135 Fifth Ave., New York, NY 10010-7193. Phone: (212) 677-5997. Back issues available from the publisher. Indexed in: BI, Education Index, Arts & Humanities Index, Readers' Guide to Periodical Literature, Book Review Index, Magazine Index.
Emphasis on the technicalities of producing theater productions. Set design for theater, film, and video. Recent issues included articles about how to deal with the problems of touring;

computer and software uses in the theater; a new product guide; and the various ways theaters have staged "A Christmas Carol."

Theatre Information Bulletin. Weekly, 1944- . New York: Proscenium Publications. LC 85-5380, ISSN 0040-5515.

Theatre Journal. Quarterly, 1949- . Baltimore, MD: The Johns Hopkins University Press in cooperation with the Association for Theatre in Higher Education (ATHE). ISSN 0192-2882. Previous title: *Educational Theatre Journal.* Subscription address: Johns Hopkins University Press, Journals Division, 701 West 40th St., Suite 275, Baltimore, MD 21211. Indexed in: MLA, Book Review Index, Humanities Index, Education Index, and Current Index to Journals in Education.

The journal's goal is to provide an outlet for scholarship and criticism in the theater arts.

Theatre News. Monthly, 1968- . Washington, DC: American Theatre Association. LC 76-321, ISSN 0563-4040. Includes *Asian Theatre Bulletin.* Back volumes available on microform from UMI.

Theatre Profiles; an illustrated reference guide to nonprofit professional theatres in the United States. Biennial, 1973- . New York: Theatre Communications Group. LC 76-641618, ISSN 0361-7947.

Theatre Quarterly (1971-1981). Continued in 1985 by *New Theatre Quarterly (NTQ).*

Theatre Studies. Semiannual, 1955- . Columbus, OH: Theatre Research Institute, Ohio State University. LC 73-640426, ISSN 0362-0964. Available on microform. Previous title: *Ohio State University Theatre Collection Bulletin.* Indexed in: MLA, American Humanities Index, Arts & Humanities Citation Index, and Abstracts of English Studies.

Theatre Survey; the American journal of theatre history. Semiannual (May and November) to members, 1960- . New York: American Society for Theatre Research (ASTR). LC 61-65338, ISSN 0040-5574. Available on microform and document delivery service of UMI. Indexed in: BI, Historical Abstracts, MLA, Humanities Index, Arts & Humanities Citation Index.

ASTR was founded in 1956 to encourage research and provide a link to the International Federation for Theatre Research. *Theatre Survey* has articles about historical topics and people in the theater, and provides reviews of new books relevant to theater interests.

Theatre Times. Bimonthly, 1982- . New York: Alliance of Resident Theatres. Address: 325 Spring St., Room 315, New York, NY 10013. Phone: (212) 989-5257. LC 82-2936, ISSN 0732-300X.

Current news of resident theaters in the New York area.

Variety. See: page 338.

THEATER LIBRARIES AND RESEARCH CENTERS

Most theater libraries in the United States are, in actuality, performing arts collections that cover film, television, and other types of live entertainment (such as the circus, magic, vaudeville, and mime). Dance and opera are often included. Each library has developed its own classification system and physical arrangement for storing, handling, and identifying the wide variety of materials in the collection. Almost every major library in the United States will have some material about the theater, and many will have special collections donated by prominent people from the entertainment industry.

The Billy Rose Theatre Collection

Address: New York Public Library at the Lincoln Center. The Billy Rose Theatre Collection. 111 Amsterdam Ave., New York, NY 10023. *Phone:* (212) 870-1639. *Hours:* Open weekdays and Saturdays; limited evening service. Hours vary daily so it is best to call.

The Billy Rose Theatre Collection is actually a large collection of theater, film, television, and radio research materials. The major strengths of the collection lie in the theater and film materials, and especially in their locally-developed historical clipping and photo files.

The theater collection was established as a separate entity in 1931 and named after Billy Rose in 1979. The collection has grown to include books, programmes and playbills from around the world; photographs and prints; posters; scenery and costume designs; periodicals; newspaper clippings; personal correspondence; manuscripts; scripts from all media; promptbooks; real objects, such as small props; and other memorabilia from the stage, film, television, radio and other areas of entertainment.

The Library has been blessed over the years by large donations of personal collections from people in the entertainment business, particularly from the New York stage and film industries. It also has a large collection of film and television program stills donated regularly over the years by film companies and distributors as well as clipping collections on film and television productions and on performers from every field. These clipping files are arranged by production title, producer, name of performer, playwright, theater or production company, and thousands of specific subjects. The Library maintains files for many productions of a particular play. The collection also provides strong historical and current coverage of the British entertainment industry, with some stage material going back to the 1600s.

Especially noteworthy is the in-house "Collection of Newspaper Clippings of Dramatic Criticism of Plays Produced in New York." It is so large that it fills one complete wall of shelving and has expanded to another one. It's a hand-clipped collection of New York newspaper reviews and articles about every play to open in New York since 1917. Since the clippings have been pasted on pages and bound in hard cover books, the collection is, by necessity, in chronological order.

Film and theater periodicals are another strong point of the collection, with many titles complete back to their first issues. And fortunately for researchers, the Library has been one of the few institutions to retain runs of old fan magazines.

Lastly, the Library created a special program in 1970 called Theatre on Film and Tape Collection (TOFT). The program films or videotapes live stage performances (both experimental theatre and commercial Broadway plays) and informal dialogues with important theatre personalities about their careers and techniques.

Mungar Memorial Library

Address: Boston University, 771 Commonwealth Avenue, Boston, MA 02215. *Phone:* (617) 353-3696. *Hours:* Call for current hours.

The Mungar Memorial Library has the largest number of privately donated collections from actors, producers, directors, and production executives around. Covers all areas of entertainment.

Harvard Theatre Collection

Address: Harvard University, Cambridge, MA 02138. *Phone:* (617) 495-1000. *Hours:* Call for current hours.

The Harvard collection was established as a separate library in 1915 with an emphasis on American and British stage materials, although all areas of the performing arts are included. The Library has made a concentrated effort to collect original theater materials and is especially strong in theater playbills, programs, costume design, and promptbooks. It is also noted for having an exceptional collection of photographs from American and British stage plays. The Library now owns the highly regarded Angus McBean Collection of 30,000 photographs of British play productions and portraits of theater personalities taken from 1937 to 1964. Just as important, it also owns the copyright to the photographs and can therefore grant the rights to use the photographs in approved projects.

The Library also has large collections of newspaper clippings, reference books, play texts, biographical information about playwrights and actors, and periodicals about the theater. In related areas, it also has a substantial collection of information about dance and ballet, as well as growing collections on other forms of live entertainment (the circus, vaudeville, and minstrel shows).

Institute of the American Musical

Address: 220 West 93rd Street, New York, NY 10025. Mail received at: P.O. Box 480144, Los Angeles, CA 90048. *Phone:* (213) 934-1221. *Hours:* by appointment.

The Institute collection covers the American musical in the theater and on film. Materials include print, audio, and video resources. It's the archives for the 1934-1951 records of New York's Paramount Theater.

Library of Congress

Address: Washington, DC 20546. *Phone numbers:* The general number is (202) 707-5521. Each division has its own phone number. *Hours:* Weekdays. Some divisions have weekend and evening hours. Call to confirm times.

Conducting theater research in the Library of Congress is difficult and confusing (and almost impossible for the novice researcher) because, unlike the other areas of the performing arts, there is no separate theater collection or expert reference staff to provide assistance. It's regrettable that the theater hasn't been accorded equal status with the other performing arts and it's a major omission in the Library's ability to provide public service. A separate reading room would establish access to what could be one of the country's most useful collections if all of the parts were pulled together in one location. As things stand, the two best ways to find theater materials in the Library of Congress are: (1) consult with the staff of the Performing Arts Library at the Kennedy Center; and (2) plan to visit and consult with several divisions of the main LC complex. The Performing Arts Library and the Key LC divisions are described in more detail below:

The Performing Arts Library is located at The John F. Kennedy Center, Washington, DC 20566. (Phone: (202) 254-9803. Hours: 11:00am-8:30 pm, Tuesday through Friday, 10:00am-6:00pm Saturday.) The Library is actually a small reading center which has about 5,000 reference books and 450 current periodical titles covering all areas of the performing arts. Its staff has the expertise to advise about theater research, but their effectiveness is hampered by the fact that virtually all of the theater materials are in the main Library of Congress facilities on the other side of the city. They will respond to telephone inquiries and do online searches on the LC databases for patrons.

If you want to do theater research at the Library of Congress, you had better know what you are looking for before you start. Assembling a complete research package of books, periodicals, and special materials is a most complex and arduous task if you have to start completely from scratch. The Library may have hundreds of thousands of plays, scripts, historical books, bibliographies, drama collections and other theater materials from around the world, but they aren't much use to anyone if you can't find them easily. Most of the theater materials are simply handled as part of the massive general collection that is stored in miles of stacks throughout the LC complex.

To find out what theater materials are in the collection, a researcher will need to start by searching the LC catalogs by author, title, or subject. Although LC has completely placed the cataloging records for its collection online, researchers have fought to keep the old card catalog intact because of the complexity and problems inherent in the new computer system; therefore, it's wise to check both under certain circumstances. Check the main card catalog for older historical titles and the online catalog for both current and historical titles. Once you have found the titles of the material you want to use, the catalog record will indicate its stack or division location.

Once you identify a title you want to see, each item must be requested separately from the reading room or the division responsible for retrieving that particular type of material from the stacks. The majority of books will need to be requested through the main reading room. Most bound periodicals are shelved in the general stacks and need to be called for from the main reading room, but current unbound issues of the same titles may be located in the **Serials Division.** Some books or sets of periodicals are only available on microform and therefore must be used in the Microform Reading Room. Still other titles can be found in several of the reading rooms. Posters, photographs and other visual media can be found in the **Prints and Photographs Division.**

The **Manuscripts Division** has the personal collections of many noted figures in all areas of the performing arts, including the theater. In general, these collections have been given to LC and often contain a variety of materials that have been gathered over the lifetime of the person. They may include books, photos, playbills, real objects, or many other types of memorabilia. The Division is also the repository for correspondence and personal papers of prominent people. Because of the variety of materials which it holds, researchers should be aware that there is some overlap with another division, **The Rare Book and Special Collections Division** which has scripts, several sets of historical theater journals, rare editions of plays, playbills, incunabula, and valuable special collections that have been donated or purchased. **The Music Division** has a number of special collections relating to the musical theater, all of the music copyrighted in the United States, voice and musical recordings, correspondence of noted musical stage composers, and journals relating to music in the theater. Theater materials from around the world may be found in the several area study Divisions that handle materials collected from specific geographical areas of the world. **The Recorded Sound Reference Center** is the access point for the Library's collection of radio and recorded sound reference information and contains a number of historical radio broadcasts of plays both here and in England. It's also a good place to hunt for recorded interviews with early stage personalities.

The **Federal Theatre Project** is the one special Library of Congress theater collection that is actually housed together in one location, and it is on permanent loan to the George Mason University Library in Fairfax, Virginia. The FTP was established in 1935 as part of the WPA and the materials in collection are the historical documents, business records, play production materials, radio programs, and other information about the 150 companies throughout the United States which participated in the Project until its end in 1939.

The Free Public Library of Philadelphia

Address: Free Public Library of Philadelphia, Theatre Collection, Logan Square, Philadelphia, PA 19103. *Phone:* (215) 686-5427. *Hours:* Monday–Friday 9:00 am.–5:00 pm.

The Free Public Library has one of the largest collections of local entertainment history, with an emphasis on collecting everything possible about the Pennsylvania and Philadelphia performing arts. The theater is most heavily represented, but significant coverage also provided for film, television, radio, the circus, minstrels, and vaudeville. Because Philadelphia has played such an important part of American entertainment history, many important events, productions, and personalities can be found in the files.

The Players Library

Address: 16 Gramercy Park, New York, NY 10003. *Phone:* (212) 475-6116. *Hours:* by appointment.

The Players Library collection contains books and other materials about the history of the American and British theaters.

The William Seymour Theater Collection

Address: Princeton University. Library. Theater Collection. Princeton, NJ 08544. *Phone:* (609) 452-3223. *Hours:* Weekdays. Visitors by appointment only.

The Collection was established in 1936 with the donation of 800 valuable theater books and other stage memorabilia from the family of William Seymour. Today, the Collection has grown to include a large number of play texts, playbills and programs, photographs, clipping files, and artifacts of both the American and British stage. The Collection has also expanded to include Princeton's film and television research resources as well as sheet music and recordings relating to musical theater. It is the home of the business records section of the Warner Brothers Archives. Film stills and movie scripts are well represented. The Library also has a large special collection of circus materials. On the local level, it has taken its responsibility seriously to document Princeton's own theater activities and follow the theatrical careers of its graduates as actors, directors, or playwrights. Many successful alumni have donated personal papers and correspondence, as have other noted people in all areas of the performing arts. Some of the personal collections that now reside at Princeton include the personal papers of such diverse people as Woody Allen, Eugene O'Neill, and James Stewart,

Humanities Research Center

Address: University of Texas at Austin. Humanities Research Center. Hoblitzelle Theatre Arts Library. P.O. Box 7219, Austin, TX 78712. *Phone:* (512) 471-9122. *Hours:* Monday–Friday 8:00 am.–5:00 pm.; Saturday by appointment only.

This is a unique collection of early American stage memorabilia and books. The initial gift that established the Library in 1956 consisted largely of posters, clipping files, playbills and programs and photographs from the 1860s to the 1920s. Of particular value is a large number of photographs of early stage performers. A few years later, a large collection of British stage materials from the 18th and 19th Centuries was added. This gave the Library a substantial number of early British playbills, photographs, historical literature, and other artifacts. More recently, the Library has regularly added film materials to the collection and now has film stills, lobby cards, scripts, and the private papers of several film industry notables. Interestingly, the Library also has a number of original autographed items from film and stage stars. Additional collections cover magic, film and stage music, circus history, band music and history, and vaudeville. Part of the collection consists of thousands of musical scores used to accompany silent films. Recent gifts and purchases have expanded and updated both the film and stage photograph collections so that nearly all eras and personalities are represented.

Theatre Arts Library

Address: University of California at Los Angeles (UCLA).
Theater Arts Library. Los Angeles, CA 90024. *Phone:* (213)
825-4880. See: FILM AND TELEVISION LIBRARIES.
Hours: Weekdays. Change with University class schedule.

Wisconsin Center For Film and Theatre Research

Address: University of Wisconsin. 816 State St., Madison,
WI 53706. *Phone:* Reading Room (608) 262-3338; Film
Archive: (608) 262-0585. *Hours:* Weekdays 10:00 am.-4:30
pm. Services: Arrangements can be made for in-house
reproduction of photographs.

The Center was established in 1960 as an archives for
collections relating to all areas of the performing arts. To
date, it has accepted over 300 gift collections from important
donors associated with the stage, screen, and television.
Important personal papers have come from writers, actors,
producers, and directors.

The theater material in the collection consists of the
production records of a number of stage companies, the
papers of prominent producers from the 1940s and 1950s,
and the current personal records of a number of stage
directors. An attempt has also been made to collect materials
from regional and experimental theater companies around
the country.

The most valuable part of the Center is the United Artists
Collection of their production company business records,
film library, film stills, and other related materials. The
Center also has hundreds of films from RKO and Warner,
along with accompanying materials such as scripts, lobby
cards, and film stills. It has received the papers of many of
the people involved in the legal problems generated by the
infamous hearings held during the 1950s by the House
Committee on Un-American Activities.

Television is represented and the collection contains shows
from the 1940s to date, including some complete early series.
Major television producers from all three networks have
contributed complete sets of their series as well as production

records for these works. It has copies of a number of live plays and variety shows from the 1950s. It has all of Rod Serling's papers covering his life of creative work. Television comedians, comedy writers, their series, and the scripts for the shows make up a special part of the collection.

The media materials in the collection include film stills from both movies and television shows, posters and lobby cards, playbills, and other visuals. Access is provided through detailed title and personal name indexes. A newspaper clipping collection contains information about thousands of personalities.

Yale Drama Library

Address: Yale University. Drama Library. P.O. Box 1903A, Yale Station, New Haven, CT 06520. Phone (203) 432-1554. Open to Yale students; other researchers must apply for permission.

The collection covers all areas of the performing arts, with 20th-Century theater making up the major part of the collection. It collects information about the Yale productions and has an expansive collection of photographs as well as set and costume designs. In addition, the Manuscripts and Archives Division of the main Yale University Library has a number of historical manuscripts and photographs that have been donated over the years.

THEATER ASSOCIATIONS AND ORGANIZATIONS

American Society for Theatre Research (ASTR). Address: c/o Theatre Arts Program, University of Pennsylvania, Philadelphia, PA 19104. Phone: (215) 898-7382. Affiliated with the International Federation for Theatre Research. Publications: *ASTR Newsletter* (Semiannual, 1972- . ISSN: 0044-7927), *Theatre Survey* (Semiannual, 1960- . ISSN: 0040-5574). Publishes occasional monographs.

Founded in 1956 to promote theater research and provide a network for theater researchers. Holds an annual conference

and presents annual theater research awards and scholarships.
Sponsors some research.

American Theatre Association. 1029 Vermont Ave., N.W.,
Washington, DC 20005. Previously: American Educational The-
atre Association. Publications to membership: *On Stage* (Quar-
terly, 1968-   .); *Annual Directory of Members* (Annual, 1949-   .
ISSN: 0065-8138); and *Summer Theatre Directory* (Annual, 1968-   .
ISSN: 0081-9387).

American Theatre Critics Association (ATCA). Address for
1991/92, c/o Clara Hieronymus, Executive Secretary, *The Ten-
nessean,* 1100 Broadway, Nashville, TN 37202. Phone: (800)
351-1752.
     Founded in 1974 for the purpose of providing closer communica-
tion between American theater critics and creating a forum for
the discussion of theater criticism. Participates in the Tony
Awards by nominating candidates for the award of Best Play
(Regional), which recognizes regional theater around the
United States.

Association of Entertainers. P.O. Box 1393, Washington, DC
20013. Phone: (202) 546-1919. Publications: *Talent Spotlight*
(quarterly), and *VICA Professional Journal* (quarterly, ISSN
0042-1839). Also publishes a membership directory. Holds semiannual convention.
     Founded in 1981 with a membership of professionals involved in
the theater (actors, managers, producers and directors, and
technicians). Serves as an intermediary in arranging theater
productions to raise money for non-profit organizations. Emphasis on live stage performances.

Costume Designers Guild. 14724 Ventura Street Building Pent-
house, Sherman Oaks, CA 91403. Phone: (818) 905-1557.
     The Guild is a chapter of the International Alliance of Theatrical
Stage Employees and Moving Picture Operators of the United
States of America. In addition to representing its members, the
Guild publishes an annual *Membership Directory,* which gives
the address and phone number, plus the stage, film and
television credits of each member listed.

Drama Desk. Address: c/o Alvin Klein, 722 Broadway, New York, NY 10003. Phone: (212) 674-4436.

Founded in 1949; membership is currently over 1000 and is made up of drama critics, editors, reporters, and other writers who cover the New York theater. Membership is from all of the media (newspapers, periodicals, radio, television, and independent services). Presents the annual Drama Desk Awards for outstanding performances in the theater. Holds a variety of meetings, including a monthly luncheon with speakers from the theatre.

Dramatists Guild. 234 West 44th St., New York, NY 10036. Phone: (212) 398-9366. Publications: *Dramatists Guild-Newsletter* (10 issues yearly) and a quarterly *Magazine.*

Founded in 1920 and is one of the oldest and most active representatives of theater professionals. The Guild represents approximately 8,000 American and British playwrights, composers, and lyricists. Presents the annual Hull-Warriner Awards. Holds seminars, play writing workshops, and other programs of interest to its members.

International Society of Dramatists. P. O. Box 1310, Miami, Fl 33153. Phone: (305) 674-0722. Publications: *The Dramatists Bible* (annual) and *The Globe* (monthly). Other publications of interest to its membership.

Founded in 1977; more of a professional service organization than an association. Provides marketing information for playwrights, scriptwriters, and dramatists. Keeps members informed of producers and companies looking for scripts and original writing in all areas (the stage, regional theater, radio, television, corporate productions, etc.), publishes requirements for scripts, and provides current information through its monthly newsletter.

International Society of Performing Arts Libraries and Museums (SIBMAS). C/o Barbo Strïbolt, Drottningsholm Theater Museum, Box 270, Stockholm, Sweden.

International Theatre Institute of the United States. 220 W. 42nd St., New York, NY 10036. Phone: (212) 944-1490.

Founded in 1948 as the American branch of the International

Theatre Institute with the goal of acting as a forum for communication between theater professionals worldwide. Works with performing arts groups, encourages theater research, and sponsors meetings of interest to the theatre community.

International Theatrical Agencies Association. 1123 North Water St., Milwaukee, WI 53202. Phone: (414) 276-8788. Publications: a monthly newsletter.

Founded in 1975 with a limited membership open only to theatrical agencies which book entertainers into live musical venues. Acts as a networking organization and placement service. Has a computerized service which links member agencies.

League of American Theatres and Producers. 226 W. 47th St., New York, NY 10036. Phone: (212) 764-1122. Previously named: The League of New York Theatres and Producers.

Established in 1930; represents legitimate theatre owners and producers in labor negotiations and acts as a lobbying organization to present members' viewpoints on local and national legislation. Conducts marketing research of interest to the theater, compiles theater statistics, holds some seminars and programs. Presents the annual Tony Awards.

New York Drama Critics' Circle. Address: c/o Richard Hummier, *Variety,* 475 Park Ave. S., New York, NY 10016. Phone: (212) 779-1100.

Founded in New York in 1935 with a small membership made up of drama critics from the New York offices of the print media (newspapers, wire services, and periodicals). Gives annual awards to plays (American or foreign) which were produced on stage in New York during the year but have not won other awards.

Outer Critic's Circle. Address: c/o Marjorie Gunner (current President), 101 West 57th St., New York, NY 10019. Phone: (212) 765-8857.

Established in 1950 with a membership of writers and critics who review New York theater activities for all areas of the media outside of New York City. Presents annual theater awards.

The Players. 16 Gramercy Park, New York, NY 10003. Phone: (212) 475-6116. Publications: their *Bulletin* (irregular).

Founded in 1888 as a private social organization for professionals in all areas of the theater. It remains so today. The public is allowed to use the Library by appointment.

Society for Theatre Research. Publications: *Theatre Notebook.*

Society of Stage Directors and Choreographers. 1501 Broadway, New York, NY 10036. Phone: (212) 391-1070. Publications: a quarterly *Journal* and a monthly *Newsletter.*

Founded in 1959; a labor union which represents theater directors and choreographers.

Theatre Guild. 226 W. 47th St., New York, NY 10036. Phone: (212) 869-5470.

Founded in 1919 and currently has over 100,000 members. The Guild exists to promote attendance at theatrical productions, supports touring companies, and sponsors the American Theatre Society (a national subscription service which provides series tickets to plays).

Theatre Historical Society of America. 2215 West North Ave., Chicago, IL 60647. Phone: (312) 252-7200. Publications: *Marquee* (quarterly) and a *Directory* of members (irregular). It also publishes some research studies.

Founded in 1969 for individuals, libraries, and historical groups interested in preserving theater history and theatrical architecture. The Society encourages theater studies, conducts research, collects archive materials. It provides speakers to other organizations upon request and provides some seminars and programs. It has its own museum. Holds an annual convention.

Theatre Library Association. 111 Amsterdam St., New York, NY 10023. Phone: (212) 870-1670. Publications to members: *Broadside;* newsletter of the Theatre Library Association (Quarterly, 1940- , n.s. 1973- .ISSN: 0068-2748). The newsletter contains news of association activities, book reviews, articles about some of the latest productions, and quality photographs. Another publication, *Performing Arts Resources* (Annual, 1974- . ISSN: 0360-

3814), is a hardcover annual containing a series of special studies and/or articles about some aspect of theater research. It also publishes an annual *Membership List* giving the names and addresses (no phones) of both personal and corporate members.

Founded in 1937 for librarians, researchers, archivists, theater professionals, and others interested in theater research. The association presents its annual book awards in May and is active in the New York theater community. An annual membership meeting is held in October.

U.S. Institute for Theatre Technology. Address: 330 W. 42nd St., Suite 1702, New York, NY 10036-6978. Phone: (212) 563-5551.

Publishes an annual *Membership Directory* which not only lists members, but also reviews significant events of the year, *Theatre Design and Technology* (quarterly), and a monthly *Newsletter.* It also provides conference information, lists awards announced during the year, and lists chapter addresses. It holds an annual conference. The Institute was founded in 1960 for educational institutions, students, and others interested in theater technology and production techniques. It both promotes and conducts research, with the emphasis on building architecture, stage design, the status of new technology, equipment use, and managerial techniques. The Institute also sponsors seminars and other programs on these subjects.

7 POPULAR MUSIC AND RECORDED SOUND RESEARCH

Popular music has always been well covered in all of the general American literature because it is such a strong part of our normal life and culture. Popular music touches our lives every day, each time we turn the radio on, buy a record, or watch television. It's in the stores where we shop, on the elevators we use, and in the restaurants where we eat. Music, the songwriters who create it, the vocalists who sing it and the musicians who play it, influence our thoughts, set our moods, and reflect the standards by which we live our lives. Occasionally, the process by which music acts as a mirror in explaining or documenting our thoughts and the events of our lives is reversed, and a musical trend or unique performer will become so commanding that the particular influence will actually change the course of our culture itself. Rock and roll and the influence of Elvis Presley did that more than any other single force in the history of popular music.

The success of popular music depends on equal doses of two main ingredients: the songwriter and the performer. Of course, other factors are involved too, but to lesser extent. The complex business of music includes music publishers, recording companies, radio stations, managers and booking agents, performing rights organizations, venue owners, and countless other personnel. But the basic creators of the art of good music are the writers of the songs and the singers and musicians who interpret them. It's a joint venture.

One has only to look at U.S. history to see that the definition of "popular music" has changed regularly over the years. Of course, there has always been a variety of music genres that, taken together, make up the body of popular music. But, in general, the term usually means the particular style of music that is the most popular at the moment.

Defining popular music used to be a much simpler process in the past because there were fewer distinctions to make than there are today. In the early days of U.S. history, the average citizen had two ways to become familiar with new music: buy sheet music and/or hear music at live performances. The most popular songs of the day were determined by the sale of sheet music and the number of people who were humming the tune. Even though modern means of communication didn't exist, music was so popular that songs could take the country by storm in the 1800s just as easily, and almost as quickly, by word of mouth. In fact, there wasn't any other way.

Live stage performances were a major factor in the making of popular music before the 1900s. In those days, every performance was a stage performance, only the style of presentation differed. Identifiable regional music sounds and styles did exist, but even this music was not too far removed from the general sound and style of the mainstream. Any city of a reasonable size had the legitimate theater, dance halls, music halls, musical reviews, vaudeville, pleasure gardens, band concerts, and recital halls. Smaller communities and the rural areas around the country had traveling medicine shows and/or variety shows, repertory theaters, local performers, county fairs and other seasonal celebrations, the circus, church socials, local high school or community bands. Neighboring families often gathered in small groups to entertain themselves. At least one or two people in every family could play a musical instrument or sing.

The mechanism for changing the face of popular music came with the commercial development of two products in the early 1900s: the phonograph and the ability to transmit radio signals. Recorded sound was invented around the turn of the century and first appeared in the form of phonocylinders before becoming vinyl records. (The physical format of recorded sound continues its never-ending evolutionary cycle today with the coming of CDs and DAT.) Once these two industries were able to develop their products to the point where the average American had access to them and could afford them, the doors opened for the creation of a wider variety of musical styles. Change came slowly at first because radio programming simply reflected popular music as it already was. Radio programmers used what they had at hand. But once the medium grew and a wider variety of programming became available, listeners and performers alike became more aware of other styles and sounds both here and abroad, and began to experiment.

Unique forms of American music, heretofore enjoying only local or regional popularity, had the chance to be heard at the national level. Country music was one of several genres that became more clearly defined and grew in popularity as a consequence of radio and records. Country music came from the hills of the Appalachians and the rural South; western music came from the Western United States. Together they make up what is defined as country music today. Most early country music was usually considered American folk music and not treated as a separate genre. This categorization is reflected in many of the indexes and research materials, where one has to look under the term "folk music" in order to find material on country music. Although country music and western music have been clearly identified as genres since the early 1900s, it has only been in the last twenty years that the indexes and reference sources have adapted the terms "country music" or "country & western music" for the genres. By the middle of the 1920s, several national country music radio programs were being broadcast to large audiences and a number of singers who had previously experienced local or regional popularity had become national recording stars. The popularity of western music was helped along in the 1920s by emergence of a new movie phenomenon, the singing cowboy. Today, country music is popular worldwide, with recordings and performances available in many countries and languages.

One could take almost any musical genre and show a similar historical development regarding popularity patterns, transitions, changes, merging styles, and cross-influences that occurred as a result of the development of radio and records, and to a lesser extent, films. Jazz went from being a local Southern style to the point of being a truly international style today. The point is that all of these things provided an easy communication system for the interrelationship of ideas and channels for quick change that didn't exist before. Up until the 1950s, changes in popular music were relatively subtle; the words and music were written by Rodgers & Hammerstein or Hoagy Carmichael and recorded by Bing Crosby, Frank Sinatra, Dinah Shore, Perry Como or Rosemary Clooney. Big band music had been popular for many decades and was a major avenue of career development for new singers. The major changes that took place in popular American music were in the emergence of new writers and artists. But although the people might be new and very talented, they fit their individuality into the existing structure and as a consequence overall music sounds and styles remained similar to those already in place.

Radio was an important factor in the development of popular music and the recorded sound industry from the moment it started. Early radio created a substantial amount of original programming; that's where the popular drama and variety series were found, this was how people got the big news stories of the day, and it was the place where records became hits. Radio made national stars out of local performers and popularized the music of songwriters who had previously been unable to get their work before an appreciative audience. Every radio station provided a variety of programs during the day, and most of the shows used music as a regular feature. All stations produced live programs from their own studios using local talent and these often included both music and talk. The stations also broadcast network shows, many of which were variety shows with singers or musicians as the stars or guests. Radio stations rarely typecast their overall programming into particular formats, generally playing all types of music together. Once in a while they might broadcast a special show of all jazz music or big band music, but for the most part they might follow a Frank Sinatra record with a popular Eddy Arnold tune or a current instrumental favorite. All of this changed in the early 1950s.

Two events forced the change in radio programming patterns: (1) the coming of television in the 1950s, and (2) the subsequent need to seek out new ideas and ways to hold on to their listeners in the 1960s and 70s. The result is what we have today, the age of the special format station.

The majority of stations in the United States today broadcast only one type of format. With few exceptions, they are either all talk or all music. And if they are all music, they usually only broadcast one type of music. National Public Radio, PBS and a few other isolated examples, provide the little original scripted programming that is produced today; virtually none of it is at the local level. Most of the scripted or serial programming that is used on local radio stations comes from companies that provide syndicated shows to satisfy the needs of particular specialized formats. Even then, much of the original scripted programming available through syndication is music oriented in the form of "weekly hits" packages or combination talk shows, interviews, or music specials about particular artists.

From the viewpoint of the radio and music industries, many of these changes have been beneficial. Once the stations decided that a one-format pattern was the answer to their problems of declining listenership in the 1960s and 70s, the next step was to start breaking the music up into different categories and conducting audience research to discover which might attract the largest audience. This could never have happened just a few years earlier when little diversity existed in popular music. However, by this time Elvis Presley and his contemporaries had changed the face of popular music forever by creating rock and roll. The music did not coexist comfortably with the rest of popular music, and yet no one could deny that it also was popular music, particularly since the rock music and artists were taking over the charts. The simple, clear definition of "popular music" was broken and would never again be so singularly identified. As a result, the stage had been set for a broader audience acceptance of what popular music is. One can see this reflected in the changing domination of different types of music as new trends develop and old ones diminish.

Today, not only have stations and record companies broken the large body of popular music into specific categories, they have taken the concept one step farther and developed subcategories. Now there are several different kinds of rock music, different generations of "oldies" music, and even several different kinds of country music. One station might play contemporary music of a particular genre, while a competing station might play the traditional sounds of the same genre.

The huge amounts of material required to satisfy the needs of radio air time have given increased attention to some genres and made it possible for more artists to enter the field. It can also serve as the platform for the introduction of new music and experimental sounds. The credit for the development of new music must be shared equally between the record and radio industries, because one could not exist without the other. One may make the product available, but the other is the voice by which it is largely heard.

Popular music today is therefore the result of a long and complex history. It is still John Philip Sousa, Perry Como, musical theater, movie themes, and love songs; but it is also Michael Jackson, Randy Travis, Whitney Houston, Manhattan Transfer, The Beatles, Dolly Parton, reggae, disco, new wave, and breakdancing. Musicians can be as popular as vocalists. It's interesting then, that one of the most popular questions still asked in libraries around the country is "Where can I get a copy of Kate Smith singing 'God Bless America'?" (The answer is easier than most people think, it's still available as a 45rpm record and appears on several albums)

Starting Your Music Research

How does a researcher cope with all of this? It helps to be aware of the cultural environment that existed during the time of the music you are researching. Such knowledge will often guide you toward the best research tools to use and the terms most likely to describe what you are looking for. If you are searching a full-text database, you can use whatever the current catch-phrase is with reasonable assurance that you will find anything it has. But if you are using a database or a printed book index that uses specific subject terms, each index may define the music differently. And if you are using reference sources that are more than a few years old, the terms may be outdated or unfamiliar.

There are thousands of music periodicals from around the world. As many as several hundred might exist for a specialized area. In addition, there are hundreds of fan club journals ranging in quality from mimeographed sheets to slick professional jobs which cover the active careers of recording artists. They're worth finding and reading if you are researching the career of a particular performer. Sometimes a fan club has lasted throughout the long career of a performer and the volume of material covered in its publications can be valuable indeed. Some fan journals exist for the purpose of remembering or paying tribute to artists who have died: Elvis Presley, Marty Robbins, Bing Crosby, and Louis Armstrong are four who come to mind. These publications frequently reprint historical literature or encourage current research; in this way, they make their own unique contribution to the body of useful music literature.

As in other areas of entertainment, most music literature is not indexed at all, indexed in sources not easily available, or not indexed in great detail. The most important index in the field, *Music Index,* includes only a few established journals from any genre, and these must compete for space with literature on classical music. There's no doubt that the *Index* is a valuable tool, but the limitations in its completeness should compel the researcher to use it only as a starting point. Fortunately, the music researcher has other places to go.

Because music is so much a part of our popular culture, it is possible to do a considerable amount of research by using general sources such as *Readers' Guide to Periodical Literature,* the *New York Times Index,* and *Biography Index.* Music can be found on a variety of databases; almost any general database with popular magazines or daily newspapers will have something: *Magazine Index, Newspaper Index, Readers' Guide to Periodical Literature, Dialog,* and *Nexis* are only a few. In addition, there is *Billboard.* But keep in mind the fact that most of the databases only go back to the late 1970s. If you are researching music halls or the big band era, they will be nearly useless. This is one place where the printed edition of the *New York Times Index* is a hundred times more valuable than their database version on *Nexis*.

Another avenue of information open to the astute researcher is the large volume of material produced by collectors. Music and recorded sound collecting is big business and a number of bibliographies and discographies have been compiled by enthusiasts. Serious collectors exist for every musical area (no matter how small) and the experts in each field are often excellent researchers. One organization, The Association for Recorded Sound Collections, has a successful mix of collectors, researchers, librarians, research institutions, and record industry professionals among its membership.

The National Academy of Recording Arts and Sciences (NARAS) has recently been pushing for a heightened awareness by the recording industry for the need to preserve their master recordings. Many of these historical master tapes are stored in vaults, storerooms, or libraries without proper physical conditions or climate-control and are in a state of slow but steady deterioration. Adding to the problem is the fact that many original or master recordings that are in these company collections lack complete documentation. In other words, not even the record companies themselves know exactly what they have or what shape it is in. Preservation programs have never been a priority of record companies because of the costs involved and the fact that the attention of corporate decision makers is usually directed toward the production and sale of current products. But now that the vinyl record is being eliminated and there is an interest in restoring historical recordings in order to reissue them on CDs, archive material has taken on a renewed importance.

The interrelationship of music with the other areas of entertainment should not be ignored and researchers should consider the value of searching stage, film, and broadcast materials if their particular project calls for it. Radio research itself is most properly defined as broadcast research and belongs with the television materials. And yet, it plays an important part in the development of popular music. As always, the dividing line is thin, and getting thinner. For example, the past few years has seen a strong market develop in spoken-word recordings and cassettes. The reading of books by noted personalities has become big business. While most of the current spoken word products are on audio cassettes, older products are often available on vinyl record albums. This is especially true for radio programs. Almost every librarian is asked at least once during her or his career how to find a copy of Orson Welles' "War of the Worlds." The answer can be found by checking both the recordings and cassette listings because it's available in several formats. The *Phonolog Reporter* and the *Schwann* catalog both list spoken word products currently available for purchase, as does such reference books like *Words on Cassette*. At any rate, "War of the Worlds" is easily available, as are many other old radio programs, and such popular public speeches as Martin Luther King's "I Have a Dream." Researchers should be careful about making artificial judgments regarding how to research recorded sound materials. The text of a play may be in a theater collection, a filmed version of the same play in the film collection, the videotaped version in a television collection, and several audio versions of the same performance housed in separate music archives! Similarly, music video performances can legitimately be placed in several different types of collections.

Changes occurring in the world of popular music today are so expansive and rapid that they are hard to keep up with unless you read some of the weekly publications regularly. The coming of the audio and video compact disk (CDs and laser disks) has merged the recorded sound and visually filmed fields in new ways, bringing with it the demand for new equipment which can handle both formats simultaneously (and several formats of each). The development of DAT tape format is expected to bring additional rapid changes. The internationalization of recorded music (largely the result of the entry of multinational business conglomerates into the recording industry) is being followed by similar ownership of American music publishing houses. And what may be the biggest impact of all is just over the horizon: the removal of trade barriers which will create a European single market by 1992. Interestingly enough, many people in the industry are forecasting that the globalization of the music market may reduce the prevailing dominance of American and British music and open the door to wider exposure for music from other countries, giving them the means to grab at the chance for more popularity. Offsetting this is the fact that the larger companies are buying up the smaller ones at what many people view as an alarming rate, thereby reducing the avenues for the introduction of new talent and the ability of the smaller independent record companies to distribute their products. Will this trend bring about the worldwide homogenization of music? Will new independent companies spring to life and creative talent survive regardless of market control by a few large companies? The next few years will be exciting ones indeed.

MUSIC REFERENCE RESOURCES

The American Dance Band Discography 1917-1942, by Brian Rust. New Rochelle, NY: Arlington House. 2 vols., 1975. LC 75-33689, ISBN 0-87000-248-1.

A huge historical work, listing virtually all of the big band recordings made up to 1942.

American Popular Music: A Reference Guide, by Mark Booth. Westport, CT: Greenwood. 212 p., 1983. LC 82-21062, ISBN 0-313-21305-4.

A guide to the literature of all types of popular American music.

American Popular Music and Its Business: The First Four Hundred Years, by Russell Sanjek. New York: Oxford University Press. 3 vols., 1988. LC 87-18605, ISBN 0-19-504028-7. An abridged and updated version was published in 1991 under the title *The American Popular Music Business in the 20th Century,* by Russell Sanjek and David Sanjek. ISBN 0-19-505828-3.

The set is actually a combination of British and American history of popular music in that the first volume covers popular music from the earliest of British history to 1790. The second volume takes us from 1790 to 1909, and the third volume covers 1900 to 1984. The author does pay substantial attention to music publishing, the recording industry, and other areas of music as well as to the songs themselves.

American Popular Songs from the Revolutionary War to the Present, by David Ewen. New York: Random House. 507 p., 1966. LC 66-12843.
The book lists over 3,600 popular songs from the late 1700s to the early 1960s. The arrangement is alphabetical by title, with each entry giving the writer, date of publication, and any public productions in which the song appeared.

American Premium Record Guide, 1915-1965: 78's, 45's and LP's Identification and Values, by L.R. Docks. Florence, AL: Books Americana. 3d ed., 378 p., 1986. LC 86-168494.

American Songwriters, by David Ewen. Bronx, NY: H.W. Wilson, 489 p., 1987. LC 86-24654, ISBN 0-8242-0744-0.
Includes biographical and career information for 144 American lyricists and composers of popular music in the fields of rock, country, jazz, gospel, Broadway, and other forms. Some of the information was compiled from other published sources, not original sources, and occasional mistakes have been carried over to this work.

Annual Review of Jazz Studies. Annual, 1982- . New Brunswick, NJ: (Institute of Jazz Studies) Transaction Periodicals Consortium, Rutgers University. LC 82-644466, ISSN 0731-0641. Indexed in: Historical Abstracts, American History & Life, MI, RILM, Jazz Index. This title supersedes the *Journal of Jazz Studies* (published 1973-1981) and incorporates another title, *Studies in Jazz Discography.*

ASCAP Biographical Dictionary, by the American Society of Composers, Authors, and Publishers (ASCAP). Irregular, Fourth edition was published in 1980. Compiled for ASCAP by Jaques Cattell Press/R.R. Bowker Company. New York, 1980. 589pp. ISBN 0-8352-1283-1, LC 80-65351.
The volume has over 8,000 entries for ASCAP member writers. Entries include biographical data and career highlights.

Audiocassette Finder: A Subject Guide to Literature Recorded on Audiocassettes. 1st ed. Albuquerque, NM: National Information Center for Educational Media (NICEM)/Access Innovations. 808 p., 1986. ISBN 0-89320-106-5. Replaces: *NICEM Index to Educational Audiotapes.*
 A comprehensive listing of books, plays, and other literary works available on audio tape. The listings include old radio programs, soundtracks, spoken-word readings of books, and poetry.

Baker's Biographical Dictionary of Musicians, by Theodore Baker. 7th ed.; revised by Nicolas Slonimsky. New York: Schirmer Books/Macmillan, 1984. 2,577p. LC 84-5595, ISBN 0-02-870270-0.
 This latest edition extends coverage to the 1980s and includes both popular and classical artists (vocal as well as instrumental). International in scope, this edition contains over 13,000 profiles of artists, both living and dead. Popular music singers and musicians are well represented. Some bibliographies and/or discographies accompany selected profiles.

Bibliographic Guide to Music, by the New York Public Library, Music Division. Annual, 1975-   . Boston: G.K. Hall. LC 76-643534, ISSN 0360-2753. Previous title: *Music Book Guide.*
 In addition to being an independent serial title, this annual also serves as the *Supplement* to the New York City *Dictionary Catalog of the Music Collection.* It includes all music and related materials cataloged by the library during the previous year. In addition, the MARC tapes relating to music from the Library of Congress are added, making for a comprehensive yearly overview of published music and the literature about music.

Bibliography of Black Music, by Dominique-Rene De Lerma. Westport, CT: Greenwood. 4 vols., 1981-1984. LC 80-24681. Vol. 1: *Reference Materials;* Vol. 2: *Afro-American Idioms;* Vol. 3: *Geographical Studies;* Vol. 4: *Theory, Education, and Related Studies.* Issued as *The Greenwood Encyclopedia of Black Music* (ISSN 0272-0264).

Bibliography of Discographies, by Michael Gray. 3 vols. New York: R.R. Bowker, 1983. LC 772261, ISBN 0-8352-1023-5. Vol.

1: *Classical Music;* Vol. 2: *Jazz* by Daniel Allen; Vol. 3: *Popular Music* by Michael Gray (205 p., 1983, LC 82-20776, ISBN: 0-8352-1683-7).

Each book lists, by performer and broad topics, detailed discographies in print from world-wide sources. Covers all fields of popular music.

A Bibliography of Jazz, by Alan P. Merriam. Philadelphia: American Folklore Society. 145 p., 1954. (The Society's Bibliographical Series, volume 4) Reprinted by DaCapa (New York) in 1970. LC 75-12782; ISBN 0-306-70036-0.

Lists over 3,000 jazz titles; arranged by author.

Billboard's Country Music Sourcebook and Directory. Annual, 1961-   . New York: Billboard Publications, 1515 Broadway, New York, NY 10036. Phone: (212) 764-7300. LC 88-660166, ISSN 1042-2544. Previous title: *Billboard Country Music Sourcebook.*

Directory of artists, agents, managers, promoters, names, and addresses of facilities which book country music acts, both domestic and foreign country music organizations. Also, music publishers, a complete list of country format radio stations, radio and television program producers and syndicators, record companies, and venue owners. Lists top awards of the year, the top single records, and other industry events of the year.

Billboard's International Buyer's Guide: The Music & Video Business-to-Business Directory. Annual, 1959-   . New York: Billboard Publications. LC 85-643923. Title varies. Previous title: *International Buyers Guide of the Music-Record Industry.*

Recent issues of the *Guide* have expanded to include the video industry. Sections of each annual provide directory information for music and video companies, retail suppliers, industry services, agents and attorneys, associations and professional organizations, licensing organizations, public relations and promotion firms, music publishers, record companies, video production companies, manufacturing plants for audio and video products, and the manufacturers and distributors of materials and supplies used in the recording and video industries. Most of the book is devoted to American listings, but an International section, arranged by country, lists similar information on a more limited scale. As might be expected, Canada, Great Britain, and some of the European countries have extensive listings.

Billboard's International Manufacturing & Packaging Directory; for the record, CD, and audio/video tape industries. Annual, 1973- . Billboard Publications, 1515 Broadway, New York, NY 10036. Phone: (212) 764-7300. LC 89-656186, ISSN 1045-1641. The title has varied frequently: *International Directory of Manufacturing and Packaging, Billboard's Audio-Video-Tape Sourcebook* and *Billboard's International Tape Directory.*

    This is an industry directory of products, services, and manufactures for professionals in the audio and video industries. Sections in the directory include "Blank Tape Product Charts", a list of audio and video tape manufactures, "Professional Audio/Video/ Tape Equipment Manufactures", "Professional Services & Supplies", "Video Music Producers/Production Facilities." Major international firms are listed separately.

Billboard's International Recording Equipment & Studio Directory. Annual, 1970- . New York, Billboard Publications. LC 86-640878, ISSN 0732-0124. Previous titles: *Billboard International Directory of Recording Studios* and *International Studio & Equipment Directory.*

    A directory of professional services, recording equipment, recording studios, and other industry needs.

Billboard's International Talent and Touring Directory; the music industry's worldwide reference source: talent, talent management, booking agencies, promoters, venue facilities, and venue services and products. Annual, 1978- . New York: Billboard Publications. LC 86-10535, ISSN 0732-0124. Previous title: *Billboard's International Talent Directory.*

Billboard's Music & Video Yearbook. Annual, 1983- . Compiled by Joel Whitburn. Available from Record Research Inc., P.O. Box 200, Menomonee Falls, WI 53051. LC 87-643337, ISSN 0006-2510. Previous titles for the years 1983-1986: *Billboard's Music Yearbook* and *Joel Whitburn's Music Yearbook* (1983-1986, LC 86-641352).

Information for albums and singles which charted in *Billboard* for the year for pop, rock, black, adult contemporary, country, and compact disks. The title was changed in 1987 to reflect the inclusion of the video charts. For other *Billboard* data compiled and marketed by Joel Whitburn, see below under WHITBURN, JOEL, pages 263-264.

The Blues: A Bibliographic Guide, by Mary L. Hart and others. New York: Garland. 500 p., 1989. LC 89-34943, ISBN 0-8240-8506-X.

The literature on the blues, arranged by broad subject category. The volume covers Europe as well as the United States from early blues history through 1985. Citations are compiled from books, journals, newspapers, and other sources. Indexing is by name of performer, songwriter, titles of works, and subjects.

Blues Who's Who: A Biographical Dictionary of Blues Singers, by Sheldon Harris. New Rochelle, NY: Arlington House, 1979. Reprinted by Da Capo (New York) in 1981. 775 p., 1981. LC 81-7873, ISBN 0-306-80155-8.

Alphabetical by the actual personal name of the singer or musician, with cross-references from stage names or nicknames. Each profile provides some biographical information, an overview of the professional career, and lists important appearances and recordings. Length of entries vary from a few lines to several pages. Lesser known local and regional personalities are included as well as international stars.

The Book of World-Famous Music: Classical, Popular and Folk, by James M. Fuld. 3d ed., rev. and enl. New York: Dover. 714 p., 1985. LC 84-21232, ISBN 0-486-24857-7.

The book traces approximately 1,300 melodies back to their original sources. Original publication dates are provided when possible, variations are cross-referenced, and first lines are given for songs. Some singers are identified.

British Music Yearbook. Annual, 1972/73-   . 11th ed. (1985), edited by Marianne Barton. New York: Schirmer Books/Macmillan, 1986. 647 p. LC 75-649724, ISSN 0306-5928. Previously published by St. Martin's Press. Continues *The Music Yearbook.*

Includes information about all types of music in Great Britain, from opera to stage and television. Part 1 of the volume is surveys and statistics; Part 2 contains directory information for offices and societies; Part 3 is a directory of professional services; Part 4 is a directory of performers; Part 5 lists festivals and competitions; Part 6 is a directory of trade information (record companies, music and book publishers, periodicals, etc.); Part 7 lists libraries, museums, and educational facilities; and Part 8 lists music in places of worship.

The Cash Box Album Charts, 1955-1974. Compiled by Frank Hoffmann & George Albert. Metuchen, NJ: Scarecrow. 512 p., 1988. LC 87-12716, ISBN 0-8108-2005-6.

The Cash Box Album Charts, 1975-1985. Compiled by Frank Hoffmann & George Albert. Metuchen, NJ: Scarecrow. 546 p., 1987. LC 86-31353, ISBN 0-8108-1939-2.

The Cash Box Black Contemporary Album Charts, 1975-1987. Compiled by Frank Hoffmann & George Albert. Metuchen, NJ: Scarecrow. 240 p., 1989. LC 88-35663, ISBN 0-8108-2212-1.

The Cash Box Black Contemporary Singles Charts, 1960-1984. Compiled by Frank Hoffmann & George Albert. Metuchen, NJ: Scarecrow. 704 p., 1986. LC 85-22078, ISBN 0-8108-1853-1.

Arranged alphabetically by name of performer, with song titles listed alphabetically after each name (with date it entered the charts, weekly position, weeks on chart, and record label/record number). Another section of the book lists the songs in alphabetical order and refers to the recording artists.

The Cash Box Country Singles Charts, 1958-1982. Compiled by George Albert and Frank Hoffmann. Metuchen, NJ: Scarecrow Press. 596 p., 1984. LC 84-1266; ISBN 0-8108-1685-7.

Titles of singles that made the charts are listed two ways: (1) under the name of the artist, and (2) by title. The date each title first appeared on the charts is given, along with its weekly position during the period it was on the chart.

The Cash Box Singles Charts, 1950-1981. Compiled by Frank Hoffmann, with the assistance of Lee Ann Hoffman. Metuchen, NJ: Scarecrow. 860 p., 1983. LC 82-19126, ISBN 0-8108-1595-8.

A Catalog of Phonorecordings of Music and Oral Data held by the Archives of Traditional Music, by Indiana University, Archives of Traditional Music. Boston, MA: G.K. Hall. 541 p., 1975. LC 75-28073, ISBN 0816111200.

A photoreproduction of the card catalog of the collection, one of the largest in the world. Voice and musical recordings from around the world, with subjects for music type, geographical locations and cultural areas, performers, recording companies, and many other subjects.

The Catalogue of Printed Music in the British Library to 1980, by the British Library. Department of Printed Books. Edited by Laureen Baillie and Robert Malchin. New York: Saur. 62 vols., 1981/86. LC 81-151651, ISBN 0-86291-300-4. Updated by *British Catalogue of Music 1957-1985* (10 vols., 1988/89, ISBN: 0-86291-395-0).

The original set compiled the entries from a variety of sources, starting from 1503.

Cavalcade of Acts & Attractions. Annual, 1973- , by Amusement Business, P.O. Box 24970, Nashville, TN 37202. Phone: (615) 748-8120. LC 75-648609. Previous title: *Cavalcade and Directory of Acts and Attractions* (ISSN 0090-2993).

An industry directory to talent in all live performing fields as well as to agents, managers, promoters, and touring shows. It also lists the major award winners each year for five music organizations: The National Academy of Recording Arts & Sciences (the Grammy); The Country Music Association; The Academy of Country Music; the Gospel Music Association (the Dove Award); and MTV Music Video. In the section on "Musical & Theatrical Entertainment" the following categories are covered: bluegrass; classical; country; Dixieland; easy listening/MOR (middle-of-the-road); ethnic; folk; gospel; jazz; bands; symphonies; nostalgia shows; rhythm and blues; and rock. Following the name of each entertainer, information is given for the performer's record company, BA (Booking

Agent), PM (Personal Manager), and the number of band
members and equipment provided by the performer.

The "Theatrical entertainment" section provides similar
booking information for dance groups of all types, comedians,
TV/movie personalities, and theatrical productions (mime,
musicals, plays, and variety shows). The "Outdoor attractions &
organized touring shows" lists carnivals and circuses. Another
section lists individual circus performers and other specialty acts
"Circus, Variety, & Specialty Acts." Here you will find air
shows, animal acts, auto racing, clowns, costumed characters,
fireworks, hot air balloon pilots, hypnotists/mentalists, ice
shows, laser and light shows, magicians, stunt shows, puppets,
rodeo companies, sports shows, ventriloquists, water shows, and
wild west shows. Lastly, the people who represent and promote
the acts are listed: promoters, producers, booking agents, and
personal managers.

CD Review Digest Annual. Volume 1: 1983-1987. Voorheesville,
NY: Peri Press. 1988. Volume 1 is published in 2 parts: Part 1:
Classical Recordings; Part 2: *Jazz, Popular, Soundtrack, Cast and
Video Recordings; Indexes.* ISSN 0893-5173, ISBN 0-9617844-0-7.
Volume 2 is titled *The Guide to Reviews of All Music on Compact
Discs* (491 p., 1989. ISBN 0-9617844).

Volume 1 is a compilation of reviews, arranged alphabetically by
record title, from 40 music periodicals representing all music
genres from 1983 to 1987; Volume 2 is a guide to reviews for
1988.

Checklist of American Music Periodicals, 1850-1900, by William
Jessel Weichlein. Detroit: Information Coordinators. Second
printing, 165 p., 1970, 1979. LC 74-15083, ISBN 0911772383.
(Detroit Studies in Music Bibliography, No. 16)

A listing of periodicals, with brief bibliographic information for
each one (starting dates, frequency, publisher, and title
changes). Extremely useful for accurate documentation regarding historical titles.

Chicorel Index to the Spoken Arts on Discs, Tapes, and Cassettes.
Edited by Marietta Chicorel. New York: Chicorel Library Publish-

ing. 3 vols., 1973, 1974. Chicorel Index Series, volume 7, 7A and 7B. LC 73-158310, ISBN 0-87729-003-9.

A listing of over 23,000 spoken word recordings, both current and out-of-print titles. Arranged in sections by title, author of the work, performer/reader, and subject.

Comedy on Record: The Complete Critical Discography, by Ronald Lande Smith. 728 p., 1988. LC 87-35969, ISBN 0-8240-8461-6.

A complete discography of American comedy albums, with a supplemental listing of some imports. Selected albums are annotated for their comedy routines. A biographical section briefly profiles hundreds of comedians from all areas of show business.

The Complete Encyclopedia of Popular Music and Jazz, 1900-1950, by Roger D. Kinkle. 4 vols., Westport, CT: Arlington House, 1974. LC 74-7109, ISBN 0-87000-229-5. Volume 1: music by year, 1900-1950; volumes 2 and 3: biographies; volume 4: award listings, charts of release dates, record collecting, numerical listings of principal record labels (1920s-1940s), and various indexes.

The Complete Entertainment Discography, from 1897 to 1942, by Brian Rust and Allen G. Debus. 2d ed., 794 p., 1989. New York: Da Capa. LC 87-33155, ISBN 0-306-7620-2. The first edition was published in 1973 under the title: *The Complete Entertainment Discography from the Mid-1890's to 1942.*

The book includes brief biographies and recording discographies of over 500 entertainers from all fields. A good place to look for recordings of early actors, radio and film stars, and stage performers who are not usually thought of as recording artists.

A Comprehensive Bibliography of Music For Film and Television, by Steven D. Wescott. Detroit, MI: Information Coordinators. 432 p., 1985. LC 85-27184, ISBN 0-89990-027-5.

International in scope, and covering over 100 years of films, the book has over 6,000 entries of music used in films and television series. Although the entries are brief, this is still the most complete work published to date. Although other books on film music exist, this work has some hard-to-find information on television music.

The Concise Baker's Biographical Dictionary of Musicians, by Nicolas Slonimsky. 8th ed., New York: Schirmer/Macmillan, 1988. 1,407 p. LC 87-32328; ISBN 0-02-872411-9.
First published in 1900, this dictionary offers brief entries for professionals in all areas of the music world. Past editions include people not listed here, so previous editions are worth retaining.

Contemporary Musicians. 1989- . Annual, with quarterly issues. Detroit: Gale. LC 89-7123, ISBN 0-8103-2211-0.
This is a biographical series which covers current performers and writers in the musical fields, with an emphasis on the many areas of popular music (pop, rock, country, folk, jazz, blues, gospel, and New Age). Each issue selects approximately 100 musicians and provides biographical information, critical essays about their work, extensive discographies, and an address where the artist may be contacted.

Country: The Music and The Musicians, by The Country Music Foundation. New York: Abbeville Press. 595 p., illus., 1988. ISBN 0-89659-868-3.
An exhaustive history of country music, including photographs, bibliographies, and discographies.

Detroit Studies in Music Bibliography. Monographic series, 1961- . Warren, MI: Harmonie Park Press. ISSN 0070-3885.
Each book is an individually numbered monograph with its own author and title. All genres of music are covered in the bibliographies, which vary in length from a few pages to several hundred.

Dictionary Catalog of the Music Collection, by New York Public Library, Research Libraries. Boston: G.K. Hall. 2d ed. 45 vols., 1982. LC 82-218268, ISBN 0-8161-0374-7. The first edition was published in 1964. Supplements update the set under the title *Bibliographic Guide To Music* (Annual, 1975- .)

This is a reproduction of the New York City Public Library catalog with updates which identify what's in its Music Collection through 1971. It's an author, title, subject book catalog that includes sheet music, recordings, programs, and other special elements of music.

Dictionary of American Pop/Rock, by Arnold Shaw. New York: Schirmer Books/Macmillan, 440 p., 1982. LC 82-50382, ISBN 0-02-872350-3.

The content of the book is broader than its title suggests and includes information on country, jazz, gospel, films, musical theater, and other aspects of modern music. Not a biographical dictionary, but rather a style and semantic dictionary.

The Directory of American 45 R.P.M. Records, by Ken Clee. Philadelphia, PA: Stak-O-Wax. 3 vols., 1981.

Discographies in two sections: artists section and record label section. The artists section lists discographies for over 400 artists who have recorded on more than one label. The record label section lists recording releases by series number. If an artist recorded on only one label, then the artist will be found only in the record label section.

Directory of Music Research Libraries; including contributors to the International Inventory of Musical Sources (RISM), by Rita Benton. 5 vols. 1967-1985. Second revised edition of some volumes, 1983. Currently published by Kassel in New York. The original 3 volumes were published by the University of Iowa (Iowa City, IA). LC 83-70846 (v.5). Part 1: United States and Canada; Part 2: 13 European countries; Part 3: Spain, France, Italy, and Portugal; Part 4: Australia, Israel, Japan, and New Zealand; Part 5: Czechoslovakia, Hungary, Poland, and Yugoslavia.

A directory of the major research libraries of the world. Great Britain is covered in part 2. Each entry includes location, brief history, and some guidance regarding the contents of the collection.

Directory of Spoken-Word Audio Cassettes. Biennial, 1972- . New York: J Norton Publishers. LC 83-227754, ISBN 0884321185. Previous title: *Audio-cassette Directory.*

A listing of audio cassettes that are available for purchase. Arranged by broad subject classification. Each title is briefly annotated and the recording company and cassette number is noted. A list of companies and suppliers accompanies each volume.

The Encyclopedia of Folk, Country, & Western, Music, by Irwin Stambler and Grelum Landon. 2d ed. New York: St. Martin's Press. 902 p., illus., 1984. LC 82-5702, ISBN 0-312-24818-0.
Covers the music and performers from the early years up to about 1980. Biographical information was compiled either directly from the performer or from other literature (mostly magazine articles). Articles vary in length and may include awards and discographies.

(1) *The Encyclopedia of Jazz,* by Leonard Feather. New York: Quartet Books. Completely revised and enlarged edition, 527 p., 1978. LC 79-305210, ISBN 0-7043-2173-4. First published in 1960 by Horizon; (2) *The Encyclopedia of Jazz in the Sixties,* by Leonard Feather. New York: Da Capo. Reprint, 312 p., 1986. LC 85-31125. Original edition published in 1966 by Horizon; and (3) *The Encyclopedia of Jazz in the Seventies,* by Leonard Feather and Ira Gitler. New York: Horizon. 393 p., 1976. LC 76-21196, ISBN 0-8180-1215-3. Reprinted by Da Capo in 1987.
This series of three biographical compilations by Leonard Feather provides histories of thousands of jazz musicians up to the mid-1970s. Extensive use of photos and discographies enhance the works. The 1970s volume includes a listing of jazz films.

Encyclopedia of Music In Canada. Edited by Helmut Kallmann, Gilles Potvin, and Kenneth Winters. Toronto: University of Toronto Press. 1,076 p., illus., 1981. cn 81-094855-9, ISBN 0-8020-5509-5.
A comprehensive work about Canadian music which covers every facet and genre. Long articles provide historical information about a wide variety of subjects and identify Canadian composers, performers, and other music industry notables. Bibliographies are provided, as are some discographies. Biographies often include a photo of the subject.

Encyclopedia of Pop, Rock, & Soul, by Irwin Stambler. Rev. ed. New York: St. Martin's. 864 p., illus., 1989. LC 88-29860, ISBN 0-312-02573-4.

This edition expands, rather replaces, the first edition since previous entries have been dropped to make room for new material. Major emphasis is on rock music, with the other musical types receiving less attention.

Festivals [year]. An annual supplement issued by the periodical, *Musical America.*

International in scope and issued each spring. It highlights the music festivals that are scheduled worldwide for the current year. Feature articles highlight special festivals from Santa Fe to Leningrad, although the emphasis is on U.S. venues. One section lists festivals in the United States and Canada (location, date, how to get tickets) while another section lists the same information for international festivals from approximately 50 countries.

Film Music: From Violins to Video, by James L. Limbacher. Metuchen, NJ: Scarecrow. 835 p., 1974. LC 73-16153, ISBN 0-8108-0651-7. See also: Limbacher's *Keeping Score* for a continuation of this work.

Information is provided for film music from the early days up through 1972. The book is divided into several sections: an overview of film music; an alphabetical list of film titles and dates of release; a chronological list of films/composers; an alphabetical list of composers/films; and an alphabetical list (by film title) of recordings of film music.

Film, Television, and Stage Music on Phonograph Records: A Discography, by Steve Harris. Jefferson, NC: McFarland. 445 p., 1988. LC 87-42509, ISBN 0-89950-251-2.

The book includes both American and British productions. In addition to primary recordings from the production itself, the book has also compiled related recordings (music inspired by the original, cover recordings, tributes, etc.).

Find That Tune: An Index to Rock, Folk-rock, Disco & Soul in Collections. Edited by William Gargan and Sue Sharma. New York: Neal-Schuman, 1984. Volume 1, 303p. LC 82-22346, ISBN

0-918212-70-7; Volume 2, (1989, 387 p., ISBN: 1-55570-019-5) updated the collections through 1985.

Volume 1 indexes more than 4,000 songs in 203 published sheet music collections, with most of the top hits from 1950 to 1981 included. Volume 2 offers some repetition, but brings the information up to 1985 and adds additional titles and collections. The information in both volumes is indexed by collection title, first line, composer-lyricist, and performer. Names and addresses of some sheet music publishers are given.

Folk Music in America: A Reference Guide, by Terry E. Miller. New York: Garland. 424 p., 1986. (Reference Library of the Humanities, Vol. 496). LC 84-48014, ISBN 0-8240-8935-9.

Arrangement is by subject, with the accompanying annotated bibliographies compiled from books, periodicals, dissertations, and other sources. A wide variety of national and regional folk and ethnic music is included as are artists, musical instruments, songs, and many other subjects.

Folklife Sourcebook: A Directory of Folklife Resources in the United States and Canada. Prepared by Peter T. Bartis and Barbara C. Fertig. Washington, DC: Library of Congress, American Folklife Center. 152 p., 1986. LC 85-600334, ISBN 0-8444-0521-3.

The directory includes archives, associations, societies, educational institutions with folklife programs, libraries and archives, and recording companies. Emphasis is on life and music of early American peoples.

Folksingers and Folksongs in America: a Handbook of Biography, Bibliography, and Discography, by Ray McKinley Lawless. New revised edition with special supplement. New York: Duell. 750 p., 1965. Reprinted by Greenwood Press (Westport, CT) in 1981. LC 81-6398, ISBN 0313231044.

Includes biographies of performers, a listing of folk songs, discographies, and information on folk music, the instruments, organizations, festivals, and other related topics.

Gospel Music Official Directory. Annual, 1972-   . Nashville, TN: Gospel Music Association. LC 83-644851, ISSN 0739-604X. Previous title: *Gospel Music Directory and Yearbook.*

Membership directory of the Gospel Music Association. Also includes people, artists, agents, companies, and products/services involved in gospel music.

The Great Song Thesaurus, by Roger Lax and Frederick Smith. 2d ed. Oxford University Press. 774 p., 1989. LC 88-31267, ISBN 0-19-505408-3.

The volume lists over 11,000 popular songs from the Elizabethan period through 1986, approximately 400 years of music. Information for each song title includes songwriting credits, dates of popularity, and some historical background on individual titles. Where known, it also includes chart information, awards, and some film/television use. The book does not, however, include date of publication and/or copyright information.

Green Book, compiled by Jeff Green. 3d ed. Smyrna, TN: Professional Desk Reference. 326 p., 1989. LC 82-220575, ISBN 0-939735-03-2.

This book lists over 15,000 song titles by subject. The book is arranged by approximately 500 subjects and lists song titles about that subject, along with recordings made of each song.

Greenwood Encyclopedia of Black Music. Irregular, 1981- . Westport, CT: Greenwood. 4 vols., 1981/84. LC 80-24681, ISSN 0272-0264. Also issued as part of the set : *Biographical Dictionary of Afro-American and African Musicians* by Eileen Southern (478 p., 1982, LC 81-2586).

Guide to Musical America, by Lynne Gusikoff. New York: Facts on File. 350 p., 1984. LC 82-7373, ISBN 0-87196-701-4.

The book is broken into geographical areas of the United States and, within each section, provides a broad overview of the music of the region. The book discusses the historical development of the music and musical styles of the different regions and notes the overlaps that have developed throughout the years. The book includes rock, country, western and western swing, jazz, and other genres; many are included in each section.

A History and Encyclopedia of Country, Western, and Gospel Music, by Linnell Gentry. Nashville: Clairmont Corporation. 2d

ed. 598 p., 1969. LC 70-7208. The first edition was published by
McQuiddy (Nashville) (380 p., 1961) and reprinted in 1972 by
Scholarly Press. LC 71-166231, ISBN 0-403-01358-5.

The volume includes an eclectic mix of information. In addition
to a biographical section of performers, it lists a comprehensive
collection of early country music radio programs and reproduces
a series of early articles about country music from popular
American magazines. Some information is outdated but the
historical information is useful.

History of Popular Music. Freeport, NY: Marshall Cavendish
Corporation. [20 vols.], 1989. Volumes 1-10 have been published
to date covering the 1950s and 1960s. Volumes 11-20 will cover the
1970s and 1980s. LC 88-21076, ISBN (set): 1-85435-015-3.

A chronological history of popular music from the 1950s to date,
with an emphasis on rock music. Heavily illustrated with many
photos in color. Articles cover major performers, musical
trends, and events on a yearly basis. Music other than rock is
treated lightly and sometimes without as much expertise as one
would like. Still, for the most part, it's a knowledgeable work
and the pictures alone are worth the price. It's a huge work
worth investigating.

An Index of Selected Folk Recordings, by Beverly B. Boggs and
Daniel Patterson. Chapel Hill, NC: Curriculum in Folklore,
University of North Carolina. 55 microfiche (10,864 p.) and hard
copy manual, 1984.

An index of approximately 500 LPs of American and British
traditional music, containing approximately 8,350 songs. Indexing is by song title, album, and performer. Relevant recording
information is given for each entry. There are also key line and
subject indexes.

Index to Record Reviews. Compiled and edited by Kurtz Myers.
Based on material originally published in *Notes,* the quarterly
journal of the Music Library Association between 1949 and 1977.
Boston: G.K. Hall. 5 vols., 1978. LC 79-101459, ISBN 0-8161-
0087-X. The first supplement to this set is *Index to Record Reviews,
1978-1983* (873 p., 1985. LC 86-135431, ISBN 0-8161-0435-2). The

second supplement is *Index to Record Reviews, 1984-1987* (560 p., 1989, ISBN 0-8161-0482-4).

Based on material originally published in *Notes,* the quarterly journal of the Music Library Association. Although it is one of the few sources available for reviews, it does not pretend to be a comprehensive index since it indexes reviews from only 25 periodicals and leans heavily toward classical music.

Index to Top-hit Tunes, 1900-1950, by John H. Chipman. Boston, MA: B. Humphries. 249 p., 1962. LC 61-11711.

A listing of over 3,000 American songs (mostly recordings) which have sold at least 100,000 copies of sheet music or records. Separate listings of the songs in alphabetical and chronological order. Each entry includes the name of the writer, date of publication, and if the song was included in a film or stage musical.

Information On Music: A Handbook of Reference Sources in European Languages, by Guy A. Marco. Littleton, Co: Libraries Unlimited. 3 vols., 1975/1984. LC (set) 74-32132, ISBN 0-87287-096-0. Volume 1: *Basic and Universal Sources* (Pt.1: Basic and universal sources; Pt.2: Sources for individual countries and regions; Pt.3: Sources for specific topics; Pt.4-5: Sources for individual musicians; Pt.6: Guide to musical editions). Volume 2: *The Americas.* Volume 3: *Europe* (1984).

The International Cyclopedia of Music and Musicians. 11th ed. Edited by Oscar Thompson. New York: Dodd, Mead. 2609 p., 1985. LC 84-13736, ISBN 0-396-08412-5.

This work covers the whole of the music field, from instruments to composers. Brief articles covering various popular music subjects are included, as are some popular personalities.

International Directory of Theatre, Dance, & Folklore Festivals, by Jennifer Merin and Elizabeth Burdick. Westport, CT: Greenwood. 480 p., 1979. LC 79-9908, ISBN 0-313-20993-6.

Arrangement is by country and city, followed by the name of the event. Each festival is annotated with the name, address, and phone of a contact, the date it is usually held, and a description of the activities that make up the event.

The International Encyclopedia of Hard Rock and Heavy Metal, by
Tony Jasper. New York: Facts on File. 400 p., illus., 1983, 1985.
LC 84-10236, ISBN 0-8160-1100-1. Worldwide coverage. Includes
discographies.

International Who's Who in Music and Musicians' Directory.
Irregular (biennial), 1935- . Cambridge, England: Melrose Press.
Distributed in the United States by Gale Research (Detroit), 12th
ed., 1,300 p., 1990. ISBN 0-948875-20-8. Continues: *Who's Who in
Music and Musicians' International Directory.* Indexed in: Biographical Dictionaries Master Index.
   An international biographical dictionary of over 12,000 living
   musicians which provides brief entries giving the birth dates,
   personal information, education, professional history, awards,
   and noted works of each person. Geographical appendices
   list musical cultural and business contacts for each area
   (organizations, colleges, music facilities, awards, and other
   information).

Jazz: The Essential Companion, by Ian Carr and others. New
York: Prentice Hall. 562 p., illus, 1988. LC 88-2498, ISBN
0-13-509274-4.
   International in scope with articles about major figures in the
   genre. Jazz terms are defined and major recordings identified. A
   good beginning reference.

Jazz Festivals International Directory. Annual, 1980- . New
York: World Jazz Society. LC 85-645977, ISSN 0882-0368.
Previous title: *World Jazz Calendar of Festivals & Events.*
   A directory of events around the world, dates of the festival
   (when known), contact people and addresses. Some information
   about performers.

The Jazz Handbook, by Barry McRae. Boston: G.K. Hall. 272 p.,
1990. LC 89-77757, ISBN 0-8161-9096-8.
   The book is designed to be a quick introduction to jazz and jazz
   musicians. Arranged by decade, the book covers the major
   musicians, styles, recordings, and industry events of the period.

Jazz Index. Annual, 1977- . Supplements. Frankfurt, Germany: N. Ruecker. LC 79-642447, ISSN 0344-5399. English and German editions.

Jazz Records 1897-1942, by Brian Rust. 5th rev. and enl. ed. See: page 528.

Jazz Reference and Research Materials: A Bibliography, by Eddie S. Meadows. New York: Garland. 300 p., 1981. LC 80-8521, ISBN 0-8240-9463-8.
   The bibliography lists books, articles, dissertations, and other materials from about 1900 to 1978. It includes information on the music, artists, and recordings. Arranged by type of literature; indexed by subject, author, and title.

Keeping Score: Film Music 1972-1979, James L. Limbacher. Metuchen, NJ: Scarecrow. 570 p., 1981. LC 80-26474, ISBN 0-8108-1390-4.
   Updates his previous work, *Film Music.* The book is organized into three main sections: films/composers, composers/films, and a discography of recorded film music.

Kingsbury's Who's Who in Country & Western Music, by Kenn Kingsbury. Edited by Kenn Kingsbury. Culver City, CA: Black Stallion Press. 304 p., 1981. LC 81-180477.
   The book provides over 700 biographical sketches of important people in the country music field, performers, musicians, and business people alike. Additionally, it provides directory information for a number of recording companies, music publishers, booking agencies, and radio stations. By now most of the directory information is outdated (and therefore inaccurate), but the biographical facts that are included still make this a useful reference source.

Laserlog. Biweekly, 1987- . Looseleaf service; basic volume with biweekly updates. San Diego: Trade Services Corporation. See also: *Phonolog Reporter.* No LC or ISSN numbers.
   Lists all CD releases, laserdiscs, and videodiscs currently

available for sale. Provides complete bibliographic and order information for each title.

Laughter on Record: A Comedy Discography, by Warren Debenham. Metuchen, NJ: Scarecrow. 369 p., 1988. LC 87-35938, ISBN 0-8108-2094-3.
A discography of over 4,000 comedy LPs, arranged alphabetically by artist.

Library research guide to music: illustrated search strategy and sources, by John E. Druesdow Jr. Ann Arbor, MI: Pierian Press. 86 p., 1982. LC 81-86634, ISBN 0-87650-139-0.

List-O-Tapes. Weekly, 1964- . Basic volume with weekly replacement sheets. Published by Trade Services Corporation,, 10996 Torreyana Rd., Box 85007, San Diego, CA 92138. Phone: (619) 457-5920. LC 67-33145, ISSN 0024-4309. See Also: *Phonolog Reporter.*
Loose-leaf tape catalog covering all types of musical and audio tape releases, open reel, cartridge and cassette.

The Literature of Jazz: A Critical Guide. Edited by Donald Kennington. Chicago: American Library Association. 2d ed., rev. 236 p., 1980. LC 81-161304, ISBN 0-85365-663-0.
Arranged by type of literature, the publication covers jazz and blues literature, periodicals, and reference resources up through 1979. International in coverage, but includes only English language books.

The Literature of Rock: 1954-1978, by Frank Hoffmann and B. Lee Cooper. Metuchen, NJ: Scarecrow Press. 337 p., 1981. LC 80-23459, ISBN 0-8108-1371-8.
Covers in bibliographic format thousands of books, periodical articles, and other materials published or produced about rock music. The book is divided into specific topics with entries listed under each topic.

The Literature of Rock II, by Frank Hoffmann and B. Lee Cooper. Metuchen, NJ: Scarecrow Press. 2 vols. (1,097 p.), 1986. LC 85-8384, ISBN 0-8108-1821-3.

Covers the period 1979-1983 and adds some new entries from the period covered in the previous volume.

The Marshall Cavendish History of Popular Music. See: *History of Popular Music.*

Media Review Digest; the only complete guide to reviews of non-book media. See: page 129.

Movie Musicals on Record: A Directory of Recordings of Motion Picture Musicals, 1927-1987. Compiled by Richard C. Lynch. Westport, CT: Greenwood Press. 392 p., 1989. LC 89-2137, ISBN 0-313-26540-2.
　　The book lists film musicals along with the sound recordings that have been made of the music (along with the appropriate discographic information for each recording). It is an excellent quick reference work, but its value is lessened by the fact that the author chose not to include dance, opera, or concert films.

Musi*Key: the reference guide of note. Bimonthly. 1505 Kirkwood Dr., Fort Collins, CO 80525. Phone: (303) 484-1062. LC 88-640972, ISSN 0895-1543.
　　Issued in two volumes with four parts: Songs (one volume); and Sheets, Books, and Personality (the second volume). The song sheets list songs alphabetically, with publisher, order number, and musical arrangement. The Songs section lists songs alphabetically that are not available in single sheet music, and gives the title of a song book where it can be found. The Books section lists song books along with their complete contents. The Personality section lists artists and composers and the books that contain their music. Each section contains complete ordering information. A directory of publishers and distributors accompanies each set. All types of music are included, from "Hail to the Redskins" to the latest country or rock song.

Music: A Guide to the Reference Literature, by William S. Brockman. Littleton, CO: Libraries Unlimited. 254 p., 1987. LC 87-26462, ISBN 0-87287-526-1.
　　The reference sources for most broad genres of music are covered. The book is divided into types of sources: general

reference, bibliographical sources, discographies, and supplementary information (associations, societies, and research centers, etc.). It doesn't pretend to cover all sources for all types of music, but is a good place to start if you want a beginning education about what is available.

Music: An Illustrated Encyclopedia, by Neil Ardley. New York: Facts on File. 192p, 1986. LC 86-6279, ISBN 0-8160-1543-0.

Music Article Guide; annotated guide to feature articles in American music periodicals geared exclusively to the special needs of school and college music educators. Quarterly, 1965- . A three year index for 1986-1988 is also available. Philadelphia, PA: Information Services. LC 80-618, ISSN 0027-4240. Available on microform from UMI.
   Selectively indexes approximately 175 American music periodicals by subject and author. Although the emphasis is on material of use to the educational field, the index is still useful for other music researchers and writers. Also, the list of periodicals used by the *Guide* is a handy list of current journals.

Music, Books on Music, and Sound Recordings. Semiannual, 1973- . Washington, DC: The Library of Congress, the National Union Catalog. ISSN 0092-2838. Previous title: *Library of Congress Catalog: Music and Phonorecords* (Annual, 1953-1972).
   This is one section of the *National Union Catalog* series from the Library of Congress which details titles that have been added to the LC collection throughout the year. It identifies all published music, works about music, and sound recordings (in their various forms) that have been received and cataloged. The most valuable source available for checking facts and bibliographic information in any area of music.

Music Business Handbook & Career Guide, by David Baskerville. 4th ed., 1985. Los Angeles: Sherwood. LC 85-50766, ISBN 0-933056-04-4.
   Divided into a number of parts and examines in detail the business of music. It covers music in the marketplace, songwriting and publishing, the copyright process, the record

industry, music in broadcasting and film, and career opportunities in each area. There is also directory information for businesses, agents, and others involved in music industry activities. An appendix provides sample contracts, agreements, and other forms useful in conducting business.

Music In Print Series. 1973- . Philadelphia, PA: Musicdata. Volumes 1-6, ISSN 0146-7883. Annual Supplements (ISSN 0192-4729, 1979-) are cumulative listings. Basic volumes are individually revised periodically.
  Choral, organ, classical, orchestral, and string music in print. Compiled from publishers catalogs and updated through an annual supplement. Covers all musical genres. Both single pieces of music issued as song sheets and collections and/or song books are included.

Music Index; a subject-author guide to over 300 current international periodicals. Monthly, 1949- . Annual cumulations. Warren, MI: Harmonie Park Press. LC 50-13627, ISSN 0027-4348. Available on CD-ROM.
  International coverage of approximately 350 music periodicals. All areas of music are covered, including popular music. Selected articles include reviews, performances, performers, musical trends, formal study, instruments, recordings, theory, and just about everything else you would want to know about music from rock to classical. Regretfully, the time lag is frequently serious, with some citations taking years to make the indexes.

Music Industry Directory. Chicago: Marquis Who's Who. 7th ed. 678 p., 1983. LC 83-645913, ISBN 0-8379-5602-1.
  Previous editions titled *Musician's Guide.* Directory of organizations, associations, industry personnel, schools, libraries, performing companies for opera and music, festivals, publishers and others associated with the music field. Lists people and organizations for all areas of the music industry. Listings include: music associations and societies; start art agencies; citizen's advocacy groups; addresses of American Federation of Musicians union locals throughout the country; music libraries; music periodicals; music editors and critics for newspapers throughout the United States and Canada; opera and symphony companies; college and

music schools and other educational programs for music students; music competitions and festivals; entertainment personnel (lawyers, booking agents, managers); record companies; and music publishers. The publication also lists music awards: country music awards, platinum records, Grammy awards, Academy Awards, and Pulitzer Prizes in music.

Music Librarianship: A Practical Guide, by E. T. Bryant. Metuchen, NJ: Scarecrow. 2d ed., 449 p., 1985. LC 84-27731, ISBN 0-8108-1785-3.

Music Librarianship, by Malcolm Jones. New York: Saur. 130 p., 1979. LC 85-242358, ISBN 0-85157-274-X. (Saur's series: Outlines of modern librarianship: 5).
Contents: music librarianship, reference sources, principles of organizing and running a music library.

Music Library Association. MLA Index and Bibliography Series, Irregular, 1964- . Canton, MA: Music Library Association. LC 79-2539, ISSN 0094-6478. Previous title: *Music Library Association. MLA Index Series.*
This is a series of monographs published as separate titles, each with a series number. The bibliographies are mostly on classical music, but a few cover popular music genres.

Music Library Association. Notes. Quarterly, 1934- . Canton, MA: Music Library Association. LC 43-45299, ISSN 0027-4380. Indexed in: MI, Book Review Digest, Humanities Index, RILM, Book Review Index, International Index.
Reviews new literature, publishes a bibliography of record reviews that have appeared in other sources, lists published music songs and scores, and identifies music publisher catalogs. Each year it includes a special section on obituaries, which is often noted separately in bibliographies because of its comprehensiveness and usefulness. In general, it keeps librarians up to date on what's new in the field.

Music Master: the 45 rpm record directory, by Paul Mawhinney. Allison Park, PA: Record-Rama. First edition. 2 vols. (author, title), 1983. ISBN (set) 0-910925-02-X.

Over 200,000 recordings of all genres are listed for the years 1947-1982.

Music Periodical Literature: An Annotated Bibliography of Indexes and Bibliographies, by Joan Meggett. Metuchen, NJ: Scarecrow. 116 p., 1978. LC 77-19120, ISBN 0-8108-1109-X.
A little outdated, but still very useful as a guide to information sources about music.

Music Reference and Research Materials: An Annotated Bibliography, by Vincent Duckles and Michael A. Keller. 4th ed. New York: Schirmer Books. 714 p., 1988. LC 88-18530, ISBN 0-02-870390-1.
Arranged by type of material, with sections for dictionaries and encyclopedias, histories and chronologies, bibliographies and biographies, discographies, yearbooks and directories, and catalogs of collections. There are especially large numbers of bibliographies listed as well as printed catalogs of libraries and special collections. A good place to go to find libraries that might have type of collection useful to your research.

Musical America International Directory of the Performing Arts. Annual, 1968-   . New York: ABC Consumer Magazines, Musical America. LC 88-640608, ISSN 0735-7788. Previous titles: *Musical America Directory of the Performing Arts* and *Musical America. Annual Directory Issue.*
A directory organized geographically by state and then city. For each state or city, it lists performers, performing companies, music schools, festivals and regular events, professional organizations and associations, agents and managers, suppliers, and others dealing with the music business.

Musical Instruments of the World: An Illustrated Encyclopedia. New York: Paddington. 320 p., 1976. LC 76-21722, ISBN 0-8467-0134-0. Reprinted by Facts on File, 1985.
A well-illustrated book of over 4,000 musical instruments. Arrangement is by type of musical instrument, so that related instruments are easy to find and close together. Some groups are further subdivided by time period or geographical area when appropriate. Some biographical information is provided for expert instrument makers.

The Musician's Guide: the directory of the world of music. Chicago: Marquis Who's Who. See: *Music Industry Directory.*

NARM *Recording Industry Index.* See: *Recording Industry Index.*

The New Grove Dictionary of American Music. 4 vols., 2,600 pp. Edited by H. Wiley Hitchcock and Stanley Sadie. New York: Grove's Dictionaries of Music, 1986. LC 86-404, ISBN 0-943818-36-2.
   Covers all areas of American music from early historical times to the present pop culture. Also includes film, musicals, and dance. Long articles on subject areas and biographies of performers as well as songwriters and musicians. Some selected bibliographies and discographies.

The New Grove Dictionary of Jazz. Edited by Barry Kernfeld. New York: Grove's Dictionaries of Music, 1988. 2 vols., 1,400 p., illus. LC 87-25452; ISBN 0-935859-39-X.
   Comprehensive overview of jazz music, including the history, jazz terms, organizations, festivals, biographies (of performers, composers, arrangers), instruments, and geographical locations important to the music. Long discographies are included for performers and special topics, important jazz literature and periodicals are covered, and there is an extensive use of photographs and actual musical examples.

The New Grove Dictionary of Music and Musicians. 6th ed. Edited by Stanley Sadie. 20 vols. New York: Grove's Dictionaries of Music. 1980. LC 79-26207, ISBN 0-333-23111-2.
   Supersedes rather than updates the previous *Grove,* and includes a number of changes. The set is more international in scope, includes more information about music technology and computers, and provides coverage of all aspects of music from classical to jazz. Long historical articles from the music of North American Indians to modern music industry problems. Popular music researchers will find long historical articles useful for background understanding of modern musical forms, well-researched biographies, articles about the different areas of popular music, performers and performing practices, and some bibliographies.

The New Grove Dictionary of Musical Instruments. 3 vols. Edited by Stanley Sadie. New York: Grove's Dictionaries of Music, 1984. Illus., 2,808p. LC 84-9062, ISBN 0-943818-05-2.

Covers all geographical areas and types of musical instruments and the artists that make the music. Heavily illustrated.

The New Harvard Dictionary of Music. Edited by Don Michael Randel. Cambridge, MA: Harvard University Press. 942 p., 1986. LC 86-4780, ISBN 0-674-61525-5. This is a revised edition of *Harvard Dictionary of Music* (2d ed., 1969).

This new edition contains over 6,000 entries. Coverage of contemporary music has been expanded.

The New Oxford Companion to Music. Edited by Denis Arnold. New York: Oxford University Press. 2 vols. (2,017 p.), 1983. LC 83-233314, ISBN 0-19-311316-3. Supersedes the *Oxford Companion To Music* by Percy Scholes.

Although popular music is only lightly covered, the set is valuable for its concise coverage of musical history, instruments, and other background facts and commentary.

New Release Reporter: weekly index to all new pop recordings. Weekly, 1959-1984. Alternate title: *One-Spot New Release Reporter.* Quarterly cumulation "Permanent file edition." Trade Service Publications/One-Spot Publishing Division, 1000 West Central Road, Mt. Prospect, IL 60056. LC 84-644807.

The publication is an index to all pop recordings reported released in the previous 13 weeks. Separate pages list new releases for the current week. Indexed by song title and artist.

Includes singles, EPs, and albums. A listing of new recordings out the week of publication, a title section for 12 weeks, and an artist section for the previous 12 weeks. Excellent source of historical information to verify release dates.

The New Trouser Press Record Guide. Edited by Ira A. Robbins. New York: Collier/Macmillan. 3d ed., 657 p., 1989. LC 88-25821, ISBN 0020363702.

A collection of over 3,000 reviews (largely albums) from *Trouser Press,* with an emphasis on "New Wave" music or other music that can be considered closely related in style and content. The book offers comprehensive coverage of a genre otherwise difficult to document.

On Cassette: a comprehensive bibliography of spoken word audiocassettes. Annual, 1985-   . New York: R.R. Bowker. LC 89-646030, ISSN 0000-1260. Previous editions were published irregularly under the title: *On Cassette,* followed by *Words On Cassette.* The series returned to the original title in 1989.
A listing of over 30,000 spoken-word recordings (and other formats) currently available from over 600 producers. Arranged in sections by title, author, subject, and reader/performer. Directory of producers/distributors. Includes instructional, educational, and professional cassettes as well as popular titles and special readings of books.

Periodical Literature on American Music, 1620-1920: a classified bibliography with annotations, by Thomas E. Warner. Warren, MI: Harmonie Press. np, 1988. LC 88-21161, ISBN 0-89990-034-8. Bibliographies in American Music, no. 11.

Phonolog Reporter. Weekly, 1948-   . Looseleaf service; basic volume with weekly updates. San Diego: Trade Services Corporation. See also: *Laserlog* and *List-O-Tapes.*
This looseleaf service can be found in every record shop and library that has a substantial record collection. It lists every recording (45 rpm, album, EP, etc.), disc, audiocassette, and other formats that are currently available for sale. Arranged in sections by title, artist, albums, classical, and several special categories.

Popular Music. Annual, 1985-   . Detroit: Gale. The original set was published in 8 volumes (now available as a 3-volume cumulation); this ongoing title supplements that set. The series continues with volume 9 (1980-1984) through volume 12 (1987) as of 1989.

Popular Music, 1920-1979. A revised cumulation. 3 vols. Edited by Nate Shapiro and Bruce Pollock. Detroit, MI: Gale, 1985. LC 85-6749, ISBN 0-8103-0847-9.
An index to all types of American popular music, from jazz to

country. Arrangement is alphabetical by song title, with each entry giving the title, any alternate titles, country of origin, writer, current publisher, copyright date, and a brief annotation describing the song's history. Title page reads: "An annotated index of over 18,000 American popular songs, cumulation and updating eight volumes of *Popular Music* and including introductory essays, lyricists and composers index, important performances index, awards index, and list of publishers." The new edition is intended to supersede the previous eight volumes. However, because this edition is arranged alphabetically, while the original set was arranged chronologically by year of publication, the older set will still serve a valuable purpose if that perspective is needed. Volume 9, covering 1980-1984, and Volume 10 covering 1985 are still the current sources of information for this title.

Popular Music, by Michael H. Gray. See: *Bibliography of Discographies.*

Popular Music: an annotated guide to recordings, by Dean Tudor. Libraries Unlimited. 647 p., 1983. LC 83-18747, ISBN 0-87287-395-1.
This is a combined revision of several individual books on jazz, black music, and popular music; listings for the new genres of Punk Rock and New Wave have been added. It lists over 6,000 recordings in all subject areas and it provides a useful directory of specialist record stores and mail order services. An artists index is included.

Popular Music: a reference guide, by Roman Iwaschkin. New York: Garland. 658 p., 1986. LC 85-45140, ISBN 0-8240-8680-5.
Covers all areas of popular music, with an emphasis on books about the various genres. Some biographical information and brief coverage on novels and poetry resulting from musical influences. An appendix lists periodicals in the English language.

Popular Music Handbook: A Resource Guide for Teachers, Librarians, and Media Specialists, by B. Lee Cooper. Libraries Unlimited. 415 p., 1984. LC 84-19448, ISBN 0-87287-393-5.

Designed to promote the study of popular music and what it reflects of American life and values, the book is divided into four parts: (1) ideas for teaching popular music in the classroom, (2) reference works on popular music, (3) discographies, and (4) Bibliographies.

Popular Music Since 1955: A Critical Guide to the Literature, by Paul Taylor. New York: Mansell. 533 p., 1985. LC 84-17080. ISBN 07201172775.
An annotated listing of over 1,600 books and 200 periodicals published between 1955 and 1982. All subjects are covered, including bibliographies about personalities.

Popular Record Guide: 78 rpm records, by William J. Haskett. Golden Memories Records, P.O. Box 217, Mooresvile, IN 46158. Phone: (317) 831-5207. 4 vols., 1981. Volumes 1-3: *Vocalists, Big Bands, Personalities, etc.;* Volume 4: *Country & Western.*
Arranged alphabetically by artist, followed by discographic information regarding the 78rpm recordings made by each artist. An excellent source of historical and obscure recording information.

Popular Song Index, by Patricia Havlice. Metuchen, NJ: Scarecrow. 933 p., 1975. LC 75-9896, ISBN 0-8108-0820-X. *First Supplement* (386 p., 1978, 77-25219, ISBN 0-8108-1099-9); *Second Supplement* (530 p., 1984, LC 83-7692, ISBN 0-8108-1642-3). *Third Supplement* (875 p., 1989, LC 89-6414, ISBN 0-8108-2204-4).
Extensive indexing of popular songs in songbooks and anthologies. The main volume and supplements cover song books published 1940-1981. Indexing is by songwriter, song title, first line. Complements Sears' *Song Index* and the deCharms/Breed *Songs in Collections.*

A Preliminary Directory of Sound Recording Collections in the United States and Canada. Compiled by the Association for Recorded Sound Collections (ARSC). New York: New York Public Library. 157 p., 1967. LC 67-31297.
The publication lists about 1,700 collections with brief descriptions of each and the libraries which house them.

The Purchaser's Guide To The Music Industries. Annual, 1897- .
Published by *Music Trades* magazine, 80 West St., P.O. Box 432,
Englewood, NJ 07631. Phone: (201) 871-1965. LC 99-2406.
Previous title: *Piano and Organ Purchaser's Guide.*
A worldwide directory of manufacturers and distributors of
musical products, with emphasis on instruments and publishers of
sheet music and computer music software. However, listings are
also given for musical supplies, finance companies, music industry
associations and organizations, trademarks, and schools. A
separate section for industry statistics for the year and a FAX
directory of industry phone numbers is also presented.

Recordaid; artists' listings and popular albums. Published monthly
from 1940 to 1974. Now out of print. Philadelphia, PA: Recordaid.
The service included bimonthly artists' listings and popular
album section, a quarterly alphabetical title section for single
records, and a listing of the latest recordings by title and artist.
Still a good and comprehensive source of information for
verifying release dates for older 45s and LPs.

Recording Industry Index. Annual, 1977-1979 (v. 1-3). Cherry
Hill, NJ: National Association of Recording Merchandisers
(NARM). LC 81-640965, ISSN 0276-6078.
Short-lived, but very good, index about the recording industry.

The Recording Locator. Annual, 1976- . Saratoga, CA: Resource
Publications. LC 88-646126, ISSN 0899-0123. Previous title:
MusiCatalog.
A directory and song catalog for religious music. Lists all
religious song titles published, the publishers and their ad-
dresses.

Research Guide to Musicology, by James Pruett and Thomas P.
Slavens. Chicago, IL: American Library Association. 175 p., 1985.
LC 84-24379, ISBN 0838903312.

*A Resource Guide to Themes in Contemporary American Song
Lyrics, 1950-1985,* by B. Lee Cooper. Westport, CT: Greenwood.
458 p., 1986. LC 85-21933, ISBN 0-313-24516-9.

An analysis of over 3,000 popular songs divided into 15 areas of popular topics, political events, or personal themes. The author illustrates how popular music has dealt with these issues.

RILM Abstracts of Music Literature. Quarterly, 1967-   . Annual cumulations. New York: International Repertory of Music Literature (International Association of Music Libraries). LC 70-20092, ISSN 0033-6955. Online: Dialog (RILM Abstracts, 1971-   .).
This index covers the field of music literature worldwide and includes many languages. It provides descriptive abstracts for articles in over 300 music journals, book reviews, dissertations, and other publications in the music field. All subjects in the field are covered.

Rolling Stones Rock Almanac: the Chronicle of Rock and Roll. New York: Collier Books/Macmillan. 371 p., 1983. LC 83-16178, ISBN 0020813201.
The book covers the development of rock and roll from 1954 to 1982 and discusses its roots from other music as well as its relationship with society attitudes over the years. Arrangement is chronological, with indexing by performer, song title, and some subjects.

Scholars' Guide To Washington, D.C. For Audio Resources: sound recordings in the arts, humanities, and social, physical, and life sciences, by James R. Heintze. Washington, DC: Smithsonian Institution Press. 395 p., 1985. LC 84-600234; ISBN: 0-87474-516-0.
This listing of audio collections in the Washington, DC area is valuable to those outside of the area because of the detailed coverage given to collections in government agencies and national associations headquartered here. In addition, it lists broadcasting organizations, research centers, publishers, distributors of sound recordings, and radio stations.

Sing Your Heart Out, Country Boy. Compiled by Dorothy Horstman. Nashville: Country Music Foundation Press. 2d ed., 432 p., 1987. LC 88-119410, ISBN 0-915608-10-3. Originally published by E.P. Dutton in 1975 and in paperback by Pocket Books in 1976.

The book prints the lyrics to nearly 400 classic country songs and provides historical background about how or why they were written. A discography is also listed of available recordings of the songs included in the book.

Song Index, by Minnie Sears. New York: H.W. Wilson. 650 p., 1926. *Supplement,* 1934. Reprinted as one volume in 1966 by Shoe String Press.
Sometimes known as *The Sears Index,* this classic publication indexes nearly 20,000 songs in over 280 collections. Indexed by title, first line, and songwriter. Especially valuable for the historical information it provides. Newer indexes by other authors supplement this work, but no other work is as complete for this time period.

Songs in Collections: an index. Compiled by Desiree deCharms and Paul F. Breed. Detroit, MI: Information Service. 588 p., 1966. LC 65-27601.

Songwriter's Market. Annual, 1979- . Cincinnati, OH: F & W Publications/Writers Digest Books. LC 78-648269, ISSN 0161-5971.
A current directory of publishers, recording companies, record producers, managers, booking agents, and others involved in the song writing and publishing part of the music industry. The book provides commentary on the songwriting market, contracts, and how to sell your work. Some international publishers are listed. A short glossary of terms is useful to researchers.

Stereo Review Compact Disc Buyers' Guide. Semiannual, 1987- . DCI Inc. (Diamandis Communications, Inc.). LC 87-640293.

Stereo Review Presents Stereo Buyers Guide. Annual, 1957- . New York: CBS Magazines. ISSN 0736-6515. Alternate title: *Stereo Buyers Guide.* Previous titles: *Stereo Directory and Buying Guide* and *Stereo Hi-Fi Directory.*

Top of the Charts: the most complete listing ever, by Nelson George. Piscataway, NJ: New Century. 470 p., 1983. ISSN 0-8329-0260-8.

This compiles weekly record charts from *Record World* from 1970 through 1981. A weekly listing of the top ten singles and albums for rock, black, jazz, and country.

Top Tens and Trivia of Rock and Roll and Rhythm and Blues, 1950-1980, by Joe Edwards. Annual Supplement. St. Louis, MO: Blueberry Hill Publishing Company. 805 p., 1981. No LC or ISSN numbers.

Trade Show & Convention Guide. Annual, 1981-   . Amusement Business, P.O. Box 24970, Nashville, TN 37202. Phone: (615) 321-4281. LC 84-643869, ISSN 0743-9709. Previous title: *Trade Show Convention Guide.*
   A directory of convention and trade shows for the forthcoming five years. Listings include associations and their shows, management companies that put together the conventions and trade shows, facilities where shows can be held (hotels, convention centers, auditoriums, etc.) and the services they provide as well as exhibit space that is available.

Variety Music Cavalcade, 1620-1969: A chronology of Vocal and Instrumental Music Popular in the U.S. Edited by Julius Hatfield. 3d ed. New York: Prentice-Hall. 766 p., 1971. LC 70-129240, ISSN 0-13-940718-9.
   Arranged in chronological sequence, music in the United States is discussed and some social and/or historical events are included to place the music in its proper frame of reference. All types of popular music is covered, including church music. Indexing is by song title and composer.

A series of books using the historical charts (the weekly charts of the top 100 popular songs in various categories) from *Billboard* have been compiled by Joel Whitburn for many years, with the beginning of each title bearing his name. (see ahead.) All are listed here in one group in order to avoid confusion since some of the same information is repeated in several volumes. They're expensive and were originally intended for use by radio stations and music industry researchers. All of the books generally follow the same arrangement. The main listing is by name of the artists, with record titles listed under the artist in chronological order by chart date. Information for each title includes the date the record first appeared on the chart, the number of weeks it remained on the chart, the highest position it obtained, indication of gold or platinum status (if obtained), and the original recording company label name and record number. Many entries include brief biographical information about the artists. Another index arranges all song titles alphabetically. There is also a year-by-year chronological listing of all singles that went to the number 1 position. Available from: Record Research, Inc., P.O. Box 200, Menomonee Falls, WI 53051. Phone: (414) 251-5408.

The Whitburn titles referred to are:

(1) *Joel Whitburn Presents Billboard's Top 10 Charts.* 1989, 600 p. A week-by-week listing of the top 10 pop singles from the *Billboard* charts, 1958-1988. The list includes the 1,550 recordings to make the top ten for the 30 years noted.

(2) Whitburn. Joel. *Pop Memories 1890-1954: compiled from America's popular music charts, 1890-1954.* 657 p., 1986. LC 86-225616, ISBN 0-89820-083-0. Arranged by artist, record title, discographic information, special chart positions. A great place to go for listings of early performers' hit records. Both Bing Crosby and Perry Como have pages of listings.

(3) *Joel Whitburn's Pop Singles Annual 1955-1986;* compiled from *Billboard.* 668 p., 1987. A complete year-by-year listing, of the nearly 18,000 singles to appear on the *Billboard* pop charts. The main section is arranged chronologically by year, with titles ranked by chart performance. A title index is also presented. In addition, the book provides some brief commentary on the important social and news events of each year, along with some of the most popular films, TV programs, and sports events. The same information has been arranged by artist and title in another publication: *Joel Whitburn's Top Pop Singles, 1955-1986* (756 p.,)

(4) Whitburn, Joel. *Joel Whitburn's Top Country Singles 1944-1988.* 535 p., 1989. ISBN 0898200717. Arranged

by artist; indexed by title. Arranged alphabetically by artist, with a chronological listing of all singles which appeared on the *Billboard* charts. Information for each title includes: record label and record number, date of initial chart appearance, weeks on the chart, and "crossover" positions on the popular charts. An index of titles refers to the name of the artist. There's also a biographical section which gives brief profiles of the more popular country stars.

(5) Whitburn, Joel. *Top Country & Western Records.* LC 72-6752. Basic volume is 1949-1971 (published in 1972) and yearly supplements. Compiled from the *Billboard* charts.

(6) *Joel Whitburn's Top Pop Albums 1955-1985.* 508 p., 1985. LC 85-216224, ISBN 0-89820-054-7. Information for the 14,000 albums listed is similar to that given for the singles: artist listings, chart positions, and discographic information. Only the titles of the albums are given; the album contents are not listed.

(7) *Joel Whitburn's Top Rhythm & Blues Singles, 1942-1988.* 1989, 624 p. The chart titles have changed over the years, but this book includes what has been variously defined as soul, Black, rhythm and blues, and urban contemporary. Artist and title sections are provided with the standard information supplied in the other volumes. Also, see the *Billboard* listing above for its *Music & Video Yearbook,* compiled by Joel Whitburn.

Who's New Wave in Music: an illustrated encyclopedia, 1976-1982, by David Bianco. Ann Arbor, MI: Pierian Press. 430 p., 1985. LC 84-61228, ISBN 0-87650-173-0.

Who's Who in Rock Music, by William York. New ed. New York: Scribner's. 413 p., 1982. LC 81-21368, ISBN 0-684-17342-5.

A comprehensive listing of rock singers, groups, musicians, and others of importance in the industry. Arranged alphabetically by the name of the person or group, the book provides brief biographical and career facts about thousands of prominent individuals. Some discography information.

Who's Who of Jazz: Storyville to Swing Street, by John Chilton. 4th ed. New York: DaCapo. 375 p., 1985. LC 84-20062, ISBN 0-306-76271-4.

An alphabetical listing of early American jazz musicians, with information about their careers. Some photos.

Words On Cassette. See: *On Cassette.*

Words On Tape. Annual, 1984- . Address: Meckler Publishing Corporation, 11 Ferry Lane West, Westport, CT 06880-5808. Phone: (203) 226-6967. LC 85-647247, ISSN 8755-3759. Available online on BRS.

An international guide to the rapidly expanding audio cassette market.

The World's Encyclopedia of Recorded Music, by Francis F. Clough and G. J. Cuming. Original volume: Gramophone Corp. (London), 1952. Reprinted by Greenwood Press (Westport, CT). 890 p., 1970. LC 71-100214, ISBN 0837130034. Greenwood reprint includes *First Supplement. Second Supplement, 1951-1952* (262 p., 1953); *Third Supplement, 1953-1955* (564 p., 1957),

The set lists recordings that were current at the time of publication as well as those which were out of print. One of the few reference sources that was international in scope at the time. Detailed bibliographic information is provided for each recording and some annotations are extensive.

Year by Year in the Rock Era: Events and Conditions Shaping the Rock Generations that Reshaped America, by Herb Hendler. Westport, CT: Greenwood. 350 p., 1983. Reprinted in 1987 by Praeger. LC 87-2381, ISBN 0-275-92708-3.

A chronological, year-by-year, history of rock music from 1954 to 1981. The social events of each time period and general American lifestyles are integrated into yearly reviews of the music, the performers, the industry activities, fashion, and slang.

MUSIC PERIODICALS

ARSC Journal (3 times yearly, 1968- .) and *ARSC Newsletter* (Quarterly, 1977- .). Silver Spring, MD: Association for Re-

corded Sound Collections. ISSN (their *Journal*): 0004-5438. The
Journal is indexed in: Arts & Humanities Citation Index,
MI, MLA, RILM Abstracts of Music Literature, Music Article
Guide.

ASCAP in Action. Quarterly, 1967- . New York: American
Society of Composers, Authors, and Publishers. ISSN 0197-7849.
Available on microform and document delivery from UMI.
Previous title: *ASCAP Today* (1967-1978). Indexed in: MI.
   Information of interest to members: legislative updates, interviews with members, ASCAP events and activities, awards won
   by members, and other special features regarding the songwriting industry. SEE ALSO: *MUSIC ORGANIZATIONS,*
   page 286.

American Music. Quarterly, 1983- . Champaign, IL: University
of Illinois Press. LC 83-643978, ISSN 0734-4392. Available on
microform from UMI. Indexed in: Arts & Humanities Citation
Index, MI, Humanities Index.
   Broad coverage of popular music in America. Long articles
   about performers, writers, organizations and events. Extensive
   review section for new books and recordings. Often includes
   bibliographies and discographies.

American Record Guide. Bimonthly, 1935- . Cincinnati, OH:
Record Guide Productions. (Temporarily ceased publication between 1972-1975). LC 42-9739, ISSN 0003-0716. Available on
microform and document delivery service of UMI. Previous title:
American Music Lover. Indexed in: Access, Readers' Guide to
Periodical Literature, MI, Music Article Guide.
   Reviews recordings of all formats and current literature in the
   field, although the emphasis is on classical. Audio records are
   reviewed, including the growing field of voice tapes of books.

American Songwriter. Bimonthly, 1985- . 27 Music Square East,
Nashville, TN 37203. LC 88-51, ISSN 0896-8993.

Amusement Business; the international newsweekly for sports &
mass entertainment. Weekly, 1961- . Amusement Business, P.O.
Box 24970, Nashville, TN 37202. Phone: (615) 321-4250. LC

63-57670, ISSN 0003-2344. A *Billboard* Publication. Formed by the union of *Funspot* and the "Show" news section of *Billboard* and assumed the volume numbering of the latter. Therefore, the first issue was as v. 73 in 1961. Back issues from 1972 to date are available from UMI.

Covers all aspects of live entertainment equally. Sections highlight entertainment promotions, performers' activities, auditorium and arena management plans and programs, programs in the athletic world, food and drink concession reports, parks and attractions, fairs and expos, and the talent marketplace.

Annual Review of Jazz Studies. See: MUSIC REFERENCE RESOURCES, page 229.

Audio. Monthly, 1947- . New York: CBS Magazines. LC 80-11244, ISSN 0004-752X. Previous title: *Audio Engineering.* Indexed in: BI, MI, Popular Magazine Review.

Audio Times. Semimonthly, 1959- . New York: International Thomson Retail Press. LC 80-218, ISSN 0519-4156.

BMI Music World. Quarterly, 1962- . New York: Broadcast Music Incorporated. ISSN 0045-317X. Previous title: *BMI: The Many Worlds of Music.* Back issues available from UMI. Indexed in: MI. See Also: page 286.

News of interest to members, awards won by members, special issues (*e.g.,* the Fall issue is about country music), and industry topics of interest to songwriters and publishers.

Billboard. Weekly, 1894- . Billboard Publications, One Astor Plaza, 1515 Broadway, New York, NY 10036. Phone: (212) 764-7300. ISSN 0006-2510. Available on microfilm from Kraus Microform (White Plains, NY) or on microform and document delivery service through UMI (Ann Arbor, MI). Indexed in: Business Index, MI, Trade and Industry Index. Available online: Dialog, Billboard Network.

The magazine is best known for its weekly record charts which indicate the top selling "singles" in every category of music. Their year-end issue is a special "Talent In Action" issue that lists the best performers and recordings in each musical category. The magazine covers all aspects of the recording industry each week, with minor coverage of radio and live talent venues. Special issues throughout the year pay tribute to people and/or organizations who are celebrating special anniversaries, highlight specific types of music (black, country, gospel, Latin, etc.), and showcase talent and recordings from foreign countries. In addition to covering the record industry, the magazine has increased coverage of the video tape industry and includes charts for the top rental and sales of video tapes in various areas.

Black Perspective in Music. Semiannual, 1973- . Cambria Heights, NY: Foundation for Research in the Afro-American Creative Arts. LC 73-642106, ISSN 0090-7790. Available on microform and through document delivery service from UMI. Indexed in: Index to Book Reviews in the Humanities, Jazz Index, Music Article Guide, MI, RILM Abstracts of Music Literature.

Bluegrass Directory. Biennial, 1981- . Murphys, CA: BD Products. LC 88-32009. Latest edition is 1985/86.
Who and where to write for bluegrass, old-time, and folk music products, services, and catalogs.

Bluegrass Unlimited. Monthly, 1966- . Address: Bluegrass Unlimited. 7533 Gary Rd., Manassas, VA 22110. Phone: (703) 361-8992. ISSN 0006-5137. Indexed in: MI. Back issues indexed in Popular Music Periodicals Index (no longer published).
Articles about Bluegrass performers, historical articles about the music, appearances and tour schedules, advertisements for festivals and/shows around the country, classified section for musical items and related ephemera, news section, and current correspondence.

CD Guide. Bimonthly, 1989- . WGE Publications, WGE Center, 70 Route 202, N. Peterborough, NH 03458-1194. LC 88-649017, ISSN 0896-3495.
A catalog of current and past releases. Useful for verifying information.

CD Review. Monthly, 1984- . Hancock, NH: WGE Publications. LC 89-6393, ISSN 1044-1700. Previous title: *Digital Audio & Compact Disc Review* (1984-1988). It also publishes a *Yearbook* as a special edition.

CD Review Digest: the International Indexing Service - an Annotated Guide to English Language Reviews of All Music Recorded on Compact and Video Laser Disks. Quarterly, 1987- . Voorheesville, NY: Peri Press. LC 88-656133, ISSN 0890-0213. Annual cumulation published as: *CD Review Digest Annual* (1983-1987, LC 89-643556, ISSN 0893-5173).

As of the middle of 1989, the *Digest* divided its title into two parts. The new titles are:

1. *CD Review Digest: Classical.* Quarterly, 1989- . Voorheesville, NY: Peri Press. LC 89-8228, ISSN 1045-0114. This title started with the Summer/Fall, 1989 issue (Volume 3, no. 2) of the previous title.

2. *CD Review Digest: Jazz, popular, etc.* Quarterly, 1989- . Voorheesville, NY: Peri Press. LC 89-8232, ISSN 1045-0122. Previous title: *CD Review Digest* (ISSN 0890-0213, LC 88-656133). This title started with the Winter, 1989 (Volume 3, no. 4) issue of the previous title.

Cadence: the American Review of Jazz & Blues. Monthly, 1976- . Redwood, NY: Cadence Jazz & Blues Magazine. LC 81-640946, ISSN 0162-6973. Indexed in: MI, Jazz Index, and in two indexes that have ceased publication: Abstracts of Popular Culture and Popular Music Periodicals Index.

Canada Country. Quarterly, 1976- . Toronto, Ont., Canada: Academy of Country Music Entertainment. LC 8730295, ISSN 0834-0560. Previous titles: *Country Music News* (1979-1985) and *What's News* (1976-1978).

Canadian Composer/Compositeur Canadien. Monthly, 1965- . Toronto, Canada: Creative Arts Co. (for the Composers, Authors, & Publishers Association of Canada). Text in English and French.

LC 88-662953, ISSN 0008-3259. Available on microform from UMI. Indexed in: Canadian Magazine Index, Canadian Periodicals Index, MI, Magazine Index, RILM Abstracts of Music Literature.

Canadian Musician. Bimonthly, 1979- . Toronto: Norris Publications. LC 84-646792, ISSN 0708-9635. Indexed in: Canadian Magazine Index, Canadian Periodical Index, MI, Jazz Index.

Cash Box; the international music/coin machine/home entertainment weekly. Weekly, 1942- . Cash Box, 330 W. 58th Street, New York, NY 10019. Phone: (212) 586-2640. LC 55-23069, ISSN 0008-7289. Indexed in: Music Index.
   Weekly industry magazine for the recording, music, radio, video, and jukebox industries. Reports popularity charts of top songs in pop, country, jazz, gospel, and dance. Also charts independent records, CDs, music videos, and film video sales. Strong on industry news and international news; profiles upcoming and long-time performers.

Compact Disk. Quarterly, 1986- . New York: ABC Consumer Magazines. LC 88-656180.
   Reviews new products and releases in all areas.

Computer Music Journal. Quarterly, 1977- . Cambridge, MA: MIT Press. LC 77-644286, ISSN 0148-9267. Available on microform and through document delivery service from UMI. Indexed in: Arts & Humanities Citation Index, Music Index, Music Article Guide, RILM Abstracts of Music Literature, Science Abstracts, Science Citation Index, Compumath Citation Index.

Country Music. Bimonthly, 1972- . New York: Silver Eagle Publishers. LC 73-641113, ISSN 0090-4007. Indexed in: Access, Magazine Index, Magazine Article Summaries (Previously: Popular Magazine Review). Back issues also indexed in Popular Music Periodicals Index (no longer published).

Country Music-USA. Monthly, 1980- . Address: 1813-B Neihardt St., Branson, MO 65616. Phone: (417) 335-2380. Editorial office in Nashville; phone: (615) 321-0404.

Publishes interviews, stories, and news of interest to country music fans. Many of the ads are for the growing country music industry in and around Missouri and Arkansas. A number of country entertainers have opened their own dinner clubs, music halls, theatres, and gift shops in Branson in recent years and this periodical is an outgrowth of their success.

Country Song Roundup. Monthly, 1947- . Derby, CT: Charlton Publications. LC 78-4666, ISSN 0011-0248. A couple of irregular annuals have been published as *Country Song Roundup Annual* (1980) and *Country Song Roundup Yearbook* (1981).

Creem. Monthly, 1969- . Los Angeles, CA: Cambray Publishing. LC 77-644802, ISSN 0011-1147. Available in microform from UMI. Indexed in: Access, MRD, MI.

Daily Variety. See: FILM PERIODICALS, page 330.

Digital Audio Compact Disc Review. See: *CD Review.*

Down Beat. Monthly, 1934- . Elmhurst, IL: Maher Publications. LC 63-4684, ISSN 0012-5768. Available on microform and document delivery service from UMI. Indexed in: Readers' Guide to Periodical Literature, Arts & Humanities Citation Index, Book Review Index, BI, MI, RILM Abstracts of Music Literature.

EAR; magazine of new music. Bimonthly, 1973- . New York: EAR, Inc. LC 84-7624, ISSN 0734-2128. Indexed in: Access, Music Article Guide, MI.

Electronic Musician. Monthly, 1976- . Berkeley, CA: Mix Publications. ISSN 0884-4720. Indexed in: America History & Life, Music Index.

Fanfare. See: page 429.

Folk Music Journal. See: page 531.

Frets Magazine; the magazine for acoustic string instruments. Monthly, 1979- . Cupertino, CA: GPI Publications. ISSN 0162-

0401. Available on microform and through document delivery service of UMI. Indexed in: MI.

Goldmine. See: page 429.

The Gospel Voice. Monthly, 1988-   . Music City News Publishing Company, 50 Music Square West, Suite 601, Nashville, TN 37203. Phone: (615) 329-2200.
    Fan and industry news of the Southern gospel scene. Features interviews with performers, latest signings and management activities, reviews of new record releases, and publishes tour schedules of performers. Publishes charts of top record activity in the gospel field for albums and singles. The April issue is a Southern Gospel Music Directory. Advertisers include both artists and booking agencies.

Grammy; official publication of the National Academy of Recording Arts & Sciences (NARAS). Monthly, 1982-   . Burbank, CA: NARAS. Articles about recording artists and industry personnel, recent important recordings, genres, and other subjects of interest. Highlights of various music seminars and industry meetings, discussions of issues in the forefront.

Gramophone. See: BRITISH MUSIC PERIODICALS.

Guitar Player. Monthly, 1967-   . Cupertino, CA: GPI Publications. LC 86-7027, ISSN 0017-5463. Available on microform and document delivery service from UMI. Indexed in: MI, Magazine Index, Popular Magazine Review.

Guitar Review. Quarterly, 1946-   . New York: Albert Augustine. LC 55-36470, ISSN 0017-5471. Indexed in: Arts & Humanities Citation Index, Music Article Guide, MI, RILM Abstracts of Music Literature.

High Fidelity. Monthly, 1951-   . New York: ABC Leisure Magazines. LC 82-8247, ISSN 0018-1455. Available on microform and document delivery service from UMI. Indexed in: Readers' Guide to Periodical Literature, BI, FLI, MI, Magazine Index, Popular Magazine Index.

Hit Parader. Monthly, 1942- . Derby, CT: Charlton Publications. ISSN 0162-0266. Indexed in: Magazine Article Summaries (Previous title: Popular Magazine Review).

International Musician. Monthly, 1901- . New York: American Federation of Musicians of the United States and Canada. LC 14-421, ISSN 0020-8051. Newsletter for members of the Association. Available on microform and document delivery service from UMI. Indexed in: Magazine Article Summaries, MI. See Also: page 286.

Jazz Educators Journal. Quarterly, 1969- . National Association for Jazz Educators, Box 724, Manhattan, KS 66502. LC 82-640362, ISSN 0730-9791. Indexed in: MI, Jazz Index. Previous titles: *National Association of Jazz Educators. Newsletter* and *NAJE Educator* (1969-1980).

Jazz Journal International. See: BRITISH MUSIC PERIODICALS, page 532.

Jazz Times. Monthly, 1972- . Silver Spring, MD: Jazz Times, Inc. LC 80-648105, ISSN 0272-572X. Supersedes: *Radio Free Jazz*. Indexed in: MI, Jazz Index.

Jazz World. Bimonthly, 1972- . New York: World Jazz Society. LC 84-643349, ISSN 0749-4564. Previous titles: *Jazz World Index, Jazz Echo,* and *The Swinging Newsletter*. Indexed in: MI, Jazz Index.

Jazziz. Bimonthly, 1983- . Gainesville, FL: Jazziz Magazine. LC 83-3749, ISSN 0741-5885.
    Covers jazz, instrumental, and improvisational music. Reviews the latest recordings in all formats, with an emphasis on CDs.

JEMF Quarterly. Quarterly, 1965- . Published for the John Edwards Memorial Foundation by the Center for Popular Music, Middle Tennessee State University, Murfreesboro, TN 37132. LC

80-640246, ISSN 0021-3632. Volume 21, No. 75/76 (Spring/Summer 1985) was published in early 1989. The publisher announced that the publication will end with the next issue at the end of 1989 and be superseded by a new title, *American Vernacular Music* to be issued semiannually. Indexed in: MI, Historical Abstracts, Parts A and B, American History and Life, MLA, Music Index, RILM.

The JEMF Quarterly has emphasized early American music history, with an emphasis on country music, western swing, and bluegrass. Recent years have included a growing amount of blues, gospel, rock, and ethnic. For the large part, recordings were the main type of format discussed. The recently announced new title will emphasize a broad spectrum of American vernacular music in all formats, with an expansion to more radio, television, and sheet music.

Journal of Country Music. 3 issues yearly, 1970- . Nashville, TN: Country Music Foundation. LC 73-646348, ISSN 0092-0517. Continues: *The Country Music Foundation Newsletter.* Indexed in: Arts & Humanities Citation Index, MLA, RILM Abstracts of Music Literature. See Also: MUSIC LIBRARIES AND RESEARCH CENTERS.

Journal of Popular Culture 1967- . See: GENERAL ENTERTAINMENT PERIODICALS, page 138.

Living Blues: a Journal of the Black American Blues Tradition. Bimonthly, 1970- . University of Mississippi, Center for the Study of Southern Culture, University, MS 38677. LC 72-620160, ISSN 0024-5232. Absorbed: *Living Bluesletter* in 1985. Available on microform from UMI. Indexed in: MI, MLA, Jazz Index, RILM Abstracts of Music Literature.

Medical Problems of Performing Artists. See: GENERAL ENTERTAINMENT PERIODICALS, page 138.

Mix: the Recording Industry Magazine. Monthly, 1977- . Berkeley, CA: Mix Publications. LC 87-659026, ISSN 0164-9957. Indexed in: Music Article Guide.

Modern Drummer: a Contemporary Publication Exclusively for Drummers. Monthly, 1977- . Cedar Grove, NJ: Modern Drummer Publications. LC 84-644936, ISSN 0194-4533. Absorbed: *Modern Percussionist* (1984-1987). Indexed in: MI.

Music City News. Monthly, 1963- . Music City News, 50 Music Square West, Suite 601, Nashville, TN 37203. Phone: (615) 329-2200. ISSN 0027-4291.

One of the longest-running country music periodicals. Covers industry and fan news alike. Features interviews with artists, latest news of television and radio programming, reviews latest record album releases, and publishes tour schedules of performers. Has a special monthly column for fan club updates of name/address changes and activities. Provides extensive coverage of June "Fan Fair" events in Nashville. Hosts own nationally televised "Music City News Country Music Awards" show each year (awards are voted by MCN subscribers). Advertisements heavily geared to products of interest to country music fans.

Music Row. Biweekly, 1981- . Nashville, TN: Music Row Publishers. ISSN 0745-5054.

A news-oriented magazine for the Nashville music professionals with articles about the recording business activities that make up the industry: copyright, contracts, accounting methods, and recording methods. Regular news columns about who is in the recording studios and working on products. Publishes special issues on recording facilities, suppliers, etc. Profiles of performers and industry people. Reviews new albums and a large number of 45 rpm single releases. Charts for album cuts and independents.

Music Trades. Monthly, 1890- . Englewood, NJ: Music Trades Corporation. ISSN 0027-4488. Available on microform and through document delivery services of UMI. Indexed in: MI, PROMT.

Musical America. Bimonthly, 1898- . New York: ABC Consumer Magazines. LC 87-640738, ISSN 1042-3443. The magazine published under its original title *Musical America* from 1898 to

1964, then was published with *High Fidelity* from 1965 to 1986, when it returned to its original title. Indexed in: MI. It issues an annual supplement, *Festivals,* which lists festivals worldwide.

   Mainly classical, but covers some popular music in an academic style. The *Festivals* supplement lists festivals of many music genres worldwide, with the majority located in the United States.

Musical Quarterly. Quarterly, 1915- . New York: Macmillan LC 16-24484, ISSN 0027-4631. Previously published by Schirmer. Available on microform from UMI. Indexed in: Readers' Guide to Periodical Literature, Humanities Index, Arts & Humanities Citation Index, Book Review Digest, Book Review Index, Music Article Guide, MI, Magazine Index, RILM Abstracts of Music Literature.

Musician. Monthly, 1976- . Gloucester, MA: Amordian Press (subsidiary of Billboard Publications). LC 82-644166, ISSN 0733-5253. Previous titles: *Musician, Player and Listener* and *Music America.* Available on microform and document delivery service of UMI. Indexed in: MI.

NAMM Music Retailing News. 6 issues yearly for members, 1947- . Carlsbad, CA: National Association of Music Merchants. LC 73-647823, ISSN 0027-5913. See Also: page 288.

Notes: the quarterly journal of the Music Library Association. Quarterly, 1948- . See: page 252.

   One of the best research sources in music because of its timely and comprehensive listing of new publications. Each issue reviews new books and publishes a long list of new literature. It also publishes an annual "Obituaries" section that has become a major source in itself.

Performance; the international touring talent weekly newspaper. Weekly, 1971- . Performance, 1020 Currie St., Fort Worth, Texas 76107. Phone: (817) 338-9444. LC 85-8542, ISSN 0746-9772. Previous title: *Performance Newspaper.*

   Weekly news magazine covering touring. Regular features

include information about planned tours, artist news, stage technology, management announcements, detailed tour schedules of performers, and box office news. Charts the top box office draws of the week by performer and by gross receipts. Features interviews with artists, articles about venues, and industry concerns. Covers the United States, with international emphasis on Canada, England, and Australia. Both venues and performers advertise in the magazine.

Perspectives of New Music. Semiannual, 1962- . Seattle, WA: Perspectives of New Music. LC 66-89176, ISSN 0031-6016. Indexed in: MI.

The journal covers contemporary music and performances; it includes interviews, festival reviews, and critical reviews of recordings. An index to the periodical has been published separately by Ann P. Basart, *Perspectives of New Music;* an index 1962-1982 (Berkeley, CA: Fallen Leaf Press, 127 p., 1984. LC 83-82609, ISBN 0-914913-00-X).

Popular Music. 3 issues yearly, 1982- . New York: Cambridge University Press. ISSN 0261-1430.

An academic look at all genres of popular music, from country to rap. Articles center around the genre, various aspects of the music industries, performers, and history. A recent issue highlighted music videos and their history. Long book and record reviews. The October issue contains an annotated booklist of all new publications received during the year.

Popular Music & Society. Quarterly, 1971- . Bowling Green, OH: Popular Press (Bowling Green State University). LC 72-627179, ISSN 0300-7766. Available on microform and document delivery service of UMI. Indexed in: Arts & Humanities Citation Index, Book Review Index, Index to Book Reviews in the Humanities, MI, RILM Abstracts of Music Literature.

Covers all genres. Historical and current perspective articles about types of popular music and performers. The effects they have on society. Record, video, and book reviews.

Pro Sound News: the International News Magazine for the Professional Recording & Sound Production Industry. Monthly,

1978-   . New York: Pro Sound News Publications. LC 78-4380, ISSN 0164-6338.

RPM Weekly (Records-Promotion-Music). Weekly, 1964-   . Toronto: RPM Music Publications. cn 76-300283, ISSN 0033-7064. Previous titles: *R.P.M. Music Weekly* (1965-1968) and *R.P.M. Records Promotion Music* (1964-1965).
   Covers music, television, radio, film, recordings, and the theater. Provides record charts for Canada.

Radio & Records (R & R). Weekly, 1973-   . Address: Radio & Records, Inc., 1930 Century Park W., Los Angeles, CA 90067. Phone: (213) 553-4330. LC 85-642968, ISSN 0277-4860.
   Industry newspaper aimed toward the radio industry and the recording industry (as it relates to broadcasting). Emphasis on news from local radio markets and stations, station ratings, market research, coverage of national meetings and events, current issues of concern to radio programmers, and personnel changes from one station to another. Charts the top songs of the week for different formats for singles and albums. Some international coverage (particularly Canada and Great Britain).

Record Collector. See: page 434.

Record Research. Bimonthly, 1955-   . Brooklyn, NY: Record Research.
   One of the older journals providing historical information about recordings.

Rock Express. Monthly, 1976-   . Toronto: Rock Express Communications. cn86-39054, ISSN 0710-6076. Previous title: *Music Express* (1976-1986).

Rolling Stone. Semimonthly, 1967-   . New York: Straight Arrow Publishers. LC 73-644466, ISSN 0035-791X. Available on microform from UMI. Indexed in: BI, Book Review Index, FLI, MI, MRD, Magazine Index, Magazine Article Summaries.

The *Schwann* has had a checkered past as far as titles go. Suffice it to say that it has been around and considered an important basic record reference tool since 1949. It started out as *Schwann,* then became *Schwann 1* and *Schwann 2.* Following that, it became *New Schwann.* Recently, a *Schwann CD* has been issued monthly and a *Schwann* on a quarterly basis. As of July, 1989, the publishers have gone to the three separate *Schwann* titles. Listed below are the various titles and frequencies.

(1) *Schwann/Spectrum.* Quarterly, 1990- . Guide to all music (except classical) on CDs, cassette tape, and LPs. Includes spoken-word recordings as well as pop, country, rock, international, folk, and soundtracks.

(2) *Schwann/Opus.* Quarterly, 1990- . Guide to classical recordings on CD, cassette tape, and LPs. ISSN: 1047-2355. An annual *Artist Issue* has also been announced.

(3) *InMusic.* Monthly, 1990- . This is a monthly newsletter which updates both quarterlies.

The following is a listing of past *Schwann* series:

(1) *Schwann Record and Tape Guide.* 1949-1971. Boston: Schwann. Triennial. ISSN 0582-1487. Published under various titles. Preceded by: *Schwann Long Playing Record Catalog.* Succeeded by: *Schwann Artist Issue.*

(2) *Schwann-1 Record and Tape Guide.* Monthly, 1972 - November, 1986. ISSN 0098-356X. Semiannual cumulation is *Schwann-2 Record and Tape Guide* (ISSN: 0271-5783). New York: ABC Consumer Magazines, Inc.

(3) *New Schwann.* Monthly, from December, 1983-1986. ISSN 0742-7239.

(4) *Schwann CD.* Monthly, 1986-1989. New York: ABC Consumer Magazines Inc., 21625 Prairie Street, Chatsworth, CA 91311. LC 89-641813, ISSN 1042-5047. Alternate title: *Schwann CD Catalog.* Previous title: *Schwann Compact*

Disc Catalog. A current catalog of new releases and current product. Useful for verifying titles, dates, and record numbers.

(5) *Schwann.* Quarterly, 1987-1989. ISSN 0893-0449.

Show Music. Quarterly, 1985- . Address: 5800 Pebble Beach Blvd., Las Vegas, NV 89108. Edited by Max O. Preeo.
An all-purpose newsletter about music from Broadway and live-entertainment shows. Reviews recordings, acts as a network for readers looking to purchase or trade show music, information about sheet music, and anything else the editor thinks will be of interest to musical theater historians.

Sing Out! The Folk Music Magazine. Quarterly, 1950- . Easton, PA: Sing Out. LC 61-45751, ISSN 0037-5624. Indexed in: MI.

Song Hits. Bimonthly, 1942- . Derby, CT: Charlton Publications. LC 78-216, ISSN 0038-1365.

Song Talk; the songwriter's newspaper. Bimonthly, 1985- . To members or by subscription. Hollywood, CA: National Academy of Songwriters. See Also: page 288.

Songwriters Guild News. New York: Songwriters Guild of America.

Spin. Monthly, 1985- . New York: Spin Publications. LC 86-646867, ISSN 0886-3032. Indexed in: MI.

Stereo Review. Monthly, 1958- . New York: DCI Inc. (Diamandis Communications, Inc.). LC 76-828, ISSN 0039-1220. Previous title: *Hi-Fi Stereo Review.* Indexed in: BI, Book Review Index, Music Article Guide, MI, Magazine Article Summaries (formerly Popular Magazine Review), RILM Abstracts of Music Literature, Readers' Guide to Periodical Literature. Available online on Dialog.

Variety. See: page 338.

Videolog. See: page 391.

Words & Music. Monthly, 1987-   . Rutherford, NJ: U.S. Publishing. LC 88-269, ISSN 0897-0300 A magazine for songwriters and lyricists.

Music Libraries and Research Centers

Popular music is the one area of entertainment where information about the subject can be found in almost any library, regardless of size. Virtually every public library system has a music collection that consists of recordings and some periodical subscriptions. In addition, popular music has always been well covered in all of the general American literature because it is such a strong part of our normal life and culture. Consequently, many of the general reference resources found in every library can be of use to researchers. It's rare to find a college or university without a music department and a library collection to support the field of study. A researcher can walk through the doors of almost any institution of higher education and expect to find music literature in a way that is not possible with film, broadcasting, or the theater.

Many larger university libraries have substantial music collections that have been enhanced over the years with special gifts. Princeton, Harvard, and UCLA immediately come to mind. Indiana University not only has a large music library but also one of the comprehensive folk music collections in the world. Many other institutions as well can point to respected collections and for this reason I have not included them in this list. Information about the music collections of institutions in your geographical area can be found in several of the reference works listed in this book.

Center For The Study Of Popular Culture

Address: Popular Culture Library and Audio Center. Bowling Green State University, Bowling Green, OH 43404. *Phone:* (419) 372-2981.

The center studies U.S. popular culture. Part of the study includes study of American music and its relationship with popular culture. A large library of over 75,000 books and nearly 500,000 recordings supports the research. It also studies American culture as it is portrayed in films, on television, and through literature.

Country Music Foundation Library

Address: Country Music Foundation. Library and Media Center. 4 Music Square East, Nashville, TN 37203. *Phone* (615) 256-1639. *Hours:* Monday-Friday 9:00 am.-5:00 pm. by appointment only.

The library has the best collection of country music literature in the world. It holds an extensive collection of current and past journals, thousands of recordings, a large collection of sheet music, and the best collection of photographs available. Its media collection is also growing and it has added a number of films and video tapes in recent years. It counts among its users journalists from many countries, record researchers, performers staffs, and the local Nashville television and production community. The Nashville Association of Musicians (Local 257 of the American Federation of Musicians) gives the Library their archive copies of their recording session contracts, thereby providing accurate documentation of historic recording sessions throughout the Nashville area.The session sheets list the musicians and technicians involved in each session, the titles of the songs recorded (and each cut of the song if more than one was made) at the session, and other information needed to assure an accurate accounting can be made.

Institute Of The American Musical

Address: 121 North Detroit St., Los Angeles, CA 90036. *Phone:* (213) 934-1221. The Library is open to approved researchers by appointment.

The Institute Study Center and Archive collects anything that documents the musical theater and film musicals:

recordings and early phonocylinders, tapes, playbills and programs, photographs, film, sheet music, scripts, books, and periodicals.

Institute Of Jazz Studies

Address: Rutgers University, 135 Bradley Hall, Newark, NJ 07102. *Phone:* (201) 648-5595. The Institute is part of the main library, but operated through an independent board of directors.

The Institute was founded in 1952 and conducts research in jazz and a number of related areas. It maintains a large archive collection of books, discographies, written music, sound recordings, oral histories, films, clippings, photographs, interview tapes and transcripts, and has received gifts of important private collections.

Indiana University

Address: Archives of Traditional Music, 057 Maxwell Hall, Bloomington, IN 47405. *Phone:* (812) 335-8632.

One of the largest collections of traditional music and oral histories in the world. International in scope, with materials about the part music plays in the culture of nearly every country. Collects and makes available phonorecordings (both musical and narrative) on nearly every aspect of its study.

Library of Congress

Address: The Library of Congress, Washington, DC 20540. As always, there are several places to conduct research on popular music in the Library of Congress. Listed below are the three main points of service:

1. **Music Division, Performing Arts Reading Room.** Madison Building, Room LM 113. *Phone:* (202) 707-5507. *Hours:* Monday-Saturday 8:30 am.–5:00 pm. Closed Sunday. This division holds the largest amount of research materials in LC and is the major area for

research. It is also the access point for requesting back issues of music journals and sheet music from the stacks.

2. **Recorded Sound Reference Center.** Madison Building, Room LM 113. *Phone:* (202) 707-7833. The Center is adjacent to the Music Division, but emphasizes recorded sound. This is the access point for research regarding radio and any type of recording.

3. **Archive of Folk Culture.** Jefferson Building, Room G 152. *Phone:* (202) 707-5510. This is the location to conduct research on traditional American music and folk music from around the world. The Division has a good selection of abstracts and indexes as well as a number of discographies and periodicals. It collects early music, oral histories, and photographs. It publishes an annual listing of folk recordings, *American Folk Music and Folklore Recordings;* a selected list.

Center For Southern Folklore (Archive)

Address: 1216 Peabody Avenue, P.O. Box 40105, Memphis, TN 38104. *Phone:* (901) 726-4205.

Founded in 1972 to preserve Southern cultural heritage and promote study and research. The Archive collects publications, photographs, recordings, and tapes.

The National Cowboy Hall Of Fame And Western Heritage Center

Address: 1700 N.E. 63rd St., Oklahoma City, OK 73111. *Phone:* (405) 478-2250.

The organization was founded in 1965 to preserve and recognize the history of the American west. It maintains a western museum and a Hall of Fame. Presents annual Western Heritage Awards for the best books, works of art, and media productions based on western history. The

Library contains a large collection of books and other materials about the West. The organization publishes a quarterly magazine called *Persimmon Hill.*

The New York Public Library, Music Division

Address: Performing Arts Library at the Lincoln Center, 111 Amsterdam Ave., New York, New York 10023. *Phone:* (212) 870-1625.

The Music Division is a large collection of books, periodicals, recordings, sheet music, and photographs. The collection also contains a large number of personal papers and donations from prominent performers and musicians.

The Southern Folklife Collection

Address: The University of North Carolina at Chapel Hill, Wilson Library, CB-3926, Chapel Hill, NC 27514. *Phone:* (919) 962-1345. *Hours:* Researchers only, by appointment.

The collection is the combination of two previously separate collections: the UNC-CH Folklore Archives and the recently-purchased John Edwards Memorial Collection of sound recordings. The JEMC consisted of the most important collection of early country music and western music recordings, literature, and correspondence held in private hands.

Following the death of John Edwards (for whom the archive is named) the collection was administered by UCLA for just over 20 years. Substantial amounts of new recordings and other materials were added during that time. By combining this collection with their own Folklore Archives, which is strong in southern traditional music, UNC-CH has been able to create a traditional American music collection of over 30,000 sound recordings of country music, gospel, blues, jazz, band, swing, and western music. It also has oral histories, periodicals, films, videos, scrapbooks, clippings, and correspondence.

Music Organizations

Academy of Country Music. P.O. Box 508, Hollywood, CA 90078. Phone: (213) 462-2351. Publications: a monthly newsletter, *Country Focus*.

American Federation of Musicians. Address: Suite 600, Paramount Building, 1501 Broadway, New York, NY 10036. Phone: (212) 869-1330. Western office: 1777 N. Vine St., Suite 410, Hollywood, CA 90028. Phone: (213) 461-3441.

American Guild of Musical Artists. Address: 1727 Broadway, New York, NY 10019-5214. Phone: (212) 265-3687. Publishes *AGMA ZINE* (5 times yearly, 1936-   .ISSN: 0002-0990).

American Society of Composers, Authors, and Publishers (ASCAP). Address: 1 Lincoln Plaza, New York, NY 10023. Phone: (212) 595-3050.

Association for Recorded Sound Collections (ARSC). Address: Box 10162, Silver Spring, MD 20904. Phone: (301) 593-6552. Publishes *ARSC Journal* and a *Membership Directory*. See entry in Chapter 10, page 431.

Broadcast Music Incorporated (BMI). 320 W. 57th St., New York, NY 10019. Phone: (212) 586-2000. Publishes *BMI: Music World*.

Canadian Recording Industry Association. 89 Bloor St. East, Toronto, ON, Canada M4W 1A9. Phone: (416) 967-7272.

Composers, Authors, & Publishers Association of Canada (CAPAC). Address: 1240 Bay St., Toronto, Ont M5R 2C2. Phone: (416) 924-4427. Publishes an irregular newsletter for members, *Canadian Composer/Compositeur Canadien*.

Country Music Association. One Music Circle South, Nashville, TN 37203. Phone: (615) 244-2840. Publications: *Close-Up*. Monthly to members, 1959-   . ISSN: 0896-372X.

Country Music Foundation. 4 Music Square East, Nashville, TN 37203. Phone: (615) 256-1639. Publications: An irregular newsletter, and the *Journal of Country Music* (3 issues yearly).

Operates the Country Music Hall of Fame, maintains a large library of country music books, periodicals, recordings, and audiovisual materials. Supports country music research.

F.I.D.O.F. (International Federation of Festival Organizations). Current President: Jim Halsey, P. O. Box 4003, Beverly Hills, CA 90024. Phone: (213) 273-2472.

An international organization for festival owners and promoters.

Gospel Music Association. 38 Music Square West, Nashville, TN 37203. Phone: (615) 242-0303. Publications: a semimonthly newsletter and a membership directory.

Established in 1964 to promote gospel music. Presents annual Dove Awards for gospel music performance and recordings.

International Bluegrass Music Association. 326 St. Elizabeth St., Owensboro, KY 42301. Phone: (502) 684-9025. Publications: a bimonthly magazine, *International Bluegrass,* and a quarterly *Bluegrass Radio News.*

A relatively new organization, established in 1985, to promote one of the oldest forms of pure American music. Promotes bluegrass music, conducts industry seminars and workshops aimed at business professionals and musicians.

International Federation of Festival Organizations (F.I.D.O.F.). See: F.I.D.O.F.

Jazz World Society. P.O. Box 777, Times Square Station, New York, NY 10108. Phone: (201) 939-0836. Publications: *Jazz World* (bimonthly industry newsletter) and occasional directories such as *European Jazz Directory* and *Jazz Festivals International.*

Established in 1969 for professionals and others actively working to promote and chronicle jazz music worldwide. Sponsors seminars, supports research, and acts as a network for professional contacts.

Music Industries Association of Canada. 415 Yonge St., 10th Floor, Toronto, Ontario, Canada M5B 2E7. Publications: *MIAC Communique.* 3 issues yearly, 1980- .

Music Library Association. P.O. Box 487, Canton, MA 02021. Phone: (617) 828-8450. Publications: *Music Library Association Newsletter* (Quarterly, 1969- . ISSN 0580-289X) and *Notes.*

Nashville Songwriters Association International. 803 18th Ave., South, Nashville, TN 37203. Phone: (615) 321-5004. Publications: a bimonthly newsletter for members, *The Leadsheet.*
    Established in 1967 to support songwriters and help them gain recognition for their work. Acts as a lobbying arm for legislation, conducts songwriting seminars and workshops, holds an annual awards program, and maintains the Songwriters Hall of Fame.

National Academy of Recording Arts & Sciences. Address: 303 N. Glenoaks Blvd., Suite 140 M, Burbank, CA 91502. Publications: *Grammy.* Phone: (213) 849-1313.

National Academy of Songwriters. 6381 Hollywood Blvd., Suite 780, Hollywood, CA 90028. Phone: (213) 463-7178 or (800) 826-7287. Publications: a bimonthly newsletter, *Songtalk* and other materials of use to its members.
    Established in 1974 for songwriters and provides services in support of songwriters. Acts as a networking organization. Conducts seminars and educational programs, provides legal assistance, runs a placement service, and lobbies for legislation. Operates a song registration service called Songbank. Maintains a library of songwriting and general music information, holds an annual awards program.

National Association of Music Merchants, Inc. Address: 5140 Avenida Encinas, Carlsbad, CA 92008. Phone: (619) 438-8001. Publishes *NAMM Music Retailer News* for members.

National Association of Recording Merchandisers (NARM). 3 Eves Dr., Suite 307, Marlton, NJ 08053. Phone: (609) 596-2221. Publications: *NARM Sounding Board* (semimonthly).
    Created in 1958 as a support organization for retailers and

distributors of records and tapes. Holds an annual convention and awards program, lobbies for legislation, and speaks on issues of interest to its membership.

National Music Publishers' Association. Address: 205 E. 42nd St., New York, NY 10017. Phone: (212) 370-5330. Publishes *National Music Publishers' Association Bulletin.*

National Sheet Music Society. 1597 Fair Park Ave., Los Angeles, CA 90041. Publications: a monthly newsletter, *The Song Sheet,* and an annual membership directory.
  Founded in 1958 as an organization for individual and organizational collectors of sheet music.

Performing Rights Organization of Canada (PRO-CAN). 41 Valleybrook Dr., Don Mills, ON Canada M3B 2S6. Phone: (416) 445-8700.

Recording Industry Association of America (RIAA). 1020 19th St., Suite 200, Washington, DC 20036. Phone: (202) 775-0101.
  Founded in 1952, this organization is the trade association for the recording industry. It conducts research, compiles industry statistics, and lobbies for legislation supported by the industry. But it is also important to researchers because it is the one which officially tracks sales figures and certifies recordings for Gold Record and Platinum Record status. In addition, it now certifies videos for gold and platinum status.

SESAC, Inc. Address: 55 Music Square East, Nashville, TN 37203. Phone: (615) 320-0055.

The Songwriters Guild of America. 276 5th Ave., Suite 306, New York, NY 10001. Phone: (212) 686-6820. Publications: *Songwriter Guild News.*

Western Music Association. 3900 East Timrod St., Tucson, AZ 85711. Phone: (602) 323-3311.
  Dedicated to the preservation and performance of Western/ cowboy music and poetry.

8 FILM RESEARCH

The film industry is probably the most heavily documented of all the entertainment fields. And today, coverage of film and film personalities continues to expand into all areas of modern media. Television stars become film stars, film stars interview on television shows, and most everyone seems to want to do a Broadway play. Films no longer find their home only in commercial movie theaters; they become television specials or series, video tapes for home viewing, and soundtrack record albums. Information about a particular product or person is therefore spread over a wide variety of sources and the modern researcher is required to hustle if a comprehensive or accurate picture of your subject needs to be assembled. You never know where interesting information will turn up; the best explanation I have ever read about the nomination procedure for getting a star in the sidewalk of the Hollywood Walk of Fame was in the *Academy of Country Music* newsletter (November, 1987). As it turns out, the Hollywood Chamber of Commerce administers this attraction.

Regarding comprehensive index services, *Film Literature Index* and *International Index to Film Periodicals* are the oldest and most comprehensive indexes covering the whole range of film subjects. Yet, both are selective in the citations they include and therefore can not be complete. The indexes constantly change the list of periodicals they include as the periodicals themselves go out of business or change titles. Occasionally they are dropped for lack of interest or because another journal has preempted the field. Therefore, it's important to have some idea of when various magazines were published. Film reference resources rarely cross over into the related fields of television and theater. In fact, if you are researching an actor, most sources will not even mention the fact that the actor may have extensive credits in those mediums too. Don't take anything for granted, go check.

If you want to compile a list of films of a particular actor, *The Motion Picture Guide* is the first place to go because it's the newest source and the most comprehensive. But it's not 100% complete in every case and therefore it's important to give a courtesy review to other filmographies.

If you are searching for film reviews, *Film Review Annual* is relatively new but extremely useful because of the breadth of reviews included and/or cited for each title. And although one never wants to rely on a single review of a film, the *New York Times Film Reviews* and the *Variety Film Reviews* are absolutely invaluable for getting started. They're the quickest way to verify dates, production credits, and other facts. Again, keep in mind that no one source will pull it all together for you. *Film Review Annual* will contain some film reviews, but not others. You will want to check the NewsBank *Review of the Arts: Film and Television* for reviews that may have appeared in over 100 newspapers. And this is one place where you also want to give one of the most basic general reference sources its due: *Readers' Guide To Periodical Literature* goes all of the way back to the beginning.

To find biographical information about an actor, start with the *Performing Arts Biography Master Index* because it will provide a list of reference books which contain biographical information about your subject. *Contemporary Theatre, Film, and Television* is another useful source because it profiles many beginners as well as established stars and updates information in previous volumes. No one reference tool will provide a complete biographical and career profile. A film sourcebook about actors may include a filmography or major works but will not mention that person's minor parts in films or theater and television work.

There are a number of directories that provide addresses and phone numbers of entertainment people and businesses. However, the quickest way to contact an actor, director, or agent, is to call the Screen Actors Guild in Los Angeles or

New York and ask for their Agent Referral Office. Actors change agents (and vice versa) so often that SAG probably has the only current listing. Following that, the *Academy Players Directory* is the most comprehensive directory of actors and the *Hollywood Reporter Studio Blu-Book Directory* one of the best for the industry in general.

There are hundreds of books written about specialized film genres. I haven't made any attempt to cover genres. However, I do want to point out the extent of the body of literature that is available if you take the time to look for it. Categories especially well covered in film include: science fiction and fantasy, musicals, B westerns, B movies of all kinds, mysteries and spies, war films, directors, "Gone With the Wind," independent films and filmmakers, and animation. In television, popular genres are: westerns, Star Trek, soap operas, and various television shows ("I Love Lucy" and "The Honeymooners" are two). In music, it's Elvis and the Beatles.

It's always helpful for a writer to have background material conveniently available. For that reason, it's nice to have books in your personal research collection that provide brief background summaries about the industry and the people in it. Many of these titles can be purchased from bookstores or ordered for a reasonable price.

Don't overlook the value of out-of-print or older editions of reference books in your research. Older biographical resources are especially worth seeking out because they will contain biographies of people who have been removed from the newer editions. If you are trying to build up your home reference collection, you may want to visit used book stores or frequent large book sales for these books. The type of information you find in directories may change constantly (corporate staff names, addresses, phone numbers), but biographical information or historical facts and statistics won't change. They may be updated, but what has already been written will remain the same (unless it was incorrect to begin with, of course). Older books are also a valuable source of historical and rare photographs.

Although libraries may appear to have collections that

duplicate each other, a closer inspection of the contents will usually show that each one has material not available in the others. In fact, they can have different versions of films and television programs if a particular piece of film was cut and titled differently during different time periods or for different countries.

When you are researching in film libraries, pay special attention to collections such as newspaper clipping files and film stills. Each library will have its own set of clippings about a specific person, subject, or film and these will include at least some material that can not be found in other libraries because they have been compiled from different newspapers or magazines.

Photograph collections can vary considerably. Even though official publicity film stills all come from the same production company, different photos find their way into each library collection. This can be explained in part by the fact that most library photo collections are assembled from donations from local film distributors, movie theaters, and private collectors. The photos that were given to the library were often the stills *not* used for publicity purposes by the companies who made the donations, and therefore differ in each geographical area. In addition, some libraries have been lucky enough to be able to acquire location stills, rehearsal photos, candid (informal photos) of actors, news photos, social events, and portraits. Many of these collections are indexed only superficially and there will be no way to tell what is in the collection without looking at the photos themselves. For example, the film stills in the Billy Rose Theatre Collection for *Mary, Queen of Scots* contain many different photos from the Library of Congress collection; and the British Film Institute collection not only had the stills, but also a large number of photos from the premiere party.

Film music sources can be found in Chapter 7 on Popular Research and Recorded Sound Research.

Reference sources about comedians are also found in Chapter 5 and comedy recording references are under Chapter 7.

FILM REFERENCE SOURCES

Academy Players Directory. Quarterly, 1937- . Academy of Motion Picture Arts and Sciences. Address: 8949 Wilshire Blvd., Beverly Hills, CA 90211. Phone: (213) 278-8990.

Each issue is a four-part directory of members available for work; Part 1 (women), Part 2 (men), Part 3 (Children), and Part 4 (character actors/comedians). A "Reference Supplement" is a separate pamphlet listing the names, addresses, and phones of the agents. The publication is intended for casting directors and others concerned with employment of motion picture, television, and radio talent. An alphabetical index for each part includes: leading players; artists with disabilities; Asian Pacific artists; Black artists; Hispanic artists; Native American artists; Artists' representatives; Writers' representatives; and Casting directors. A photo of each actor or actress is included, along with the address and phone number of the representing agent.

Acquisitions & Development Directory. Annual, 1986- . Published with quarterly updates. Los Angeles: Omniartists Management Group. LC 88-649898, ISSN 0897-5183.

An international directory of companies which develop and produce programs for film companies, television networks, and cable. The emphasis is on the financial end of the industry. Supporting services are also listed such as financial backers and services, commissions, and other information useful to production companies and potential investors and/or developers of programs.

An Actor Guide to the Talkies: a comprehensive listing of 8,000 feature-length films from January, 1948, until December, 1964, by Richard Bertrand Dimmitt. Metuchen, NJ: Scarecrow. 2 vols., 1967/1968. LC 67-12057.

This set is one of the more convenient ways of identifying actor credits in films. Volume 1 is an alphabetical listing of films with full cast credits; volume 2 indexes alphabetically by name all of the actors listed in the cast credits with reference to their film appearances in volume 1. See Also: *A Title Guide to the Talkies,* by Richard Bertrand Dimmitt.

An Actor Guide to the Talkies, 1965 through 1974, by Andrew
Aros. Metuchen, NJ: Scarecrow Press. 771 p., 1977. LC 77-21589,
ISBN 0-8108-1052-2.
   This publication continues the Dimmitt set by adding 3,500 films
   for 1965-1974 and following the same format. See Also: *A Title
   Guide to the Talkies, 1975 through 1984,* by Andrew Aros.

*An Alphabetical Guide to Motion Picture, Television, and Video
Tape Production,* by Eli Levitan. New York: McGraw-Hill. 797 p.,
1970.
   Arranged alphabetically, the book defines words and phrases,
   explains technical processes, and discusses theory. Outdated if
   you want current definitions, but useful for historical purposes.

American Actors and Actresses: a guide to information sources, by
Stephen M. Archer. 710 p., 1983. Gale Performing Arts Information Guide Series, Vol.8. LC 82-15685, ISBN 0-8103-1495-9.
   This is a good basic bibliography arranged by name of stage and
   film actors, followed by a listing of articles about that person.
   For the large part, the articles are taken from journals you are
   likely to be able to find in your local public or college library.

American Film & Video Review. Annual, 1962-   . St. Davids, PA:
Eastern College, American Educational Film and Video Center.
Previous title: *American Film Review* (1962-1986).

American Film Festival Guide. Annual, 1959-   . LaGrange Park,
IL: American Film & Video Association (Previously, the Educa-
tional Film Library Association). Previous title: *Festival Film
Guide.*

The American Film Industry: A Historical Dictionary, by Anthony
Slide. Westport, CT: Greenwood. 431 p., 1986. ISBN 0-313-24693-
9, LC 85-27260.
   A concise overview of the film industry listing production and
   distribution studios, discussing technology and techniques,
   covering genres, and providing directory information for organizations and research facilities.

The American Film Institute Catalog of Motion Pictures. New York: R.R. Bowker. Although a number of volumes are planned, only three have actually been published to date: F1 is titled *Feature Films, 1911-1920* (2 vols, 1988, LC 88-040245, ISBN 0-520-06301-5); Volume F2 is titled *Feature Films, 1921-1930* (1971, ISBN 0-8352-04405); Volume F6 is titled *Feature Films, 1961-1970* (1976, LC 79-128587, ISBN 0-8352-0453-7).

A listing of feature length films released for commercial theater showing in the United States for the dates indicated on the volumes. Includes foreign films shown commercially in the U.S. if they were over 45 minutes in length and were in English or had subtitles. Information given includes cast and production credits along with a brief synopsis, length, genre, copyright date. A number of detailed indexes provide access by personal name, producer/director, genre, geographical area, and subject. The volume for 1911-1920 includes brief bibliographies for reviews of the film cited.

American Film Institute Guide to College Courses in Film and Television. 8th ed. LC 90-630, ISBN 0139255947. Published jointly by the American Film Institute and New York: Simon & Schuster.

An international listing of colleges and universities offering degrees and/or programs. Provides details about each program as well as the production facilities available at each institution.

The American Film Musical, by Rick Altman. Bloomington, IN: Indiana University Press. Illus., 386 p., 1987. ISBN 0-253-30413-X, LC 86-45473.

Includes information about hundreds of films; also provides extensive discussions about theory, history, and criticism of the film musical.

Annual Index to Motion Picture Credits. Annual, 1976- . Los Angeles,CA: Academy of Motion Picture Arts and Sciences. ISSN: 0163-5123. Previous title: *Screen Achievement Records Bulletin* (1976-1977).

This annual publication lists films that have been released for at least one week during the eligible period in a commercial theater in Los Angeles area and gives cast and complete production credits. Arrangement is alphabetically by film title, with indexes for actors, directors, cinematographers, editors, music, producers, sound, and releasing companies.

ArtsAmerica Fine Art Film and Video Source Book. Annual, 1987- . Address: ArtsAmerica, 125 Greenwich Ave., Greenwich, CT 06830. Phone: (203) 637-1454.
Lists fine-art videos and films (including documentaries). Has subject listing as well as title and distributor. Good source for information about museums and their collections. Includes some directory information for leaders in the field.

Back Stage. TV, Film, & Tape Production Directory. Annual, 1965- . New York: Backstage Productions. See: TELEVISION AND REFERENCE RESOURCES, page 365.

Bibliography of Film Bibliographies, by Hans Jurgen Wulff. New York: K.G. Saur. 326 p., 1987. LC 88-171898, ISBN 3598106300.
Lists over 1,000 published bibliographies about film and television personalities, history, genres, productions, and other subject areas.

A Biographical Dictionary of Film, by David Thomson. New York: Morrow. 2d rev. ed. 682 p., 1981. LC 80-20500, ISBN 0-688-00132-7.
A comprehensive and concise biographies of film personalities and others of importance to the industry. Does not offer complete filmographies for those cited.

British Film Actors' Credits, 1895-1987, by Scott Palmer. Metuchen, NJ: Scarecrow. 935 p., 1988. LC 87-31098, ISBN 0-89950-316-0. See: BRITISH FILM REFERENCE RESOURCES. Chapter 11, page 493.

The British Film Catalog: 1895-1985, by Denis Gifford. New York: Facts on File. Unpaged [1152 p.], 1986. LC 86-6281, ISBN 0-8160-1554-6. See: BRITISH FILM REFERENCE RESOURCES, Chapter 11, page 493.

Brooks Standard Rate Book. Annual, 1956- . Publisher: Stanley J. Brooks Company, 1416 Westwood Blvd., Suite 201, Los

Angeles, CA 90024. Phone: (213) 470-2849. LC 79-643357, ISSN 0193-2314.

If you want to know how much people in the film, television, and theater industries get paid, this is the place to go. It publishes wage schedules and agreements with the major industry unions and guilds for the West Coast and location pay for various places around the country. Indexed by occupational title, it lists wages for everyone from actors, to film editors, to wranglers.

Celebrity Articles From The Screen Guild Magazine. Edited by Anna Kate Sterling. Metuchen, NJ: Scarecrow. 172 p., illus., 1987. LC 86-31389, ISBN 0-8108-1962-7.

Anthology of articles from *The Screen Guild Magazine,* which contains many profiles of early screen stars and industry personnel.

Cinema Booklist, by George Rehrauer. Scarecrow Press, Metuchen, NJ. 473 p., 1972. LC 70-188378, ISBN 0-8108-0501-4. Also published: *Supplement I* (405 pp., 1977, LC 77-371983); *Supplement II* (470 pp., 1977). Index to *Supplement II* covers all three volumes. Comprehensive list of film publications, including books, periodicals, and published scripts.

Cinema Sequels and Remakes, 1903-1987, by Robert A. Nowlan and Gwendolyn Wright Nowlan. Jefferson, NC: McFarland. 966 p., illus., 1988. LC 88-42640, ISBN 0-89950-314-4.

A comprehensive listing of films that have sequels or have been made more than once. The book includes all films from silents to date in the genres of drama, adventure, romance, comedy, and thrillers which have at least one remake or sequel. Each entry includes plot synopsis, cast and production credits, and a comparison of the various versions.

Cinematographers, Production Designers, Costume Designers & Film Editors Guide, 1988. 2d ed., 302 p., 1990. Compiled and edited by Susan Avallone. Lone Eagle Publishing, 9903 Santa Monica Blvd., Beverly Hills, CA 90012. Phone: (213) 471-8066. 120 p., 1988. LC 89-643541, ISSN 0894-8674, ISBN 0-943728-29-0.

A directory of prominent professionals in the fields listed in the title. Each entry includes artistic credits in film or television, address and phone number of the person or an agent, membership in professional organizations or unions. Not comprehensive, but the best source available for contacting people in these areas. There are a few entries for deceased people if they were prominent in their field and are considered to have made lasting contributions.

The Complete Dictionary of Television and Film, by Lynne Naylor Ensign and Robyn Eileen Knapton. See: TELEVISION AND RADIO REFERENCE RESOURCES, page 370.

The Complete Film Dictionary, by Ira Konigsberg. New American Library (NAL), 1633 Broadway, New York, NY 10019. 420 p., 1987. ISBN 0-453-00564-0, LC 87-5747.
    Extensive listing of over 3000 film terms and topics with frequent in-depth coverage. Covers technical terms, equipment, styles, genres, business slang, and film history.

Contemporary Theatre, Film & Television. See: Chapter 6, page 176, and Chapter 8, page 291.

The Critical Index: a bibliography of articles on film in English, 1946-1973, by John C. Gerlach and Lana Gerlach. New York: Teachers College Press. 726 p., 1974. LC 74-1959.
    The authors have indexed 22 film periodicals for the time period indicated; selected annotations are provided. An alphabetical names section which includes actors, directors, and other prominent people in the industry is especially useful. A subject section is arranged by broad topic. Author and title indexes are supplied. This publication is an effective supplement to some of the newer indexing services that lack historical coverage (for example, the *Film Literature Index* and the *International Index to Film Periodicals,* as important as they are, only started in the early 1970s).

Dictionary of Film Terms, by Frank E. Beaver. New York: McGraw-Hill. 392 p., illus., 1983. LC 82-14046, ISBN 0-07-004216-0.
    Good source of information for the non-industry researcher. Strong on historical aspects of the industry and includes film companies, genres, a variety of industry notables, and important events.

Directory of Members. Annual, 1967- . Directors Guild of America. For address, see: page 357. ISSN 0419-2052.
  Directory gives phone numbers and addresses of DGA members or their agents. Occasionally both home and business phones are given.

DVE Productions publishes a series of directories of Hollywood film and television production companies. Each directory lists the name of the company, address and phone, key personnel (officers and creative staff), and production credits. Some are only a few pages in length, but all are updated frequently and therefore are worth including here. Their address is 3017 Santa Monica Blvd., Suite 149, Santa Monica, CA 90404. Phone: (213) 281-7637. The titles are: *Feature Film Producers* (three times yearly, previously titled *Feature Script Submission Directory*); *The TV Producers* (three times yearly); *The TV Syndication Contact Sheet* (annual); and *Distributors* (twice yearly). Another publication, *Overall Deals At The Studios* (three times yearly), provides details about contractual relationships and current deals between the major studios and stars, producers, and writers.

Educational Film-Video Locator; of the consortium of university film centers and R.R. Bowker. 2 vols. New York: R.R. Bowker. 3d ed., 1986. LC 81-645009, ISBN 0-8352-2179-2, ISSN 0000-0973. Volume 1 contains subject, title, and audience indexes, plus A-H of the title listing. Volume 2 contains titles I-Z.
  Lists films available to rent from the Consortium of University Film Centers. The set has title and subject indexes. Each title has a brief annotation.

Film: A Reference Guide, by Robert A. Armour. Westport, CT: Greenwood Press. 251 p., 1980. LC 79-6566, ISBN 0-313-22241-X.
  The book is divided into chapters about filmmaking (film production, actors, directors, etc.) with bibliographies. Special chapters about reference works and periodicals enhance the work.

Film Actors Guide: Western Europe, by James R. Parish. Metuchen, NJ: Scarecrow Press. 606 p., illus., 1977. LC 77-22485, ISBN 0-8108-1044-1.

Arranged alphabetically by name of actor, with a chronological listing of films that person made (only the film title and year of release is given). A brief, but concise listing. Extremely useful for quick, clean checklists.

Film & Video Finder (NICEM). See: pages 372-373.

Film and Video Makers Directory. Annual, 1973-   . Carnegie Institute, Museum of Art, Pittsburgh, PA.

The Film Book Bibliography 1940-1975, by Jack C. Ellis, Charles Derry, and Sharon Kern. Metuchen, NJ: Scarecrow. 752 p., 1979. LC 78-4055, ISBN 0-8108-1127-8.

The Film Buff's Checklist of Motion Pictures. Edited by Richard D. Baer. Hollywood, CA: Hollywood Film Archive. 321 p., 1979. LC 79-14820, ISBN 0193616036.
The book is a simple, straight, alphabetical listing of over 19,000 films released from 1912 to 1979. Lead actors, film company, and release date are provided for each title. In addition to the major releases, the book also includes "B" films, documentaries, shorts, animated films, and some movies made for television.

Film Canada Yearbook. Annual, 1977-   . Address: 1430 Yonge St., Suite 214, Toronto, ONT. M4T 1Y6. Phone: (416) 922-5772. ISSN 0831-5175. Previous title: *Canadian Film Digest Yearbook* (1977-1985).
A complete review and analysis of the Canadian year in film. Good statistics for the industry, including figures for box office receipts, theaters and drive-ins, audience demographics, and other information. Provides directory information for Canadian film and television businesses, including studios, production companies, suppliers, and services.

Film Daily Year Book. Published annually from 1919 to 1970; no longer published. New York: Film Daily. Listed films from 1915 through 1970; gives cast and production credits.

Film Directors: a complete guide. Compiled and edited by Michael Singer. Annual, 1983- . Lone Eagle, 9903 Santa Monica Blvd., Beverly Hills, CA 90212. Phone: (213) 471-8066. ISSN 0740-2872. (8th annual international edition, 1990. 558 p. ISBN 0-943728-35-5.) ISSN 0740-2872.

Each annual includes several short biographical interviews with directors. The body of the volume is an alphabetical listing of directors. Each entry contains brief biographical information about the director, a listing of his/her works, and an address an/or agent where the director may be contacted. Indexed by director, film titles. There is a separate index of agents representing directors.

Film Directors Guide: Western Europe, by James R. Parish. Metuchen, NJ: Scarecrow. 292 p., illus., 1976. LC 76-1891, ISBN 0-8108-0908-7.

The Film Encyclopedia, by Ephraim Katz. Address: Crowell, New York, NY. 1979. 1266 p. LC 79-7089, ISBN 0-690-01204-7.

Biographical information covers people in all parts of the film industry. Arrangement is alphabetical by name; filmographies accompany some entries.

The Film Index: a bibliography. 3 vols. White Plains, NY: Kraus International. Volume 1: *The Film as Art* (ISBN 0-527-29329-6) was published in 1941 by H.W. Wilson and reprinted in 1985 by Kraus; Volume 2: *The Film as Industry* (1985, ISBN 0-527-29334-2); Volume 3: *The Film in Society* (1985, ISBN 0-527-29335-0). LC 87-35288, ISBN (set): 0-527-29326-1. Online: Wilsondisc.

Compiled in the 1930s by the Writers Program of the Work Projects Administration (WPA) of the City of New York, with the cooperation of the Museum of Modern Art (New York), each volume is an extensive bibliography of books and periodical articles covering the theme of the book. A good guide to historical literature.

Film Literature Index. Quarterly, 1973- . Annual cumulations. Film and Television Documentation Center. Address: Richardson 390, State University of New York, Albany, NY 12222. Phone: (518) 442-5745. LC 74-642396, ISSN 0093-6758.

Each issue is divided into two sections: (1) Film, and (2) Television/Video. The index covers film, television, and video subjects and performers from articles published in over 200 film periodicals worldwide. It also includes film reviews from non-industry periodicals whenever possible. Although there is some-times a serious time lag before material is included, it's the most extensive and comprehensive reference source of film information available. An in-house document delivery service will provide, for a fee, copies of any of the articles listed in the publication.

Film Producers, Studios, Agents and Casting Directors. Edited by Susan Avallone and Jack Lechner. Lone Eagle. 282p., 1990. ISBN: 0-943728-28-2.

Film Review Annual. Annual, 1981- . Jerome S. Ozer, Publisher, 340 Tenafly Rd., Englewood, NJ 07631. ISSN 0737-9080.
This annual publishes detailed reviews for films released during the year. Arrangement is alphabetically by film title, with a series of indexes. Reviews are reprinted in their entirety of full-length films released in major American markets from approximately twenty major newspapers and periodicals. Each citation includes selected reviews plus complete production credits for the film, including the MPAA rating. There are separate indexes for film critic, publications cited, cast, produc-ers, directors, screenwriters, cinematographers, film editors, music, and production crew. Each volume also lists major international film awards for the year; uniquely, the nominees are listed as well as the award winners.

Film Review Index. Edited by Patricia King Hanson and Stephen L. Hanson. Address: Oryx Press, Phoenix, AZ. 1986. Volume 1: *1882-1949* (397p., ISBN 0-89774-153-6; Volume 2: *1950-1985* (400 pp., ISBN 0-89774-331-8).
Not very comprehensive. The set cites film reviews from a variety of sources (periodicals and books) for approximately 6,000 American and a few foreign films. Indexed by film title, chronological (year of production), director, and country.

Film Superlist: 1894-1959, by Walter E. Hurst. Various volumes published and updated frequently. Publisher: Seven Arts Press,

6253 Hollywood Blvd., Suite 1100, Los Angeles, CA 90028. ISSN 0071-0695. Phone: (213) 469-7209.

This series of volumes lists approximately 50,000 motion pictures that are believed to be in the U. S. public domain either because the film's copyright has expired or is no longer valid. There are a number of important and popular titles on the list and the compilation makes for fascinating reading.

Film, Television, and Video Periodicals: a comprehensive annotated list, by Katharine Loughney. New York: Garland. 1991, 431 p. LC 90-14071. ISBN 0-8240-0647-X.

This is the newest and most authoritative listing of periodicals completed for many years, with information current through 1988. International in scope (with English and foreign-language titles), each citation includes current and past titles and publishing history, publisher's address and phone number, and OCLC and ISSN numbers. A descriptive annotation accompanies each entry.

Film-Video Canadiana; a guide to Canadian films and videos produced in [current year]. Biennial, 1969- . (Frequency has varied) Address: Moving Image and Sound Archives, Documentation and Public Service, 395 Wellington Street, Ottawa, Ontario, KIA 0N3 Canada. ISSN 0386-1002. Supersedes *Film Canadiana* (1972- .) and the Canadian Film Institute *Yearbook of Canadian Cinema* (published 1969-1980). Published in English and French.

The publication is a joint project of several major organizations and documents Canadian films made and/or released during the year. Production information, distributor, and synopsis is provided for each title.

Filmed Books and Plays: a list of books and plays from which films have been made, 1928-1986, by A.G.S. Enser. Lexington, MA: Lexington Books/Heath. 770 p., 1987. ISBN 0-566-03564-2. Previous editions were for the years 1928-1974 and 1975-1981. Originally published in London by Gower.

A listing of English-language films, with information about both the films and the books and plays from which they were adapted. An author index provides a list of films made from the writer's works. Especially helpful is a "change of original title" index which identifies titles of books that were changed for the film.

Filmmaker's Dictionary, by Ralph S. Singleton. Beverly Hills, CA: Lone Eagle Publishing. 188 p., 1986. LC 86-15303 ISBN 0-943728-08-8.

Concise, short entries for film industry terms. Covers legal, technical, literary, scriptwriting, acronyms for organizations, and business terms used throughout the industry.

The Focal Encyclopedia of Film and Television Techniques. Edited by Raymond Spottiswoode. New York: Hastings House. 1,100 p., 1969, 1981. LC 73-7135, ISBN 0240506545.

A major work in its time. So much has changed since its publication that it is largely outdated. However, it remains extremely useful for historical purposes and for general background information. Arranged alphabetically, it ranges from giving simple word definitions to longer articles on film procedures, theory, and various other subjects. Has some good illustrations that are useful to researchers.

Footage 89: North American Film and Video Sources. Edited by Richard Prelinger and Celeste R. Hoffnar. Publisher: Prelinger Associates, 430 West 14th St., Room 403, New York, NY 10014. Phone: (212) 633-2134. 795 p., 1989. LC 88-90769, ISBN 0-927347-01-6.

A major new research source which lists 1,600 film and video collections throughout North America. Both educational institutions and commercial firms are listed and a detailed synopsis is given of the contents of each collection. Special materials and unique collections are noted wherever possible. The book begins with a number of articles about how to do research in the field, how to do copyright research, an overview of the stock footage industry, and restoration techniques. In addition to listings about historical films, there is considerable information about newsreel footage as well as sources of film for television programs.

Forty Years of Screen Credits, 1929-1969. Compiled by John T. Weaver. Metuchen, NJ: Scarecrow Press. 1970. 2 vols. ISBN 0-8108-0299-6.

Arranged in alphabetical order by performer's name. The set includes both American and British actors and includes brief biographical information and, as completely as possible, film titles in which the subject appeared (listed in chronological order). An extensive work, it features regular players as well as stars.

Gaffers, Grips, and Best Boys, by Eric Taub. New York: St. Martin's Press. 200 p., 1987. LC 87-16364, ISBN 0312011504.
This is not a reference book, but rather a popularly-written book which explains what people do in specialized jobs throughout the film production process. It starts at the preproduction stage and goes through postproduction; along the way it clearly discusses what scriptwriters, stuntmen and women, technicians, editors, and many other people do on their jobs and how their work contributes to the final product. It's the kind of book writers and entertainment industry researchers can use to develop a quick understanding of how the industry works on the inside.

A Guide To American Film Directors: the sound era: 1929-1979, by Larry Langman. Metuchen, NJ: Scarecrow. 2 vols, 1981. LC 81-14536, ISBN: 0-8108-1467-6.

Guide to Critical Reviews, Part IV: The Screenplay. by James M. Salem. See: page 181.

A Guide to World Cinema: Covering 7,300 Films of 1950-84 including Capsule Reviews and Stills from the Programmes of the National Film Theatre, London. Edited by Elkan Allan. Published in London by Whittet Books; distributed in the United States by Gale (Detroit, MI). 682 p., 1985. ISBN 0-905483-33-2.
The work is actually a listing of films shown at the British Film Institute from 1950 through 1984. Its value to researchers is the detailed bibliographic record and plot summary supplied for each film and the fact that (from an American viewpoint) this is a significant source of foreign film information. The value is enhanced by the fact that both major and minor films are included without prejudice to coverage. Photos accompany many entries.

Halliwell's Film Guide, by Leslie Halliwell. New York: Scribner. 7th ed. 1,264 p., 1990. LC 89-45159. ISBN 0-06-016322-4.

An alphabetical listing of over 16,000 films. Each entry includes selected technical and cast credits, release date, and a brief plot synopsis.

Halliwell's Filmgoer's and Video Viewer's Companion, by Leslie Halliwell. New York: Scribner. 9th ed. 786 p., 1989. LC 88-29818, ISBN 0-684-19063-X. Paperback edition published by Harper & Row (1,000 p., 1990, LC 89-45916, ISBN 0-06-096392-1).

Similar in some ways to the *Guide,* but with information about films which are available on video. In addition to the alphabetical listing of films, this title includes entries for actors, some screenwriters, directors, producers, and other important film people.

Halliwell's Television Companion. See: page 511.

A Handbook For Film Archives II. Edited by Eileen Bowser and John Kulper. New York: Garland. 200 p., 1990. ISBN 0-8240-3533-X.

A basic manual for film archive management. Covers all aspects of setting up and running a library or archive, with sections on selection, cataloging, and preservation. Special attention is paid to handling films, photos, scripts, posters, and other special materials.

Hollywood Creative Directory. Address: 3000 Olympic Blvd., Suite 2413, Santa Monica, CA 90404. Phone: (213) 315-4815. This company publishes three directories for use by the Hollywood film and television industries. Each directory is an annual with three updates during the year. The *Hollywood Creative Directory* (LC 88-8914, ISSN 0897-7674) lists the names, phone numbers, key personnel, and production credits for film studios, television networks, independent producers, and cable channels. One section lists studio deals between studios and production companies or individuals. It also lists writers, directors, and actors. The *Hollywood Agents Directory* lists names, addresses, and phone numbers for both talent and literary agencies and independent agents. The *Hollywood Distributors Directory* lists business information for both American and foreign film and television programming distributors. In addition, it publishes two other useful directories: *Feature Writers, '80-'89; their credits & their agents* and *The Complete Reference Guide to Movies Made for TV and Miniseries: September 1, 1984 to July 1, 1989.*

Hollywood Reporter Studio Blu-Book Directory. Annual, 1978-   .
Address: The Hollywood Reporter, 6715 Sunset Blvd., Hollywood, CA 90028. ISSN 0278-419X.
   A comprehensive directory that covers all aspects of the film industry, from agents and contacts for performers, names and addresses of film associations and organizations, technical and specialized services, press and publications, and all service industries needed by the film industry for production support. Emphasis is on the West Coast, particularly the Los Angeles area. One section provides a complete list of award winners for over fifty major awards in film, television, music, and the theater; Canadian and British awards are also included. The complete Emmy division awards are given.

The Hollywood Who Done It. Irregular. Publisher's address: P. O. Box 206, Culver City, CA 90232-9870. Information for the 1990 edition: Volume 1: *Films* (614 p., 1990, ISBN 1-878499-01-7) and Volume 2: *Credits* (760 p., 1990, ISBN 1-878499-02-5).
   Each edition has complete film credits for approximately the last five years of film production. For example, the 1990 set has credits for over 1,800 films that were made from 1984 through 1989. Extensively cross-referenced by film title and major film categories (actors, directors, animal trainers, etc.).

The Holt Foreign Film Guide, Ronald Bergan and Robyn Karney. New York: Holt. 638 p., 1989. LC 88-45750, ISBN 0-8050-0991-4. Originally published in 1988 in England under the title *Bloomsbury Foreign Film Guide.*
   An alphabetical listing of films, with each entry giving the original release date, partial technical and cast credits, running time, and a brief plot synopsis. Awards are noted. The book contains a large number of British films as well as classics from

around the world. Films are listed under their British release titles and/or original foreign release titles, with a cross-reference to their American titles. Although this may be an inconvenience for the casual home viewer who uses the book to determine which old movie to watch on television, it is a decidedly valuable approach for the film researcher who needs to sort out multiple titles given to the same film as it was released in different countries. If you don't live near a large film library, this would be a useful reference book to purchase for your home library collection.

I.D.A. Directory. Annual, 1984-   . International Documentary Association. See: page 357.
   Membership includes all areas of film production. The entry for each member contains brief biographical information, filmography, address, and phone.

The Illustrated Directory of Film Stars, by David Quinlan. See: page 394.

The Illustrated Encyclopedia of Movie Character Actors, by David Quinlan. New York: Harmony Books/Crown. 325 p., 1986, 1985. LC 85-27126, ISBN 0517561719. Originally published in England under the title: *The Illustrated Directory of Film Character Actors.*
   The book is a collection of biographies, photos, and filmographies of respected British and American character actors. It profiles some actors who are difficult to find in other sources.

The Illustrated Guide to Film Directors, by David Quinlan. Totowa, NJ: Barnes & Noble. 335 p., 1983. LC 83-10572, ISBN 0-389-20408-0.
   Arrangement is alphabetical by the name of the director. Each entry includes some biographical information, a career review, and a filmography. A photo of the director or a film still from one of the director's films accompanies most profiles.

The Illustrated Who's Who of the Cinema. Edited by Ann Lloyd and Graham Fuller. New York: Macmillan. Updated edition, 480 p., 1987. LC 87-11701.

The *Guide* covers all areas of filmmaking and is useful for its coverage of earlier film people. Some filmographies.

Index to Critical Film Reviews in British and American Film Periodicals, by Stephen E. Bowles. New York: Burt Franklin, 1975. 3 vols. (in two bound volumes). LC 74-12109, ISBN 0-89102-040-3.

This publication indexes film reviews that appeared in 32 film magazines between 1932-1971. Also includes reviews of books about films.

Index to Motion Pictures Reviewed by Variety, 1907-1980, by Max Joseph Alvarez. Metuchen, NJ: Scarecrow Press. 510p., 1982. LC 81-23236, ISBN 0-8108-1514-X.

The book provides a concise alphabetical listing of all motion pictures indexed in *Variety* from 1907-1980. The date and page number of the *Variety* review follows the title. This quick index can also be used as a guide to the bound multivolume set of *Variety Film Reviews* (published by Garland).

The International Dictionary of Films and Filmmakers. Edited by Christopher Lyon and Susan Doll. Chicago: St. James. 5 vols. Volume 1: *Films* (2d ed., 1,300 p., 1990, ISBN 1-55862-037-0); Volume 2: *Directors/Filmmakers* (2d ed, 1,200 p., 1991, ISBN 1-55862-038-9); Volume 3 : *Actors & Actresses* (670 p., 1986, LC 83-24616, ISBN 0-912289-08-2); Volume 4: *Writers & Production Artists* (484 p., 1987, LC 83-24616, ISBN 0-912289-09-0); and Volume 5: *Title Index* (494 p., 1987, ISBN 0-912289-86-4).

Not a comprehensive index to films in general, but a critical evaluation of selected films. The volumes cover what are judged to be the most widely studied films and filmmakers from around the world. The *Films* volume includes production credits and an extensive bibliography for each title included as well as an extensive essay by a noted critic or scholar. Similarly, the other volumes provide a historical overview of each person's work and an essay on their accomplishments. Some personal biographical material is included.

International Directory of Cinematographers, Set, and Costume Designers in Film. Edited by Alfred Krautz; compiled by the

International Federation of Film Archives (FIAF). 10 vols.; H.G. Saur, 175 Fifth Ave., New York, NY 10010. Phone: (212) 982-1302. LC 82-162615,
The volumes produced so far cover film industry personnel in Europe and the East European countries in considerable detail. Each directory has a short biography and complete filmography for each person listed.

International Directory of Film and TV Documentation Centers. Edited by Frances Thorpe. Chicago and London: St. James Press. 3d ed. 140 p., 1988. LC 89-20268, ISBN 0912289295.
The book is a worldwide survey of what the editor considers to be the best film and television research collections; a listing of over 100 collections from forty countries. The entry for each facility includes address, phone, staff, a detailed description of the types of information in the center and any special collections that are available for use. In addition, each entry notes the availability of photocopy and/or commercial copying services and policies.

International Film and TV Yearbook. Annual, 1955- . London: King Publications. Previous title: *British Film and TV Yearbook* (1955-1976).
Covers the British film industry and people. An extensive directory of organizations associated with all aspects of the industry.

International Film Guide. See: *Variety International Film Guide,* pages 495-496.

The International Film Industry: a historical dictionary, by Anthony Slide. Greenwood, Westport, CT. 423 p., 1989. ISBN 0-313-25635-7, LC 88-25103.
Everything you might want to know about the international film industry briefly identified. Alphabetical arrangement covers countries, organizations, production companies, technical terms, film language, festivals and other meetings, awards, and periodicals and other literary publications.

International Film Necrology, by William T. Stewart, Arthur F. McClure, and Ken D. Jones. New York: Garland. 328 p., 1981. LC 80-17636, ISBN 0824095529.

A listing of over 11,000 people from all areas of the entertainment field and the dates of their birth and death. Place of birth and some limited professional information is also given.

International Film, Radio, and Television Journals, by Anthony Slide. Westport, CT: Greenwood Press. 428 p., 1985. LC 84-8929, ISBN: 0-313-23759-X. (Greenwood series: *Historical Guides to the World's Periodicals.* ISSN 0742-5538)

A comprehensive guide to popular and trade magazines for the fields of film, radio, and television. Each title is profiled in detail, with bibliographic documentation completed as far as possible. One unique feature is its inclusion of fan club journals. Arrangement is by entertainment field and title. Lists are also provided by subject and country of origin.

International Index to Film Periodicals. Annual, 1972- . International Federation of Film Archives (FIAF). Address: 113 Canalot Studios, 222 Kensal Rd., London W1O 5BN. Phone: 01-960 1001. American distributor: New York: R.R. Bowker, 1972, 1973. St. Martin's Press, 1974-1978. Distributed in the U.S. since 1979 by The American Film Institute. LC 72-1964, ISSN 0000-0388.

The service started out as a cooperative indexing venture between several major European film libraries through the sponsorship of FIAF. The original product was distributed via subscription for card sets. The one flaw in this series is that information presented is not current due to the infrequent publication schedule. Indexing is international in scope with an occasionally changing list of 75 to 80 film journals which have been selected from many countries. Not as extensive as the *Film Literature Index,* but enough differences exist to make this a worthwhile source too. Indexed by broad subject, film title, biography (individuals), and director.

International Index to Television Periodicals. See: pages 374-375.

International Motion Picture Almanac. Annual, 1929- . New York: Quigley Publishing, 159 West 53rd St., New York, NY 10019. Phone: (212) 247-3100. ISSN 0074-7084. Continues: *Motion*

Picture and Television Almanac. Available on microform, 1929-1986, from Brookhaven Press (LaCrosse, WI).

A major film industry reference book. Provides brief biographical information about important people in the industry (leaders as well as the stars). Also provides production credits and film reviews from the *Motion Picture Product Digest* for the past year. Publishes a commentary about the year in review with emphasis on problems, trends, and notable events. Canada, Great Britain, and Ireland are given separate attention and another section briefly covers the rest of the world market. A wide variety of supporting statistics are available for ticket grosses, attendance by age group, how the recreation dollar is spent by the average person. The all-time top 100 motion pictures are listed as are the top movies for the year covered. Complete lists of Academy Award winners for the year can be found in each volume, along with the major winners for previous years. The volume also provides directory information for suppliers of equipment and supplies; stock film libraries; film and television studios and production companies; organizations and associations which represent or deal with the industry; buying and booking agents; film festivals and fairs; awards and polls; and a list of independent theaters. It prints the complete text of Rules and Regulations of the Classification and Rating Administration, which forms the rationale for the rating of motion pictures. One interesting bit of unique information: there is a list of all drive-ins in the United States (in geographic order by state, city, and name/address of the drive-in).

Inventory of the Collections of the National Film, Television, and Sound Archives. Compiled under the direction of Jean T. Guenette and Jacques Gagne. Ottawa: Public Archives. 227 p., 1983. ISBN 0-662-12438-3.

A catalog of the major Canadian archive for film, television, and sound recordings.

Kemps International Film & TV Yearbook. Annual, 1956- . Address: The Kemps Group, 1-5 Bath St., London EC1V 9QA England. Phone: 01-253 4761. ISSN 8665-1563. Previous title: *Kemps Film and Television Directory.*

Major coverage focuses on the British film, television, and video industries and people. It supplies management names, addresses and phone numbers, and a description of services offered by each business listed: production companies, facilities, equipment suppliers, location services, and others associated with filmmaking. Recent volumes have increased international coverage. For more detail, see: BRITISH FILM REFERENCE SOURCES, page 494.

Landers Film Reviews. Quarterly, 1956-   . Annual index. Landers Associates, P.O. Box 27309, Escondido, CA 92027. LC 85-23709, ISSN 0023-785X. Previous title: *Bertha Landers Film Reviews* (LC 67-6334). Indexed in: MRD.

One of the older and most-used review sources for libraries and educational institutions. Reviews and rates films and other audiovisual materials. Provides source of supplier.

Leonard Maltin's TV Movies & Video Guide, by Leonard Maltin. Revised annually. New York: Signet.

If you own only one quick research tool listing films, this is it. Even though it's designed for television viewers who want a quick summary of a film, the information in the book is correct and the list exhaustive. It's an alphabetical listing of nearly 20,000 films likely to be shown on television or made available on video tape. Entries include title, major cast members, date of release, brief plot synopsis and a personal evaluation, and availability on video. Film researchers will need more information than this book provides, but it's a great way to get started on your research in the comfort of your home and the latest edition is available in any bookstore.

The Macmillan Film Bibliography: A Critical Guide to the Literature of the Motion Picture, by George Rehrauer. New York: Macmillan. 2 vols, 1982. Volume 1 is the bibliography; Volume 2 provides indexing by author, broad subjects, and scripts. LC 82-20870, ISBN 0-02-6964000-7.

An annotated bibliography of nearly 7,000 books on film. Coverage is international in scope; many annotations are descriptive and thorough. Indexes provided: author, subject (with film titles and some personal names), script index.

Magill's Cinema Annual. Annual, 1982-   . Salem Press, P.O. Box 50062, Pasadena, CA 91105. ISSN 0739-2141.

This annual supplements *Magill's Survey of Cinema* and provides signed critical reviews of films released in the United States for the previous year. Technical and cast credits are given along with the MPAA rating and the running time. Some films are fully reviewed while others are briefly noted. A brief bibliography of reviews from periodicals follows the main entry. Obituary and award sections are included along with several detailed indexes.

Magill's Survey of Cinema, edited by Frank N. Magill. Pasadena, CA: Salem Press. The title is an umbrella for a series of multivolume sets published over a period of years: The first series was published as *Magill's Survey of Cinema: English Language Films* (4 vols, 1980); the second series was published as the *Second Series* (6 vols., 1981). The third series was *Magill's Survey of Cinema: Silent Films* (3 vols., 1982). The latest in the series is *Magill's Survey of Cinema: Foreign Language Films* (8 vols., 1985).

Each set is arranged in alphabetical order by film title. Technical and cast credits are given for each film along with a plot summary and extensive reviews. Not a comprehensive tool. International in coverage, the series provides long reviews and evaluations of each film in addition to production credits. Extensive indexing.

Media Review Digest. Annual, 1970-   . Semiannual supplements. Ann Arbor, MI: Pierian Press. LC 73-172772. ISSN 0363-7778. Previous title: *Multi-Media Reviews Index.*

Arrangement is by film or media title. Reviews and evaluates non-book media (audio, video, films and filmstrips) in over 140 periodicals and reviewing services. For users from educational institutions and libraries. Indexes provided: general subject, producer and distributor index which includes addresses (no phones).

Motion Picture Almanac. See: *International Motion Picture Almanac.*

The Motion Picture Annual. Annual, 1986- . Address: Cinebooks, P.O. Box 1407, 990 Grove St., Evanston, IL 60204. Phone: (312) 475-8400. LC 88-640845, ISBN 0-933997-17-5.
Includes a listing, with production credits and synopsis, of American films released for the year. Also includes major film awards and obituaries of film personnel who died during the year.

Motion Picture Directors: A Bibliography of Magazine and Periodical Articles, 1900-1972, by Mel Schuster. Metuchen, NJ: Scarecrow. 418 pp., 1973. LC 73-780, ISBN 0-818-0590-1.
Arranged alphabetically by name of director. Includes film and television.

The Motion Picture Guide, by Jay Robert Nash and Stanley Ralph Ross. Address: Cinebooks, Chicago, IL. (Distributed by R.R. Bowker) 1985, 12 volumes plus annual yearbooks. ISBN 0-933997-00-0, LC 85-071145. Annual supplement titled: *The Motion Picture Guide Annual.*
Volumes 1-9: film titles in alphabetical order up through 1984. Volume 9 includes a separate section for films released in 1984. Volume 10: silent films. Index in additional two volumes: artist name index, alternate title index, series index, and an awards index. Annual volumes include profiles on newcomers and obituaries of people who died during the past year. Covers English-language theatrical films produced from 1927 to 1984 as well as major silent films and some foreign films. It does not include made-for-television films, documentaries, or serials. Information provided for each film includes year of release, cast and roles played, production credits, production and distribution companies, original running time, critical ratings, cast and credits, a plot summary, and occasionally some background information about the making of the film. Index by performer, production personnel, and awards.

Motion Picture Performers: A Bibliography of Magazine and Periodical Articles, 1900-1969, by Mel Schuster. Metuchen, NJ:

Scarecrow. 702 p., 1971. LC 70-154300, ISBN 0-8108-0407-7.
Supplement 1: (1970-1974, 783 pp., 1976; ISBN 0-8108-0879-X).
  One of the best places to start your research about an American
  or British actor. The volumes are arranged alphabetically by
  name, followed by a list of articles about that person. Journal
  articles were selected from an international list of industry and
  popular periodicals.

*Motion Picture, TV & Theatre Directory: for Services and Prod-
ucts.* Semiannual, 1960-   . Address: Motion Picture Enterprises
Publications, Box 276, Tarrytown, NY 10591. Phone: (212)
245-0969. LC 87-648216, ISSN 0580-0412.
  Directory of companies in the New York area involved with
  film, television, stage and video production. Includes agents,
  equipment rental, costumers, specialty stores, and other industry services.

*Motion Pictures: A Catalog of Books, Periodicals, Screenplays,
Television Scripts, and Production Stills,* by University of California, Los Angeles (UCLA). Theater Arts Library. 2d rev. ed.
Boston, MA: G.K. Hall. 775 p., 1976.
  A listing of the cards from the catalog of this major film library.
  The collection is divided into five sections: (1) author listing
  (personal, corporate title), periodicals, personal papers and gift
  collections, and archive materials; (2) published scripts; (3)
  unpublished scripts; (4) television scripts and other information;
  (5) stills, photos, posters, pressbooks, and other memorabilia.
  See Also: FILM LIBRARIES.

*Motion Pictures, Television, and Radio: A Union Catalogue of
Manuscript and Special Collections in the Western United States,* by
Linda Mehr. See: pages 129, 144.

Movie Comedians: the Complete Guide, by James L. Neibar.
Jefferson, NC: McFarland. 255 p., illus., 1986. LC 84-43204, ISBN
0-89950-163-X.
  An alphabetical listing by name of the comedian, with brief
  biographical information and extensive filmographies.

The Movie List Book: a Reference Guide to Film Themes, Settings, and Series, by Richard B. Armstrong and Mary Willems Armstrong. Jefferson, NC: McFarland. 400 p., 1990. LC 89-43692, ISBN 0-89950-240-7.

This book lists movie titles by a broad range of approximately 450 subjects, themes, geographical or physical settings, and well known characters. If you want to know what films had librarians or bounty hunters in them, this is the book to use.

Moving Pictures: an annotated guide to selected film literature, with suggestions for the study of film, by Eileen Sheahan. New York: A.S. Barnes. 146 p., 1979. LC 78-55576, ISBN 0-498-02296-X.

The book is designed for academic study at the college level and organizes film literature by type of publication (indexes, encyclopedias, periodicals, etc.) as well as archives and museums, organizations, festivals, and some awards. Although the directory information is beginning to be outdated by now, the book is still useful for the published reference materials it annotates.

National Union Catalog. Audiovisual Materials. Washington, D.C.: Library of Congress. Quarterly, 1953- . Previous titles: *Library of Congress Catalog. Motion Pictures and Filmstrips,* and *Audiovisual Materials & Films and Other Materials for Projection.*

This is the quarterly publication which identifies all audio visual materials added to the Library of Congress collection for the previous quarter. Extremely valuable because it includes many titles that are never listed in commercial review publications.

The New Film Index: a bibliography of magazine articles in English, 1930-1970, by Richard D. MacCann and Edward S. Perry. New York: Dutton. 1975. 522 pp.

Bibliography of articles indexed from 35 film and popular magazines, with additional citations from other sources. Brief annotations arranged in broad categories by film type. Indexing mostly by director. Difficult to use if you are looking for specific and/or detailed subjects.

The New York Times Encyclopedia of Film, 1896-1979. Edited by Gene Brown. 13 vols., 1984. Originally published by the New York

Times, the set is currently published and distributed by Garland
(New York). LC 81-3607, ISBN (set): 0-8129-1059-1.

The set excludes film reviews (available in *The New York Times
Film Reviews*) and obituaries (available in *The New York Times
Biographical Service*), but otherwise reproduces in chronological order all writings relating to films that have been published in
the *New York Times* from 1896 through 1979. Coverage includes
news articles, historical pieces, interviews with celebrities, and
financial reports. Volumes are chronological in order, with the
last one being the index volume for names and subjects. It's an
extremely valuable reference source that is sometimes difficult
to use if you don't already know the date of the information you
need. The indexing lacks detail; it's limited to film title, selected
important names, and broad subject areas. Only the names of
the lead players of the film are indexed. Similarly, only the
person who is the main subject of the article is indexed even
though others may be mentioned. You will be able to find
performers from other fields of entertainment if they appeared
in films. And although the reproductions of articles, photos, and
advertisements for film openings or in-person appearances are
occasionally of uneven quality, if you need a specific *New York
Times* article it is far easier to come to this set to read it than it
would be to use film or fiche. All in all, it's a wonderful source of
information, particularly offering a unique historical perspective
on the early film stars and the development of the industry.

The New York Times Film Reviews. Ongoing set, with volumes
1-18 reproducing reviews from 1913 to 1988. Biennial, with
additional volumes in progress. Originally published by the New
York Times, the set is currently being published and distributed by
Garland (New York). ISSN 0362-3688.

The series provides complete reproductions of original film
reviews from the *New York Times*. Reviews are arranged
chronologically. The set is indexed by film title, names of cast
and major production personnel, and film company. As with the
other *New York Times* sets, the chronological arrangement
makes it difficult to use if you do not already know the date of
the information you need, but it's still a valuable source of
reviews. It's also another place to start when trying to compile a
list of films of a particular performer.

NICEM Film & Video Finder. See: *Film & Video Finder,* pages 372-373.

NICEM Index to Producers and Distributors. Annual, 1971- . See: *AV Producers and Distributors,* BROADCAST REFERENCE RESOURCES.

NICEM Index to 16mm Educational Films. See: *Film and Video Finder,* pages 372-373.

On Location Directory: the national film and videotape production directory. Annual, 1977- . On Location Publishing, 6777 Hollywood Blvd., Suite 501, Hollywood, CA 90028. Phone: (213) 467-1268. LC 79-644140, ISSN 0740-1159. Title varies.
 National directory of production facilities, services and suppliers, and other businesses in the film and video industry. Organized geographically by state and city. Also includes local and national licensing commissions, a geographical breakdown of available film locations, and other information useful for planning on-location filming.

On the Screen; a film, television, and video research guide, by Kim N. Fisher. Littleton, CO: Libraries Unlimited. 209 p., 1986. LC 86-20965, ISBN 0-87287-448-6.
 The book lists reference sources, data bases, and research centers for the film and television industries. Detailed and well-written annotations accompany each entry.

The Oxford Companion to Film. Edited by Liz-Anne Bawden. New York: Oxford University Press. 767 p., 1976. LC 76-1463, ISBN 0192115413.
 This one-volume work covers a wide range of topics from production techniques to important people in the business. Long entries for film styles, theory, history, genres, and other major subjects. A good, quick source of film history.

Pacific Coast Studio Directory. Quarterly, 1920- . Address: 6313 Yucca St., Hollywood, CA 90028. Phone: (213) 467-2920. LC 81-3335, ISSN 0731-2059.

A frequently updated directory of support businesses and organizations needed for film and television production on the West Coast. Lists suppliers for everything from equipment to animals.

Player's Guide: the annual pictorial directory for stage, screen, radio, and television. Annual, 1944-   . New York: Player's Guide. See: Chapter 6, page 189.

The Producer's Masterguide: the international production manual for motion pictures, television, commercials, cable, and video tape industries in the United States, Canada, and the United Kingdom. Annual, 1979-   . Address: New York Production Manual, Inc., 330 W. 42nd St., 16th Floor, New York, NY 10109-0753. Phone: (212) 465-8889. ISSN 0732-6653, ISBN 0-935744-04-5, LC 83-641703. Previous title: *New York Production Manual.*
Production information of interest to producers. Includes local production information by state (U.S.), by territory (Canada), and for England. Information includes location sites, local permit procedures and regulatory authorities, and businesses which can provide support services. It also has an overview of the film rating system and gives guidelines and procedures for applying for a rating. Copyright registration procedures are provided. Also includes local union information. Has a chapter on awards: Oscars, Golden Palm, Emmies, CLIOs.

Reel Facts: the movie book of records, by Ken Schessler. Updated edition. New York: Vintage. 477 p., 1982.
Broken into sections by subject, the book presents lists of facts about the film industry. It includes financial information and production statistics, market statistics, as well as popular information about stars and awards. The "best" and "worst" in many categories.

Reminder List of Eligible Releases. Annual, 1927-   . Beverly Hills, CA: Academy of Motion Picture Arts and Sciences.
Yearly official list of films eligible for consideration for the Oscar awards.

Retrospective Index to Film Periodicals, 1930-1971, by Linda Batty. New York: R.R. Bowker. 1975. LC 74-34246, ISBN 0-8352-0660-2.

An index to fourteen film periodicals during the time period noted. Indexes provided: film title, subject, and book review citations (by author). The work is another source that helps fill a gap in the indexing of historical film literature.

NewsBank. *Review of the Arts: Film and Television.* See: Chapter 5, pages 129-130.

Science Fiction, Horror & Fantasy Film and Television Credits, by Harris M. Lentz. See: page 380.

Screen International Film and T.V. Yearbook. Annual, 1945-   . London: King Publications. Previous titles: *International Film and T.V. Yearbook,* and *British Film and T.V. Yearbook.* See: pages 380-381.

Screen World. Annual, 1949-   . Address: Crown, 225 Park Avenue South, New York, NY 10003. Phone: (212) 254-1600. Alternate title: *John Willis' Screen World.* LC 50-3023, ISBN (for 1988 volume): 0-517-56963-9.
   Annual listing of films released during the previous year in the United States, both domestic and foreign. Includes photos. Some biographical information on selected performers; obituaries for the past year. Name and title indexes.

Selected Film Criticism. Edited by Anthony Slide. Metuchen, NJ: Scarecrow Press. 7 vols., 1982-1985. LC 81-23344.
   Six volumes reproduce film reviews from a number of sources and cover the years 1896-1960; the seventh volume covers foreign films from 1930 to 1950. The original film reviews are completely reprinted as published, and therefore provide a valuable insight into historical film literature.

Star Guide: how to reach movie, TV stars and other celebrities. Annual, 1984-   . Ann Arbor, MI: Axiom Information Services. Previous title: *Celebrity Directory.*
   A rather broad list of personalities in many fields. Many addresses are for the representatives of the people listed.

Studio Blu-Book Directory. See: *Hollywood Reporter Studio Blu-Book Directory.*

Title Guide to the Talkies: a comprehensive listing of 16,000 feature-length films from October, 1927, until December, 1963, by Richard Bertrand Dimmitt. Metuchen, NJ: Scarecrow. 2 vols., 1965.
The purpose of this work is to identify the literary source from which the film was developed. Films are listed alphabetically with reference to the original work and author. Useful in identifying which films are derived from novels, biographies, plays, and other works. It's also useful as a quick source of screenwriter credits.

A Title Guide to the Talkies, 1964 through 1974, by Andrew Aros. (344 p., 1977; LC 76-40451, ISBN: 0-8108-0976-1). *A Title Guide to the Talkies, 1975 through 1984.* (355 p., 1986; LC 85-27682, ISBN: 0-8108-1868-X). Metuchen, NJ: Scarecrow.
Both of these titles update the original Dimmitt work and expand it by including more foreign films and by adding books and/or novels that have been derived from the films themselves. See also the companion set, *An Actor Guide To the Talkies.*

Union List of Film Periodicals: holdings of selected American collections. Compiled and edited by Anna Brady. Address: Westport, CT: Greenwood Press. 316 p., 1984. ISBN 0-313-23702-6, LC 83-22585.
Information for the periodical holdings of 35 American libraries goes up through 1981. The book provides a listing of approximately 1600 film periodicals by title and gives a publishing history for each one (date of first issue, title changes, ISSN numbers, country of issue). A geographical breakdown, giving titles by country, is also presented. Participating libraries and their holdings are identified for each title. Excellent source for locating out-of-print and/or minor film journals. Useful for Interlibrary loan programs. A directory of the participating libraries includes an address for each one.

Variety Film Reviews, 1907-1984. New York: Garland. 19 vols., 1983-1986. Volume 16 the index to v.1-15; v.18 indexes v.17-18; v. 19 indexes 1985-1986. ISSN 0897-4373.

This is a complete set of all film reviews published in *Variety* from 1907 to 1986. The reviews are not photo reproductions of the originals (as are the *New York Times* reviews), but new typeset true-text copies of the originals. The set is arranged in chronological order, following the same format as the *New York Times* series. Only full length feature film reviews are included although short films also appeared until 1927. No made-for television movies or other television programming is included. Indexing is by film title.

Variety International Film Guide. Annual, 1964-   . London: Andre Deutsch; U.S. Distributor: Hollywood: Samuel French. ISSN 0074-6053, See: pages 495-496.

Variety International Show Business Reference. Edited by Mike Kaplan. New York: Garland Publishing, 1981. 1,135 p. See: page 134.

Variety Obits: An Index to Obituaries in Variety, 1905-1978, by Jeb H. Perry. Metuchen, NJ: Scarecrow Press. 311 p., 1980. ISBN 0-8108-1289-4, LC 80-10424.
   A concise alphabetical list of names of show business professionals from all areas of entertainment whose obituaries appeared in *Variety*. Each entry includes: name, age, date of death, principal profession, and date of *Variety* publication.

Variety Obituaries, 1905-1988. Edited by Chuck Bartelt and Barbara Bergeron. Garland Publishing, 136 Madison Ave., New York, NY 10016. 12 vols., 1989. LC 87-25931.
   The set reprints all *Variety* obituaries through 1988 (over 90,000) in chronological order by their publication date in *Variety,* in 10 volumes (1905-1986); volume 11 is an alphabetical index to the original set and volume 12 updates the set through 1988. The entries do not necessarily provide a complete review of a performer's career. Includes obituaries for all fields of entertainment.

Variety Presents: the Complete Book of Major U.S. Show Business Awards. Edited by Mike Kaplan. New York: Garland Publishing, 564 p., 1985. LC 84-18734, ISBN 0-8240-8730-5.

The book lists the nominees and award winners for Oscars, Tonys, Emmys and Grammys. Organized in body of work by award, indexed by name and title.

Variety Source Book 1: Broadcast-Video. See page 389.

Variety TV Reviews. See: page 390.

Variety Who's Who in Show Business. 3d ed. Edited by Mike Kaplan. New York: R.R. Bowker. 412 p., 1989. LC 85-20578, ISBN 0835226654.
Over 6,500 biographies of artists and film industry personnel.

Variety's Complete Home Video Directory. See: *Bowker's Complete Video Directory,* page 366.

Who Was Who On Screen, by Evelyn M. Truitt. New York: R.R. Bowker, 3d ed. 788 p., 1983. ISBN 0-8352-1578-4.
Provides about 13,000 brief entries for film performers who died between 1905 and 1982. Coverage is worldwide, although emphasis is on American, British, French, and German actors and actresses. A valuable source of information about bit players as well as major stars. No television personalities are included unless they also appeared in films. Extensive filmographies are also provided for each entry. This is especially useful for the lesser known artists.

Who's Who in Canadian Film and Television. Irregular, 1985- .
Address: Academy of Canadian Cinema & Television. 653 Yonge St., 2nd Floor, Toronto, Canada M4Y 1Z9. Phone: (416) 967-0315. LC 86-30678, ISSN 0831-6309.
Includes actors, directors, producers, and other industry notables. Some bibliographies and filmographies.

Who's Who in the Motion Picture Industry. Annual, 1981- .
Address: Packard Publishing, P.O. Box 10372, Beverly Hills, CA. LC 81-645741, ISSN 0278-6516. See Also: *Who's Who in Television,* Chapter 9.

Includes names from all areas of the film industry. Includes TV and cable personnel. Gives credits and business addresses. Emphasis is on California.

A Who's Who of Australian and New Zealand Film Actors: The Sound Era, by Scott Palmer. Metuchen, NJ: Scarecrow. 171 p., 1988. LC 87-32215, ISBN 0-8108-2090-0.
The book includes both major and minor actors in both countries and provides brief biographies and filmographies.

A Who's Who of British Film Actors, by Scott Palmer. Metuchen, NJ: Scarecrow. 561 p., illus., 1981. LC 80-26016, ISBN 0-8108-1388-2.
Arranged alphabetically by name of actor, the book provides a comprehensive listing of actors and their film credits (titles and years of release).

The World Almanac Who's Who of Film. Edited by Thomas G. Aylesworth and John S. Bowman. New York: World Almanac/Pharos Books. 448 p., 1987. LC 87-50075, ISBN 0-88687-308-8.
Brief biographies and selected film titles of major film stars. Some photographs. Not much depth, but useful for birth and death dates, and a quick check.

World Film Directors. Bronx, NY: H.W. Wilson. 2 vols., illustrated. Volume 1: *1890-1945* (1,247 p., 1987, LC 87-29569, ISBN 0-8242-0757-2); Volume 2: *1945-1985* (1,205 p., 1988, LC 87-29560, ISBN 0-8242-0763-7).
Comprehensive articles about the careers of each of the 419 selected directors include a detailed biography, filmography, and lengthy bibliography.

FILM PERIODICALS

Access. Biweekly, 1974-   . National Citizens Committee for Broadcasting. Address: P.O. Box 12038, Washington, D.C. 20005. ISSN: 0149-9262.

An organization concerned with access to television programming by all segments of American society, particularly minority groups. Their magazine reports on current issues of interest and legislative and regulatory actions relating to their goals.

American Cinematographer. Monthly, 1920- . ASC Holding Company. American Society of Cinematographers Corporation. Address: 1782 N. Orange Dr., Hollywood, CA 90028. Phone: (213) 876-5080. ISSN 0002-7928.
Emphasis on the technical and production end of film. Articles about the making of films, interviews, evaluation of new equipment, book reviews. Available on microfilm from University Microfilms. Indexed in: BI, FLI, IIFP, IITP, ICFR, and Chemical Abstracts.

American Classic Screen. Bimonthly, 1976-1984. No longer published. Shawnee Mission, KS: American Classic Screen (National Film Society). ISSN 0195- 8267. If you can find the back issues this is an excellent source for film history. Indexed in Film Literature Index.

American Film: magazine of film, video, and television arts. Monthly, 1975-1991. (Available by subscription or membership in The American Film Institute). Published by Billboard Publications. Editorial office: 6671 Sunset Blvd., Suite 1520, Hollywood, CA 90028. Phone: (213) 856-5350. Subscription address: P.O. Box 2046, Marion, OH 43305. Phone: (800) 347-6969. ISSN 0361-4751. Previous title: *A F I News.* Back issues available from UMI. Indexed in: BI, FLI, IIFP, IITP, and MRD.
Provides current coverage about both American and foreign films. Interviews film producers and directors as well as performers. Includes some coverage of television and video. Reviews new theater releases, videos, and literature of interest to the industry. The magazine's want-ads section covers everything from scripts to memorabilia.

Animation. Quarterly, 1987- . Address: Animation Magazine, P.O. Box 25547, Los Angeles, CA 90025. ISSN 1041-617X.
A new magazine which covers the field of animation and includes news, interviews, technical developments, in-depth

stories and special projects. Articles are illustrated with examples of the films or projects discussed.

Back Stage. See: THEATER PERIODICALS, Chapter 6.

The Big Reel. Monthly, 1973- . Address: Empire Publishing Company, R.R. 3, Box 83, Madison, NC 27025. Phone: (919) 427-5850. ISSN 0744-723X.
For the film collector. The largest part of each issue consists of lists of films for sale from private collectors. Some foreign films, television shows, and videos are also listed. Sales lists include memorabilia such as posters, lobby cards, photos, periodical issues, and autographs. Short articles and a few book reviews. Heavy emphasis on 16mm and 35m films; lots of westerns. Information on film festivals and meetings geared to collectors.

Billboard. See: MUSIC PERIODICALS.

Boxoffice. Weekly, 1932- . Address: RLD Communications, 203 N. Wabash Ave., Suite 800, Chicago, IL 60601. Phone: (312) 922-9326. Editorial offices: 1800 N. Highland Ave., Suite 710, Hollywood, CA 90028-4526. ISSN 0006-8527. Indexed in: FLI.
Detailed box office ticket sale reports and other financial information and statistics from throughout the United States for movie theaters and other venues. National and regional sections. Also contains articles of interest to theater owners about equipment, technology, and services for use in theaters. Reviews new film releases. The magazine also publishes an annual buyer's directory.

Business and Home TV Screen. See: *Back Stage.*

CTVD: Cinema TV Digest; a quarterly review of the serious foreign-language cinema-TV press. Irregular, 1962- . Newberry, SC: Hampton Books. ISSN 0007-9219.

Cineaste. Quarterly, 1967- . Cineaste Publishers. Subscription address: P.O. Box 2242, New York, NY 10009. Phone: (212) 982-1241. ISSN 0009-7004. Available on microfilm from UMI.

Indexed in: FLI, FRA, ICFR, IIFP, MRD, Alternative Press Index, and Sociological Abstracts.

Provides good coverage of independent filmmakers, both foreign and domestic. Each issue includes articles about the making of particular films, interviews (with performers, directors, screenwriters, or others in the industry), book and film reviews, and news of interest.

Cinefantastique. 5 issues yearly, 1970- . Address: Cinefantastique, P.O. Box 270, Oak Park, IL 60303. Phone: (312) 366-5566. ISSN 0145-6032. Indexed in: FLI, MRD.

Fantasy and science fiction magazine for film and television shows. Extensive coverage of the skill and techniques used to create special effects. Reviews new releases and some literature.

Cinema Canada. Monthly, 1967- . Address: Cinema Canada, P.O. Box 398, Outremont Station, Montreal, Canada H2V 4N3. Phone: (514) 272-5354. ISSN 0009-7071. Previous titles: *Canadian Cinematography.* Incorporated *Cinemag,* and *Cinema Canada Trade News North.* Indexed in: FLI, IIFP, and MRD.

Covers Canadian film and television industries. Articles on current productions and interviews with popular performers and directors/producers. Reviews latest film releases and television shows.

Cinema Journal. Quarterly, 1961- . University of Illinois Press, 54 East Gregory Dr., Champaign, IL 61820. ISSN 0009-7101. Previous title: *Society of Cinematologists Journal.* Indexed in: FLI, ICFR.

Literary and scholarly approach to film for those who teach it. Articles cover a broad range of subjects, including film history, book and film reviews, methods and technology, information about upcoming conferences, workshops, and sources of financial support (educational grants, etc.). Indexed in: Art and Humanities Citation Index, Film Literature Index, International Index to Film Periodicals.

Cinemascore; the film music journal. Semiannual, 1979- . Fandom Unlimited Enterprises, Box 70868, Sunnyvale, CA 94086. Phone: (415) 960-1151. ISSN 0277-9803. Indexed in: FLI.

Classic Images. Monthly, 1962- . Muscatine Journal, 301 East 3rd St., Muscatine, IA 52761. Phone (319) 263-2331. ISSN 0164-5560. Previous titles: *Classic Film/Video Images, Classic Film Collector, Eight MM Collector.* Phone: (319) 263-2331. Indexed in FLI, MRD.

Aimed toward the film historian, collector, and film buff. Articles cover film history, careers of performers, and overviews of film genres. Filmographies are published in each issue. Advertisements for all types of film memorabilia and lists of films for sale. Indexed in *Film Literature Index;* back volumes available on microfilm from UMI. Articles available through their document delivery service.

Critic. Bimonthly, 1955- . Address: American Federation of Film Societies, 144 Bleecker St., New York, NY 10012. ISSN 0090-9831. Previous titles: *Film Society Newsletter* and *Film Society Review.*

Geared toward those interested in the impact film and television have on society and social issues and vice versa. Reviews latest releases and literature.

Daily Variety. Weekdays, 1933- . Address: Daily Variety, 1400 N. Cahuenga Blvd., Hollywood, CA 90028. Phone: 469-1144. ISSN 0011-5509.

The daily newspaper of the film industry. Special annual index issue for their film reviews "Daily Variety Film Reviews, October-September" published in October of each year. Also reviews television shows, theater/stage plays, and other live on-stage performances.

Emmy. Bimonthly, 1979- . Academy of Television Arts and Sciences. See: page 395.

Film. Monthly, 1954- . London: British Federation of Film Societies. See: page 497.

Film & History. Quarterly, 1971- . Historians Film Committee. Address: The History Faculty, New Jersey Institute of Technology, Newark, NJ 07102. ISSN 0360-3695. Supersedes *Historians Film Committee Newsletter.* Indexed in: IFP, FLI.

Periodical covering the use of history in films (both fictional drama and documentaries). Emphasis on both academic history and film studies. Reviews current releases and relevant literature.

Film Bulletin: America's independent motion picture journal. Biweekly, 1933- . Address: Wax Publications, 1239 Vine St., Philadelphia, PA 19107. Phone: (215) 568-0950. ISSN 0015-1165. Indexed in: FLI.

A trade journal for industry personnel interested in release dates for new productions, booking information for theater operations, current events, financial news, company activities, and boxoffice forecasts.

Film Comment. Bimonthly, 1962- . Address: Film Society of Lincoln Center, 140 West 65th St., New York, NY 10023. ISSN 0015-119X. Previous title: *Vision; a journal of film comment.* Available on microfilm from UMI. Document delivery from UMI, ISI. Indexed: BI, FLI, ICFR, IIFP, IITP, MRD, Readers' Guide, Humanities Index, Arts & Humanities Citation Index.

Covers both American and foreign films, some television. Interviews performers and influential industry personnel, offers critical reviews of new releases, and special articles on film theory.

Film Culture. Irregular, 1955- . Address: Film Culture, GPO Box 1499, New York, NY 10001. ISSN 0015-1211. Indexed in: FLI, ICFR, IIFP.

A "new ideas" magazine for people interested in independent filmmaking. Promotes new performers and directors, concepts, and technical techniques.

Film History. Quarterly, 1987- . Address: American Museum of the Moving Image, 34-12 36th St., Astoria, NY 11106. ISSN 0892-2160.

As the title indicates, the magazine is interested in the historical development of the film industry, both here and abroad. Emphasis is on scholarly research and use of film libraries and archive facilities.

Film Journal. Monthly, 1937-   . Address: Pubsun Corporation, 244 West 49th St., Suite 305, New York, NY 10019. Phone: (212) 246-6460. ISSN 0199-7300. Previous title: *Independent Film Journal.* Indexed in: FLI, ICFR.

Emphasis on new film releases from mainstream film studios. Covers business topics of the industry and includes articles/ interviews of interest to industry personnel. Includes a regular "Buying and Booking Guide" and an annual "Distribution Guide." Includes frequent cumulative indexes.

Film Library Quarterly (1967-1984). See: *Sightlines.*

Film Literature Index. See: pages 302-303.

Film Literature Quarterly. Quarterly, 1973-   . Salisbury, MD: Salisbury State University. See: *Literature/Film Quarterly.*

Film News International. Monthly, 1982-   . Address: V.P.A., 1800 Avenue of the Stars, Los Angeles, CA 90067. Phone: (213) 552-5315. ISSN 0741-0492.

Industry newsletter for film, television, video, and cable business news and activities. Also includes information about equipment and services.

Film Quarterly. Quarterly, 1945 -   . Address: University of California Press, Berkeley, CA 94720. Previous titles: *Hollywood Quarterly,* and *Quarterly of Film, Radio, & Television.* ISSN 0015-1386. Available on microfilm from UMI. Indexed in: BI, FLI, FRA, ICFR, IIFP, IITP, MRD, Humanities Index, Readers' Guide, Art Index, Book Review Index.

Scholarly and/or educational approach to articles, interviews, and reviews (film and book). Includes reviews, interviews, and articles about mainstream and special types of films.

Film Review Digest. See: *Sightlines.*

Filmfacts. UCLA, Los Angeles, CA. Semimonthly from 1958 to 1977. No longer published. ISSN 0015-153X. Indexed in: ICFR.

Excellent source for older film reviews. Compiled reviews from about a dozen of the major film periodicals.

Films and Filming. Monthly, 1954- . See: BRITISH FILM PERIODICALS, page 497.

Films in Review. Monthly, 1950- . Address: National Board of Review of Motion Pictures, P.O. Box 589, Lenox Hill Station, New York, NY 10021. Phone: (212) 628-1594. ISSN 0015-1688. Previous titles: *National Board of Review Magazine* (1926-1944) and *New Movies: The National Board of Review Magazine* (1945-1949). Indexed in: Art Index, BI, FLI, FRA, ICFR, IIFP, IITP, MRD.
Contains articles on films and filmmaking, filmographies of performers, reviews of films, television movies, and books. Has regular features on film music. Some information on collecting.

Graffiti. See: FILM ORGANIZATIONS (International Animated Film Society), page 357.

Historical Journal of Film, Radio, and Television. See: BRITISH FILM PERIODICALS.

Hollywood Acting Coaches and Teachers Directory. Quarterly, 1984- . Address: Acting World Books, Box 3044, Hollywood, CA 90078. Phone: (213) 466-4297.
Directory of acting courses, teachers, and other information about the study of acting in the Los Angeles area.

The Hollywood Reporter. Daily (Monday through Friday), 1930- . Address: The Hollywood Reporter, Inc., 6715 Sunset Blvd., Hollywood, CA 90028. Phone: (213) 464-7411. In New York: 1501 Broadway, New York, NY 10036. Phone: (212) 354-1858. ISSN 0018-3660.
A trade newspaper covering all aspects of the film and television industries. Includes financial news, ratings, box office standings, personnel changes, current and future productions, and legal matters. It also publishes special theme issues such as their annual special on film and television music.

Hollywood Studio Magazine. See: COLLECTING.

Hollywood Stuntmen's Hall of Fame News. Bimonthly, 1978- .
Moab, UT: Hollywood Stuntmen's Hall of Fame, Inc. Previous
title: *Falling for Stars News.*

Image. See: FILM LIBRARIES (International Museum of Photography at George Eastman House).

In Motion. Monthly, 1982- . Address: 421 Fourth St., Annapolis,
MD 21403. Phone: (301) 269-0605. ISSN 0889-6208.
   Production news, tips, and the latest techniques for film, video,
   and media personnel. Geared toward the MidAtlantic region,
   but articles would be useful to any filmmaker.

The Independent; film and video monthly. Monthly, 1976- .
Association of Independent Video and Filmakers/Foundation for
Independent Video and Film. Address: Foundation for Independent Video and Film, 625 Broadway, 9th Floor, New York, NY
10012. Phone: (212) 473-3400. ISSN 0731-5198. Previous title:
Association of Independent Video and Filmmakers Newsletter.
Indexed in: FLI, Alternative Press Index.
   Published for the independent filmmaker and makers of non-
   fiction film and television programming. Includes news, services, directory information as well as articles about the latest
   trends and productions.

Journal of Film and Video. Quarterly, 1949- . University Film
and Video Association, Rosary College, 79 East Division St.,
River Forest, IL 60305. ISSN 0742-4671. Previous titles: *Journal of
the University Film Producers Association, Journal of the University Film Association,* and *Journal of the University Film and Video
Association.* Indexed in: IIFP.
   Academic journal for the teaching of film and video techniques
   at the college level. Reviews new literature and film releases.

Journal of Popular Film and Television. Quarterly, 1972- .
Heldref Publications, 4000 Albemarle St., Washington, DC 20016.
ISSN 0195-6051. Previous title: *Journal of Popular Film.* Corre-

spondence to: Editor, *Journal of Popular Film and Television,* Popular Culture Center, Bowling Green State University, Bowling Green, OH 43403. Volumes 1-9 available on microform from UMI; volumes 10 to date available from Heldref Publications. Indexed in: FLI, MRD, IIFP, IITP, Abstracts of Popular Culture, Historical Abstracts, International Index to Television Periodicals.

Publishes articles of popular interest about film and television subjects and personalities, with an emphasis about how the subjects related to modern culture. Some filmographies and reviews of films, television shows, and current literature.

Landers Film Reviews. See: page 314.

Literature/Film Quarterly. Quarterly, 1973- . Salisbury State College, Salisbury, MD 21801. ISSN 0090-4260. Indexed in: FLI, IIFP, MRD, Humanities Index.

Academic journal which discusses good literature that has been made into film. Reviews and evaluates films and the literary works from which they were taken. Reviews new films and related literature. Indexed in: International Index to Film Periodicals, Film Literature Index, PMLA Bibliography, Humanities Index.

Millimeter. Monthly, 1973- . Cleveland, OH: Penton Publishing. LC 78-648363, ISSN 0164-9655. Back issues from: University Microfilms. Indexed in: MRD, FLI.

Film and television production magazine centering on the audio and image technology aspects of production. Articles focus on interviews with producers/directors, new techniques and technology in services, and equipment. Provides names and addresses of support services.

Modern Screen. Monthly, 1930- . Sterling's Magazines, 355 Lexington Ave., New York, NY 10017. Phone: (212) 391-1400. ISSN 0026-8429. Incorporated: *Radio Stars.*

Fan magazine featuring interviews and photos of film and television stars. A good resource for older biographical information and photos.

Monthly Film Bulletin. Monthly, 1934-   . London: British Film Institute. ISSN 0027-0407. See: pages 498-499.

Motion Picture Investor: newsletter on analysis of private and public values of movies and movie stock. Monthly, 1984-   . Carmel, CA: Paul Kagan. ISSN 0742-8839.

Movie Life. Monthly, 1937-   . Ideal Publishing, 2 Park Ave., New York, NY 10016. ISSN 0027-2698.
Fan magazine featuring film and television stars. Good source for historical biographical information and photographs.

Moviegoer. Monthly, 1982-   . Address: 13-30 Corporation, 505 Market St., Knoxville, TN 37902.
Reviews latest theater film releases; heavily illustrated and provides some background on the actors in each production.

Photo Screen. Bimonthly, 1965-   . New York: Sterling's Magazines. ISSN 0031-8566.
Fan oriented; articles about film stars, movie history, interviews.

Photoplay. Monthly, 1911-   . Macfadden Group, 215 Lexington Avenue, New York, NY 10016. ISSN 0162-5195. Incorporated: *Movie Mirror.*
Fan oriented; articles and news about film stars and current films. Good, candid photos often used. Early issues cover some popular radio personalities who were also film stars.

Premiere. Bimonthly, 1987-   . Premiere Publishing, 2 Park Avenue, New York, NY 10016. ISSN 0894-9263. Indexed in: FLI.
The American version of a French magazine. Long interviews with film personalities, articles about the industry, and comprehensive critical reviews of new releases. It uses a multitude of photos, both color and black/white.

Pre-Production Newsletter. Monthly. National Film Sources, 10 East 39th St., Suite 1017, New York, NY 10016. Phone: 1-800-222-3844.
A source of current job information for actors and other people

involved in filmmaking. Lists jobs available and production companies who are looking for talent for upcoming projects.

Productions-in-Progress. Bimonthly, 1987- . Address: P.O. Box 23562, L'Enfant Plaza, Washington, DC 20026. Phone: (202) 488-0717.
Industry magazine providing news about current and planned film and television productions.

Quarterly Review of Film and Video. Quarterly, 1976- . Redgrave Publishing, P.O. Box 786, Cooper Station, NY 10276. ISSN 0146-0013. Previous title: *Quarterly Review of Film Studies.* Indexed in: IIFP, IITP.
Academic and literary journal of film theory and criticism. Reviews current films and film literature.

RTS Music Gazette. Bimonthly, 1973- . Address: RTS, Box 1829, Dept. BW, Novato, CA 94948.
Newsletter covering film music and soundtrack recordings.

Screen Stars. Monthly, 1944- . Magazine Management, Office of Publications, 575 Madison Ave., New York, NY 10022.
Fan magazine featuring film and television stars. Good source of historical information and photos.

Screen World. Monthly, 1949- . New York: Crown Publishers. ISSN 0080-8288.
Fan oriented; articles about film stars and the latest movies.

Sight and Sound; international film quarterly. Quarterly, 1932- . London: British Film Institute. See: page 500.

Sightlines. Quarterly, 1967- . The American Film & Video Association, 920 Barnsdale Rd., Suite 152, LaGrange Park, IL 60525. Phone: (312) 482-4000. Formed by the merger of the *EFLA Bulletin, Filmlist,* and *Film Review Digest.* Incorporated *Film Library Quarterly* in 1985. ISSN 0037-4830. Indexed in: FLI, MRD, Library Literature.

A popular approach to subjects of interest to film historians and educators. Each issue may include such diverse topics as reviews of business videos, the career of a film pioneer, an overview of jazz in film, and computer animation in the same issue. Reviews films, videos, and books.

Starlog; magazine of the future. See: page 398.

Variety. New York: Variety, Inc. Weekly. 1905 - . Annual index issue in January. ISSN 0042-2738. Publication policy: in-house staff only. Address in New York: 154 W. 46th St., New York, NY 10036. Phone: (212) 869-5700. In Los Angeles: 1400 N. Cahuenga Blvd., Hollywood, CA 90028. Phone: (213) 469-1141. Also has offices in other cities and countries. Publishes a separate London edition. Index for the previous year in a late January issue. Indexed in: FLI, IIFP, IITP, MI, MRD.
     Special issues throughout the year cover important meetings or highlight film industries in various parts of the world. Major focus is on the film industry. Extensive film reviews in each issue, detailed coverage of television programming and, to a lesser extent, reviews Broadway plays and sometimes the London theater, including cast credits. It also has sections reporting regularly on the radio, recording, and video industries. See Also: *Daily Variety.*

Wide Angle: a film quarterly of theory, criticism, and practice. Quarterly, 1978- . Baltimore: Johns Hopkins University Press (Athens Center for Film and Video). ISSN: 0160-6840. Available on microform from UMI. Indexed in: FLI, IIFP, MRD, MLA, Arts and Humanities Citation Index.

FILM, TELEVISION AND BROADCASTING LIBRARIES AND ARCHIVES

It is the intent of this section to cover only the major libraries and museums. In addition to these, many large public libraries and university libraries have extensive film and entertainment literature collections.

Academy of Motion Picture Arts & Sciences:
Margaret Herrick Library

Address: Academy of Motion Picture Arts and Sciences (AMPAS). Margaret Herrick Library. 333 S. LaCienega Blvd. (the corner of Olympic and LaCienega) in Beverly Hills, CA 90211. *Phone:* (213) 247-3020. *Hours:* Open weekdays (except Wednesday); hours vary. Visiting researchers by appointment only; visitors would be wise to write ahead of time and request information sheets about library rules and regulations. Limited photocopy services are available for a fee. Requests for information or photographs received by mail are handled by the Academy's National Film Information Service at the same address. Copies of film stills can be purchased, although the Academy does not give publication or reproduction rights.

The Library was founded in 1931 and has a large collection of books, periodicals, clippings, published and unpublished scripts, stills and portrait photos, costume designs, memorabilia, and correspondence. Major collections include: film stills from most films; production files for individual films; scripts (drafts, cutting continuities, etc.); manuscripts; personal papers; and other film resources. Since its major strength is film, it has only a small amount of information on television. The library is especially strong in information about the Academy Awards and numerous personal collections donated by the major studios and stars of Hollywood.

American Film Institute:
Louis B. Mayer Library

Address: The American Film Institute. Louis B. Mayer Library. P.O. Box 27999, 2021 N. Western Ave., Los Angeles, CA 90027. *Phone:* (213) 856-7655. *Hours:* Monday-Friday 10:30 am-5:30 pm. The Library is for the AFI staff and students of the AFI. Outside researchers should arrange for appointment.

Founded in 1969, the Library is relatively small in size compared to the others discussed in this section. It has a basic collection of books, periodicals, clippings, and memorabilia. It has some complete sets of historical film periodicals. The emphasis is on film; although the television and video collection is growing. It has some film and television scripts and stills. Special collections include: oral histories with film pioneers and private collections donated by industry personnel.

Annenberg School of Communications Library

See: University of Southern California (USC).

Annenberg Script Collection

See: University of Pennsylvania.

Anthology Film Archives:
The Jerome Hill Library

Address: Anthology Film Archives, 32 Second Ave. at Second St., New York, NY 10003. *Phone:* (212) 505-5181. Open to the public by appointment. Copies of film stills can be purchased.

The Library specializes in films, videos, and information about independent and avant garde filmmaking. It has film stills, posters, files on independent film productions and the people who make them. It also has some production documentation that has been donated by independent film companies and several private collections of papers and correspondence that have been donated by industry personnel. The Library also has files on organizations involved in independent filmmaking and video art. It also holds an international collection of periodicals on the subject.

AFVA Film Library

Address: American Film & Video Association. Film Library. 920 Barnsdale Rd., Suite 152, LaGrange Park, Illinois 60525. *Phone:* (312) 482-4000. *Hours:* By appointment.

The collection consists of books, films, clippings, and other materials geared toward the interest and needs of teachers, librarians, and others involved in the educational process.

Brigham Young University
Arts And Communications Archives

Address: Arts and Communications Archives, Brigham Young University, 5030 Harold B. Lee Library. *Phone:* (801) 378-3514. *Hours:* Monday-Friday during the day; closed weekends. Keeps university schedule. Visitors should make arrangements to use the collection prior to visit.

The Archive has a growing collection of film materials and is working hard to become an important film research center. Its major strength lies in donations of private collections from major film industry personnel. It has the papers, correspondence, and other private documents of Cecil B. DeMille relating to his life and films. In addition, substantial donations have been made by director John Ford, screenwriter Art Arthur, producer Howard W. Hawks, and others. It also has a number of production records of small film companies. The Library has a strong collection about film music, including collections of papers, recordings, and music donated by composers such as Hugo Friedhofer and Max Steiner as well as music from film companies; a major collection is the Republic Pictures Music Archives. It has the personal collections of Mary Astor, Harry Carey, Laraine Day, Andy Devine, and James Stewart.

Broadcast Pioneers Library

Address: Broadcast Pioneers Library. 1771 N St., N.W., Washington, DC 20036. *Phone:* (202) 223-0088. *Hours:* 9:00 am-5:00 pm. Visitors by appointment only and payment of a research fee. Reproductions of photos can be purchased; no rights are given.

This is a small, but unique library on broadcasting history. Its Collection contains books, historical and current runs of periodicals, approximately 20,000 photographs, oral history interviews, and reports covering radio and television.

CBS News Archives

Address: CBS News Archives. 524 W. 57th St., New York, NY 10019. *Phone:* (212) 975-2834.

More of a commercial research service than an archive, this is CBS film footage that is available for sale.

Federal Communications Commission Library

Address: Federal Communications Commission Library. 1919 M St., N.W., Washington, DC 20554. *Phone:* (202) 632-7100. *Hours:* weekdays; open to the public by appointment only. The primary purpose of the Library is to provide research facilities to the FCC staff. Identification required to enter agency. Photocopy service available.

A large and fairly technical collection covering the broadcasting industry and its ownership, management, station activities and market studies. The Collection includes books, periodicals, technical reports, and law materials. It has no "popular" type of material. This Collection covers television, radio, cable, and telecommunications.

Hollywood Film Archive Library

Address: Hollywood Film Archive Library. 8344 Melrose Ave., Los Angeles, CA 90069. *Phone:* (213) 933-3345. Private. Researchers admitted by special appointment.

This Library has books, periodicals, and clippings. It also has a unique online database of film production credits and other information.

International Museum of Photography: George Eastman House

Address: International Museum of Photography at George Eastman House. 900 East Avenue, Rochester, NY 14607.

Phone: (716) 271-3361. Publications: *Image* (quarterly; highlights collections of the Museum), *Newsletter* (quarterly, for members and donors). *Hours:* Monday-Friday 10:00 am-4:30 pm. Researchers should make arrangements ahead of time to use the collection or view films.

The Museum has a huge collection of several million film stills. In addition, it also has books, periodicals, and films relating to photography and film production. The Museum's collection is international in scope. It also covers some television programming.

Library of Congress

Address: Library of Congress. Motion Picture, Broadcasting, and Recorded Sound Division. Madison Building. Washington, DC 20540. *Phone:* (202) 707-1000. *Hours:* Monday-Friday 8:30 am-5:00 pm. Services: Pay photocopy machine available (bring change). Stills may be copied (by in-house service) only with written permission of the film company. Apply to view films three days in advance.

This Library houses the largest international film and television collection in the United States. The Division receives the Copyright Office depository copies of film/television/video productions. The Library has large reference collection, extensive clipping files of film and TV program reviews, files about personalities and specific productions, scripts from films and television programs, and memorabilia. Its vast collection of nearly 100,000 film stills was put on an optical disk system several years ago and is available for use in the Library's Reading Room.

The American Television and Radio Archives (ATRA) was established in 1976 as part of the Motion Picture, Broadcasting, and Recorded Music Division and contains special collections about radio and television. In addition to thousands of radio program disks, ATRA has a growing number of television programs. The largest collection by far is the NBC-TV program collection. In 1986, the network gave The Library a nearly complete collection of NBC-TV programs broadcast from 1935 to 1985. A detailed microfiche file, the NBC Television Program Analysis File, provides access to the collection. Information for each program includes production information, stars and guests, date of each broadcast, storyline, and credits. The collection itself is still in the processing stage and not yet available for viewing.

The Library also has many special collections that have been purchased or donated over the years. They also have back issues of periodicals published worldwide. Some historical journal collections are only available in microform and must be viewed in a separate area of the library at the Microform Reading Room.

Another important research center is the Recorded Sound Reference Center, located in Room LM 113, in the Madison Building of the Library of Congress, Washington, DC 20540. (Phone: (202) 707-7833. Hours: Weekdays; open to the public.) The Center focuses on radio history and recorded sound. It has a particularly strong collection of rare radio disks and transcriptions going back to the beginning of Broadcasting. Additionally, it has a number of BBC radio programs and the indexes to the BBC's programming.

Museum of Broadcast Communications

Address: Museum of Broadcast Communications. 800 South Wells St., Chicago, IL 60607-4529. *Phone:* (312) 565-1950.

The Museum opened in 1987 and exhibits memorabilia from both radio and television history, and the personalities who headlined in the early days. In addition to the museum itself, there is the A. C. Nielsen Research Center which houses film and tape of early television and radio programs. Although the collection is national in scope, the Center is working to collect programs from the Chicago area.

Museum of Television and Radio

Address: Museum of Television and Radio (formerly Museum of Broadcasting). 25 West 52nd St., New York, NY 10019. *Phone:* (212) 621-6600. Publications: *M.B. News* (quarterly). *Hours:* Tuesday-Saturday Noon-5:00 pm.

An Archive for television and radio broadcasts that has the heavy support of the industry behind it, thanks to the late William S. Paley who founded it in 1976. This is not a traditional research center in that one can not do research there beyond identifying and viewing programs. There are no print or published research resources. The emphasis of the Museum is on collecting copies of actual television and radio programs. In fact, its 30,000 title collection probably makes the Museum the largest repository in the United States outside of the Library of Congress. Viewing time is limited and there is an admission charge to the facility. All of the funding seems to go for purchasing the collection or paying housing costs; it appears that little has been spent on identifying the collection itself. Items in the collection are poorly identified in a combination card catalog and loose-leaf binder system. Because of these problems, researchers should come, or call ahead of time, with full information about the program or programs they want to view.

Museum of Modern Art

Address: Museum of Modern Art. Film Study Center and the Film Stills Archive. 11 West 53rd St., New York, NY 10019. *Phone:* for the Film Study Center: (212) 708-9613; and for the Film Stills Archive: (212) 708-9602. *Hours:* Open only to researchers by appointment during weekday afternoons. Publications about the Museum Collection: *Catalog of the Library of the Museum of Modern Art, New York City.* Boston, G.K. Hall, 1976. 14 volumes. A more recent publication is: *The Film Catalog;* a list of holdings in the Museum of Modern Art. Edited by Jon Gartenberg. New York: G. K. Hall/Museum of Modern Art. 443 p., 1987. Researchers may purchase copies of the film stills upon approval. No rights are given.

The Museum has an important collection of nearly 6,000 rare and early films. It also is known for its large collection of film stills. The Film Study Center has books, scripts, films, clippings, and memorabilia. It also has special collections dealing with D. W. Griffith, silent films, and the collections of various film personalities.

National Archives

Address: National Archives and Records Service (NARS). 8th St. and Pennsylvania Avenue, N.W., Washington, DC 20408. There are two branches in NARS that are of interest to film and television researchers: Motion Picture, Sound, and Video Branch, phone: (202) 786-0041; and the Stills Picture Branch, phone: (202) 523-3236. *Hours:* Monday-Friday 8:45 am-5:00 pm. Some research areas are also open on Saturday. The NARS main reading rooms and research facilities are open to the public. Other areas, or offices in the various divisions are accessible only by permission and appointment.

This government agency holds the Stock Film Library collection of stock footage owned by the federal government. A number of special collections contain war films, labor history and other topics of interest. There are also thousands of film stills of news events and people important to world history. One of the most requested series of photos is a sequence of about a dozen photographs taken of Elvis Presley and President Nixon together during a surprise Elvis visit to the White House.

National Association of Broadcasters Library

Address: National Association of Broadcasters. Library and Information Center. 1771 N St., N.W., Washington, DC 20036. *Phone:* (202) 429-5490. *Hours:* Weekdays; open to the public during the afternoon hours by appointment only. Call ahead.

Small, but excellent collection of books and periodicals covering television and radio as well as the broadcasting industry in general. The collection covers new technology, production, advertising, commentary, regulation, historical materials, government reports. The library has a good collection of current literature and periodical subscriptions.

National Public Radio

Address: National Public Radio (NPR). 2025 M St., NW, Washington, DC 20036. *Phone:* (202) 822-2000. Public

Information Office: (202) 822-2300. Audience Services Department: (202) 822-2323.

NPR has a library, but researchers can gain entrance by permission only. Of more value to researchers is NPR's vast archive of radio programs. In addition to drama and documentary programs, there are countless valuable interviews, music programs, commentaries, and news events. The collection is fairly well indexed and researchers can purchase copies of programming for research purposes. It helps if you know what you want, but the NPR Audience Services Department will do a limited amount of searching for you. You can make your requests by phone or letter. In addition, NPR has a number of their broadcasts available for sale on audio cassettes; write for their catalog if you are interested.

NBC News Archives

Address: NBC News Archives. 30 Rockefeller Plaza, Room 902, New York, NY 10020. *Phone:* (212) 664-3271. Not open to the public. Requests should be submitted in writing.

The Archives have film footage from the 1950s to date. It is possible to purchase film for research or production purposes.

The New York Public Library at the Lincoln Center: The Billy Rose Theatre Collection

Address: The Billy Rose Theatre Collection. New York Public Library at Lincoln Center. Performing Arts Research Center. 111 Amsterdam Ave. New York, NY 10023. *Phone:* (212) 870-1639. *Hours:* Monday and Thursday 10:00 am-7:45 pm.; Tuesday, Wednesday, Friday, and Saturday 10:00 am-5:45 pm. Services: Photocopy service available. *Hours:* Vary; call ahead to confirm openings. Permission can be obtained to copy stills; a release is required. A private photographer may be used or the Library will do the work in-house.

The Library has premier film, television, and theater collections. It also provides some radio coverage. The

Collection includes books, periodicals, scripts, and memorabilia. It has extensive clipping files, which include reviews of film and television productions as well as information about personalities. There is also a large international stills collection arranged by production title and personality. Special collections have been donated to the Library by both celebrities and organizations. The Library is equally strong in theater materials. Among its special collections are filmed/videotaped Broadway productions. See Also: Chapter 6 on theater libraries for more detail.

Pacific Film Archive

Address: Pacific Film Archive. University of California, Berkeley. University Film Museum. 2625 Durant Ave., Berkeley, CA 94720. *Phone:* (415) 642-1437.

Besides clippings, stills, and film literature, this Archive also has an extensive collection of Japanese feature films.

PBS Archive

Address: Public Broadcasting System (PBS). Archives. 1320 Braddock Place, Alexandria, VA 22314-1698. *Phone:* (703) 739-5380. *Hours:* Monday-Friday 9:00 am-5:00 pm.

The PBS Archive Collection contains the PBS's historical programming from 1953 to the present. There are viewing facilities. However, there is limited indexing of the collection.

Television Information Office

Address: Television Information Office. 745 Fifth Ave., New York, NY 10151. Disbanded in early 1989. Its collection was donated to the Museum of Television and Radio.

University of California at Los Angeles (UCLA)

The University of California at Los Angeles (UCLA) has two collections that are designed to service the film and entertainment community: (1) the Theater Arts Library and (2) the Film and Television Archives.

The Theater Arts Library is located at 405 Hilgard Ave., Los Angeles, CA 90024. (Phone: (213) 825-7253; Special Collections Department (213) 825-4879.) The Library's hours vary according to the University's schedule. To learn more about the Library consult its publication: *Motion Pictures: A Catalog of Books, Periodicals, Screenplays, Television Scripts, and Production Stills.* (Compiled by Audree Malkin. 2d ed., rev. and exp. Boston: G.K. Hall, 1976. 775 p.) This book is a partial guide to the UCLA collection.

The Theater Arts Collection covers theater, film, and television. It has the largest television collection in the country and made an effort to collect material long before other libraries did so. The Library has books and periodicals, screenplays, unpublished television scripts, production stills, clippings, and film and video. It also has special collections on film and TV stills; film and TV series scripts; personal papers of film personalities; Twentieth Century Fox corporate files; film music; the Star Trek series; files from MGM, Paramount, RKO, and Columbia; and collections from major film studios.

The UCLA Film and Television Archive is also located at 405 Hilgard Ave., Los Angeles, CA 90024-1622. Phone: (213) 206-8013. The hours of the Archive Research and Study Center are Tuesdays, 9:00 am-5:00 pm, but researchers must make advance appointments. The Archive publications are: *Film/TV/Radio;* and *A Guide to Media Research Resources at UCLA* (24 p., no date.) The latter pamphlet covers all of the UCLA research libraries and highlights what performing arts materials might be found in the libraries' collections.

The Archive has a film collection of over 40,000 titles from the 1890s to today; over 30,000 television programs from the mid 1940s to date; and a rapidly growing news broadcast collection of nearly 100,000 recent programs. Moreover, it has millions of feet of old newsreels. The Archive covers some local and international programming as well as national television programming. It also has a smaller amount of radio programs. Much of the collection has been catalogued on the University's Orion online system which the University plans to make available publicly in the future.

University of California, Riverside:
The Library

Address: University of California, Riverside. 4045 Canyon Crest Dr., P.O. Box 5900, Riverside, CA 92517. *Phone:* (714) 787-3233. *Hours:* Monday-Friday 9:00 am–5:00 pm. Publications: *Dictionary Catalog of the J. Lloyd Eaton Collection of Science Fiction and Fantasy Literature.* G.K. Hall, 1982.

The Library has a large science fiction and fantasy collection: the Eaton Collection. The Collection is international in scope, and includes films, books, periodicals, and memorabilia.

University of Pennsylvania:
The Annenberg School of Communications,
Television Script Archive

Address: University of Pennsylvania, The Annenberg School of Communications, Television Script Archive, 3620 Walnut St., Philadelphia, PA 19104. Access to the collection is by appointment only by written application to this address. A fee is charged to non-university researchers. Oryx Press has recently published two books about the collection: *Index to the Annenberg Television Script Archive* and *Thesaurus of Subject Headings For Television.* See Chapter 9 on Broadcast Research for information about these books.

Although the Archive has only been open since 1988, it is already recognized as a major research institution for the television industry. The collection is comprised of over 30,000 television scripts from 1976 to the present. Approximately 1,500 new titles are received each year. It includes series, specials, movies made for television, soap operas, and other materials from all of the major networks (NBC, ABC, CBS, and Fox). The core of the collection is donations made from

TV Guide. The scripts often represent various stages of production and may be drafts, working scripts, or final versions. The Archive is in the process of creating a database of its collection called TSAR (Television Script Archive database).

University of Southern California, Los Angeles (USC)

USC has two collections of note, although the Cinema-Television Library is by far the larger collection:

The **Annenberg School of Communications, The Library,** is located at the University of Southern California, University Park, Los Angeles, CA 90089-0281. (Phone: (213) 743-4114.) The Library keeps university hours.

The Library is a small, but highly concentrated collection of books and periodicals about broadcast communications. It is designed to support the faculty and staff of the school, but will assist members of the public as time allows.

The **Cinema-Television Library and Archives of Performing Arts** is located at the University Library, Los Angeles, CA 90089. *Phone:* (213) 743-6058. *Hours:* Call the Library for its current schedule. In general, however, the Library keeps university hours and may not be open evenings, weekends or holidays. Also, write for visitor regulations to Reading Room use. Consult *Primary Cinema Resources: An Index to Screenplays, Interviews, and Special Collections at the University of Southern California.* (Compiled by Christopher D. Wheaton and Richard B. Jewell. Boston: G.K. Hall, 321 p., 1975.) for information about the contents of the Library. The Index is one of the few sources listing interviews. The Library's stacks are closed and all material not located in the reading room area must be requested from the staff. The Library has special catalogs of the Warner Bros. collection as well as catalogs for their scripts, videos, and stills collections.

The Library was started in the 1930s and the scope of the collection covers both film and television. It includes books, periodicals, clipping files, scripts, film stills and other photos, pressbooks, recordings, audio tapes of interviews, and memorabilia. It has also collected on the international level and is especially strong in East European cinema. Its special collections include scripts of the Burns and Allen radio and television shows and collections from various personalities, producers, directors, and others involved in the industry. It also has scripts and production records from Twentieth Century-Fox, Universal, MGM, and other studios. The Library is the main Warner Bros. Archives and maintains Warner's film and television records.

Vanderbilt University:
Vanderbilt Television News Archives

Address: Vanderbilt Television News Archives. Vanderbilt University. The Jean and Alexander Heard Library, 419 21st Ave., South, Nashville, TN 37203. *Phone:* (615) 322-2927. *Hours:* Monday-Friday 8:00 am-5:00 pm.; Saturday by appointment. Researchers should make appointments. Publications: *Television News Index and Abstracts.*

The major part of the collection consists of the evening network news broadcasts of NBC, CBS, and ABC from 1968 to the present. Other broadcasts and televised specials of a news or documentary, or political nature are included. Some of the programs are available for rent.

Walt Disney Archives

Address: Walt Disney Archives. 500 South Buena Vista St., Burbank, CA 91521. *Phone:* (818) 560-5424. *Hours:* Open weekdays. Open to the Disney staff and to visiting researchers by appointment.

The Archives was established in 1970 to preserve the works and history of Walt Disney and the Disney enterprises. The collection includes all facets of Disney activities, although the emphasis is on film, television, and animation. The Archive holds most of the personal Walt Disney collection: correspondence, and other personal items. It also has a large collection of photographs, a number of books and comics published about Disney or his cartoon characters, recordings of music used in the films, and an extensive historical clipping collection about Disney characters. Of major importance is the fact that it is the official archive for Disney business activities, including the theme parks. It has the film scripts and production files of all Disney film and television shows, including the daily call sheets for films, the drawings for the animated films, and some props and costumes. The Archives also maintain collections of Disney newsletters, phone books, a history of the licensing and merchandise agreements covering Disney characters, annual reports, and other Disney business records.

Warner Research Collection

Address: Warner Research Collection. Burbank Public Library 110 North Glenoaks Blvd., Burbank, CA 91502. *Phone:* (818) 953-9743. The collection is a commercial research service which charges fees for the work conducted. Available to perspective clients by appointment only.

This collection was formerly the research library of Warner Brothers Studios and is now a separate research facility within the Burbank Public Library. The collection is geared toward providing research services needed by the film industry and is therefore not strictly a collection of materials dealing with film history. The staff will research information needed for script development, commercials, and the verification of facts.

Wesleyan Cinema Archives

Address: Wesleyan University. Wesleyan Cinema Archives. 301 Washington Terrace, Middletown, CT 06457. *Phone:* (203) 347-9411, extension 2259.

This relatively new archive has made a name for itself the past few years by aggressively going after prestigious collections. Consequently, the Archive has succeeded in acquiring the private papers and collections of a number of noted film industry people, among them Elia Kazan, Frank Capra,

Ingrid Bergman, and Clint Eastwood. It also seeks out film scripts, production records, and other primary materials. It has a complete set of the historical "Omnibus" television programs.

Wisconsin Center for Film & Theater Research

Address: Wisconsin Center for Film and Theater Research. The Archives-Manuscripts Reading Room is located at the State Historical Society, 816 State St., Madison, WI 53706. *Phone:* (608) 262-3338. The Film and Photo Archive is in the same building, room 412; the phone is: (608) 262-0585. *Hours:* Monday-Friday 10:00 am-4:30 pm. Publications: *The Wisconsin Center for Film and Theater Research.* Available upon request. Also useful is: *Sources for Mass Communications, Film, and Theater Research.*

This Archive was founded in 1960 and is a joint venture between the University of Wisconsin, Madison, and the State Historical Society of Wisconsin. It is designed to cover the major aspects of the performing arts and has extensive film, television, and theater collections. It has a major script collection. See Chapter 6, Theater Libraries for a detailed description of the collection.

FILM PROFESSIONAL ASSOCIATIONS AND ORGANIZATIONS

Academy of Canadian Cinema and Television. 653 Yonge St., 2d Floor, Toronto, Ontario, Canada M4Y 1Z9. Publications: *Infocus* (quarterly).

Academy of Motion Picture Arts and Sciences. 8949 Wilshire Blvd., Beverly Hills, CA 90211. Phone: (213) 278-8990. Founded in 1927. Publications: *Annual Index to Motion Picture Credits* (annual), *The Bulletin* (1928-1981).

Academy of Science Fiction, Fantasy, and Horror Films. 334 W. 54th St., Los Angeles, CA 90037. Phone: (213) 752-5811. Founded in 1927. Membership: industry personnel. Membership services: lectures, seminars, conferences.

Academy of Television Arts and Sciences. 3500 W. Olive Ave., Suite 700, Burbank, CA 91505-4268. Phone: (818) 953-7575. Membership: Television and film industry professionals. Publications: *Emmy Magazine* (bimonthly), and *Emmy Directory*. Sponsors the television archive collection at UCLA.

Actor's Equity Association. 165 West 46th St., New York, NY 10036. Phone: (212) 869-8530. In California: 6430 Sunset Blvd., Suite 1002, Hollywood, CA 90028. Phone: (213)462-2334. Founded in 1913. Membership: Members of the acting profession. Contact source for theater actors. Publication: *Equity*.

Alliance of Motion Picture and Television Producers. Address: 14144 Ventura Blvd., 3rd Floor, Sherman Oaks, CA 91423-2794. Phone: (818) 995-3600. Membership is made up of film companies, independent producers, and other film personnel.

American Cinema Editors. Address: 4416-1/2 Finley Ave., Los Angeles, CA 90027. Phone: (213) 660-4425.

American Federation of Film Societies. Three Washington Square Village, New York, NY 10012. Phone: (212) 254-8688. Publications: *Film Society Bulletin* (nine issues yearly).

American Federation of Television and Radio Artists (AFTRA). 260 Madison Ave., New York, NY 10016. Phone: (212) 532-0800. In California: 1717 N. Highland Ave., Hollywood, CA 90028. Phone: 461-8111. Labor organization representing professionals in the radio and television industries.

American Film and Video Association. Address: 920 Barnsdale Rd., Suite 152, LaGrange Park, IL 60525. Phone: (312) 482-4000. Founded in 1943. Previously named the Educational Film Library Association. A nonprofit organization established to provide information about non-print media, with emphasis on films. Membership: open to individuals and organizations. Publications: *American Film Festival Guide* (Annual), *Sightlines* (Quarterly).

Sightlines was formed by the merger of *EFLA Bulletin, Filmlist,* and *Film Review Digest.* ISSN 0037-4830.

American Film Institute. The John F. Kennedy Center for the Performing Arts, Washington, DC 20566. Phone: (202) 828-4000. AFI West Coast Office: P.O. Box 27999, 2021 N. Western Ave., Los Angeles, CA 90027. Publications: *American Film* (monthly), *A.F.I. Close-up* (quarterly), *AFI Education Newsletter* (bimonthly), *Factfile* series (irregular), *Preview* (bimonthly).

American Guild of Variety Artists (AFL-CIO). 184 Fifth Ave., New York, NY 10010. Phone: (212) 675-1003. Founded: 1939. Members: Stage and film performers.

American Society of Cinematographers. 1782 North Orange Dr., Hollywood, CA 90028. Phone: (213) 876-5080. Founded: 1919. Membership: members of the profession.

Associated Actors and Artistes of America (AFL-CIO). 165 West 46th St., New York, NY 10036. Phone: (212) 869-0358. Founded: 1919. Membership: Members of the profession.

Association of Independent Video and Filmmakers. 625 Broadway, 9th Floor, New York, NY 10012. Phone: (212) 473-3400. Membership: Industry personnel and others.

Association of Motion Picture and Television Producers, Inc. 8480 Beverly Blvd., Los Angeles, CA 90048. Phone: (213) 653-2200. Founded: 1924. Membership: Film studios and producers.

Association of Talent Agents. Address: 9255 Sunset Blvd., Suite 318, Los Angeles, CA 90069. Phone: (213)274-0628. Founded: 1937 as Artists' Managers Guild. Name changed in 1979. Members: Talent agents.

Authors' Guild, Inc. 234 West 44th St., New York, NY 10036. Phone: (212) 398-0838.

The Authors League of America, Inc. 234 West 44th St., New York, NY 10036. Phone: (212) 391-9198.

Canadian Film Institute. 75 Albert St., Ottawa, Ontario, Canada K1P 5E7

Council on International Nontheatrical Events (CINE). 1201 16th St., N.W., Washington, DC 20036. Phone: (202) 785-1136 or 1137. Founded: 1957. A nonprofit association that selects entries for film festivals and competitions; international in scope.

Directors Guild of America. 7950 Sunset Blvd., Hollywood, CA 90046. Phone: (213) 656-1220. New York Office: 110 West 57th St., New York, NY 10019. Phone: (212) 581-0370. Publications: *Action!* (bimonthly) and *Directory of Members* (Annual) for the Guild's membership.

The Dramatists Guild, Inc. Address: 234 W. 44th St., New York, NY 10036. Phone: (212) 398-9366.

Educational Film Library Association. See: American Film & Video Association.

International Alliance of Theatrical Stage Employees & Moving Picture Machine Operators of the U.S. and Canada (AFL-CIO). 1515 Broadway, New York, NY 10036. Phone: (212) 730-1770. Founded: 1893. Membership: The organization is an alliance of approximately 900 local unions in the United States and Canada. The locals cover personnel in the production, distribution, and exhibition parts of the industry.

International Animated Film Society (ASIFA-Hollywood Chapter). 5301 Laurel Canyon Blvd., No. 219, North Hollywood, CA 91607. Phone: (818) 508-5224. Publications: *Graffiti* (bimonthly, for members only).

International Documentary Association. 1551 South Robertson Blvd., Los Angeles, CA 90035. Phone: (213) 284-8422. Publications: *I.D.A. Directory* (annual). Professional association for film personnel interested in non-fictional productions.

Motion Picture Association of America, Inc. 1600 Eye St., Washington, DC 20006. Phone: (202) 293-1966. California office:

6464 Sunset Blvd., Suite 520, Hollywood, CA 90028. Phone: (213) 464-3117. Purpose: To develop the market for films, to speak out about legislation. Public relations, lobbying, film industry representation on topics and issues of interest to the film industry. Membership: Major U.S. film producers.

National Academy of Television Arts and Sciences. 111 West 57th St., New York, NY 10020. Phone: (212) 586-8424. Membership: Awards: Emmy Awards for daytime, sports, and local programs. Publications: *Television Quarterly.*

National Association of Broadcasters. 1771 N St., N.W., Washington, DC 20036. Phone: (202) 429-5300. Represents the radio and television industries in lobbying efforts. Speaks out on ideas and issues of interest. Membership: Industry organizations and personnel. Membership services: placement service. Publications: *Highlights, Radioactive.*

National Film Society. 8340 Mission Rd., Suite 106, Prairie Village, KS 66206. Phone: (913) 341-1919. Founded in 1975. Membership: Anyone interested in film preservation or screen history. Publications: *American Classic Screen.*

Producers Guild of America. 400 Beverly Dr., Suite 211, Beverly Hills, CA 90212. Phone: (213) 557-0807. Founded: 1950. Membership: Film producers. Publications: *The Journal of the Producers Guild of America* (quarterly to members).

Screen Actors Guild. 7065 Hollywood Blvd., Hollywood, CA 90028. Phone: (213) 465-4600. Agent Referral Office: 856-6737. New York Office: 1515 Broadway, 18th Floor, New York, NY 10019. Phone: (212) 944-1030. New York Agent Referral Office number: 944-6797. Founded: 1933. Members: Actors. Publications: *Reel* (semi-annual, from the New York office). *S.A.G. Hollywood Close-up* (monthly).

Society for Cinema Studies. c/o Dr. John Fell, Film Department, San Francisco State University, 1600 Holloway Ave., San Francisco, CA 94132. Phone: (415) 731-0595. Membership: People interested in the study of film history. Publications: *Cinema Journal.*

Society of Motion Picture and Television Engineers (SMPTE). Address: 595 Hartsdale Ave., White Plains, NY 10607. Phone: (914)472-6606. Publications: *SMPTE Journal.*

Women In Communication. See: TELEVISION ORGANIZATIONS.

Women In Film. Address: 6464 Sunset Blvd., Suite 900, Los Angeles, CA. 90028 Phone: (213) 463-6040. Offices also in New York, Washington, DC, and Atlanta.

Writers Guild of America, East. 555 West 57th St., New York, NY 10019. Phone: (212) 245-6180.

Writers Guild of America, West. 8955 Beverly Blvd., Los Angeles, CA 90048. Phone: (213) 550-1000.

9   BROADCAST RESEARCH
(Television, Radio, and Video)

Film and television research may appear to be similar in nature, but some important differences exist. While most of the libraries that have large film collections also have television materials, the film and television literature rarely mix the two mediums. Indexes to film literature don't include television periodicals, and vice versa. One of the few exceptions is *Film Literature Index,* which indexes both film and television periodicals. A book that lists film credits for actors will usually not list that person's television credits; and again, the reverse is true. Consequently, you can not assume that one reference source has given you everything you need to know about a particular person or subject.

Because television is still considered a relatively new industry, many libraries with large film collections only started to collect television materials within the past few years, and therefore their resources may not contain as much depth as a researcher would desire. Many early television programs have been lost because the networks or local stations failed to save them, and much printed material went unsaved. Although some institutions are working hard to correct this situation, it is simply too late in some cases. The Library of Congress was fortunate recently when NBC donated many years of its programs to the Motion Picture Division. Once this is fully available to the public, an important gap in television history will be filled.

Broadcasting is heavily commercialized and much of the current literature has to do with the business end of the television and video industries. Market research is heavily used and ratings virtually control the decision-making process at many stations. Two research and ratings services dominate the field and their weekly or quarterly reports are anxiously awaited at both the national and local levels: Nielsen Media Research, (Nielsen Plaza, Northbrook, IL 60062. Phone: (312) 498-6300) and Arbitron Ratings Company (142 W. 57th Street, New York, NY 10019. Phone: (212) 887-1300)

The worlds of radio and television survive in part on the Arbitron and Nielsen ratings because these two ratings services, more than any of the others, measure the popularity of programming and the numbers of viewers and/or listeners for programs and stations. And as far as the broadcast industry is concerned, ratings are the only measure of commercial success. In order to provide information about viewing or listening audiences at the local, regional, and national levels, the services have created "market areas" that are reached by the signals of individual radio or television stations. Nielsen calls them Designated Market Areas (DMA) and Arbitron uses the term Areas of Dominant Influence (ADI). Geographically, all of the counties in the United States are assigned to one of these market areas, and the area is then ranked in importance by the size of population it contains. The highest ranked markets have the largest populations. The numbers published by these services have an important impact on the advertising dollar, and therefore station incomes. Measurements have become more sophisticated in recent years and the services can now break down audience characteristics into precise age groups, listening habits for a particular age group, which programs they watch and how long they stay with a particular station, and other factors of importance to programmers and advertisers. These figures are then used by advertisers who want to target a certain audience (they will pay to place ads on the station with that audience) and by stations who want to attract advertisers to their station.

Nielsen supplies television rating information for local, regional and national areas. Their main prominence in the public eye is at the national level, where they have no major competition. The Nielsen weekly network television program rating results are published in many local newspapers. They also conduct quarterly seasonal "sweeps" in which all of the markets are measured at one time to measure viewer preference of network programming. And they do "overnights," a quick audience sampling, but generally consider these statistics to be less reliable.

Arbitron provides ratings for both radio and television, but only at the local level. Although smaller firms exist, Arbitron measurements are the dominate factor in radio ratings. Radio reports differ from television because there are many more radio stations in a market area; as a result, the audience is more fragmented. Therefore, measurements are discussed in terms of "shares" and "cumulative audience," meaning that station's share of the radio audience when compared with stations that broadcast a similar format and the station's part of the total audience in the market area.

The publications of both companies are issued as part of an overall contractual or subscription service and also through their own database services, but are generally far too expensive and specialized for most libraries to justify purchasing. The places most likely to have them are your local radio or TV stations or private libraries of large businesses associated with the broadcasting industry.

Researching television programs or series is more difficult than researching a motion picture. It's possible to combine reference sources which list the programs for each yearly season, sources that identify series episodes by title, and information in the *TV Guide Index* in order to compile a complete overview of a particular series. Once you have this information, you can go to a library and read the back issues of *TV Guide* or purchase the issues outright (see Chapter 10, FANS AND COLLECTING, for sales outlets).

Astute fans of old movies use the *Television Programming Source Books* to find which packages contain the movies they want to see, and then monitor cable channels or correspond with a network of friends around the country to identify channels which are broadcasting the series. Once they identify where the series is being shown, it's only a matter of time until the movie they want will be shown.

Radio still plays an important role in this country, but is the hardest of the broadcast media to research. Part of the reason is that the content of radio programming has changed considerably over the years. Much of the early programming was scripted drama or variety shows; today, the majority of programming is recorded music, followed by current news. As a reflection of these program patterns, the research resources are also divided. The early radio stars were profiled in the fan magazines and often had film and stage experience as well. Many of radio's biggest names went on to become television stars. But, with one or two exceptions, radio personalities rarely receive that kind of attention today. One is more likely to find information about radio personalities in recording industry journals such as *Billboard* rather than fan magazines. National Public Radio and some local stations are about the only current sources of drama or variety programming.

TELEVISION AND RADIO REFERENCE SOURCES

A.B.C. News Index. Quarterly, 1986- . Annual cumulations. Research Publications, 12 Lunar Dr., Woodbridge, CT 06525. Phone: 1-800-732-2477. ISSN 0891-8775.
  Transcripts of television programs produced by ABC News (evening news and other programs) are available from this organization. The *Index* is a fairly thin publication (each issue averages about 90 pages) which provides subject, title, and personal name access to this material.

Actors' Television Credits, 1950-1972, by James Robert Parish. SEE: *The Complete Actors' Television Credits, 1948-1988* by James Robert Parish and Vincent Terrace.

All TV Publicity Outlets - Nationwide. Semiannual, 1970- . Address: Public Relations Plus, P.O. Drawer 1197, New Milford, CT 06776. LC 88-648762, ISSN 0889-2717. Previous titles: *TV Publicity Outlets, nationwide.* The publication absorbed: *Cable TV Publicity Outlets, Nationwide.*
  Looseleaf directory of advertisers, ad agencies, and publicity firms dealing with television producers and stations.

All TV & Cable Publicity Outlets Nationwide. Kent, CT: Resource Media. 1989. LC 89-61115, ISBN 0-925133-02-7.

American Broadcasting: a source book on the history of radio and television. Compiled by Lawrence W. Lichty and Malachi C. Topping. New York: Hastings House. 723 p., 1975. LC 74-2024, ISBN 0803803621.
  An extensive bibliography covering all areas of broadcasting. Although it's too old now to contain current material, it is useful for historical materials.

American Radio. Quarterly, 1976-   . Indianapolis, IN: Duncan's American Radio. LC 0738-8675, LC 78-642306.
  This is one of the major ratings books for the radio industry. Issued quarterly, plus an additional "Small Market" issue, it provides ratings and program information for all of the radio markets. It uses Arbitron and Birch Radio estimates as the basic data for its charts.

Arbitron Ratings Company, 142 W. 57th St., New York, NY 10019. Phone: (212) 887-1300. Listed below are some of the titles published by Arbitron:

  Arbitron ADI Market Guide.
  Arbitron Ratings; Radio and Television City Book.
  Arbitron Television Audience Estimates in the Arbitron Market of [name of area].
  Arbitron Television Population Book.
  Arbitron Ratings: Television.

A V Market Place. Annual, 1969-   . New York: Bowker. LC 89-29207, ISSN 1044-0445. Previous title: *Audio Visual Market Place* (1969-1988).
  A directory of manufacturers, suppliers, retailers, associations and organizations, film and TV commissions, distributors of audiovisual and video programs and related equipment and supplies, and conventions and meetings. It also has a good section about industry periodicals and reference books. The section on awards lists some lesser known ones not usually found.

AudioVideo Review Digest. Three issues yearly, 1989-   . Annual cumulations. Detroit: Gale. LC 89-7607, ISSN 1043-4038.

This is a new entry into the growing body of literature for audio and video reviews. Each issue will index reviews from over 200 review sources for films, video tapes, recordings, and the multiple formats for each field.

BCTV: Bibliography on Cable Television. Annual, 1975-   . Issued with monthly updates. San Francisco, CA: Communications Institute, 1550 Bryant St., San Francisco, CA 94310. LC 84-8040, ISSN 0742-4914.

A yearly bibliography and directory of resources about cable television.

Back Stage. TV, Film, & Tape Production Directory. Annual, 1982-. Address: 330 W. 42nd St., New York, NY 10036. Phone: (212) 947-0020. LC 82-645474, ISSN 0734-9777.

The directory from *Back Stage* which lists industry production companies and services for TV, film, and video tape. Directory information is furnished for photographers, agents, technical services, equipment suppliers, trade organizations, screening rooms and studios, music and recording services, and other businesses which are part of the entertainment industry. Organized geographically, with nearly half of the book covering the New York City area. Chicago, California, and several other areas are covered to a smaller extent. See Also: *Back Stage* magazine in Chapter 6 (theater periodicals).

Bacon's Radio - TV Directory. Annual, 1987-   . Chicago, IL: Bacon's Publishing Company.

The Big Broadcast, 1920-1950, by Frank Buxton and Bill Owen. New York: Viking Press. 301 p., 1972. LC 73-149272, ISBN 0-670-16240-X. (A revised and expanded edition of *Radio's Golden Age, the complete reference work*).

A valuable radio research tool which lists radio shows which appeared on national networks from 1920 through 1950. Each show entry includes cast and production credits, dates aired, and a description of the show's ongoing plot or style.

Bowker's Complete Video Directory. Annual, 1988-   . New York: R.R. Bowker. Available on a Bowker CD-ROM program. Published in 2 volumes. Volume 1: *Entertainment;* Volume 2: *Education/Special Interest.* ISBN 0-8352-2891-6. Previous title: *Variety's Complete Home Video Directory.*

This was *Variety's* entry into the home video reference race in 1988, but recently renamed to the Bowker title. The volume provides a listing of approximately 62,000 videos that are available for home purchasing and viewing. In addition to feature films, it lists television series which are available on video, educational films, and special interest videos (such as industry training films). However, one confusing element is that a video of a series episode may only be identified by the episode title, with no cross-reference for the series title. Consequently, if you do not know your material, you may mistakenly believe a title is something it is not. Arrangement is by title, with each entry including major cast members, plot summary, order information, and production credits. Indexing is by title, genre, major cast member, and director. A list of names and addresses of distributors and manufacturers is also included for ordering purposes. Special indexes include: a Spanish language index of Spanish videos, a closed-caption index, a laser video index, and an awards index indicating which films in the volume have won awards.

The Broadcast Communications Dictionary, by Lincoln Diamant. 3d ed., rev. and exp. Westport, CT: Greenwood Press. 255 p., 1989. LC 88-25093, ISBN 031326502X.

The dictionary tries to provide a wide range of terms, from slang to technical names that cover the broadcasting industry (television, radio, satellite communications, and cable). It includes British terminology as well, and distinguishes between American and British meanings when necessary.

Broadcast Television: a research guide, by Fay C. Schreibman. Los Angeles: American Film Institute. 62 p., 1983. LC 84-186073, ISBN 0-89093-571-8

A brief, but helpful guide to a sparsely covered field.

The Broadcaster's Dictionary, by James McDonald. Rev. ed. Broomfield, CO: Wind River Books. 198 p., 1987. LC 86-9215, ISBN 0938023047.

Broadcasting Bibliography: a guide to the literature of radio and television. Edited by Susan M. Hill; compiled by the staff of the NAB Library. 3d ed. Washington, DC: National Association of Broadcasters. 74 p., 1989. ISBN 0-89324-076-1.

A brief but excellent guide to literature in the field of broadcasting lists over 500 books and reference sources. They cover such topics as business, regulation, program production, new technology, telecommunications and systems. In addition, there is a list of 110 trade periodicals useful in keeping current with industry events and issues.

Broadcasting - Cable Yearbook. Annual, 1935- . Address: Broadcasting Publications, 1705 DeSales St., Washington, DC 20036. Phone: (202) 659-2340. ISSN 0732-7196. Available on microform. Indexed in: *Statistical Reference Index.* Previous title: *Cable Yearbook.* Combines to previous titles: *Broadcasting Cable Sourcebook* and *Broadcasting Yearbook.*

A comprehensive directory listing all television, radio stations, and satellite/cable organizations in the United States and Canada. Listings include call letters, station phone numbers/ addresses and personnel, advertising agencies, attorneys, services, and other important information. It has a separate listing of all radio and television stations alphabetically by call letters, another listing of radio stations by formats, and lists of which radio stations broadcast in AM, FM, or stereo (radio and TV). Section A is a comprehensive history and evolution of the broadcasting media, spells out station application procedures, reviews laws and legislation, provides a directory of regulatory agencies, and lists station and cable ownership. Section B covers radio broadcasting and provides directory information for stations, a review of U.S. international radio broadcasting, call letters, AM/FM stations, programming and formats, frequencies, and a guide to the Arbitron stations. Section C covers the television industry in much the same manner and adds a list of pending applications, a large section about the television marketplace which includes a list of the 212 "ADI" stations according to Arbitron Television and tables from the Nielsen Marketing Research. Section D provides a short overview of the cable industry and provides detailed statistical and directory information for the industry. Section E covers satellite programming and services in North America. Section F provides information about programming for each media. Directory information is provided for producers, distributors, and production services. It also lists stations by subject format, support services offering news and music, and other special programming material. Section G presents directory information for the advertising and marketing services that deal with radio or TV accounts. This section also provides current studies and statistics about radio and TV audiences (their characteristics, set usage, etc.). Section H is a technology and equipment section which reviews new developments of the year and provides directory listings for manufacturers and suppliers for each medium. Lastly, Section I lists professional services, such as consultants, talent agents, attorneys, research services, and employment services. Associations, societies, and other organizations are also listed. Broadcasting schools and other educational programs are noted. A review of new books published during the year is international in scope and covers all areas of broadcasting.

Broadcasting Index. 1972-1981. Washington, DC: Broadcasting Publications. No longer published. LC 33-14221.
It was good while it lasted, and the back volumes are still useful if you can find them.

C.B.S. News Index. Annual, 1975-   . Ann Arbor, MI: UMI. ISSN 0362-3238.
Indexes all programs produced by CBS News (the evening news and special programs such as "60 Minutes," "Face the Nation," and "West 57th"). It's comprehensive, but the time lag is about three years. The 1986 edition was published in 1989.

Cable and Station Coverage Atlas and Zone Maps. Annual, 1966-   . Warren Publishing, 2115 Ward Ct., NW, Washington, DC 20037. Phone: (202) 872-9200. ISSN 0193-3639. Previous titles: *Cable and Station Coverage Atlas and 35-Mile Zone Maps* and *Television Digest's Cable & Station Coverage Atlas.*

A comprehensive directory for cable, satellite, and television stations and companies in the United States. Organized geographically by state. Lists call letters, phones/addresses, personnel, and other information for each station or company. The Atlas section shows 35 and 55 mile zone maps and Grade B Contour maps used for identifying broadcast signal areas. Also lists government regulatory agencies and other organizations with an interest in the industries covered. Lists related equipment and service vendors.

Cable Contacts Yearbook. Annual, 1983- . Supplemented by a monthly newsletter and daily updating service. New York: Larimi Media Directories. LC 85-23484.
   The directory lists all cable systems, satellite networks, independent program producers, news services, and system operators. Programs are listed along with the following information: contact person and/or office, guest information, product usage, technical and visual support requirements, subscriber figures, and pre-produced program placement opportunities.

Canadian Radio-Television and Telecommunications Commission. *Annual Report.* Annual, 1976- . Ottawa, Canada: The Commission. Text in English and French. LC 79-642670, ISSN 0704-2019. Formed by the merger of the Telecommunications Committee of the Canadian Transport Commission and the Canadian Radio-Television Commission in 1976. The *Annual Report* was previously issued as the annual report of the Canadian Radio-Television Commission from 1968 to 1976.

Communication Yearbook. Annual, 1976- . Newbury Park, CA: published by Sage Publications for the International Communication Association.
   The yearbook identifies ongoing research in the field of communications and reviews major developments and activities in the industry for the year. It presents a broad coverage, from the social effects of communications to recent technical achievements.

Communications Abstracts. Quarterly, 1978- . Newbury Park, CA: Sage Publications. LC 78-645162, ISSN 0162-2811.

The index provides long abstracts to articles of interest to people in the communications fields. The periodicals abstracted change constantly and the October issue lists the titles covered regularly. While most of the citations pertain to technical matters, radio and television articles are included that are about history, popular culture, music, and general-interest themes. There are a number of citations for audience research.

The Complete Actors' Television Credits, 1948-1988, by James Robert Parish and Vincent Terrace. 2d ed. Volume 1: *Actors* (560 p., 1990, LC 89-10607, ISBN 0-8108-2204-0). Volume 2: *Actresses* 2nd ed., (389 p., 1990, LC 89-10607, ISBN 0-8108-2204-0). The first edition of this set was: *Actors' Television Credits, 1950-1972,* by James Robert Parish. Metuchen, NJ: Scarecrow. 869 p., 1973. LC 73-9914, ISBN: 0-8108-673-8. *Supplement I: 1973-1976* (423 p., 1978, ISBN 0-8108-1053-0, LC 77-10741); *Supplement II: 1977-1981* (327 p., 1982, ISBN 0-8108-1559-1, LC 82-5961). *Supplement III: 1982-1985* (449 p., 1986, LC 86-17691, ISBN: 0-8108-1928-7).
  Each volume is an extensive listing, by actor's name, of his/her television performances. This source is particularly valuable for two reasons: (1) it lists a large number of supporting actors as well as stars, and (2) the titles of some series episodes are mentioned as well as the main series titles.

The Complete Dictionary of Television and Film, by Lynne Naylor Ensign and Robyn Eileen Knapton. New York: Stein and Day. 256 p., 1985. LC 83-42634, ISBN 0812829220.
  A good basic dictionary still useful today. Sticks close to a straight definition of technical words and terms rather than launching off into essays. Includes broadcasting, cable, television, and film language.

The Complete Directory to Prime Time Network TV Shows, 1946-Present, by Tim Brooks and Earle Marsh. 4th ed. New York: Ballantine. 1,063 p., 1988. LC 87-91863, ISBN 0-345-35610-1. Paperback.
  An alphabetical listing of all network and top syndicated TV series from 1946 to 1986. Each entry includes cast and technical credits, broadcast dates, synopsis, and some history. Network

television schedules are listed for each year. The book also includes a list of hit songs that were theme songs of series and a complete list of Emmy award winners.

The Complete Directory to Prime Time TV Stars: 1946 - Present, by Tim Brooks. New York: Ballantine. 1,086 p., 1987. LC 86-92108, ISBN 0-345-32681-4. Paperback.

An alphabetical listing of anyone who has ever had a regular role in a primetime television series or miniseries. Besides actors, it includes newscasters, musicians, emcees, announcers, and sportscasters. Length of entries varies from a couple of lines to comprehensive biographical and career reviews of major performers. Notable guest appearances are listed in addition to series credits. Several lists will be of interest to the trivia fan: a birthday calendar listing stars' birthdates; a city and state listing of performers' place of birth; a list of performers in the TV Academy Hall of Fame; and a special trivia appendix with questions and answers. It's a good place to start when you are trying to find the names of the shows performers appeared on regularly.

The Complete Encyclopedia of Television Programs, 1947-1979, by Vincent Terrace. 2d ed., rev. New York and London: A.S. Barnes, 1979. 2 vols. (3,500 p.). LC 77-89651, ISBN 0-498-02177-7.

Provides information on network and syndicated American television programs or programs imported for showing on American television. Not limited to series, but provides incomplete coverage. Each program listing includes: cast credits, broadcast dates, production information, music, plot summary, and other information.

The Complete Reference Guide to Movies Made for TV and Miniseries: September 1, 1984 to July 1, 1989, by Maj Canton. Los Angeles: Hollywood Creative Directory. 204 p., 1989.

The book lists over 600 movies alphabetically and provides broadcast dates, full production credits, ratings share, and a brief synopsis of the plot. Indexing is by subject, production credits, and names.

Directory of Experts, Authorities, & Spokespersons; the talk show guest directory. Annual, 1984-   . Washington, DC: Broadcast Interview Source. See: page 126.

Directory of Free Programs, Performing Talent, and Attractions. Annual, 1983-   . See: page 126.

Directory of Religious Broadcasting. Annual, 1972-   . National Religious Broadcasters. P.O. Box 1926, Morristown, NJ 07960. Phone: (201) 428-5400. ISSN 0731-0331.
     Directory of radio and television stations, program suppliers, people in the industry, and related equipment and service vendors who supply religious programming needs. Also lists NRB award winners.

Duncan's Radio Market Guide. Annual, 1984-   . Duncan's American Radio Inc., P.O. Box 2966, Kalamazoo, MI 49003. LC 89-646564, ISSN 0743-7498.
     A nationwide directory of radio stations, radio market information, and other information and statistics geared toward advertisers and the commercial end of the industry.

Encyclopedia of Television: Series, Pilots, and Specials; 1937-1973, by Vincent Terrace. [Volume 1] New York Zoetrope, 80 East 11th St., New York, NY 10003. ISBN 0-918432-69-3, LC 84-61786. Updates have the same title, with the years identifying the volume. Volume 2: *Encyclopedia . . . 1974-1984* (458 p., 1985, ISBN: 0-918432-61-8), and Volume 3: *Encyclopedia . . . 1937-1984* (662 p., 1986, ISBN: 0-918432-71-5).
     Volume 3 is an index to the other volumes and a "who's who" listing of names with their TV credits. The first two volumes in the series are alphabetical listings of television series, pilots, and specials with cast and production credits, music credits, dates broadcast, network, and time provided for each entry. Listings are for programs of all lengths, with some guest appearances by stars on series episodes noted. There are separate indexes for performers, directors, writers, and producers. Names may appear in more than one index.

Film & Video Finder. Albuquerque, NM: National Information Center for Educational Media (NICEM). 1st ed., 3 vols., 1987.

ISBN 0-89320-110-3. This title supercedes and replaces the *NICEM Index to 16mm Educational Films* and the *NICEM Index to Educational Videotapes*.

A bibliographic guide to nearly 100,000 commercially produced 16mm films and videotapes. Volume 1: Subject listing of films or videos and a directory of producers/distributors; Volume 2 and Volume 3: Listings by title. Available online under the title "AV Online" on Dialog (File 46).

Film Literature Index. See: pages 302-303.

Film, Television, and Video Periodicals, by Katharine Loughney. New York: Garland. 1991. See: FILM REFERENCE RESOURCES.

Gale Directory of Publications and Broadcast Media. See: Chapter 4, page 106.

Global Guide to Media & Communications, by John Lent. New York: K.G. Saur. 145 p., 1987. LC 88-128965, ISBN 3598107463.

A broad-based bibliography to international literature about broadcasting. Covers all forms of communications: books, periodicals, newspapers, radio, television, and film.

Halliwell's Television Companion. See: BRITISH TELEVISION REFERENCE RESOURCES, Chapter 11, page 511.

A History of Broadcasting in the United States, by Erik Barnouw. New York: Oxford University Press. 3 vols., 1966/70. LC 66-22258.

The set is a thoroughly researched history of broadcasting, with commentary by experts and extensive bibliographical references. Volume 1: *A Tower in Babel* covers the beginning of American broadcasting up to 1933; Volume 2: *The Golden Web* covers 1933 to 1953; and Volume 3: *The Image Empire* is about 1953 through the 1960s.

The Home Video Yearbook. Annual, 1981-   . White Plains, NY: Knowledge Industry Publications. LC 83-642584, ISSN 0277-9226.

The publication covers the business of the home video industry:

cable, satellite, video tapes, and computers. It has directory information on companies, manufacturers, suppliers, associations and organizations, and products. It also includes a list of meetings for the year and a bibliography of professional journals.

Home Viewer's Official Video Software Directory Annual. Annual, 1985- . Home Viewer Publications, 11 North 2d St., Philadelphia, PA 19106. No LC or ISBN numbers.

A comprehensive directory of organizations, associations, distributors, vendors and businesses involved in the video business. Detailed information is given about each corporation listed. It also provides a wide range of yearly statistics concerning the video industry and video use by American households. For example, it has charts on the number of VCRs in households and the amount of VCR and videotape sales for the year.

Index to the Annenberg Television Script Archive. Volume 1: 1976-1977. Edited by Sharon Black and Elizabeth Sue Moersh. Phoenix, AZ: Oryx Press. 206 p., 1990. LC 89-16199, ISBN 0-89774-553-1.

This is the first in a number of volumes planned as indexes to the scripts in the University of Pennsylvania's Annenberg Television Script Archives. This volume lists 2,400 scripts written in 1976-1977, with each entry in alphabetical order by series title and including the episode title, authors, dates of script and broadcast, which draft (first, final, etc.), and other information that may be available. A companion publication, *Thesaurus of Subject Headings for Television,* was developed specifically for use with the collection.

International Encyclopedia of Communications. New York: Oxford University Press in conjunction with the Annenberg School of Communications. 4 vols., 1989. LC 88-18132, ISBN 0195049942.

A comprehensive look at all areas of communications (film, television, radio, video, publishing) through long articles by noted experts in each field.

International Index to Television Periodicals. Biennial, 1979- . F.I.A.F. (International Federation of Film Archives), 113 Canalot

Studios, 222 Kensal Road, London W10 5BN, England. Phone: 01-960 1001. ISSN 0143-5663; ISBN 23-7-8806060212.

A comprehensive index to television periodicals. Indexing is provided for nearly 100 titles from various countries. Originally distributed as a card service. Access is by subject, title, and personal name. See: Chapter 11 on Research Resources in Great Britain, page 512 for a full description. See Also: *International Index to Film Periodicals.*

International Motion Picture Almanac. Annual, 1929- . See: pages 312-313.

International Television and Video Almanac. Annual, 1938- . Quigley Publishing Company, 159 West 53rd St., New York, NY 10019. LC 87-644123, ISSN 0539-0761. Previous titles: *Television Almanac* and *International Television Almanac.* Available on microfilm, 1938-1986, from Brookline Press, LaCrosse, WI.

Major focus is on the U.S. industry. Contents include: a review of the year, Emmy awards, a comprehensive biographical section of industry people, talent and literary agencies, advertising and publicity representatives, equipment, companies, producers-distributors, television stations (call letters and addresses), programs, home video statistics and industry directory information, major retail stores and chains, cable television directory, advertising agencies, organizations and professional associations, the industry in England and Ireland, the world market, and international film festivals. It also lists current television series, miniseries, and movies made for television during the year.

International TV & Video Guide. 1982- . London. See: *Variety International Television Guide.*

Kagan Associates, also known as Paul Kagan Associates (126 Clock Tower Place, Carmel, CA 93923-8734. Phone: (408) 624-1536) is one of the largest publishers of newsletters, special studies, and reference books for businesses dealing in cable or pay TV, broadcasting, TV program syndication, the film industry, and home video. The publications are highly technical and deal in investment and financial analysis. Altogether, Kagan publishes 25 newsletters and a half dozen annuals. Some of the more important titles are:

Annuals:

Kagan Census of Cable & TV. Annual. Statistics about cable and pay TV subscribers.

Kagan Census of Cable System Ownership. Semi-annual, 1975-   . Address: Paul Kagan Associates, 125 Clock Tower Place, Carmel, CA 93923. Phone: (408) 624-1536. ISSN 0732-2283. Semiannual compilation of cable systems throughout the United States and statistics about the systems. Information includes: date the system began operation, number of subscribers, rates charged, income received, and other information.

The Cable TV Financial Databook. Annual sourcebook of statistics on the financial data of cable.

Newsletters:

Broadcast Investor. News for investors in privately owned radio and television stations, public company financial news, and financial analysis.

Broadcast Stats. Market billings, expenditures, station sales, FCC data, for radio and TV stations.

Cable TV Franchising, Cable TV Investor, Cable TV Programming, Cable TV Advertising, Cable TV Technology, Cable TV Tax Letter, and *Cable TV Law Reporter* are all newsletters which deal with the business of cable television.

Motion Picture Investor. News for the investor in film production and distribution.

TV Program Investor. Market news about trends in television program syndication, and the different financial values on programs, companies, and businesses involved in selling programs.

Longman Dictionary of Mass Media & Communication, by Tracy Daniel Connors. New York: Longman. 255 p., 1982. LC 82-92, ISBN 0-582-28337-X.

I'm fond of this dictionary because it has a good selection of terms and defines them as they are commonly used by industry personnel, as opposed to the usual academic approach. The dictionary covers language used in advertising, TV, radio, film, publishing, theater, and public relations. If the term is used differently in the various media, it lists the meanings separately and identifies the field. They had the best definition of "actuality" that I've read in any dictionary (if it could be found at all).

Motion Pictures, Television, and Radio; a union catalogue of manuscript and special collections in the western United States. Compiled by Linda Mehr. See: page 129.

Movies Made For Television, the telefeature and the mini-series 1964-1986, by Alvin H. Marill. New York: New York Zoetrope. A Baseline book. 576 p., 1987. LC 87-43022, ISBN 0-918432-80-4. A previous edition covered 1964-1984.

Over 2,000 productions are listed. Arrangement is alphabetical by film title. Each entry provides a plot summary, cast and production credits, broadcast date, running time, network, and some background data. Indexing is by major cast members and producers. A separate list of alternate titles, with cross-references, is provided.

NewsBank. *Review of the Arts: Film and Television.* See: pages 129-130.

Primetime Proverbs: the book of TV quotes. Compiled by Jack Mingo. New York: Harmony/Crown. 255 p., 1989. LC 89-2221, ISBN 0-517-572-84-2.

A book of the most notable quotes from television series and characters throughout the history of television. Quotes are divided into sections by subject, with credit for each quote provided for the show and or character who made the statement.

Public Broadcasting Directory, by the Corporation For Public Broadcasting. Annual, 1982-   . 1111 16th St., NW, Washington, DC . Phone: (202) 955-5100. ISBN (1987-88 ed.): 0-89776-1049. LC 89-29839.

Previous title: *CPB Public Broadcasting Directory.* This yearbook of public broadcasting lists national, regional, and local public radio and television network/stations. Each station or network is fully described, major personnel listed, and production information provided. Separate indexes are provided by geographical area, names of personnel, call letters, and type of license for both television and radio stations.

Public Television Transcripts Index. Quarterly, 1987-   . Annual cumulations. Research Publications, 12 Lunar Dr., Woodbridge, CT 06525. Phone: 800-732-2477, or (203) 397-2600. ISSN 0897-9642.

An index of programs airing on public television (PBS) from 1973 to 1986. Indexing is in one alphabet by subject, personal names, and program title. The company also provides transcripts to a number of the PBS news/commentary series. Publications are timely sources of information.

R & R Program Suppliers Guide [year]. Annual. Los Angeles, CA: Radio & Records.

An annual publication in newspaper format listing all of the suppliers of radio programming for sale to radio stations. The publication lists programs by type: music features (daily, weekly, special or seasonal); news programming; entertainment news; comedy; sports; talk shows; public affairs; drama; and self-help series. It also lists program services (software, jingles and station IDs, special formats, etc.) and provides a directory of suppliers of the programs which are listed. An index lists programs alphabetically by title.

R & R Ratings Report & Directory. Los Angeles: Radio & Records. 1979-   . LC 81-644066, ISSN 0276-1831. Previous title: *Radio & Records Ratings Report.*

Published as a special supplement to *Radio & Records,* this annual directory emphasizes information useful to the radio industry. Feature articles review such industry topics as ratings, format leaders of the year, the top personalities and stations, the top 100 market profiles. A wide variety of charts and statistics are presented. Industry directory information is given for broadcast schools, consultants, employment services, equipment and service companies, media and press representatives, film studios and production companies, record companies, and research firms.

Radio: a reference guide, by Thomas Allen Greenfield. Westport, CT: Greenwood. 185 p., 1989. LC 88-24647, ISBN 0-313-22276-2.
This book is one of the few research sources which centers on radio. It starts with a broad history of radio and then follows with chapters on stations and networks, radio programming (entertainment, news, sports) and various industry topics. It lists books, periodicals, organizations, and special collections that are useful to radio researchers. Altogether, it lists about 500 radio research sources.

Radio and Television: a selected, annotated bibliography. Compiled by William E. McCavitt. Metuchen, NJ: Scarecrow. 229 p., 1978. *Supplement One: 1977-1981* (155 p., 1982, LC 82-5743, ISBN 0-8108-1556-7). *Supplement Two: 1982-1986* compiled by Peter K. Pringle and Helen E. Clinton (249 p., 1989, LC 88-23968, ISBN: 0-8108-2158-3.
The basic volume is a bibliography of broadcasting literature from 1926 to 1976. Arrangement is by broad subject classification and lists reports, books, pamphlets, and serials. Supplements update the basic volume through 1986.

Radio Contacts Directory. Annual, 1970-   . 2 vols., with monthly updates. New York: Larimi Communications Associates. LC 77-649268, ISBN 8230-8511-2, ISBN 8230-8501-3.
The directory is a geographical list of radio stations arranged first by state, then city. The following information is given for each station: call letters, address and phone, key personnel and job titles, station format, target audience, and a description of any in-house produced programming. The set also includes

network and syndicate listings, program contacts, guest requirements for programs, and guest placements.

Radio Soundtracks: a reference guide, by Michael R. Pitts.
Metuchen, NJ: Scarecrow. 2d ed. 337 p., 1986. LC 85-30409, ISBN
0-8108-1875-2.
   A listing of radio programs which are available for purchase on
   recordings and/or audio tape. It includes both serial programming and radio specials. One section of the book lists records on
   which radio stars have appeared and record album compilations
   of radio programs. All in all, a one-of-a-kind source.

Radio's Golden Years: encyclopedia of radio programs, 1930-1960,
by Vincent Terrace. Published in London by Tantivy; distributed
in the United States by A.S. Barnes (San Diego). 308 p.,
illustrated, 1981. LC 79-87791, ISBN 0-498-02393-1.
   Approximately 1,500 network and syndicated programs are listed.
   Arrangement is alphabetical by program name. Technical and cast
   credits are given, dates of broadcast, and a brief description of
   each program. A name index is useful for identifying performers
   and the programs on which they appeared.

Review of the Arts: Film and Television (NewsBank). See: pages
129-130.

Science Fiction, Horror, & Fantasy Film and Television Credits, by
Harris M. Lentz III. Jefferson, NC: McFarland. 2 vols (1,400 p.),
1983. LC 82-23956, ISBN (set): 0-89950-071-4. *Supplement:
through 1987* (936 p., 1988, LC 88-42646, ISBN: 0-89950-364-0).
   A comprehensive index to the genre. Section 1: actors and
   actresses; Section 2: Directors, screenwriters, and other production credits; Section 3: Index of films; Section 4: Index of
   television programs; and Section 5: alternate title index.

Screen International Film and TV Year Book. Annual, 1947-   .
Edited by Peter Noble. London: A Screen International Publication. ISBN 0-900925-18-3.
   Information about the British film and television industry
   directories of industry personnel, equipment, agents, artists,
   organizations, studios, and services. An international directory

and who's who section covers other countries. See: Chapter 11, page 495.

Special Edition: a guide to network television documentary series and special news reports, 1955-1979, by Daniel Einstein. Metuchen, NJ: Scarecrow. 1,069 p., 1987. LC 86-6599, ISBN 0-8108-1898-1.
A comprehensive listing of special television programs that are difficult to find elsewhere.

Studio Blu-Book Directory. The Hollywood Reporter. See: FILM REFERENCE SOURCES.

Syndicated Television: the first forty years, 1947-1987, by Hal Erickson. McFarland, Box 611, Jefferson, NC 28640. 432 p., 1989. ISBN 0-89950-410-8; LC 89-42583.
The volume lists hundreds of non-network syndicated programs. The programs are series either independently produced or past network series that have been shown in syndication. A number of programs are listed that have not been included in reference works that cover only network programming. Some good history about syndicated television is also presented.

Television; a guide to the literature, by Mary Cassata and Thomas Skill. Phoenix, AZ: Oryx Press. 148 p., 1985. LC 83-43236, ISBN 0897741404.
A brief book, divided into chapters by broad social subjects (politics, children, news, etc.). The major part of each chapter is an essay about that particular area of television, followed by reference sources for that topic. No in-depth coverage.

Television: 1970-1980, by Vincent Terrace. San Diego, CA: A.S. Barnes, 1981. 322 p. Additional section brings coverage to March, 1981. LC 81-3580, ISBN 0-498-02577-2.
This work includes a detailed listing of television series and other programming (variety specials, pilots, etc.) for the decade. Section 1 lists network and syndicated series, section 2 covers pilot films, and section 3 chronicles variety specials. Indexing is by actor and director. However, if you know the series title you want, check for it; don't rely on the index. I found the index to

be incomplete; although the syndicated series of one performer was listed properly, his name was not in the index.

Television and Cable Factbook. Annual, 1944-   . Washington, DC: Warren Publishing. 2115 Ward Ct., NW, Washington, DC 20037. Phone: (202) 872-9200. ISSN 0732-8648. Previous title: *Television Factbook* (ISSN: 0082-268X). Volume 1: *Stations.* Volume 2: *Cable and Services.* Online services: Will provide specialized data on disks or tape.

The set provides information on the television industry worldwide. It lists all television stations in the United States, Canada, and major foreign markets; local programs produced by each station; equipment used in its operations; market ratings for U.S. stations; ownership and control of stations; applications pending for new stations; a buyers guide for products and services; and all cable systems in the U.S. and Canada. Lists major manufacturers, networks, government agencies, professional associations, and organizations. Also, includes a directory of important people. A supplementary pamphlet, *Handy Pocket Directory of Television Stations in Operation [year]* accompanies the annual. Updated information published regularly in the publisher's journal, *Television Digest.*

Television & Video Almanac. See: *International Television & Video Almanac.*

Television Comedy Series: an episode guide to 153 TV sitcoms in syndication, by Joel Eisner and David Krinsky. Jefferson, NC: McFarland. 880 p., 1984. LC 83-42901, ISBN 0-89950-088-9.

Gives complete information on an episode-by-episode basis: title, dates of broadcast, guest stars, plot, and production credits.

Television Contacts. Annual, 1977-   . Supplemented by a monthly newsletter and daily updating service. New York: Larimi Communications. LC 77-646567, ISSN 0147-3352.

A directory of television programming: national, syndicated, and local programs. Information for each program: address and phone, contact person, guest and information requirements, and affiliation.

Television Drama Series Programming: A Comprehensive Chronicle, 1947-1959, by Larry James Gianakos. Metuchen, NJ: Scarecrow Press, 565 p., 1980. ISBN 0-8108-1330-0, LC 80-17023. Additional volumes of the same series and title include: *1959-1975* (794 p., 1978, LC 78-650, ISBN: 0-8108-1116-2.); *1975-1980* (457 p., 1981, LC 81-5319, ISBN: 0-8108-1438-2); *1980-1982* (678 p., 1983, LC 83-3388, ISBN: 0-8108-1626-1); *1982-1984* (830 p., 1987, LC 85-30428, ISBN: 0-8108-1876-0.

This guide to TV series gives individual episode titles, dates of broadcast, and production credits. Each volume updates the previous volumes. An overview at the beginning of each volume lists the days and times of network program schedules. Programs are listed chronologically. Several appendices list literary works that have been produced for television. This set is one of the few places where episode titles are listed for series. It makes a point, however, that not all series gave names to their episodes, so this information simply does not exist for every series.

Television Index. Address: 4029 27 St., Long Island City, NY 11101. Phone: (718) 937-3990. See: TELEVISION AND RADIO PERIODICALS, page 399.

Television Network Daytime and Late-night Programming, 1959-1989, by Mitchell E. Shapiro. Jefferson, NC: McFarland. 300 p., 1990. LC 90-52508, ISBN 0-89950-526-0.

Information about daytime programs and late-night shows that appeared on the major networks. A good place to find elusive information about game shows, soap operas, and talk shows.

Television Network Movies. Annual, 1973- . Television Index, 40/29 27th St., Long Island City, NY 11101. Phone: (718) 937-3990. ISSN 0149-7359.

Annual listing of information about made-for-television movies 90 minutes or longer that were shown separately or as part of an anthology, feature films shown on network television, series pilots that are not part of a series, and other special feature length programs made for television during the past season. Each issue is about 30 pages and covers the major networks only; it does not include cable networks. Arrangement is alphabetical by title and includes network which broadcast the film, length, date of broadcast, package release date, stars, and writer/director.

Television Network Prime-Time Programming, 1948-1988, by Mitchell E. Shapiro. Jefferson, NC: McFarland. 764 p., 1989. LC 89-45006, ISBN 0-89950-412-4.
The volume lists the network schedules for each season, program changes, and other information about the programs broadcast each year. Indexed by title. The book is divided into the seven nights of the week and notes all schedules and changes.

Television News Index and Abstracts. Monthly, 1972-   . Nashville, TN: Vanderbilt Television News Archives, Jean and Alexander Heard Library. ISSN: 0085-7157.
Published as a guide and an index to network evening news (ABC, CBS, and NBC) programs. Includes program, subject, geographical location, and name indexing.

Television Programming Source Books. Annual, 1949-   . BIB Channels (A Division of Act III Publishing), 401 Park Ave. South, New York, NY 10016. Phone: (212) 302-2680. The set is published in three volumes. Volume 1 is published in two parts (*Films/Alphabetical A-L,* and *Films/Alphabetical M-Z*); Volume 2 is *Film Packages;* Volume 3 is *Series.* ISBN (set): 0-943174-14-7. Previous titles, issued separately from 1949 through 1988, were: *TV Feature Film Source Book; TV Series, Serials, & Packages;* and *TV Series, Serials & Packages: Foreign Language Edition.*
Volume 1 (*Films*) is an industry directory of approximately 30,000 films available for rent to television stations. The listing includes theatrical motion picture features, made-for-television movies, and made-for-cable television films. Information for each title entry includes genre (drama, comedy, etc.), original release dates, production and cast credits, review rating, distributor (U.S, and International), and brief synopsis. Movies made for television are noted by the term "telefeature."
Volume 2 (*Film Packages*) is a companion to Volume 1 and lists "packages" of films that can be rented as a group, which is the way most local stations handle the films they rent for showing. While many film titles are included in both volumes, some titles appear only in the first volume since not all films are marketed as part of a package. This is especially true of older

films and foreign language imports. Films are cross-referenced by title, distributor, individual packages, and genre. For detailed production information about each title, the reader should use Volume 1. Indexing is by title, distributor, film package (a listing of all of the films in each package), distributors (key personnel, address, phone), a holiday/themes index (identifies films suitable for specific holidays), and a glossary. A special Genre section lists films by horror/science fiction, Westerns, Spanish language packages, Canadian packages, and language packages. A brief glossary is at the end.

Volume 3 (*Series*) lists approximately 20,000 domestic and international series, specials, and miniseries available for rent to television stations. The book divides the programs into four time segments by length: long form, hour form, half hour form, short form. Within each segment, titles are listed according to genre (action-adventure, cartoons, daytime, religious, etc.). Each program entry has detailed bibliographic/production information; running time (original and edited), brief broadcast history, number of episodes, years produced, cast, plot synopsis, debut year, rerun dates, original producer, and U.S./International distributor. The Long Form section contains series that have episodes which run longer than 60 minutes, the Hour Form lists series from 31 to 60 minutes in length, the Half-Hour Form contains titles 16 to 30 minutes long, the Half-Hour Comedy Form lists comedies from 16 to 30 minutes long, and the Short Form lists series with a running time of less than 16 minutes. The Language Index identifies which U.S, series are available in foreign languages (either through dubbing or subtitles). This is primarily an aid to foreign firms who want to rent series for showing in other countries. This index is organized by language and lists the series which are available in each language. A separate Spanish Language Index lists series available in that language. A Holiday/themes Index identifies series which have special holiday approaches or particular ongoing themes (Black history, Heritage, Adult, etc.). The Barter Index lists those titles sold for a barter agreement. The Distributors section lists distributors, suppliers, and producers who are sources of programming supply. Each company entry includes a list of the titles they manage, key personnel, address, and phone. A brief Glossary defines television and financial terms.

Thesaurus of Subject Headings for Television: a vocabulary for indexing script collections, by Sharon Black. Phoenix, AZ: Oryx Press. 84 p., 1990. LC 88-34570, ISBN 0-89774-552-3.

Although the book is a list of the terms used to index the Annenberg Script collection, this is an extremely useful book to use as a guideline in researching television anywhere. The introduction has an excellent discussion about indexing television collections which could easily serve as a basic introduction to television research. A small book, but a valuable one.

Three Decades of Television: a catalog of television programs acquired by the Library of Congress, 1949-1979, Library of Congress, Motion Picture, Broadcasting, and Recorded Sound Division. Edited by Sarah Rouse and Katharine Loughney. 1989. LC 86-20098, ISBN 0-8444-0544-2.

Tony, Grammy, Emmy, Country: a Broadway, television, and records awards reference. Compiled by Don Franks. Jefferson, NC: McFarland. 202 p, 1986. LC 85-43577, ISBN 0-89950-204-0.

Complete listings of winners for four major awards: The Emmy (Academy of Television Arts and Sciences), the "Tony" (American Theatre Wing), the Grammy (National Academy of Recording Arts and Sciences), and the Country Music Association awards.

Total Television; a Comprehensive Guide to Programming from 1948 to 1980, by Alex McNeil. New York: Penguin. 2d ed. 1,027p., 1984. ISBN 0-14-00-4911-8.

Lists both network and syndicated series. Although it provides fewer production credits than other sources, it makes up for this deficiency by including longer plot profiles and more information about actors' guest appearances on series episodes. It does give the broadcast dates for each program and some brief comments covering the broadcast history of long-running series. Indexing is by series and performer.

Tune In Yesterday: the ultimate encyclopedia of old-time radio, 1925-1976, by John Dunning. Englewood Cliffs, NJ: Prentice-Hall. 703 p., 1976. LC 76-28369, ISBN 0-13-932616-2.

This historical review of radio programs provides a listing of the major popular network and syndicated radio programming from 1925 to 1976. Arrangement is alphabetical by show name. Although it's limited to prime-time drama, comedy, and variety, it's still a valuable source of information. In addition, hard-to-find biographical information about many of the radio stars is also included.

TV and Radio Directory. (Volume 3 of the set, *The Working Press of the Nation*). See: pages 118-119.

TV Dimensions. Irregular (Biennial), 1983-   . Media Dynamics. Address: 322 East 50th St., New York, NY 10022. Phone: (212) 838-1467. The 1989 volume is the latest edition.
This yearbook presents as complete a picture of the television viewing audience as you could ever hope to find. It contains statistics on audience demographics, attentiveness, and exposure to programming and commercials. It analyzes audience reactions to what they see by various ways and includes breakdowns by gender, age, households, geographical areas, and income. It has surveys about VCR use, children viewing habits, studies about popularity trends in shows over several decades, network shares 1950-1988, syndicated program viewing by genre, and numbers of TV sets and VCRs per household. It uses data acquired from other industry sources, including Simmons, Nielsen, and Arbitron data.

TV Facts, by Cobbett Steinberg. Rev. ed. New York: Facts on File, 478 p., 1986. LC 82-15528, ISBN 0-87196-733-2.
A compilation of various statistics, charts, and lists of information about television audiences, the shows, and industry profiles. For programs, it lists prime time network schedules from 1950 to 1985, the longest running series, and the costs of programming. For viewers, it charts the number of TV households in America, viewers with color and cable TV, and viewing habits and attitudes. The section on ratings explains how ratings are conducted, lists the top series, the top movies, and top-rated programs of all time. The section on advertising includes a discussion about advertising techniques and includes charts for revenues, the top markets, a comparison of radio and TV revenues, and TV's share of the advertising dollar. The awards

section includes complete historical listings of awards from associations and/or publications associated with the television industry. Some of the award listings include the nominees as well as the winners. There's a complete listing of Emmy award nominees and winners from 1948 to 1984. Lastly, a section covers the networks and individual stations. It presents a brief history of television broadcasting from 1949 to date and charts profits or losses by various categories. Ownership and employment statistics are also charted.

TV Feature Film Source Book. Annual with supplement, 1949-   . New York: Broadcast Information Bureau. This publication underwent a title change in 1989. See: *Television Programming Source Books* (Volume 1: Films).

TV Guide 25 Year Index; by author and subject. Radnor, PA: Triangle Publications. 506 p., 1979. LC 79-67725; ISBN: 0-9603684. *TV Guide Index* supplements bring this basic volume up to date: *1978-1982* (176 p., 1983, LC 83-51316, ISBN: 0-9603684-3-4); *1983* (64 p., 1984, LC 84-52336, ISBN: 0-9603684-4-2); *1984* (68 p., 1985, LC 85-51243, ISBN: 0-9603684-5-0); *1985* (70 p., 1986, LC 86-050728, ISBN: 0-9603684-6-9); *1986* (78 p., 1987, no LC number in volume, ISBN: 0-9603684-7-7; a *Cumulated Supplement,* 1988.

I consider this an invaluable reference source that should be in all public and research libraries. The series indexes all articles and brief profiles published in the *TV Guide* national edition from April, 1953 through December, 1977. The only disappointment is that it does *not* index the program listings themselves. Indexing is alphabetical by personalities, titles of programs, and subject areas.

T.V. News. Annual, 1977-   . Basic volume with daily updating service. New York: Larimi Communications. ISBN (1987) 0935224351.

A directory of television news departments and contacts. It lists television stations geographically by state and city, national and regional networks, and news services. It includes major staff of each news department, news directors, assignment editors, and programs produced by news departments (along with the contact person and program description), subjects covered, and whether or not guests or specialists are used on the programs.

TV Series, Serials & Packages. Annual, 1949- . New York: Broadcast Information Bureau. Previous title: *TV Film Source Book; Series, Serials, and Packages.* (ISSN:0082-1373). This title underwent a title change in 1989. See: *Television Programming Source Books.*

TV Series, Serials & Packages; foreign language edition. Annual, New York: Broadcast Information Bureau. This title underwent a title change in 1989 and is now absorbed into Volume 3 (*Series*) of *Television Programming Source Books.*

Unsold Television Pilots, 1955-1989, by Lee Goldberg. Jefferson, NC: McFarland. 655p., 1990. LC 89-42717, ISBN 0-89950-373-X.
This volume compiles information about all of the television series that reached the development stage at television networks but were never produced. Information was compiled from news reports in interviews, press releases, articles from magazines and reports in *TV Guide, Variety, Hollywood Reporter,* and *Electronic Media.* Pilots are listed chronologically by year, then by title, and include as much information as is known about each one. Some photos. Indexing is by title, actor, director, and scriptwriter.

Variety Radio Directory. 1937-1941. No longer published. New York: Variety. LC 37-19432.

Variety Source Book 1: Broadcast-Video, by Marilyn J. Matelski and David O. Thomas. Boston: Focal Press. 124 p., 1990. LC 90-153819, ISSN 0959-1486, ISBN 0-240-80067-2.
This is the first volume of a title that plans to alternate each year between broadcast/video and film/theater industry information. Each volume will provide industry statistics, review current events, and discuss industry trends. Information is compiled from the past year of *Variety* for television, cable, home video, radio, and other forms of communications. Coverage is international. The current volume includes information about current television programming trends, charts for VCR sales and many other topics, and a glossary of terms used regularly in *Variety.*

Valuable information for the short time it was published. Each volume included a listing of network shows and the guests on each broadcast, biographies of industry leaders, and a breakdown of local programming by state and station.

Variety TV Reviews, 1923-1988. Edited by Howard H. Prouty. New York: Garland. 15 vols., 1989. LC 89-17088. Volumes 1 and 2 index reviews from *Daily Variety* for 1946-1960; volumes 3-14 index the weekly *Variety* television reviews. Volume 15 is the index to the set. Supplemental volumes are planned biannually.

Following the same chronological and print format as the other Garland *Variety* review tools, this set reproduces in facsimile every television review published in the weekly *Variety* from 1930 through 1986 and the approximately 42,000 reviews published in *Daily Variety* from 1946 through 1960. It contains reviews of local programs, daytime shows, foreign programs, syndicated programs, specials, series (both network and independent), sports, and many other types of programs.

Variety's Complete Home Video Directory. SEE: *Bowker's Complete Video Directory.*

The Video Register and Teleconferencing Resources Directory. Annual, 1979- . Address: Knowledge Industry Publications, 701 Westchester Ave., White Plains, NY 10604. Phone: (914) 328-9157. LC 79-640381, ISSN: 0087-3836.

A video industry directory which contains listings for manufacturers of audio/video equipment and related products; teleconferencing services and equipment; product dealers; production/post-production facilities; local cable systems and facilities where local cable programs can be produced; and program distributors. A unique feature is its identification of the major users of these resources (in the fields of business, government, education, and the arts). There's also a useful section for educational seminars, trade organizations, industry publications, and upcoming trade shows of interest to the industry professional.

The Video Source Book. Annual, 1979- . Detroit: Gale. LC 82-61690, ISSN 0748-0881.

Provides information on over 50,000 videos and video disks of all formats from approximately 1,300 sources. In addition to feature films and television programs, the volume lists music, educational, cultural, how-to, and sports videos. Indexes provided: title, subject, videodisc, 8mm, closed-caption, main cast, distribution sources. An unforgivable flaw is the fact that the main cast index is woefully incomplete, listing only 410 selected actors. Each title entry has information for year of release, time, color or black/white, cast, brief plot summary, and the name of the distributor/supplier.

Videolog. Weekly, 1948- . San Diego, CA: Trade Service Publications. LC 84-7822, ISSN 0746-7699.

A current, comprehensive listing of videos available for sale along with manufacturers, label numbers, and other information needed to order each title. Weekly looseleaf updates for changes.

Webster's New World Dictionary of Media and Communications, by Richard Weiner. New York: Prentice-Hall. 533p., 1990. LC 90-31012, ISBN 0-13-969759-4.

This is a new dictionary with over 30,000 words and terms (including slang) defined fully and in clear language. All areas of communications are included. When more than one meaning can be used for a term, each definition for the term is identified in the context of its use.

Who's Who in Television and Cable, by Steven H. Scheuer. New York: Facts on File, 1983. (Illus., 579 pp.) ISBN 0-87196-747-2, LC 82-12045.

Profiles producers, directors, corporate executives, set designers, critics, writers, agents, and on-camera personalities. The emphasis is on industry people rather than popular performers. Includes photos whenever possible.

Who's Who on Television, compiled by ITC books. See: Chapter 11, page 513.

World Radio-TV Handbook. Annual, 1947- . Billboard Publications Sales Office, 1515 Broadway, New York, NY 10036. ISBN (1989 edition): 0-8230-5920-0.

An international guide to broadcasting, with offices in New York, London, Denmark, and The Netherlands. The largest part of the book lists broadcasters by country. The book is divided into sections for world radio, world television, world maps showing the transmission areas, a reference section for frequency bands and frequency lists around the world, and a directory of international organizations and businesses dealing with broadcasting. An excellent source of worldwide statistics and current activity in radio and television broadcasting.

Yearbook of Radio & Television. Annual, 1964- . New York: Television Daily. Previous titles: *Radio Annual* (1938-1949) and *Radio Annual and Television Year Book* (1950-1963).

TELEVISION AND RADIO PERIODICALS

Amusement Business. See: pages 123, 135-136.

Audio-visual Communications. Monthly, 1967- . Media Horizons, 50 West 23rd St., New York, NY 10010. ISSN 0004-7562. Previous title: *Film and Audio Visual Communications.*
  Journal for personnel involved in the production and marketing of audiovisual productions. Interviews with major successful figures, articles on new techniques and equipment, graphics and computer visuals, and production planning and control. Reviews new equipment and current productions.

Back Stage. Weekly, 1960- . See: THEATER PERIODICALS, Chapter 6.

Billboard. See: MUSIC PERIODICALS. See also: DATABASES.

Broadcaster. Semiannual, with monthly updates, 1942- . Toronto, Canada: Northern Miner Press. ISSN 0008-3038. Indexed in: *Canadian Business Index.* Previous title: *Canadian Broadcaster.*

Provides a detailed review of the Canadian television and radio industries. Technical in nature.

Broadcasting; the fifth estate. Weekly, 1931- . Broadcasting Publications, 1705 DeSales St., Washington, DC 20036. Phone: (202) 659-2340. ISSN 0007-2028. Available on microfilm and reprint service of UMI. Indexed in: BI, *Business Periodicals Index, Business Index, PROMPT* (Predicasts), and *Trade & Industry Index.* Online with: Dialog.
   Industry journal for television, cable, and radio personnel. News, current issues, legal matters, government rules and regulations, latest personnel changes, cable and satellite, new shows, innovative ideas, and anything else of interest.

Cable Age. Biweekly, 1981- . 1270 Avenue of the Americas, New York, NY 10020. Phone: (212) 757-8400. Indexed in: IITP.
   Published as a section of *Television/Radio Age* since 1983.

Cable Choice; the magazine of cable entertainment. Monthly, 1986- . Boston: Cable Publications.
   Cable program listings.

Cable Guide (Horsham); America's cable magazine. Monthly, 1980-. New York: TVSM. Previous title: *Cable Today.*
   Monthly listing of programs on cable stations.

Cable Libraries. Monthly, 1973- . Newsletter from ASIS (American Society for Information Science). Available from: Tepfer Publishing, 607 Main St., Ridgefield, CT 06877. ISSN 0161-7605.
   Newsletter for libraries which operate and/or participate in cable operations and programming.

Cable Marketing; management magazine for cable television executives. Monthly, 1981- . Associated Cable Enterprises, 352 Park Ave. South, New York, NY 10010. Phone: (212) 696-5318. ISSN 0279-8891.

Cable Television Business. Biweekly, 1963- . Cardiff Publishing Co., 6300 S. Syracuse Way, Suite 650, Englewood, CO 80111. Phone: (303) 220-0600. ISSN 0745-2802. Previous titles: *TVC* and

TV Communications. Index: PROMPT. Available on microform from UMI; also available through their document delivery service.
The magazine covers business issues of interest to the cable industry.

Cable TV Magazine. Monthly, 1981-   . Available from: National Mediarep, 50 East 42nd St., New York, NY 10017. Phone: (212) 953-7755. ISSN 0277-1462.
Publishes monthly program guides for major cable stations in the United States.

CableVision; information and analysis for cable television management. Weekly, 1974-   . International Thomson Communications, 600 S. Cherry St., Suite 400, Denver, CO 80217. Phone: (303) 860-0111. ISSN 0361-8374.
Weekly news, technical developments, legislation, and program information for cable system subscribers, owners and operators.

Cableage. See: *Television-Radio Age.*

Cash Box. See: page 234.

Channels; the business of communications. Monthly, 1981-   . Act III Publishing, Television Division, 401 Park Ave. South, New York, NY 10016. Phone: (212) 302-2680. ISSN 0895-642X. Previous title: *Channels of Communication.* Indexed in: IIFP.
Current news about the business of television broadcasting. Covers all aspects, from the technical developments to social issues, with an emphasis on the financial and business end.

Children's Video Report. Bimonthly, 1975-   . Address: 145 W. 96th St., Suite 76, New York, NY 10025. ISSN 0883-6922.
This serial provides detailed annotated reviews of videos suitable for children.

Classic TV. See: page 418.

Communications Daily. Weekdays, 1981-   . Washington, DC: Warren Publishing. ISSN 0277-0679. Available online: Meade Data, NewsNet.

Community Television Review. Quarterly, 1977-   . National Federation of Local Cable Programmers, 4530 16th St., NW, Washington, DC 20011. Phone: (202) 829-7186.

Daily Variety. See: page 330.

Daytime TV Presents. Monthly, 1969-   . Sterling's Magazines, 355 Lexington Ave., New York, NY 10017. Phone: (212) 391-1400. ISSN: 0011-7129. Previous title: *Daytime TV.*
   Fan magazine featuring interviews and news about soap opera performers. It also provides synopses of the plots of the programs.

Emmy, the magazine of the Academy of Television Arts & Sciences. Bimonthly, 1979-   . Academy of Television Arts and Sciences (ATAS), 3500 West Olive Ave., Suite 700, Burbank, CA 91505. ISSN 0164-3495. On microform from UMI. Indexed in: Access, IITP.
   Articles about the history of television as well as current events and issues; features on series and performers along with information about agents, scriptwriting, legislation and new technology.

Facts, Figures, Film & TV. See: *TV Facts, Figures, & Film.*

FM Guide. Monthly, 1962-   . New York: Hampton International Communications. ISSN 0014-5971.
   Newsletter for FM radio stations. Contains news, film and play reviews, and other regular features.

The Gavin Report. Weekly, 1954-   . San Francisco, CA: Gavin Report.
   Published for radio stations, the weekly periodical provides charts for albums and singles of all of the music formats, rates new record releases, and covers station news and activities. Publishes both "top 40" charts and "up and coming" charts for music by genre.

Historical Journal of Film, Radio, & Television. See: BRITISH FILM PERIODICALS, Chapter 11, page 498.

Home Viewer. Monthly, 1981- . Home Video Publications, 11 North 2d St., Philadelphia, PA 19106.
   Reviews latest releases for the home video market. Articles feature interviews with performers and updates on latest news of interest to consumers. Some new product reviews.

INTV Journal. Bimonthly, 1985- . View Communications Corp., 80 5th Ave., New York, NY 10011. Phone: (212) 807-9595. ISSN 0882-2271. Previous title: *INTV Quarterly.* Alternate title: *Independent Television Journal.*
   A magazine for independent television personnel with articles on the business aspects of the industry.

Inside Radio. Weekly, 1975- . Cherry Hill, NJ: Inside Radio Inc. LC 82-2244, ISSN 0731-9312.
   News, trends, and information about the radio business.

International Television News. Monthly, 1970- . Irving, TX: Inez Wehrli Publishers. Journal of the International Television Association. Previous titles: *International Television News Journal, Industrial Television News,* and *NITA News.*

Journal of Broadcasting and Electronic Media. Quarterly, 1956- . Broadcast Education Association, 1771 N Street, NW, Washington, DC 20036. Phone: (202) 4295355. ISSN 0883-8151. Available on microform from UMI and through their document delivery service. Indexed in: IIFP, Humanities Index, Legal Periodicals Index, P.A.I.S., Social Science Citation Index, Sociological Abstracts, and Current Index to Journals in Education. Previous title: *Journal of Broadcasting.*
   Scholarly journal on broadcasting covering the media's influence on culture and politics as well as evaluations of programs and their impact on viewers. Reviews new books and other products.

Journal of Popular Film and Television. Quarterly, 1971- . See: FILM PERIODICALS.

On Cable. Monthly, 1980- . On Cable Publications, 25 Van Zant St., Norwalk, CT 06855. ISSN 0273-5636.

Similar to *TV Guide,* only for cable television. Publishes 54 regional editions and provides program listings for cable stations and articles of interest to viewers.

Panorama. Monthly, 1980-   . Triangle Communications, 850 3rd Ave., New York, NY 10022. ISSN 0191-8591.
Reviews television programming, compares network coverage of major events, and provides background articles about specials and how they were filmed. Articles also covers current affairs and timely topics of interest to educated viewers.

Photoplay. See: page 336.

Public Broadcasting Report. Biweekly, 1978-   . Washington, DC: Warren Publishing, Inc. ISSN 0193-3663. Available online: NewsNet.

The Pulse Of Radio; radio's management weekly. Weekly, 1985-   . Streamline Publishing, 1212 U.S. Highway One, North Palm Beach, FL 33408. Phone: (407) 626-3774.
Latest radio industry news for station managers, with emphasis on personnel changes from one station to another. Articles on current topics such as market research and programming trends.

Radio & Records. See: page 278.

Radio Only. Monthly, 1978-   . Cherry Hill, NJ: Inside Radio Inc. ISSN 0731-8294.
Published for radio managers; contains information on the latest trends, ideas, and program styles.

RadioWeek. Weekly, . National Association of Broadcasters, 1771 N St., NY, Washington, DC 20036. Phone: (202) 429-5350. Incorporates *Radioactive* (1975-1988).
Association news for members, articles of interest on managing radio stations, financial analysis, and programming issues.

Radio World. Semimonthly, 1977-   . Falls Church, VA: Industrial Marketing Advisory Services, Inc. ISSN 0279-151-X.

Religious Broadcasting. Monthly, 1969- . Morristown, NJ: National Religious Broadcasters. ISSN 0034-4079. Indexed in: Christian Periodical Index.

Reruns; the magazine of television history. Irregular, 1980- . See: page 419.

Ross Reports Television. Monthly, 1949- . Television Index, 40/29 27th St., Second Floor, Long Island City, NY 11101. Phone: (718) 937-3990. ISSN 0035-8355.
   Casting and production information for the television industry. Provides information about upcoming productions, directory information (names, addresses, phones) for agents, directors, producers, professional and trade organizations, studios, and producers of programs.

Satellite Orbit. Monthly, 1982- . Boise, ID: Comm Tek Publishing Co. ISSN 0732-7668. Previous title: *Satguide.*
   TV viewing/program guide for satellite dish owners.

Satellite Week. Weekly, 1979- . Washington, DC: Warren Publishing Co. Online on: NewsNet.

Soap Opera Digest. Biweekly, 1976- . P.O. Box 359036, Palm Coast, FL 32037. ISSN 0164-3584.
   News and story lines of all of the day and evening soap operas.

Soap Opera People. Bimonthly, 1985- . Tempo Publishing, 475 Park Ave., South, Suite 2201, New York, NY 10016.
   Fan magazine covering the daily soap operas and their stars.

Soap Opera Update. 18 issues yearly, 1988- . Address: Soap Opera Update Magazine, 158 Linwood Plaza, Fort Lee, NJ 07024. ISSN 0898-1485.
   Fan magazine for soap opera buffs emphasizes photo displays of the shows. Provides synopses of storylines of current daytime series.

Starlog; magazine of the future. Monthly, 1976- . New York: Starlog Group, Inc. ISSN 0191-4626.
   Magazine of science fiction television and film programs.

Take One; the video entertainment newsletter. Monthly, 1981- .
Little Rock, AR: Falcon Publications.

TBI: Television Business International. Monthly, 1988- . New
York: Act Three Communications.

Television Contacts. Annual,1976- . See: page 382.

Television Digest; with consumer electronics. Weekly, 1945- .
Warren Publishing, 2115 Ward Ct., NW, Washington, DC 20037.
Phone: (202) 872-9200. ISSN 0497-1515. Previous title: *Television
Digest.* Indexed in: Business Index, Trade & Industry Index.
Online in: NewsNet, Dialog.
  A weekly newsletter of industry people and events in broadcast-
  ing, cable, and consumer electronics. New equipment and
  products, current legislation, lobbying activity by various associ-
  ations, copyright rules and regulations, and any other news
  affecting the industry.

Television Index; television network program and production
reporting service. Weekly, 1949- . Television Index, 40-29 27th
St., Long Island City, NY 11101. Phone: (718) 937-3990. ISSN
0739-5531.

Television International Magazine. Bimonthly, 1956- . Television
International Publications/Al Preiss, Ltd., Box 2430, Hollywood,
CA 90028. Phone: (213) 462-1099. Previous title: *Telefilm Interna-
tional Magazine.*

Television Quarterly. Quarterly, 1962- . The National Academy
of Television Arts and Sciences, 111 West 57th St., New York, NY
10019. Phone: (212) 586-8424. ISSN 0040-2796. Available as part
of membership services. Subscriptions available to nonmembers.
  Articles of interest to the membership. Historical articles about
  trends and personalities as well as current issues.

Television/Radio Age. Biweekly, 1953- . Television Editorial
Corp., 1270 Avenue of the Americas, New York, NY 10020.
Phone: (212) 757-8400. ISSN 0040-277X. Previous title: *Television*

Age. Incorporated *Cableage.* Indexed in: Business Periodicals Index, BPI, IITP. Online: Business Periodicals Index.
   Current news of interest to broadcasting executives. Articles about networks, program suppliers, programming trends, corporate trends, and financial interests.

TV and Movie Screen. Bimonthly, 1953- . Sterling's Magazines, 355 Lexington Ave., New York, NY 10017. Phone: (212) 391-1400. ISSN 0041-4492.
   One of the older fan magazines covering film and television stars. Emphasis is on interviews and photographs. Some rock music stars have been included in recent years. A good source of historical photos and biographical information.

The TV Collector. See: page 419.

T.V. Entertainment Monthly. Monthly, 1982- . Cable publications, 333 Congress St., Boston, MA 02210. Phone: (617) 574-9400. Previous titles: *CableTV Guide* and *Cabletime.*
   Publishes detailed monthly program guides of cable channels.

TV Facts, Figures, & Film; the magazine of syndicated programming. Monthly, 1973- . Address: 100 Lafayette Dr., Syosset, NY: Broadcast Information Bureau (a division of the National Video Clearinghouse). Previous title: *Facts, Figures, and Film* (ISSN 0046-3124). Phone: (516) 496-3355. Reprint articles available.
   Provides current information about the syndicating of programs. Articles about series, personalities, and business activities in the industry. News for stations, people, and production companies involved in syndicated programming. News on both old and new programs available for syndication and the business end of the industry. Articles on program ideas from around the country.

TV Guide. Weekly, 1953- . Radnor, PA: Triangle Publications. ISSN 0039-8543. Regional publications throughout the United States. Its 35-year cumulative index includes articles (but not the program listings). Feature articles indexed in: BI, Access, Magazine Index, PROMT (Predicasts) and on corresponding databases.

TV News Magazine. Weekly, 1950- . Carmel, IN: Carter Publications, Inc.

TV Pro-Log; television programs and production news. Weekly, 1939- . Long Island City, NY: Television Index, Inc. ISSN 0739-5574.

A weekly industry newsletter which provides information about television programs currently under production and projected plans for new ones.

Video. Monthly, 1978- . Address: Reese Communications, 460 W. 34th St., 20th Floor, New York, NY 10001. Phone: (212) 947-6500. ISSN 0147-8907. Indexed in: BI.

The Video Librarian. Monthly, 1987- . Published by Randy Pitman, P.O. Box 2725, Bremerton, WA 98310. Phone: (206) 377-2231. ISSN 0887-6851.

A comprehensive listing, rating, and review source for new video releases. Geared toward libraries and schools, but useful for anyone. Brief, but well-written critical reviews cover all types of videos; good selection of made-for-video productions. Some issues highlight particular subjects or discuss issues of concern to the video marketplace.

Video Marketplace. Bimonthly, 1987- . World Publishing Company, 990 Grove St., Evanston, IL 60201. ISSN 0895-2892.

Industry news for the retailer. Includes listings of videos available for direct purchase.

Video Review. Monthly, 1980- . New York: Viare Publishing. ISSN 0196-8793. 902 Broadway, New York, NY 10010. Phone: (212) 477-2200.

One of the longest running video publications. Emphasis is on new equipment and product reviews, industry news and developments, some how-to-do-it articles about using video equipment, and reviews of the latest video tapes and discs. Successfully covers all levels of interest, from consumers to industry personnel.

Video Software Dealer. Monthly, 1985- . VSD Publications, 5519 Centinela Ave., Los Angeles, CA 90066. Phone: (213) 306-2907. ISSN 0894-3001.

Geared toward the video store owner and managers, the publication has news of latest releases, industry trends and marketing activities, distribution services, chain operations, and new equipment reviews and evaluations. Reviews of new video releases.

Video Trade News. Monthly, 1975- . Address: C.S. Tepfer Publishing Co., 56 Branchville Road, Ridgefield, CT 06877. Phone: (203) 438-7224.

Newsletter aimed toward video business personnel.

Video Week. Weekly, 1980- . Washington, DC: Warren Publishing. ISSN 0196-5905. Available online: NewsNet.

Videodisc Newsletter. See: pages 500-501.

VideoMania. See: page 420.

TELEVISION, RADIO, AND VIDEO ORGANIZATIONS

Academy of Television Arts and Sciences. Address: 3500 W. Olive Ave., Suite 700, Burbank, CA 91505. Phone: (818) 953-7575. Publishes *Emmy Magazine* and awards Emmys for television prime time (night time) programming.

American Federation of Television and Radio Artists (AFTRA) Address: 260 Madison Ave., New York, NY 10016. Phone: (212) 532-0800.

American Guild of Variety Artists (AGVA/AFL-CIO). Address: 184 Fifth Ave., New York, NY 10010. Phone: (212) 675-1003.

American Video Association. Address: 557 East Juanita Ave., Suite 3, Mesa, AZ 85204. Phone: (602) 892-8553. Established in

1980 as a trade organization that serves the interests of independent video dealers.

Associated Actors and Artistes of America (AAAA/AFL-CIO).
165 W. 46th St., New York, NY 10036. Phone: (212) 869-0358. An association made up of a number of other unions and groups representing entertainers.

Association of Independent Television Stations. Address: 1200 18th St., N.W., Suite 502, Washington, DC 20036. Phone: (202) 887-1970.

Association of Independent Video and Filmmakers. Address: 625 Broadway, 9th Floor, New York, NY 10012. Phone: (212) 473-3400. Represents the independent media producers and personnel.

Broadcast Pioneers Library. Address: 1771 N St. NW. Washington, DC 20036. Phone (202) 223-0088. Publications: *Broadcast Pioneers Library Reports* (quarterly). The library is available to researchers, who should call ahead of time to make an appointment.

Corporation for Public Broadcasting. Address: 1111 16th St., N.W., Washington, DC 20036. Phone: (202) 955-5100.

Federal Communications Commission. Address: 1919 M St., N.W., Washington, DC 20054. Phone: (202) 632-7000.

International Radio and Television Society, Inc. Address: 420 Lexington Ave., Suite 531, New York, NY 10170. Phone: (212) 867-6650.

International Teleproduction Society. Address: 990 Avenue of the Americas, Suite 21E, New York, NY 10018. Phone: (212) 629-3266. Nonprofit international trade association which also provides an educational function regarding the production of videos.

National Academy of Television Arts and Sciences. Address: 110 W. 57th St., New York, NY 10019. Phone: (212) 586-8424.

Publications: *Television Quarterly*. Awards Emmys for daytime, children's, religious, sports, and news documentary programming.

National Association of Broadcasters. Address: 1771 N St., N.W., Washington, D.C. 20036. Phone: (202) 429-5300.

National Association of Television Program Executives, Inc. Address: 10100 Santa Monica Blvd., Suite 300, Los Angeles, CA 90067. Phone: (213) 282-8801.

National Cable Television Association. Address: 1724 Massachusetts Ave., N.W., Washington, DC 20036. Phone: (202) 775-3550. Represents the cable television industry.

National Federation of Local Cable Programmers. Address: 4530 16th St., Washington, DC 20003. Phone: (202) 829-7186.

National Public Radio. 2025 M St., N.W., Washington, DC 20036. Phone: (202) 822-2000.

National Religious Broadcasters. CN 1926, Morristown, NJ 07960. Phone: (201) 428-5400. Publications: *The Directory of Religious Broadcasting*.

Station Representatives Association, Inc. Address: 230 Park Ave., New York, NY 10169. Phone: (212) 687-2484.

Television Bureau of Advertising. Address: 477 Madison Ave., New York, NY 10022. Phone: (212) 486-1111.

Video Software Dealers Association. Address: 1008-F Astoria Blvd., Cherry Hill, NJ 08003. Phone: (609) 424-7117.

Women In Communication, Inc. Address: Two Colonial Place, 2101 Wilson Blvd., Arlington, VA 22201.

10 THE FAN ELEMENT: COLLECTORS AND COLLECTING

It doesn't detract from a performer's success to suggest that the credit for some of this success belongs to the fans who have supported the artist through the good and the bad. The people who have been willing to buy products, tickets to films or performances, or with their hard-earned dollars indicate that they want to see that artist. The artist couldn't have any of it without the faith of the audience. And in the end, it's often the fans who do the most to assure that a performer is remembered through the years. When it comes to collecting, it's the fans who are in the forefront. It's usually the fans' collections that are found in libraries and archives and make it possible for some future writer to put together an accurate and complete story of a performer's career.

Not only are fans excellent collectors, much of the best detailed research comes from people who are fans of a particular person or genre. Most bibliographies, filmographies, discographies, and other detailed compilations of particular subjects are written by people who readily admit to a strong appreciation of the subject they have researched. Why? It goes back to what I said in our initial discussion about research: it is a strong emotional involvement in your work that is the basis to keep going. These research materials often take years to compile, sometimes they represent a lifetime of knowledge and work, and would be virtually impossible to complete without a long term intense commitment.

As we have already discussed, most performers don't collect information about themselves and often are the worst source about factual data regarding their careers. Their

families and staff members sometimes do have their own
personal collections. It's worth seeking them out whenever
possible. Libraries may have extensive collections, but often
can't identify the contents of what they have in great detail.
Even though entertainment periodicals have tremendously
valuable collections of information in their pages over the
years, most of the information isn't indexed.

Who has it? The fans. Fans are the most able of
information hunters; they have their "networking" skills
fully developed, and are sometimes organized at a worldwide
level. They're the ones who buy, clip, save, and spend
exorbitant amounts of effort and money to find everything:
records, publications, films, photographs, ads, posters, tour
books, post cards, fan club newsletters, sales objects, radio
and TV interviews, correspondence, and especially autographs. They buy, sell, trade, bid, and do whatever it takes to
collect everything about the artist or a particular subject in
which they have an interest. They frequently do it for years.
They also tend to carry cameras and take photographs of
every event they attend. Therefore, they become excellent
sources for historical pictures. They carry audio recorders
and video cameras with them and tape performances.
Long-time collectors may have substantial archive collections that will include important historical information not
available anywhere else.

Fan clubs and good fan club presidents have been known
to play an important part in the success of individual
performers. When a performer is just starting out, the
enthusiasm and support of an organized group of fans can go
a long way in promoting that artist's career. Club presidents
may work so closely with the artist that they function as
unofficial staff members and often handle some publicity
functions. Most journalists have at one time or another
received substantial help from the fan club president or other
prominent fans of an artist. If you need a substantial amount
of historical background material about an artist, the fan club
may be the best place to go. Fan club journals are one of the
best sources of history about a performer and will include
everything the artist was doing at the time each issue was
published as well as projects that have been announced for

the future. They frequently include copies of newspaper articles or references to magazine articles, interviews, and performance reviews. The journals are also one of the best sources for photographs that cover the artist's whole career.

In the past, most fan club presidents were fans who came from the ranks of the club membership. Today many fan club presidents are paid staff members of the performer's office and are, in fact, designated "fan club presidents" as one part of their total job responsibilities. This is especially true where performers maintain a regular office and hire several staff people to handle the business of their careers. The fan clubs are merged into their other business activities and can be more easily monitored if direct control is in the hands of the regular staff. However, this is not to say that the traditional approach is gone. It's not; it is just not as prevalent now.

There are several different types of fan clubs. First, there is the most common type of fan club, the active club for a current performing artist. The purpose of the club is to provide the fans with current news of the artist's activities and provide other information and/or products the fans may want. The clubs are designed to be fun for the fans and frequently include such benefits as contests and prizes, back stage visits with the performer at a concert, and special products that are available only through the fan club. This should not be viewed as crass commercialism on behalf of the artist; anyone who has dealt with fans will know that they strongly demand such products as tee shirts, posters, and other items. And if the items are not provided through the performer's office, they will quickly be supplied through an underground black market. In fact, the same can be said for the club itself; if a performer does not furnish a club directly, or authorize one indirectly, unofficial fan clubs may well spring up anyway as fans of a particular performer find one another and establish a correspondence network.

Fan clubs also come in the form of "societies." These may be formed in the memory of deceased artists; Elvis Presley, Bing Crosby, Marilyn Monroe, and James Dean are a few of the many performers so honored. Or, societies may be formed for literary figures: Shakespeare, Ibsen, Jane

Austen, G.B. Shaw, and T. E. Lawrence. Others may exist as organizations for people who are interested in a particular genre of music or film; there are jazz appreciation societies, "B" western societies, bluegrass clubs, and theater societies worldwide. Still others may serve as a home for people interested in a particular television series or film; Star Trek, The Avengers, and The Prisoner are three series with societies of substantial membership and the film, "Gone With the Wind" has several historical study groups.

That's the positive side. The negative? The private collections of fans are often poorly documented and some fans do not want to share what they do have with anyone else. This happens when fans relate their collections to a perceived personal tie between themselves and the performer, even though the items in the collection (clippings, articles, etc.) may never have been in the hands of that performer. They want to feel they have something exclusive, out of feeling a personal closeness and, therefore, are reluctant to even make copies . . . especially if they are in possession of something that is rare or one-of-a-kind document. Of course, they would be doing more for the artist involved if they did share, but it's most difficult to explain this to someone who feels an importance by having something in their collection that no one else has. It's understandable for people to want to keep originals, less so when they don't want to provide copies.

There are two major types of collectors:

(1) Commercial collectors who do it with the intention of buying, selling, or trading.

(2) Collectors who collect everything about a particular subject or public personality with the intention of keeping the information private.

FINDING SPECIAL COLLECTIONS IN RESEARCH CENTERS

There are catalogs and brochures about particular libraries, reference books designed to highlight collections in special areas, and special resources which seek to publicize collections, etc. Often, if a special collection has received no publicity, it's virtually impossible to find it except by word of mouth from a knowledgeable source.

When private collections are donated to libraries or museums, they become available for enjoyment by the industry and public, are well cared for, and benefit other performers as well by ensuring that this special part of entertainment is well documented. The sharing of collections and memories with everyone is a wonderful example for other people to follow; we are all better for it.

THE MEMORABILIA MARKETPLACE

There's a huge market in memorabilia in all areas of the entertainment world. The memorabia marketplace consists of specialized shops, local and regional weekend "fairs" or marketplaces, and newsletters or magazines that specialize in a certain area and have ads from shops and private collectors. Some libraries will keep lists of places that sell memorabilia as a response to patron interest.

A FAN'S GUIDE TO COLLECTING

Finding What You Want

If you want to start a collection, or expand the one you have, you can find material about your subject by reading newsletters or magazines, attending weekend get-togethers with people of similar interests, or joining fan clubs. Try for the shot in the dark: contact people who have advertised that they have similar types of material, even if they haven't advertised that they have exactly what you want. Get out and take the chance to know people because word of mouth and/or personal referrals can be especially helpful.

But any kind of collecting is definitely a "buyer beware"

world. Most collectors or dealers are honest, and a surprising number of them will go to a lot of effort to help you out at no cost at all. But, there are a few people who charge outrageous prices, fail to deliver the quality they promise, or simply don't deliver at all. If you intend to collect, acquire a little experience in your area of interest and take the time to make contacts with experts on whose advice you can rely; this will help you quickly weed out the few undesirables who are around. In general, personal collecting is an area that most people are into because of their love and enthusiasm for the medium. Sellers generally started out as collectors (and most still maintain personal collections). There isn't usually enough money in the average collection environment to get rich on. Again, most everyone knows everyone else and are quick to pass the word when someone is dishonest or difficult to deal with.

Finding Fans

A number of fan-oriented periodicals in film, television, and music, such as *Movie Collector's World* and *Music City News,* regularly provide current information about fan club names/ addresses and activities. There are also several books which compile fan club information.

Books and Periodicals

Christensen's Ultimate Movie, TV, & Rock 'n' Roll Directory. Compiled by Roger and Karen Christensen. 3d ed., 1,005 p., 1988. Cardiff-By-The-Sea Publishing, 6065 Mission Gorge Rd., San Diego, CA 92121. ISBN 0-960-80383-1. Infrequent updates provided to the basic volume.

A directory of fan club and other information of interest to fans in virtually all areas of the entertainment field. In addition to listing fan clubs and unofficial groups interested in particular personalities or subjects in the entertainment fields, the book lists current addresses of film stars and reproduces facsimiles of autographs. It also has a section for periodicals of interest to fans. This publication is a good place to start, but the information provided may not be current due to lack of frequent updates.

The Fan Club Directory. 2730 Baltimore Ave., Pueblo, Co 81003. Editor: Blanehe Trinajstick.

Fanclubs. Bedford Hills, NY: Ackerman/Rothfeld/Kazer. Distributed in the UK by David Gold & Sons, London. 2d annual edition, 1984. ISBN 0-947952-00-4.
  The book lists fan club addresses in both the United States and England. The majority of clubs listed are for pop or rock stars.

Fandom Directory. Edited by Mariane S. Hopkins. Fandata Publications, 7761 Asterella Ct., Springfield, VA 22152-3133. Number 11, 1989-1990 edition. 493 p., 1989. ISSN: 8756-8349, ISBN: 0-933215-11-8.
  A directory of fans, fan clubs, services, and research libraries. The emphasis is on science fiction, fantasy, and comic book collectors, but information is also provided for the general film collector and classic television fan. Listings appear for: fan clubs; fan periodicals and fan club newsletters; retail stores (indexed by state); a convention index; advertisers; and a geographic listing of fans' names and addresses. The book also has a section on artists and their work. Lastly, there is a section covering over 118 libraries which have research collections of interest to genre fans.

Ulrich's International Periodicals Directory under the subject heading "Clubs." Their listing of fan clubs has grown steadily over the years and now occupies several pages of small print.

Organizations

International Fan Club Organization (IFCO). The Johnson Sisters. P.O. Box 40328, Nashville, TN 37204-0328. Publishes *I F C O Journal* (3 yearly, 1965-).
  This organization works with country music fan clubs and actually rates them in terms of their services and effectiveness. It works with them, provides advice and assistance when needed, and promotes fan club activities worldwide.

COLLECTING AUTOGRAPHS

Autographs are a particularly risky business. Unless you are standing face-to-face with the performer when he or she signs, there is absolutely no way you can be sure the autograph is authentic. Still, I've purchased some autographs in the last few years and I'm very fond of what I have. The best advice I can give is to deal with reputable business people and have a good idea what the signature and handwriting should look like of the performer you want. Deal with someone who tries to guarantee the authenticity of the autograph and will refund your money if you are dissatisfied.

Regarding where to purchase autographs, I've listed several of the largest autograph dealers, but there are hundreds around. Many of the places which sell memorabilia also sell autographs, as do rare book dealers. Most film magazines will have some advertisements for dealers, as will the most popular periodicals in the other entertainment fields. *Movie Collector's World, Classic Images,* and *The Big Reel* have a large number of advertisers.

Books and Periodicals

Autograph Collector's Journal. 1948-   . See: *Manuscripts.*

The Autograph Collector's Magazine. 8 issues yearly, 1985- . Address: P.O. Box 55328, Stockton, CA 95205-8828. Phone: (209) 473-0570.

Magazine for dealers and collectors alike includes information about all types of autographs: the arts, music, sports, politicians, historical figures, and anyone else whose signature might be worth something. Recent articles covered what one needs to know about appraisals, jazz signatures, identifying facsimile signatures, collecting country music autographs, and baseball Hall of Fame postcards. A large number of dealers advertise in this publication. International in scope. The magazine sells lists of autograph collectors worldwide; the lists can be ordered by geographical area.

The Autograph Review. Bimonthly, 1978-   . Syracuse, NY: J.W. Morey.

Celebrity Autographs, by Roger Christensen. San Diego, CA: Cardiff-By-The-Sea Publishing. 1 vol., 1988. ISBN 096080384X.
    The main section of this book is a collection of over 6,000 autograph facsimiles. This was originally part of another Christensen book, the *Ultimate Movie, TV and Rock Directory.* A large number of celebrity signatures are reproduced, with the majority verified as having been obtained in person. He covers all fields, but is especially strong in film, TV, and rock music. In addition, the book lists fan clubs and autograph dealers.

Collecting Autographs, by Herman M. Darvick. New York: Messner. 96 p., 1981. LC 81-1847, ISBN 0671340255.
    A guide for the beginner which discusses the best areas to collect, how to determine the value of an autograph, ideas on how to collect autographs, and suggestions for displaying your collection.

Collecting Autographs and Manuscripts, by Charles Hamilton. Norman, OK: University of Oklahoma Press. 2d ed., 269 p., 1987. LC 87-51437, ISBN 0870695053.

Manuscripts. Quarterly, 1948-   . Published by The Manuscript Society. 350 North Niagara St., Burbank, CA 91505. ISBN 0025-262X. Previous title: *Autograph Collectors' Journal.*
    A quarterly journal published by an international society for members who are involved in all areas of autograph collecting. The society also publishes a newsletter.

The Pen & Quill. Universal Autograph Collectors Club (UACC). P.O. Box 467, Rockville Center, NY 11571.

The Price Guide to Autographs, by George Sanders and Helen Sanders. 2nd ed. Radnor, PA: Wallace-Homestead Book Company. 608 p., 1991. LC 90-70547, ISBN 0-87069-567-3.
    The book is a detailed guide to the prices you can expect to pay or obtain for the autographs of public personalities, performers, and historical figures.

Autograph Dealers

Authentic Autographs. P.O. Box 129, Everett, MA 02149. Catalog. Celebrity and sports autographs.

B.J.S. Autographs, P.O. Box 886, Forest Hills, NY 11375. Phone: (718) 897-7275.
   Autographs from film, opera, singers, composers. Photographs, letters, programs, and manuscripts.

Thomas Burford Autographs. 20 Sunnyside Ave., A241, Mill Valley, CA 94941. Phone: (415) 389-8133. Buys, sells, and trades autographs of celebrities.

Celebrities International. P.O. Box 36-D-71, Los Angeles, CA 90036. Phone: (213) 930-0539. Supplies lists by subject. Celebrity autographs on photos and cards; includes all areas of entertainment. They also sell film and stage memorabilia.

Elmer's Nostalgia. 3 Putnam St., Sanford, ME 04073. Phone: (207) 324-2166. Monthly catalog. Entertainment, political, historical, literary, and pop culture autographs and memorabilia.

The Follansbee Archives. Box 50352, Santa Barbara, CA 93150. Quality autographs, letters, and documents.

Phyllis Goldman. 404 E. 75th St., New York, NY 10021. Phone: (212) 628-4474. Catalog available. Movie star autographs and related items.

Gross. 2675 Hewlett, Merrick, NY 11566. Autographs.

Paul Hartunian Autographs. 127-B East Bradford Avenue., Cedar Grove, NJ 07009. Phone: (201) 857-7275.

Mike Hirsch. 11 Philips Mill Dr., N. Middletown, NJ 07734. Phone: (201) 787-1202. Autographed stills and cards. Lists available.

JD and Bob's Autographs. RR 1, Box 150, York, ME 03909. No phone number available. Autographs of film and TV stars, pop and country singers, writers, sports figures, and politicians.

Brian Kathenes Autographs and Collectibles. P.O. Box 77296, West Trenton, NJ 08628. Phone: (609) 530-1350. Autographs from public figures and well-known people as well as stage and film personalities.

Andrew B. Korton. 305 Columbia Blvd., Cherry Hill, NJ 08002. Phone: (609) 779-2788. Film, television, and music stars from the past to the present. Appears to specialize in some television shows such as Star Trek, Honeymooners, and Batman.

Robert Kuhn Autographs. P.O. Box 5223, San Francisco, CA 94101. Phone: (415) 474-6981. No lists available. Buys and sells. Autographs from all types of public figures, including film/TV, political, sports, literary, bands, country music, and composers.

Jim Larson's Autographs. 645 So. Harrison St., Denver, CO 80209. Phone: (303) 778-6462. Autographed photos and cards of film and television stars.

Alan Levine. P.O. Box 1577, Bloomfield, NJ 07003. Phone: (201) 743-5288. Celebrity autographs from screen, television, and stage.

William Linehan Autographs. Box 1203, 7 Summer St., Concord, NH 03301. Phone: 1-800-346-9827.

Lone Star Autographs. P.O. Box 500, Kaufman, TX 75142. Phone: (214) 563-2115 (day), (214) 932-6050 (evenings). Catalog available. Autographs of politicians, literary, scientific, film, and music people.

Nate's Autographs. P.O. Box 459, Stevenson, MD 21153. Phone: (301) 484-9392. A full range of autographs, from the common to the rare.

Oregon State Autograph Company. Box 1, Umpqua, OR 97486. Phones: (503) 459-4730 or 1-800-544-3836. Monthly newspaper catalog of autographs. Buys and sells letters, documents, books, and photographs signed by entertainers, writers, politicians, and other public figures.

Cordelia and Tom Platt. 1598 River Rd., Belle Mead, NJ 08502. Phone: (201) 359-7959. Emphasis on rare and special autographs of performers, literary figures, and politicians. Photos, letters, manuscripts.

R & R Enterprises. P.O. Box 52, Newton, Centre, MA 02159. Phone: (617) 444-3360. Monthly catalog of autographs available. Deals with all public figures as well as show business personalities and sports figures. Some rare materials.

Charles Rogers Autographs. 8721 Santa Monica Blvd., Suite 105, West Hollywood, CA 90069. Phone: (213) 464-3146. Autographed books, photos, and programs.

Safka & Bareis Autographs. P.O. Box 886, Forest Hills, NY 11375. Phone: (718) 897-7275. Catalog available. Autographed photos, letters, cards.

Janet Schray. 6721 Troost Ave., #5, North Hollywood, CA 91606. Phone: (818) 982-5099. Autographed photos and cards. List available.

Georgia Terry. 840 N.E. Cochran Ave., Gresham, OR 97030. Phone: (503) 667-0950. Catalog available. Celebrity autographs.

Louis Trotter Autographs. P.O. Box 410924, San Francisco, CA 94141-0924. Phone: (415) 626-7392. Free catalog. Film and TV autographs.

Joe Tufano. 107-25 79th St., Ozone Park, NY 11417-1106. Phone: (212) 836-3252.

COLLECTING FILM, TELEVISION & VIDEO MEMORABILIA

Books

Turning Paper to Gold: how to make money with old books, magazines, comics, sheet music, and other printed paper collectibles, by Joseph Raymond LeFontaine. Betterway Publications. 288 p., 1988. ISBN: 0-932620-97-3, LC 88-2838.
  A guide to finding and collecting material noted in the title. Useful information includes book search services and dealers.

Warren's Movie Poster Price Guide: complete index and price guide to movie posters: 1930-1959, by Jon R. Warren. New York: Harmony. 404 p., 1986. LC 85-24857, ISBN 0-517-56167-0, ISSN 0884-3791.
  A well-written and illustrated book which covers posters, lobby cards, one-sheets, half-sheets, window cards, and title cards. If these terms have always confused you, this book clearly defines each one and provides an illustrated example. It has sections on pricing, restoration and repair, foreign posters (of American films), a market review, and a 385-page alphabetical listing of films and the price of their posters and cards. This first volume covers what the author calls "the golden age of Hollywood" with future books planned on other areas and film genres.

Periodicals and Newsletters

B Westerns in Perspective. Monthly, 1983- . P.O. Box 591, Stokesdale, NC 27357.
  Newsletter of interest to western film fans covers the early films and actors.

The Big Reel. Monthly, 1973-   . Address: Route 3, Madison, NC 27025. Phone: (919) 427-5850. ISSN: 0744-723X.
  One of the oldest collectors resources around. Emphasis is on 16mm films; includes ads for stills, posters, old issues of film

magazines, lobby cards, and autographs. Largest section covers old films for sale, trade, or bid. Growing coverage of videotape and old television shows. Articles about film personalities and special subjects, such as westerns. Regular updated listing of film festivals. Ads from private collectors of all interests. International in scope. Frequently available on newsstands.

Classic Images. Monthly, 1962- . Address: P.O. Box 4079, Davenport, IA 52808. Phone: (319) 383-2377. Previous titles: *Classic Film/Video Images, Classic Film Collector, Eight MM Collector*. ISSN: 0275-8423. Back volumes available from UMI and articles available through their document delivery service. Indexed in *Film Literature Index*.
   Written for the film historian and collector, and knowledgeable film buff. Comprehensive articles cover film history, careers of performers, and overviews of film genres. Sometimes reprints appropriate articles from other magazines. Ads for all types of film memorabilia; lists of films for sale.

Classic TV. Monthly, 1988- . Address: 2980 College Ave., Suite 2, Box 25, Berkeley, CA 94705.
   A new magazine for buffs of 1950s and 1960s television. Lists old programs that are being shown on cable and other stations around the country. Historical articles about series, and information for collectors.

Disc Deals. Monthly, 1985- . Address: Disc Deals, P.O. Box 391, Pine Lake, GA 30072. ISSN: 0882-2794.
   Newsletter for the buying, selling and trading of discs (laser, audio, and video). Articles on current trends and developments in the industry and marketplace. Reviews new equipment and products.

Hollywood Studio Magazine. Monthly, 1966- . Hollywood Studio Magazine, 3960 Laurel Canyon Blvd., Suite 450, Studio City, CA 91604-3791. ISSN: 0894-2188. Indexed in: FLI.
   A collector's magazine emphasizing older Hollywood movies and film stars. Lots of ads and collector's notices.

International Directory of 16mm Film Collectors. Irregular, 1971- . ISSN: 0074-462X. Address: 16mm Filmland, P.O. Drawer F, Mobile, AL 36601. Phone: (205) 432-8406.

Movie Collector's World. Biweekly. Address: P.O. Box 309, Fraser, MI 48026. ISSN: 8750-5401. Previous titles: *Film Collector's World* and *Movie & Film Collector's World.* Incorporated *Video Shopper* in 1988.

Newspaper format consisting of advertisements and sales lists for film and TV memorabilia (lobby cards, posters, stills, autographs, etc.). Also lists for sale or trade: films, video tapes of TV programs, and international products. Collectors with special interests list what they are looking for. If you're selling, you can find a lot of listings for dealers looking to buy material. Publishes a Fan Club Directory section in each issue that updates the latest club addresses and activities. Reviews the latest book and video releases. Provides listings of upcoming collector's get-togethers and shows around the country.

Reruns: the magazine of television history. Three times yearly, 1980- . P.O. Box 1057, Safford, AZ 85548. Phone: (602) 428-0307. ISSN: 0278-6397.

Articles about vintage television programs, complete listings of series programs (including episode titles, synopsis of the story, cast credits, and broadcast dates), and overviews of television seasons by year. Extensive classified ad section for collectors of old programs. Beyond being an excellent contact source between collectors, there's a lot of good television research published here that's hard to find in the more academic journals.

The TV Collector. Monthly, 1982- . Published by Stephen W. and Diane L. Albert, P.O. Box 188, Needham, MA 02192. Phone: (617) 238-1179. ISSN: 0887-5847.

Newsletter for collectors of TV memorabilia and programming. It also publishes articles about historical television series and lists of series' episodes. News of fan clubs and appreciation societies, book reviews about television shows and personalities, announcements of new film and TV video releases, and ads for sales and trades.

VideoMania. P.O. Box 47, Princeton, WI 54968. Phone: (414) 295-6813.
   A newspaper format monthly similar to the movie collectors periodicals, but strictly for video buffs. Covers all areas of interest with lots of ads.

Video Shopper. See: *Movie Collector's World.*

Commercial Sources of Memorabilia

Another World Books and Comics. 1615 Colorado Blvd., Los Angeles, CA 90041. (213) 257-7757.

Artist's & Writer's Store. 1405 S. DeSoto Ave., Tampa, FL 33606. (813) 254-0561.

B & B Nostalgia. 14621 E. Poulter Dr., Whittier, CA 90604. (213) 941-8309.

Back Lot Books and Movie Items. 7278-A Sunset Blvd., Hollywood, CA 90046. (213) 876-6070.

Bijou. 10250 Santa Monica Blvd., Century City Shopping Center, Los Angeles, CA 90067. (213) 277-0637.

Book City Collectables. 6625 Hollywood Blvd., Hollywood, CA 90028. (213) 466-0120.

Eddie Brandt's Saturday Matinee. 6310 Colfax Ave., North Hollywood, CA 91609. (818) 856-7660.

Mike Brennan. 3013 South Lincoln, Springfield, IL 62704. Inexpensive photographs and stills of film and TV personalities.

Bridgeway to Hollywood. Ms. Jan Wahl, 1207 F. Bridgeway, Sausalito, CA 94965. (415) 332-1225.

Burbank Book Castle. 200 N. Golden Mall, Burbank, CA 91502. (213) 845-1563.

Chapman's Picture Palace. 1757 N. Las Palmas Ave., Hollywood, CA 90028. (213) 467-1739.

Chic A Boom. 6905 Melrose Ave., Hollywood, CA 90038. (213) 931-7441.

Chuck & Rita's. 5515 Lankershim Blvd., North Hollywood, CA 90068. (213) 761-2201.

Cine Monde. 1932-A Polk, San Francisco, CA 94109. Lobby cards, posters.(415) 776-9988. Good source of posters and film stills.

Cinema City. 1735 Peck Street, P.O. Box 1012, Muskegon, MI 49441. Material only goes back to the 1970s.

Cinema Collectors. 1507 Wilcox Ave., Hollywood, CA 90028 (At Sunset and Wilcox). (213) 461-6516. Open 7 days a week. Free catalog. Large supply of posters, photos, and books. Free catalog; will deal by mail.

Cinema Graphics. Box 10761, Denver, CO 80210. Posters, lobby cards, press books, photos.

The Cinema Shop. 526 O'Farrell St., San Francisco, CA 94102. Phone: (415) 885-6785. Posters, stills, pressbooks, lobby cards from film and television.

Collectors Book Store. 1708 N. Vine St., Hollywood, CA 90028. (located at Hollywood and Vine). (213) 467-3296. Stills, pressbooks, posters, scripts, magazines, books; some costumes and props.

Collectors Bookcase. 820 E. Chapman Ave., Fullerton, CA 92631. (714) 526-1645.

Ray Courts. P.O. Box 5040, Spring Hill, FL 34606. Phone: (904) 683-5110. Huge selection of used 16mm films for sale.

Creative Film Society. 7237 Canby Ave., Reseda, CA 91335. (213) 881-3887.

Dorothy's Surrender. 7985 Santa Monica Blvd., West Hollywood, CA 90046. (213) 650-4111.

Duncan Poster Service. 132 1/2 N. Beckley, Dallas, TX 75203. (214) 943-6918.

Larry Edmunds Bookshop. 6658 Hollywood Blvd., Hollywood, CA 90028. (213) 463-3273. One of the largest and best known shops. Publishes a monthly booklist of new titles received.

Fantasies Come True. 7408 Melrose Ave., Los Angeles, CA 90046. (213) 655-2636. Walt Disney items only.

Film Favorites. P.O. Box 133, Canton, OK 73724. Phone: (405) 886-3358. Good source for lesser known film stills. Also have photos from radio and television shows. Will accept "want lists."

Film Finders. P.O. Box 4351, Hollywood, CA 90078. Locater for hard to find films.

Flicker Arts. 7920 Chambersburg Rd., #201, Huber Heights, OH 45424.

Front Row Center Theatre Memorabilia. 8127 W. 3rd St., Los Angeles, CA 90048. (213) 852-0149.

Gaines Films & Video. P.O. Box 2067. Van Nuys, CA 91404. (213) 781-0331.

The Galactic Starport. 333 Jefferson St., #23, San Francisco, CA 94133. (415) 766-2821.

Phyllis Goldman. 404 East 75th St., New York, NY 10021. Autographs.

Granada Posters. P.O. Box 64980-226, Dallas, TX 75206. Phone: (214) 821-8864. Posters and one sheets.

Hollywood Book & Poster Company. 6349 Hollywood Blvd., Hollywood, CA 90028. (213) 465-8764.

Hollywood Book Service. 1654 Cherokee St., Hollywood, CA 90028. (213) 464-4164.

Hollywood Collectibles. P.O. Box 7498, Rego Park, NY 11374. Catalog available. Posters, photographs, other memorabilia.

Hollywood Dream Factory. 1842 Sylvania Ave., Toledo, Ohio 43613. Phone: (419) 474-3065. Books, magazines, and film products.

Hollywood Home of the Stars. 706 N. Gardner St., Los Angeles, CA 90046. (213) 653-4809.

Hollywood Movie Posters. 6727 1/2 Hollywood Blvd., Hollywood, CA 90028. Phone: (213) 463-1792.

Hollywood Poster Exchange. 965 N. La Cienega Blvd., Los Angeles, CA 90069. (213) 657-2461.

Hollywood Poster Gallery. 672 1/2 Hollywood Blvd., Hollywood, CA 90028. (213) 463-1792.

Jim's TV Guides. 3975 Arizona St., Ste.4, San Diego, CA 92104. Phone: (619) 298-1953.
  Sells back issues of *TV Guide* and the Canadian *TV Guide.* Also sells other TV memorabilia: photos, books, comics, toys, gum cards, and other products associated with television programs. A catalog of TV collectables is available.

Elliot M. Katt (books only). 8568 Melrose Ave., Los Angeles, CA 90069. (213) 652-5178. The bookstore stocks books in all areas of the performing arts, with an emphasis on technical and reference books on cinema, acting, music, and writing. Has a lot of publications from small publishers that are not easily found elsewhere. Catalog available upon request.

La Belle Epoque. 1111 Gayley, Los Angeles, CA 90024. (213) 208-8449. Rare posters. Free search service.

Werner Lehmann. 16 Alden Pl., Bronxville, NY 10708. Posters and props, American and foreign.

Leonardo's. P.O. Box 971, Palos Verdes Estates, CA 90274. Film stills and portraits of stars. Catalog available.

Limelight Bookstore. 1803 Market St., San Francisco, CA 94103. (415) 864-2265.

Little Shop of Posters. 5 Berkshire Ct., Westhampton, NJ 08060. Phone: (609) 267-0277. Lobby cards, posters.

Luton's Original Theater Poster Exchange. 2780 Frayser Blvd.-D, Memphis, TN 38127. Phone: (901) 357-1649. Warehouse and retail store for large selection of movie posters.

Marlow's Bookshop. 6609 Hollywood Blvd., Hollywood, CA 90028. (213) 465-8295.

Memory Lanes Antique Mall. 14251 Frampton Ave., Harbor City, CA 90710. (213) 530-8180.

Memory Shop West. 3450 16th St., San Francisco, CA 94114. (415) 625-4873. Open: Mon-Sat.

Milton Moore. P.O. Box 140280, Dallas, TX 75214-0280. Movie star photos. Some candids and portraits. Good selection of film and TV stills. Good source for old television program photos.

Motion Picture Arts Gallery. 133 E. 58th St., New York, NY Phone: (212) 223-1009.

Movie Galleria. 3111 University Dr., Suite 320, Coral Springs, FL 33065. Posters, photos, and nostalgia products.

The Movie Gallery. 2072 Front St., East Meadow, NY 11554. Phone: (516) 794-0294. Posters, lobby cards, and pressbooks.

Movie Memories. 131 Parker Ave., Hawthorne, NJ 07506. Phone: (201) 427-0709 or 427-7542. Posters.

Movie Poster Place. P.O. Box 128, Lansdowne, PA 19050-0128. Phone: (215) 352-0888.

Movie Poster Service. P.O. Box 517. Canton, OK 73724. (405) 886-2248.

Movie Poster Warehouse. 1550 Westwood Blvd., West Los Angeles, CA 90024. (213) 470-3050.

Movie Posters. 8961 Mint Ave., Westminster, CA 92683. Phone: (714) 841-1314. Posters from 1900 to date; will buy, sell, or trade.

Movie Star News. 212 East 14th St., New York, NY 10003. Phone: (212) 777-5564, 982-8364. Stills, posters, and pressbooks.

Neale Lanigan Autographs. 1 West Butler Ave., Ambler, PA 19002.

Nickelodeon. 13820 Ventura Blvd., Sherman Oaks, CA 91423. (213) 981-5325.

Nostalgia Enterprises. 11702 Venice Blvd., West Los Angeles, CA 90066. (213) 390-6564.

Jerry Ohlinger's Movie Material. 242 W. 14th St., New York, NY 10011. (212) 674-8474. Open daily. One of the largest and most comprehensive dealers for film and TV material, particularly stills and posters. Has a variety of small pamphlets listing what they have on various subjects.

Quality First. c/o 6546 Hollywood Blvd., Suite 201, Hollywood, CA 90028. Mail order only. Large supply of photos and stills. Also has posters, lobby cards, back issues of magazines, and other memorabilia.

Rick's Movie Graphics. Suite 3, 1105 N. Main, Gainesville, FL 32601. (904) 373-7202. Stills, lobby cares, posters (U.S. and foreign), and scripts from the 1950s.

Walter Rigdon. 136 Stony Hollow Rd., Greenlawn, NY 11740. American and British movie magazines and sheet music. European film memorabilia.

Ralph S. Secinaro. P.O. Box 100, Haddon Heights, NJ 08035. Phone: (609) 546-0731. Buys and sells. Posters and lobby cards.

Shokus Video. P.O. Box 8434, Van Nuys, CA 91409. Phone: 1-800-541-6219. Specializes in video tapes of vintage television programs. Catalog available.

Silver Screen. 119 E. 14th St., New York, NY 10003. Phone: (212) 677-4485.

Sy Sussman. 2962 S. Mann St., Las Vegas, NV 98102. Phone: (702) 873-2574. Large collection of photographs of performers (mostly in the film industry) for sale at very inexpensive prices.

Michael J. Tam. P.O. Box 3211, San Leandro, CA 94578. Large selection of inexpensive celebrity photos.

TV Guide Specialists. Box 20, Macomb, IL 61455. Sells back issues of *TV Guide,* 1948-1988. Catalog available.

The Tape and Record Room. 201 E. Broadway, Long Beach, CA 90802. (213) 432-7602.

Texas Movie Emporium. P.O. Box 12965, Austin, TX 78711. Phone: (512) 458-2676.

Theatre Poster Exchange. 2780 Frayser Blvd., P.O. Box 27621, Memphis, TN 38127. Phone: (901) 357-1649. Posters and stills. Will accept for "want lists."

Tiberio. 458 N. Robertson Blvd., West Los Angeles, CA 90048. (213) 659-5777.

Harry A. Victor. 1408 18th Ave., San Francisco, CA 94122. Phone: (415) 664-4286. Specializes in cigarette, food, and beverage cards with pictures of film stars or scenes from films on them. Catalog available.

Video Finders. Address: P.O. Box 4351, Los Angeles, CA 90078. A search service for hard-to-find films.

Xanadu Galleries. 212 N. Orange Ave., Glendale, CA 91203. (213) 244-0828.

Canada

Mnemonics, Ltd. Dept. "G" #9, 3600 21st St., Calgary, Alberta, T2E 6V6 Canada. Phone: 1-800-661-6538. Posters and photos.

Shelly Wallach. 32 Kern Rd., Don Mills, Ontario Canada M3B 1T1. Phone: (416) 444-8461. Posters and lobby cards.

MUSIC AND RECORD COLLECTING

Books

American Premium Record Guide, 1915-1965: 78's, 45's and LP's identification and value, by L. R. Docks. Florence, AL: Books Americana. 3d ed., 378 p., 1986.
> One of the standards in the field and used as a discographic guide to popular music by many researchers. Arranged alphabetically by performer, it includes such diverse music genres as pop, jazz, blues, country, big band, and some rock.

Country Music Buyers-Sellers Reference Book & Price Guide, by Jerry Osborne. Osborne Enterprises, Tempe, AZ. 1985, 320 p.
> Organized by performer, the book lists all of the albums released by that artist, along with the date, label name, catalog number, and estimated worth on the collector's market.

International Bibliography of Discographies: classical music and jazz & blues, 1962-1972; a reference book for collectors, dealers, and libraries, by David Edwin Cooper. Littleton, CO: Libraries Unlimited. 272 p., 1975.
> A detailed listing of recordings for the decade, intended to update previous literature which listed earlier recordings of the same genres.

Movie/TV Soundtracks and Original Cast Albums Price Guide, by Jerry Osborne. Also titled: *Osborne and Hamilton's Original Cast Albums Price Guide.* 177 p., 1981. LC 81-11079, ISBN 0-89019-077-1.

The Official Price Guide to Records, by Jerry Osborne. 8th ed. House of Collectibles. 1,004 p. 1988. Titles for previous editions varied, but the best known is *Popular & Rock Price Guide For 45's.*
   A comprehensive listing of records from 1950-1985 along with collector's price estimates for various editions. Indexed both by title and artist. The book includes tips and advice for the beginning collector; two large sections cover Elvis Presley and The Beatles.

Popular Music: an annotated guide to recordings, by Dan Tudor. See: Chapter 7.

Rock Records: a collector's directory of Rock Albums and musicians, by Terry Hounsome. New York: Facts on File. 738 p., 1987. ISBN 0-8160-1754-9.
   An alphabetical listing by artist, with a discography of their album releases. No 45s are included, although some EPs can be found. Listings are more complete for rock artists than for some of the related talent also listed.

Periodicals

APM Monograph Series (Antique Phonograph Monthly). Brooklyn: APM Press. Monthly, 1973-   . ISSN 0361-2147. Address: APM Press, 502 East 17th St., Brooklyn, NY 11226. Phone: (718) 941-6835. Indexed in: RILM Abstracts of Music Literature.
   Covers early recorded sound (1877-1930).

American Record Guide. See: MUSIC PERIODICALS, Chapter 7.

Blitz; the rock and roll magazine for thinking people. Bimonthly, 1975-   . Los Angeles: Blitz.
   Articles and information of interest to collectors.

Disc Collector. Monthly, 1950-   . Cheswold, DE: Disc Collector Publications. ISSN 0731-843X. Previous title: *Disc Collector's Newsletter.*

DISCoveries. Monthly, 1988- . Osborne Enterprises, P.O. Box 255, Port Townsend, WA 98368. Phone: (206) 385-1200. LC 88-178, ISSN 0896-8322.
> For collectors of records, tapes, and discs of all kinds of music in the out-of-print record market. Articles on collecting, performers, and historical reviews of music and the recording industry. Set sale, auction, and trade lists.

Down Home Music Newsletter. Irregular, 1978- . El Cerrito, CA: Down Home Music Inc.
> A newsletter of imported recordings for sale, mostly from England and Australia. Emphasis on rock and country.

Fanfare; the magazine for serious record collectors. Bimonthly, 1977- . Address: Fanfare, Inc., P.O. Box 720, Tenafly, NJ 07620. Phone: (201) 567-3908. ISSN 0148-9364. Indexed in: Music Index.
> Rather scholarly articles cover music collecting from classical to country. Lengthy book and audio reviews. International in scope. Classified ads section for reader/collector inquiries.

Goldmine; the record collector's marketplace. Bi-weekly, 1974- . Address: Krause Publications, 700 E. State St., Iola, WI 54945. ISSN 0271-2520. Available on microform from UMI.
> This magazine has the largest circulation of all of the collector's magazines. It features articles, interviews, information for record collectors in all music fields, with an emphasis on rock. Advertisements for dealers sales and auction lists make up a large part of the publication. Articles include in-depth discographies for both recording artists and record companies. In addition to records of all formats, it has ads for sheet music, an ongoing convention calendar, and reviews new publications. Includes a small amount of video tape, television programming and film.

Horn Speaker; the newspaper for the hobbyist of vintage electronics and sound. Monthly, 1972- . Address: Jim Cranshaw, Publisher, Box 53012, Dallas, TX 75253. Phone: (214) 286-1673.

I.A.J.R.C. Journal. Quarterly, 1967- . Islington, Ontario, Canada: International Association of Jazz Record Collectors. ISSN 0098-9487. Indexed in: Music Index.

Jukebox Collector Newsletter. Address: 2545 S.E. 60th Ct., De Moines, IA 50317-5099. Phone: (515) 265-8324. ISSN 0882-4908.

Music Clubs Magazine. Quarterly, 1922- . Indianapolis, IN: National Federation of Music Clubs. ISSN 0161-2654.

Paul's Record Magazine. Enfield, CT: Paul E. Bezanker, Editor and Publisher. Irregular, 1975- . ISSN 0360-2109.

Record Collector. See: page 434.

Record Collector's Monthly. Irregular (4 to 6 issues yearly), 1982- . Mendham, NJ: Record Collector's Monthly. ISSN 8755-6154.
  Similar to *Goldmine* in scope and content. Record collecting in all areas of popular music, with emphasis on the 1950s and 1960s.

Record Exchanger. Quarterly, 1969- . Orange, CA: Vintage Records. ISSN 0557-9147.

The Record Finder. Monthly, 1984- . P.O. Box 1047, Glen Allen, VA 23060. Phone: (804) 273-9141 or 266-1154.
  Source for records of all interests. Also a source for sheet music, reel tapes, disks. Information about conventions. Few articles; the magazine is made up mostly of auction and sales lists from collectors.

Schwann Record & Tape Guide. See: pages 279-280.

Sheet Music Exchange. Bimonthly, 1983- . Quicksburg, VA: Sheet Music Exchange. ISSN 0741-7780.

Show Music. Quarterly, 1981- . Las Vegas, NV: Show Music. 87-658664, ISSN 8755-9560.
  For collectors of theater, musical shows of all kinds. Information about cast recordings, musical shows, nostalgia records, and reissues. Reviews new recordings, relevant books, and some videos.

Organizations

Association For Recorded Sound Collections. The Association publishes two publications: a *Newsletter* and its *Membership Directory* (which includes a brief listing of the collections and interests of each member).

The *Newsletter* contains announcements and newsnotes about ongoing projects of the membership, records or equipment being sought by members, current restoration work, new publications, and new record releases of interest to members.

THEATER MEMORABILIA

Applause Theatre Books. 211 W. 71st St. New York, NY 10023. Phone: (212) 496-7511.

Backstage Books. P.O. Box 53383, Washington, DC 20009.

Cinemabilia Inc., Film Book Graphic Center, 611 Broadway, The Cable Building, Suite 203, New York, NY 10012.

Drama Books. 511 Geary St., San Francisco, CA 94102.

Drama Book Shop. 723 7th Ave., New York, NY 10019. Phone: (212) 944-0595.

Samuel French Theater and Film Bookshop. 7623 Sunset Blvd, Hollywood, CA 90046. One of the biggest and best known bookstores for international theater books covering all aspects of the industry.

Golden Legend, Inc. 7615 Sunset Blvd., Los Angeles, CA 90046.

Image Theatre Art. Box 949, Kenwood, CA 95452.

Howard Karno Books. P.O. Box 431, Santa Monica, CA 90406.

Pagent Book and Print Shop. 109 East Ninth St., New York, NY 10003. Phone: (212) 674-5296.

Anna Sosenko, 76 West 82 St., New York, NY 10024.

Richard Stoddard. 18 East 16th St., New York, NY 10003. Phone: (212) 645-9576.

Strand Book Store. 828 Broadway, New York, NY 10003. Phone: (212) 473-1452.

Theatre Arts Bookshop. 405 West 42nd St., New York, NY 10036. Phone: (212) 564-0402.

Theatricana. P.O. Box 4244, Campus Station, Athens, GA 30605.

Triton Gallery. 323 West 45 St., New York, NY 10036. Phone: (212) 765-2472.

BRITISH FANS & COLLECTING RESOURCES

Fans

Fanclubs. See: FANS.

The Theatre

A.E. Cox. 21 Cecil Rd., Itchen, Southampton SO2 7HX. Phone: 0703-447989. One of the best known dealers in theatre books, posters, stills, play programs, and out-of-print periodicals. He also has a large cinema collection.

Anne Fitzsimons. The Retreat, The Green, Wetheral, Carlisle, Cumbria CA4 8ET.

French's Theatre Bookshop. 52 Fitzroy St., London W1P 6JR. Phone: 01-387 9373.

Gaby Goldscheider. 29 Temple Rd., Windsor, Berkshire, England SL4 1HP.

Langton Gallery, Limited. 3 Langton St., London SW10 0JL.

Ed Meredith. Circus Crafts, 4 Argyil St., Ryde, Isle of Wight PO33 3BZ.

C. D. Paramor. 25 St. Mary's Sq., Newmarket, Suffolk CB8 0HZ. Phone: 0638 664416. Conducts business by mail only. A good source of historical theater programs, posters, periodicals, and other materials. Current and out-of-print books.

Peter Wood. 20 Stonehill Rd., Great Shelford, Cambridge CB2 5JL. Specializes in rare items from all areas of the performing arts.

Photography

The Photographic Collector. Quarterly, 1980- . Bishopsgate Press, 37 Union St., London SE1 1SE. Phone: 01-403 6544. ISSN 0260-5155.
   An interesting journal with articles on photo collections in libraries and museums, some private collections, and information of interest to collectors. Lists collectors clubs and runs advertising associated with collectors.

Picture Researcher's Handbook: an international guide to picture sources. See: page 144.

Film and Television

Inter Film Collector. 15 Wallace Ave., W. Worthing, West Sussex BN11 5RA England.

Bookshops

Cinema Bookshop. 13 Great Russell St., London WC1. Phone 01-637 0206.

Decorum Books. 24 Cloudesley Sq., London N1. Dealers in secondhand film and television books and periodicals.

Flashbacks. 6 Silver Pl., Beak St., London W1R 3LJ. Phone: 01-437 8562.

Motley Books. Mottisfont Abbey, Romsey, Hampshire SO5 0LP. A mail order business dealing in early cinema literature and memorabilia.

That's Entertainment. 43 The Market, Covent Garden, London WC2E. Phone: 01-240 3490.

U.K. Poster Dealer. Sylvia Edwards, 23 Marchmont Rd., Edinburgh, EH9 1HY Scotland. Posters, lobby cards, stills.

The Vintage Magazine Shop. 39-41 Brewer St., London W1V 7HF. Phone: 01-439 8525. A large collection of British film and television magazines, as well as other British journals.

Weinberg. 51 Carmarthen Ave., Portsmouth, England. British posters, stills, pressbooks.

Record Collecting

Collectors Items. John A. Holly, 10 Rydens Rd., Walton-on-Thames, Surrey KT12 3BX England. Phone: 0932 242862. Bimonthly, 1980-   . ISSN: 0261-2550.

Record Collector. Monthly, 1948-   . Ipswich: Record Collector. LC 61-40750, ISSN: 0034-155X. Address: Heanor Record Centre, Ltd., 47 Derby Road, Heanor, Derbyshire DE7 7QH. Previous title: *Record Buyer.*

Record Collector. Monthly, 1980-   . London: Diamond Publishing Group. ISSN: 0261-250X.

Vintage Record Mart. Bimonthly, 1970-   . Address: London Hill, Rayleigh, Essex SS6 7HP.

11   RESEARCH RESOURCES IN GREAT BRITAIN

The purpose of this chapter is to give a general overview of how to conduct entertainment research in Great Britain and cover the major research centers and materials that are unique to that country.

If you do entertainment research on a regular basis, you know that there's a strong tie between the theater, film, and music industries of Great Britain and the United States. And if you do very much historical research, it won't be long before you find yourself in England in spirit, if not in body.

One thing to keep in mind: Britain is much smaller in both population and geographical area than the United States and therefore can't be expected to have the numbers of special collections or facilities that we do. It's a country where World War II still impacts the life of the average person. It's still common in Britain to be told during a visit to an institution that they used to have more, but so much was lost in the bombing during the war. Lastly, the economy is different from the United States. Consequently, people and organizations give serious thought to the way they spend even the smallest amount of money in an effort to make the best use of what they have. It's a careful approach because funds arc limited. In spite of all of this, they have built and maintained an impressive collection of historical materials.

Funding from the government is scarce today. Most organizations are scrambling to find sources of support and are often competing for the same dollars. As a result, Britain is pretty much of a fee-based society in everything it does. Expect to pay for what you use. And take enough money along to join some of the organizations whose libraries you plan to use because it's often less expensive to become a member for a year than pay a daily fee for several days of access to a research facility.

I have to provide a word of caution about getting around: many buildings in Britain lack elevators or escalators and it's often necessary to walk up one or more flights of stairs to get to your destination. This is true in the Underground too; there are a lot of stairs in most of the stations, even the ones with escalators. If you are handicapped in your ability to move around easily, be sure to inquire about access when you make your plans. It appeared to me that access, particularly for people in wheelchairs, was simply not possible in many cases.

You can avoid some initial frustrations by realizing that there are occasionally significant differences in the meanings of some words between American and British English language. The quicker you can identify them the better off you will be. On my first trip to England I had trouble getting directions to subway stations the first few times I asked for them until I finally figured out that there was a language problem involved. It may be a small matter, but the subway system in London is called "The Underground," or sometimes "The Tube." It is NEVER called a subway. The term "Subway" in England is used for walkways or sidewalks that go under a road; if you ask directions to the subway, you will find yourself at the entrance to a tunnel.

THE RESEARCHER IN ENGLAND

Let me preface this section by saying that most institutions in England lack sufficient staff and sometimes the physical facilities to deal with more than a few people at a time and therefore by necessity must limit the number of patrons they can serve on a particular day. Because of these limitations, and the desire to protect their resources (some of which are fragile, old, or rare), their rules are somewhat different than we normally encounter in the United States. Most libraries have "closed collections," meaning that the stack or storage areas are closed to everyone but the staff. Therefore researchers cannot browse or retrieve materials themselves; rather they must request what they want and wait for the material to be brought to them, which is often a slow process. Of course, the same procedures apply in American libraries that have collections of rare materials.

Before you visit British facilities, you need to give some thought as to what they expect from you rather than just thinking about what you expect from them. This calls for a different frame of mind for Americans, who are used to walking into libraries unannounced and virtually demanding a full range of services at no waiting and no cost. It doesn't work that way in England. Each side has a role to play and expectations to meet.

The patron has certain responsibilities that must be met before he or she can expect to receive the services of a particular special library:

(1) You MUST write and request permission to use the collection, provide references if requested, and wait to receive approval for your visit. All of this demands quite a bit of time, persistence, and patience. Be sure to build in the time needed to accomplish this before you even start planning your trip or there may be no trip to take.

(2) You MUST have a specific purpose for your visit; you can't go to "browse." Many of the special libraries see themselves as a "library of last resort" and encourage researchers to do as much of their research as possible in public or college libraries before they contact them. Therefore, be prepared to make a convincing argument that you can't find the material any place else.

(3) You frequently MUST be able to state exactly what material you wish to use in the collection.

(4) Manners are expected. (Show up on time, do as requested, follow rules, and write thank-you notes.)

The copyright law is taken seriously in Britain. Photocopying the material yourself is no excuse for avoiding the law.

Photocopy services are expensive and not every library has a machine available for public use. Most public libraries do have at least one coin-operated machine in a public area, but many private research libraries do not. Sometimes machines aren't available at all and material may not be copied under any circumstances. In many places, you will have to leave the material to be copied and come back after it another day. One word of advice, the British coins are big and heavy; take some sort of coin pouch with you if you plan on using very many coins. They will never fit in a regular American billfold.

While researchers may be a little "put off" at some of the rules and procedures, there are reasons for the rules and regulations you encounter and you will have to learn to live with them. Conversely, since very little has been put on microform or copied, it's an exciting experience to be able to hold a rare book in your hand; it makes the effort it took to get there worth every second. I think you will find that the British librarians are most helpful once they know you are serious about your work.

Since many of the special libraries require advance application from visitors and/or see themselves as a "library of last resort," where do foreign visitors go to do some quick research of a general nature? The answer is, the public libraries. The Guildhall Library, the Westminster City Library, and The British Library's Newspaper Library at Colindale are especially good places to conduct quick general research. All three are discussed later in this chapter.

GENERAL RESEARCH REFERENCE RESOURCES

Reference Books, Abstracts, and Indexes

Artistes and Their Agents. Annual, 1980-   . John Oxford Publications, 12 The Avenue, Eastbourne, East Sussex BN21 3YA. Phone: Eastbourne (0323) 645871. ISSN 0143-8131; ISBN (1986 ed.) 0-903931-69-9. Incorporates: *Entertainment Event Information Directory.*

A directory of British entertainment artists from all fields and their agents or representatives.

Arts & Humanities Citation Index. 3 issues yearly, 1977- . See: page 98.

Aslib Directory of Information Sources in the United Kingdom. Edited by Ellen M. Codlin. London: Aslib. Fifth edition, 2 vols., 1982/84. Volume 1: *Science, Technology, and Commerce* (1982); Volume 2: *Social Sciences, Medicine, and the Humanities* (1984). ISBN 0851421849.
    A subject listing of British reference books, serials, and periodicals.

Benn's Media Directory. Annual, 1846- . Tonbridge, Kent: Benn's Business Information Services. Issued in two volumes: International (LC 86-648222) and United Kingdom (LC 86-648221). Previous titles: *Benn's Press Directory* (1978-1985) and *Newspaper Press Directory* (1846-1978).
    An annual directory of newspapers, periodicals, and other serial titles published in the United Kingdom. Each entry provides the address, phone, beginning date, general description of content and style, and the geographical area served.

Bibliographic Index. See: page 99.

British and Irish Library Resources, by Robert B. Downs and Elizabeth C. Downs. London: Mansell; distributed in the United States by H.W. Wilson. Revised and updated edition. 427 p., 1981. LC 82-210249, ISBN 072011604X.
    An extensive bibliography listing descriptive information about libraries throughout Great Britain. The book lists published catalogs of library collections, in-print descriptions of special collections, articles about British libraries, and other publications (such as pamphlets and reports).

British Book News. Monthly, 1940- . The British Council, 10 Spring Garden, London SW1A 2BN. Phone: 071-499 8011. LC

53-39085, ISSN 0007-0343. Previous title: *Selection of Recent Books Published in Great Britain* (1940-1941).
The major review source for new publications in England.

British Books In Print. Annual, 1874- . London: Whitaker & Sons. LC 02-7496, ISSN 0068-1350. Distributed in the U.S. by R.R. Bowker, New York. Previous title: *The Reference Catalogue of Current Literature*. Available online: Dialog.
A listing of new books published during the year. Arrangement is alphabetical by author, title, and broad subject area. A current directory of British publishers is also included.

British Education Index. 3 issues yearly, 1954- . Annual cumulation. British Library, Bibliographical Services Division, 2 Sheraton St., London W1V 4BH. LC 61-45718, ISSN 0007-0637.
Indexes over 300 English-language periodicals by broad subject; coverage not limited to education, despite the title.

British Humanities Index. Quarterly, 1915- . Annual cumulative volumes. Library Association, 7 Ridgmount St., London WC1E 1AE. ISSN 0007-0815. Previous title: *The Subject Index to Periodicals* (1915-1961).
A subject index to approximately 375 British periodicals (and some newspapers) in the humanities and social sciences. See also the American *Humanities Index*.

British Library Directory. Chicago: St. James. 162 p., 1989. ISBN 1-55862-043-5.
A listing of public and special libraries in Great Britain and Northern Ireland. It gives the name, address, and phone of the libraries and brief descriptions of their collections.

British National Bibliography. Weekly, 1950- . Quarterly and annual cumulations. London: British Library, Bibliographic Services Division, 2 Sheraton St., London W1V 4BH. Phone: 071-636 1544. LC 51-6468, ISSN 0007-1544. Also available on microfiche and online.
This is a national bibliography of books received by the Copyright Office of the British Library. Arrangement is by subject, with author and title indexes. Series are included, but

periodicals are identified separately after 1980 in their *Serials in the British Library* (Quarterly, 1981-). It's often used as an extension of the British Library *General Catalog* because of its subject arrangement and completeness in current information.

British Performing Arts Yearbook. Annual, 1988- . Rhinegold Publishing, 241 Shaftesbury Ave., London WC2H 8EH. Phone: 071-240 5740. LC 89-18399, ISSN 0951-5208.
This is the first edition of a yearbook and directory of entertainment facilities, organizations, and suppliers which covers all of Great Britain. It lists venues in the larger cities and throughout each country, performers and companies in the musical and performing arts, and agents for music and entertainment artists. In addition, it provides information on associations and arts councils and identifies arts festivals.

British Technology Index; a current subject guide to articles in British technical journals. Published 1962-1980. ISSN 0007-1889. Previously published as: *The Subject Index to Periodicals* (1915-1961). Superseded by: *Current Technology Index* (1981- .).

British Union Catalogue of Periodicals. See: *Serials in the British Library*.

Contacts. See: *Spotlight Contacts*.

Current British Directories. Irregular, 1953- . C.B.D. Research, 154 High St., Beckenham, Kent, BR3 1EA. LC 53-26894, ISSN 0070-1858.
A listing of several thousand directories of professional associations, organizations, and other membership groups throughout the British Commonwealth.

Current Technology Index. Monthly, 1981- . Annual volume. London: The Library Association. LC 81-644003, ISSN 0260-6593. A supplement is currently issued under the title *Catchword and Trade Name Index* (Quarterly, 1981- ; ISSN 0261-0191). Continues *British Technology Index* (1962-1980). Before that, it was part of the *Subject Index to Periodicals* (1915-1961). Available on microform from Oxford Microform Publications.

The Dictionary of National Biography. London: Smith, Elder. 63 vols., 1885/1900. *Supplements* through 1960 published by the Oxford University Press (London).

The most important British biographical source. Includes information about people from all fields. Although all the people included have gained respect in their profession, many are not well known outside of their chosen profession. Consequently, this set is worth using if you need to find information about the less noted entertainers.

Directory of British Associations and Associations of Ireland. Irregular, 1965-   . LC 83-7346. 9th ed., 1988 (ISBN 0-900246-49-9). Edited by Henderson, G.P. and Henderson, S.P.A.. Published by CBD Research, Ltd., 15 Wickham Rd., Beckenham, Kent BR3 2JS. Phone: 081-650 7745. ISSN 0070-5152. Distributed in the United States by Gale Research (Detroit).

A directory covering all types of associations, societies, and organizations in Great Britain. Each entry gives the address, phone, and a brief profile of the organization.

Fan Clubs. See: pages 432-434.

International Who's Who. Annual, 1935-   . LC 35-10257, ISSN 0074-9613. Europa Publications, 18 Bedford Sq., London WC1B 3JN.

The Libraries of London. Edited by Raymond Irwin, and Ronald Staveley. 2nd rev. ed. 332 p., 1961. London: The Library Association. LC 62-1104.

The Library Student's London, by Brian H. Baumfield and Kenneth Roy McColvin. London: Association of Assistant Librarians (South Eastern Division). 2nd ed. 196 p., 1969. LC 74-429354.

A good guide on research facilities of interest to library school students. It also has a very useful chapter on used bookshops and places where one can purchase back issues of periodicals.

The Newspaper Press In Britain: an annotated bibliography. Edited by David Linton and Ray Boston. 361 p., 1987. London: Mansell Publishing. LC 86-23837, ISBN 0-7201-1792-5.

An extensive listing of British newspapers, both current and past, with information about their publishing history. An excellent place to find out what newspapers are published in a particular geographical area of Great Britain or specific details about a particular title.

Picture Researcher's Handbook: an international guide to Picture Sources and how to use them, by Hilary Evans. See: PHOTO RESEARCH in Chapter 5.

Picture Sources UK. Edited by Dr. Rosemary Eakins. Published by Macdonalds & Co., Maxwell House, 74 Worship St., London EC2A 2EN. 474 p., 1985. LC 86-127772, ISBN 0-356-10078-2.
An excellent guide to research facilities and commercial sources of photographs. If you are seeking to purchase photographs, there are lists of professional photographers and their collections, organizations and/or libraries that have photo collections, and stores that sell stills and other related materials.

Poole's Index to Periodical Literature. 1802-1881. *Supplements* (1882-1887, 1888-1908). A *Cumulative Author Index, 1802-1906* is available from Pierian Press (Ann Arbor). See: SMALL TOWN RESEARCH, Chapter 4, page 112, for detailed description.

Serials in the British Library, together with locations and holdings of other British and Irish libraries. Quarterly, 1981- . Annual cumulation. British Library, Bibliographic Services. Address: 2 Sheraton St., London W1V 4BH. Phone: 071-323 7077. ISSN 0260-0005. Continues the *British Union Catalogue of Periodicals* (BUCOP), which ceased at the end of 1980.

Showcall. Annual, 1973/74- . Published by Carson and Comerford, Stage House, 47 Bermondsey St., London SE1 3XT. Phone: 071-403 1818. ISSN 0264-4150, ISBN (1988, 2v.) 0-9010-48-23-2.
A long-running directory of artists and their representatives. The main body of the directory is an alphabetical listing of artists and attractions available for work. The remainder of the volume lists directory information for agents, management firms, venues, services, suppliers, and associations and organizations. The

publishers also put out *Stage and Television Today,* Britain's leading theatrical newspaper.

The Showman's Directory. Annual, 1968- . Since 1982, the annual is published in two parts, September and December. Stephen & Jean Lance Publications, Brook House, Mint St., Godalming, Surrey, GU7 1HE. Phone: 048 6822184. ISBN 0946-509-17-4.
     A directory of venues, suppliers, and services; everything one needs to put on a show.

Spotlight Casting Directory. Annual, 1928- . Published by The Spotlight, 42-43 Cranbourn St., London WC2H 7AP. Phone: 071-437 7631.
     A several-part directory of British actresses, actors, and children available for work. Each entry includes a photo, physical description of the person, agent and phone number.

Spotlight Contacts. Annual, 1947- . Published by The Spotlight, 42-43 Cranbourn St., London WC2H 7AP. Phone: 071-437 7631. ISSN 0010-7344.
     An extensive directory of organizations, manufacturers, and services associated with the entertainment industry in Great Britain. The directory lists agents and representatives, Arts associations, associations and unions, production companies, venues, promoters, newspaper critics, stage and film theaters, press cutting agencies (newspaper clipping services), periodicals and other publications, photographers, touring companies, film and television companies, and many other businesses.

Subject Index to Periodicals. 1915-1961. No longer published. London: Library Association. Previous title: *Athenaeum Subject Index to Periodicals* (1915-1919). This index was split into two separate titles and continued by *British Humanities Index* and *British Technology Index* (itself continued by *Current Technology Index*).
     The major index to periodicals in England during its time. Still valuable as a research tool if you can find it because the *British Humanities Index* only started where it left off.

Whitaker's Almanack. Annual, 1869-   . J. Whitaker & Sons, 13 Bedford Sq., London WC1B 3JE. Alternate title: *An Almanac.* ISSN 0083-9256. Distributed in the United States by Gale Research (Detroit, MI).

Similar to the American *World Almanac,* each volume notes important events of the year, compiles statistics, and identifies important people in British government and society. Addresses of associations, societies, and clubs are included.

Who's Who: an annual biographical dictionary. Annual, 1849-   . LC 04-16933, ISSN 0083-937X. A & C Black, Publishers. Address: 35 Bedford Row, London WC1R 4JH. Published in the U.S. by St. Martin's Press, New York.

The original *Who's Who;* all similar titles took their formats from this one. Each volume is a listing of important people in the British Isles. Back volumes are valuable for the historical information they contain. A *Who Was Who* (1897-   . LC 20-14622) series is also published about those who have died.

Willing's Press Guide: a guide to the press of the United Kingdom and to the principal publications of Europe, Australasia, the Far East, Middle East, Africa and the Americas. Annual, 1874-   . British Media Publications: Windsor Ct., East Grinstead House, East Grinstead, West Sussex RH19 1XE. LC 53-36485, ISSN 0000-0213. Previous titles: *Willing's Press Guide and Advertisers' Directory and Handbook* (1899-1927) and *Willing's Press Guide* (1874-1899). Current title started in 1928.

Covers the newspaper and periodical industries of the countries named in the title.

Writers' & Artists' Yearbook. Annual, 1906-   . London: A & C Black. LC 08-22320, ISSN 0084-2664. Distributed in the United States by Writer's Digest Books (current volumes published in the United States under the title: *International Writers' & Artists' Yearbook*). Similar in content format to the American *Writer's Market* annual.

The book is arranged in two parts: (1) a directory of markets for articles, books, scripts (stage, film, radio, and TV), photographs, poetry, music, and research; and (2) general information of interest to writers, with articles about financial matters, laws and regulations, publishing practices, research techniques and manuscript preparation, and associations. There's also a section listing literary agents.

Databases

Automated database services are just now coming into their own in Great Britain. Few libraries are able to provide public services in this area yet, and those who can offer automated reference searching have many of the same databases available in the United States. *Nexis* and *Dialog* are the most common. When it comes to British databases, *World Reporter* is just about the only commercial media database around.

The majority of the databases developed in England are of specialized collections, such as the British Library *Catalog* and *British Books In Print*. This follows the general European style of smaller, single file, specialized databases rather than large, multi-file systems. Most European countries are small and the commercial market for each service is therefore limited. Just as important, there is the need to provide information in each of the many foreign languages throughout Europe and the desire by Europeans to have their own publications indexed. The larger databases tend to reflect a strong American bias (at the expense of an international perspective) because they were developed in the United States and largely contain American publications. And as with the broadcasting industry and other industries throughout much of the world, many of the databases may be government funded or otherwise regulated. Many countries do not share the American political view that government involvement in various industries is a conflict of interest. As a result, it is not considered unusual or undesirable for newly developing industries to receive financial support from their government or be closely regulated. Similar to the early stages of American development, the databases to be most heavily marketed are the financial information systems. This is where the money is, and businesses are the most viable market for the product.

BLAISE (British Library Automated Information Service). This database has two services: *BLAISE-LINE* is geared to the library market and contains the *UKMARC* and *LCMARC* files of bibliographic cataloging records as well as *WHITAKERS* (British Books in Print) database. It offers access to the following British Library collections: Cartographic materials, Humanities and Social Sciences, Music Library, and Science. The *BLAISE-LINE* system also offers access to the American National Library of Medicine files.

British Books in Print. Available on *BLAISE-LINE* and *Dialog.*

British Catalogue of Audio-Visual Materials. British Library, Bibliographic Services. 2 Sheraton St., London. W1V 4BH England. Available at the British Library.

British National Bibliography. British Library, Bibliographic Services. Available at the British Library and by subscription.

Current Research in Britain. Humanities. British Library, Document Supply Center. Available online on *Pergamon Infoline.*

Financial Times. Available on *World Reporter, Dialog,* and *Nexis* (Mead Data).

Manchester Guardian Weekly. Available on *Nexis.*

World Reporter database. Available only in England at this time. British newspapers indexed on the system: *The Guardian, The Financial Times, The Telegraph, Today, The Times,* and *The Sunday Times.*

Newspapers and Periodicals

Great Britain is rich in daily newspapers and many of them have played an important part in recording popular entertainment history. In addition to the newspapers and periodicals listed below, the following newspapers have published reviews of plays, films, and television shows over the years and are the most often quoted sources: *Daily Express, Daily*

Mail, Daily Mirror, Daily Telegraph, The Guardian, Mail on Sunday, and the *Standard.*

Celebrity Bulletin. Semiweekly, 1952- . ISSN: 0045-6020. Celebrity Service, 93-97 Regent St., London W1R 7TA. Phone: 071 439 9840.

Information regarding the daily activities of celebrities, with emphasis on the London area. The publication notes arrivals and departures, public appearances, work under way, and the names and phone numbers of agents and other representatives where celebrities may be contacted. Primarily for use of the press and other professionals in the entertainment business.

Illustrated London News. Bimonthly, 1842- . Illustrated London News, Elm House, 10-16 Elm St., London WC1X 0BP. Phone: 071-278 2345. LC 82-6899, ISSN 0019-2422. Back volumes available on microform from UMI. Indexed in: BHI, BTI, and BRI.

A longstanding popular magazine, with articles on all fields of the entertainment industry throughout the years, especially noted performers. Extensive use of photographs and line drawings. A good source for historical theater and film reviews (often with photos or artwork).

Manchester Guardian Weekly. Weekly, 1919- . Cheshire: Guardian Publications. LC 85-54168, ISSN 0025-200X. Index available. Back issues are on microform and articles can be obtained through document delivery service of UMI. Recent years are available online from Lexis/Nexis database service.

Media, Culture, and Society. Quarterly, 1979- . London: Sage. ISSN 0163-4437. Indexed in: IITP.

The emphasis of the periodical is on the impact of film, broadcasting, and other media forms on British society and culture.

Observer. Weekly (Sunday), 1791- . The Observer, Ltd., 8 St. Andrews Hill, London EC4V 5JA. Phone: 071-236 0202. LC 85-21111, ISSN 0029-7712. Available on microform from publisher. Indexed in: British Humanities Index, Book Review Index.

A popular magazine with frequent coverage of the performing

arts and performers. Stage and film reviews. Strong use of original photographs.

Performance: the review of live art. Bimonthly, 1979- . 14 Peto Pl., London NW1. Phone: 071-936 2714. ISSN: 0144-5901.
Covers all of the performing arts with in-depth articles and photos. Good interviews and profiles of personalities. Extensive reviews of film, television, radio, and stage. Listings of shows and performances throughout England.

The Spectator. Weekly, 1828- . 56 Doughty St., London WC1N 2LL. LC 04-12682, ISSN 0038-6952.
A generally conservative magazine with longstanding reviews of films, plays, television, and radio programs. Illustrated.

Sunday Express. Weekly, 1918- . London: Express Newspapers. LC 88-63928, ISSN 0039-5196. Available on microfilm from UMI.

Sunday Times Magazine. Weekly, 1822- . Times Newspapers, 200 Gray's Inn Rd., London WC1X 8EZ. Phone: 071-837 1234.
Popular articles include some about personalities. Color and b/w photos.

Tatler and Bystander . 1901- . London.

Telegraph Sunday Magazine. Weekly, 1976- . London: Daily Telegraph, 135 Fleet St., London EC4P 4BL. Phone: 071-353 4242. Available on microfilm from publisher. Indexed in: BHI. Previous titles: *Daily Telegraph Magazine* and *Weekend Telegraph.*
A popular Sunday magazine which frequently includes reviews and articles about many areas of the entertainment industry and personalities. Good photos.

The Times. Daily (except Sunday), 1785- . London: The Times. Available in the U.S. on CD-ROM. LC 85-54080, ISSN 0140-0460. Published briefly under the titles: *The Daily Universal Register* (1785-1787) and *The Times, or, Daily Universal Register* (1788). There are several indexes to *The Times,* and the titles and frequency of publication have varied. There is a *Times* index for 1785-1790 and *Palmer's Index to the 'Times'* (1790-1939). In 1906,

The Times started publishing its own index on a regular basis. In addition, there is an *Obituaries from the Times* series (1951-1975, 3 vols.).

TLS; the *Times* literary supplement. Weekly, 1902-   . Annual index. London: The Times Newspapers. LC 75-644287, ISSN 0307-661X. Previous title: *Times Literary Supplement.* Also available: *Cumulative Index, 1902-1980* (2 volumes). Indexed in: BHI, HI, Book Review Index, Book Review Digest.
   One of the older review publications. The performing arts are well covered over the years.

Weekend. Weekly, 1904-   . London: Mail Newspapers. ISSN: 0043-0390.

RESEARCH LIBRARIES IN GREAT BRITAIN

The British Library

The British Library is a huge organization that is responsible for three areas of documentation of British resources:

(1) The British Library itself is a huge complex of buildings and collections which maintains one of the most valuable collections in the world.

(2) The Library publishes the *British National Bibliography,* a listing of new books and other materials received for copyright in Great Britain. This is also available online and can be accessed by author, title, or subject.

(3) It operates the British Library Document Supply Centre, a commercial document delivery service that does business worldwide.

The British Library was a part of the British Museum until 1973, when it became a separate legal entity. The Library is actually an expansive collection of libraries and reading rooms at a number of locations. The Main Library is still physically located in the British Museum at Great Russell Street. Because of the large number of reading rooms and services, only the collections of most interest to entertainment researchers are covered in this chapter (The Main Library, the Newspaper Library, and the National Sound Archives).

It's difficult to keep track of all the British Library activities. The following publications are issued in order to assist those who need information regarding their collections and services . Most of the publications listed below can be ordered from: The British Library, Bibliographic Services Division Publications, 2 Sheraton St., London W1V 4BH. Phone 071-636 1544.

The British Library Bibliographic Services Division Newsletter. Quarterly, 1976-   . ISSN: 0308-230X. The best way to keep up with what's going on inside of the British Library complex of offices and services. Articles explain their ongoing computerization efforts, expanding business operations, and program changes.

British Library News. Monthly, 1976-   . ISSN: 0307-3481. A newsletter about the inner activities of the library including staff changes, new publications for sale, and some division activities.

The British Library Research and Development Newsletter (Semi-annual, 1974-   . ISSN: 0305-1714) and *British Library Research Reviews* (Irregular, 1981-   . ISSN: 0261-2178). These two publications keep the public informed about library and information research sponsored and supported by the Library. New technological developments are often covered here.

The Catalogue of Printed Music in the British Library to 1980. See: page 527.

British Museum. Department of Printed Books. *General Catalogue of Printed Books.* Photolithographic edition to 1955. 263 vols., 1959/1966. *Supplements* through 1975, 39 vols. After 1975, all supplements for sale to the public have been produced only in microfiche. A complete CD-ROM version of the *Catalogue* is being marketed by Chadwyck-Healey (London), to be available in 1991. A complete record of the books in the Library from the 15th Century through 1955, with the exception of the Oriental collection. *Supplements* were issued 1971-1975. Mainly indexed by author.

British Library Research Facilities

The British Library (Main Building)

Address: Great Russell Street, London WC1B 3DG. The British Library shares the same building with the British Museum.

Phone: 071-636 1544.

Hours: Opens at 9:00 am Monday through Saturday; closes at 5:00pm (Monday, Friday, and Saturday) and at 9:00pm (Tues-Thurs). Closed British holidays, the end of October, and other days as necessary. Check for hours of opening before you plan your trip!

The Underground: There are two stations within close walking distance: the Tottenham Court Road Station and the Russell Square Station.

Reading rooms of the British Library (at the Great Russell Street Location): The main building is made up of a number of large reading rooms with each offering reference book collections in a particular subject area and/or specialized services. They are: Humanities and Social Sciences (The Main Reading Room); the North Library (rare books); the North Library Gallery (microforms or oversized and/or fragile books); Department of Manuscripts; Map Library; Music Reading Area; Official Publications and Social Sciences Service Reading Room; and the Philatelic Collection.

Other Collections and Their locations: The Oriental Collection is at 14 Store St., London WC1E 7DG; and the India

Office Library and Records is at 197 Blackfriars Rd., London SE1 8NG. The Science Reference and Information Service maintains collections in science, technology, commerce (business), and patents and trademarks. The Main Reading Room (Holborn) is located at 25 Southampton Buildings, Chancery La., London WC2A 1AW, with a smaller reading room (Aldwych) at 9 Kean St., Drury Lane. London WC2B 4AT.

General information: The Humanities and Social Sciences Division houses the Main Reading Room, the main Enquiry Desk, and the main reference collection and most of the services.

Services: A separate room is available to accommodate people who wish to bring in typewriters. The Library does not supply typewriters. Microfilm and fiche machines are available, but should be requested ahead of time. Sound-proof cubicles are available for readers who want to use dictating machines or blind readers with amanuenses. A number of services and aids are available for handicapped persons; anyone interested in this assistance should contact the Library ahead of time in order to assure the most complete service that can be provided.

Reference services: Start at the Enquiry Desk.

Computer search services: A number of subscription services are available and all searching is done for a fee. This includes automated programs that supply catalog information for the British Library *Current Catalogue* and their *British National Bibliography.* No online systems or terminals are available in the reading rooms for free public use. The point of contact is the Main Reading Room Enquiry Desk. Searches are conducted with the requester present and print-outs are usually supplied within 2 to 5 days (depending on the search). The following online programs are available:

BLAISE-LINE, the British Library's own automated information service.

The *Current Catalogue* of the British Library. This includes most books acquired and cataloged by the British Library Humanities and Social Sciences since 1976, some 1971-75 titles, MARC records created by the Oriental Manuscripts and Printed Books offices for material acquired since 1980 (excluding Japanese, Korean, and Chinese), and the India Office Library and Records monographs from 1983 to date.

The following *UK MARC* online catalogs of books and other materials are the computerized records used in creating the *British National Bibliography: UKMARC 50/70* (1950-1970), *UKMARC 71/76* (1971-1976), and *UK MARC* (the current file from 1977 to date). They can be searched by author, title, or subject.

The following catalogs are also available online and may be helpful in your research. The *DSC Catalogue* is a listing of books in Western European languages (1980 to date) housed at the British Library Document Supply Centre, the *ESTC* online file is a catalogue of printed materials published in the eighteenth century, the *ISTC* file (Incunable Short Title Catalogue) records the locations of all materials printed from movable type before 1501, and the Library of Congress' *LCMARC* and *REMARC* databases of material acquired and/or catalogued from 1897 to date.

In addition to the above bibliographic databases, the library also has a number of information databases available. While many of these are available in the United States, several are compiled from exclusively British publications: the *British Education Index, Whitaker* (current in-print and forthcoming books published in the UK), and *Polis* (UK Parliamentary issues, proceedings, and documents).

Newspaper and news-related databases are located at the Newspaper Library, Colindale. The major British online service is *World Reporter.*

Photocopy services: No immediate, self-serve or coin-operated machines. All photocopy work must be prepaid when ordered and, as far as I can tell, picked up another day. You will be given a date for pick-up at the time you order the copying and may have the material mailed to you if desired. There are a great many special restrictions and all work must conform with copyright laws. Photocopy service can be ordered by mail. All told, it might be quicker and more convenient to order what you need in the way of periodical articles and pages from other current publications from the Document Supply Centre. You will pay a fee either way.

Interlibrary loan: This is handled through the Document Supply Centre.

Publications: See above. In addition, the Library publishes a multitude of 6- to 10-page free pamphlets that are guides to using the Reading Room and its collections.

Research services: The staff of the British Library does not do photocopying or research for patrons. The library does, however, maintain a list of names and addresses of people who are available to do the work on a salaried basis.

Visitor requirements: Everyone wishing to use the British Library must apply for (and be issued) a photo pass at the Reader Admissions Office. Passes are issued immediately upon approval of application. Passes can not be issued by mail or ahead of time because a photo is required on the pass itself. Passes are issued for various time periods from a few days to several years, and are not normally given to those under 21 years of age. While most of the Reading Rooms require the passes, others do not and the reader may apply directly to them for permission to visit. The Department of Manuscripts requires a supplementary pass and the India Office Library and Records requires a letter of recommendation or official stamp from the applicant's institution or university. The Library collection is deemed to be open to those needing materials not available elsewhere or, by virtue of their research work, need access to the materials located there.

Readers are expected to obey regulations governing conduct in the reading rooms. The regulations are spelled out in a pamphlet.

The Stacks: The stacks are closed. To request books from the stacks, the reader must identify each title by using reference books or Library catalogues, and fill out a call slip. Books shelved on site may be delivered to the reader in about an hour. Books that are housed off-site should be requested at least 24 hours ahead of time.

The Catalogue: The catalog is not the traditional card catalog familiar to most Americans. Rather, the Catalogue is a set of bound volumes in which typed strips of paper (entries for each new title) have been hand-pasted on blank pages. Another adjustment Americans will have to make is the fact that the Catalogue is by personal name (author) *or* title *or* issuing institution (and sometimes only author!). Personal names may be followed by books by or about that person. There are no subject terms in the books. Actually, there are two main catalogues: (1) The *General Catalog* lists all books catalogued up to 1970 plus acquisitions for 1971 to 1975 listed in blue pages in the back of each volume; (2) the *Current Catalog* is on microfiche and lists books received from 1976 to date. There is also a small card catalog for books that have never been placed in the main catalogs, and for the Oriental Collections. Separate catalogs also exist for books shelved in the Main Reading Room, the Music Collection, the Map Collection, and for the Newspaper Catalogue. The Science Reference and Information Service Catalogue is on microfiche and must be requested at the Enquiry Desk. There are a number of additional indexes and catalogs beyond the ones listed here.

Subject indexing is superficial at best. This is true of nearly all European libraries. There is a far greater reliance on the use of published bibliographies by researchers in England and the rest of Europe because library subject cataloging has never been prominently conducted. It's a small, but vital, difference in the way research is conducted. Subject indexes to both catalogs are shelved in another part of the reading room and may be missed completely if you aren't aware of their existence. Even then, they're not complete and occasionally not accurate regarding the pressmark. Your best bet, as advised by the Library itself, is to use one of the many subject bibliographies shelved in the Main Reading Room. The *British National Bibliography* can be used for publications from 1950 to date. Lastly, some of the computer services that are available may be useful in subject searching. The best answer, of course, is to do your subject searching elsewhere and then come armed with a list of books to search in the two main catalogs.

There is no separate catalog for periodicals. Periodicals in the *Current Catalog* are listed by title. Periodicals in the *General Catalog* are entered one of three ways: either under their title, *place* of the issuing organization (followed by the institution's name and then the name of the periodical), or under a section in "P" titled PERIODICAL PUBLICATIONS.

Most daily and weekly newspapers or periodicals are housed at Colindale and are not in the *General Catalog*. However, London newspapers published before 1801 are housed at Bloomsbury in the Burney collection along with several other exceptions. Catalogs of the Colindale and Bloomsbury collections are available in the Main Reading Room.

Suffice it to say that it is all very confusing and requires a considerable amount of time and effort to complete a thorough search. You had better know exactly what you want before you go there.

The British Library: National Sound Archive

Address: The main Archive is located at 29 Exhibition Rd., London SW7 2AS. A small regional reading room is located in the reading room of the British Library Document Supply Centre at Boston Spa near Wetherby in West Yorkshire.

Phone: 071-589 6603/4.

The Underground: South Kensington.

Hours: Weekdays 9:30 am - 4:30 pm (Thursdays until 9:00pm). Listening facilities are available during those hours. No pass is required to enter.

Services: Facilities are available to listen to recordings. Appointments must be made in advance to assure service.

Publications: The National Sound Archive General Catalog. In addition, the Archive contributes to the *National Discography.*

Automated services: The Archive is in the process of automating its card catalog. In addition, it expects to have the *National Discography* program available when it goes online.

General information: The National Sound Archive was originally the British Institute of Recorded Sound until 1983, when it became part of the British Library and acquired its current name.

The Collection: The collected materials include music, voice recordings, all types of sound effects and nature recordings, political speeches, theater performances, writers and playwrights reading and discussing their works, and the music and voice recordings and broadcasts (in the original language) from many other countries. The original collection was oriented toward opera and classical music. In addition to historical sound recordings going back to the 1890s, the Archive holds all current British commercial record releases and has recently branched out to include videos and CDs in addition to the traditional cylinders, vinyl, and audio tape recordings. Thousands of the recordings are unpublished and not available anywhere else. It has a complete duplicate set of BBC Sound Archive Recordings. Since BBC archive and research collections are limited to its own in-house staff, this is the only place that allows public access.

Voice recordings make up an important part of the Archives. The Archive is especially strong in actuality and documentary recordings, worldwide radio broadcasts, interviews and other voice recordings from famous people. Its Recorded Literature and Theatre Collection features 20th-Century writers and playwrights reading and talking about their own work, live theater recordings made over a quarter of a century, and interviews and/or workshops made with leading actors, directors, and other personalities. The Oral History collection also has interviews with notable people in British entertainment. Their extensive sound effects collection has weather and nature sounds, animals, industrial noise, vehicles, city sounds, and just about anything else you can imagine.

The Music collection covers all types of music worldwide. Live performances by artists, BBC musical radio and television broadcasts, interviews, studio recording sessions, and talks supplement the musical recordings. The Archive is especially strong on classical, popular music, and jazz. The Archive has an ongoing collection of jazz interview materials through their Oral History of British Jazz program. In addition, the Archive has a large international Traditional Music collection which features both commercial recordings and "field recordings" from many countries.

Among the reference resources available for readers to use are the catalogues to the BBC Sound Archives, the BBC song title indexes, various published indexes and music catalogues, and historical runs of important periodicals related to broadcasting and music. The reference section also maintains a National Register of Sound Collections, which identifies recorded sound collections throughout the UK.

The Archive's large collection of nearly 100,000 musical scores is housed at its Boston Spa facility and may be viewed there.

Under certain circumstances, such as educational and media use, the Archive will supply copies of its materials provided that copyright clearance has been obtained.

British Library: Newspaper Division—Colindale

Address: Colindale Ave., London NW9 5HE

Phone: general enquiries: 071-323 7353; for photocopy enquiries: 071-323 7355.

The Underground: The Colindale Station (close to the end of the Edgware branch of the Northern Line). The Library is across the street, slightly to the right, of the station. The surrounding area is largely residential.

Hours: 10:00am - 5:00pm Monday through Saturday. No requests accepted after 4:15pm.

Publications: Catalogue of the Newspaper Library, Co-lindale. London: Published by British Museum Publications. 8 volumes, 1975. Volume 1 lists London newspapers; Volume 2 lists England, Wales, Scotland, and Ireland; Volumes 3-4 list overseas titles; and Volume 5-8 is an alphabetical listing of the complete collection.

Services: The Library supplies a wide range of photocopy and photographic services, none of which can be provided on a same-day basis. No public self-service machines are available. Prepayment required. Will provide service by mail.

Computer search services are available, with access to *BLAISE, Dialog,* and *World Reporter.* The Information Officer at the Library is responsible for the service.

If you plan to spend the day, be prepared to eat in a small vending machine room or bring your own food.

The two reading room areas together have just over 100 seats, of which about one-third are at microform readers. Be sure to get there early, especially on Saturday.

General information: This Library contains newspapers from the provinces, Wales, Scotland, and Ireland. (Pre-1801 London newspapers and Oriental newspapers, however, are at the British Museum location). Part of the collection of provincial and Irish newspapers was destroyed by a bomb during World War II, but the Library is still the largest single newspaper library in the world. Altogether, the Library has about 40,000 titles of both current and discontinued newspapers. This collection contains over 600,000 bound volumes of original newspapers and over 250,000 reels of microfilm; each year the Library adds approximately 6,000 bound volumes and 11,000 reels of film.

The collection contains daily and weekly newspapers and periodicals from London (1801 to date) and from about 1840 to date (a few go back as far as 1700) for all of the British provinces, Ireland, Scotland, and Wales. It also holds comprehensive historical collections of the Commonwealth countries and foreign newspapers. It tries to collect the principal newspapers in western and Slavonic languages from all countries.

United Kingdom newspapers are microfilmed and/or bound before they are available to readers; therefore, the most recent issues of British newspapers may not be available to readers for up to three years. An exception is that current files of the most popular newspapers such as *The Times* and *The Observer* are made available to readers by the mainte-nance of duplicate copies. The way to compensate for this problem is to do your research that requires the use of current newspapers in other libraries, reserving your histori-cal research for this Library.

The Reference collection located throughout the reading rooms is excellent. It has a large number of newspaper indexes from around the world. British newspaper indexes include: *Financial Times, The Glasgow Herald, Picture Post Index, The Guardian Index,* and the various *Times* indexes.

The Catalog of the collection is both in looseleaf volumes and a traditional card catalog.

The British Library Document Supply Centre

Address: The British Library Document Supply Centre is located at Boston Spa, Wetherby, West Yorkshire LS23 7BQ.

Phone: 0937 546070.

Hours: Weekdays, 9:15 am - 4:30pm.

Publications: Interlending and Document Supply (Quarterly, 1971- . ISSN: 0264-1615). Available by subscription from the above address. The publication is international in scope and covers lending and document supply policies, practices, and developments. It also publishes *Current Serials Received* (Annual, ISSN: 03090655) which lists all titles current

received by the Document Supply Centre and the Science
Reference and Information Service. It also publishes other
titles about serial and periodical collections.

General information: The main function of the Document
Supply Centre is to operate a commercial document delivery
service and interlibrary loan program. It will loan documents
to other libraries, but the major part of the program is
devoted to supplying photocopy or microform copies of
periodical articles, books, and other documents for a fee. Its
services are available to the public worldwide and it is an
unparalleled source of rare and valuable research material.

Collections and services: This facility is also the British
Library service for northern England and supplies public
reference and reading services through its Northern Listening Service Reading Room. It offers free listening service for
most of the National Sound Archive Collection (based in
London). Arrangements should be made a week ahead of
time with the London Archive office. The Library's extensive collection of sheet music and scores are housed at the
Document Supply Centre and are therefore easily accessible.

Libraries in the City of London

Guildhall Library

Address: Aldermanbury, London EC2P 2EJ

Phone: (071) 606 3030

The Underground: St. Paul's Station or Bank Station are the
closest. Mansion House and Moorgate are also in the area.

Hours: 9:30 am - 5:00 pm, Monday through Saturday. Some
services are limited or unavailable on Saturday, so it would
be wise to call ahead if you plan to work on that day. The
Prints & Maps section is closed on Saturday.

Services: The Guildhall Library is open to the public and no appointment is required. Because of the rare nature of most of the collection, most of the stack area is closed to access and the materials must be requested by filling out call slips and having the material retrieved, a process that generally takes only about fifteen minutes. Two days notice is necessary if a reader wants to use materials stored off site (this includes many of the 19th century periodicals). Identification may be required in order to use some of the rarer and more valuable materials. Photocopy service is available. And the photographic reproduction and microfilming of rare items can be arranged with approval. The Library has available, upon request, a short list of professional researchers who can be hired. The Library is accessible to the handicapped.

General information: This is probably the most useful of London's public libraries for nonresident researchers in need of a quick and convenient large collection in which to do general research. The Library is divided into three sections (Printed Books, Manuscripts, and Prints & Maps) each with its own reading room, card catalog, and staff. The core of the Library is its extensive collection of London material, which includes monographs, poll-books, and hundreds of years of official publications and records of local government bodies throughout the London area. Of interest to theater researchers are the holdings of 19th century English plays, theater programs, and playbills. The Library also has a large collection of files, newspapers and periodicals, and publications dealing with all aspects of English history.

The Printed Books Section of the Library is located on the main floor and includes the general reference collection, major historical resources such as the calendars of state papers, and the general card catalog. A separate room holds the library's most used periodicals and newspapers. A list of newspapers and journals that are available in the library collection is kept at the reference desk. Some of the Library's rare book collection is located in the adjacent Whittington Room. There are complete sets of the House of Commons and House of Lords debates and journals as well as other public and local official documents.

The Manuscripts section includes company records, parish registers, and a wide variety of other historical documents. It is the official repository for historical records relating to London, with holdings dating from the 11th century. Any researcher working in this area will be required to use a pencil for their work as no other writing tool is permitted. Some material dating back to the 1600s is stored in another building and must be requested a day or two ahead of time. A large number of frequently used records have been microfilmed and may be used in this form. The Manuscript section staff will assist visitors in identifying and interpreting manuscripts, but can not do their research for them. Because of the strong interest in genealogical research, the Library suggests that researchers who can not visit the library in person (or who may need extensive help) should consider employing a professional record agent. The following organization maintains a list of agents for hire: The Secretary, Association of Genealogists and Record Agents, 1 Woodside Close, Caterham, Surrey CR3 6AU. Enclose 55 pence or five international reply coupons for the list.

The Prints & Maps section also centers on the history of London and the surrounding area, with a large collection of portraits, satirical prints, and maps dating back to the mid-16th century. This section also includes photographs, theater bills and programs, playing cards, and other visual materials.

Barbican Library

Address: The Library is located on Level 7 of the Barbican Centre EC2Y 8DS.

Phone: (071) General information 638 0569, Music Library 638 0672.

The Underground: The Barbican station.

Hours: 9:30 am - 5:30 pm weekdays, 9:30 am - 12:30 pm Saturday.

Services: Photocopy service is available. Listening booths are provided for recorded sound material.

General information: Much of the collection is designed to reflect a strong interest in the arts. Entertainment researchers will find comprehensive areas on the theater, cinema, and music. The Music Library provides books, scores, and recorded materials.

City Business Library

Address: Gillett House, Basinghall St. EC2V 5BX. Located close to Guildhall Library.

Hours: 9:30 am - 5:00 pm, Monday through Friday. Closed Saturdays.

Phone: (071) 638 8215/6

The Underground: The Moorgate station is the closest.

General information: The Library provides the daily information needs of the London business community. It contains large collections of local and international directories, collections about various industries, and a large number of periodicals and newspapers. Photocopy and facsimile transmission services are available.

Other London Area Libraries

Westminster City Library (Central Reference Library)

Address: St. Martin's St., London WC2H 7HP. Just off Leicester Square.

Phone: (071) 798 2034.

Hours: 10:00 am - 7:00 pm, Monday through Friday, 10:00 am - 5:00 pm on Saturday.

The Underground: The Charing Cross or Leicester Square stations.

Services: Coin-operated photocopy machines are available. Some online search services.

General information: The Library acts as "A library of first resort" for students and researchers of the performing arts and much of the collection is immediately available to patrons in open stacks in the Main Reading Room. It has a large collection of performing arts information, with over 6,000 books and several hundred periodical and serial titles covering the theater, film, television, radio, dance and ballet, costumes, and the circus. The Library has a strong collection of directories and other current reference materials. It has a collection of *The Spotlight* which goes back to 1940 and back copies of a number of annuals and periodicals. Its other titles of note include: *Who's Who in the Theatre, The London Stage Series, London Theatre Record, The Era,* and *The Stage.* Its Fine Arts Library section includes additional information (theater architecture, posters, etc.) and the Commercial Library section holds information on companies, market research, and statistics. The main card catalog provides author/title/subject access. The Library also has in-house vertical file material (clippings, pamphlets, etc.) on performing arts people and subjects. Some back years of periodicals are on microfilm.

Westminster City Library (Victoria Library)

Address: 160 Buckingham Palace Rd., London W2 5HR.

Phone: (071) 798 2187.

Hours: 9:30 am - 7:00 pm Monday Through Friday, 9:30 am - 5:00 pm Saturday.

The Underground: Victoria Station.

Services: Photocopy machine and audio-visual listening equipment are available.

General information: A large central music library is located here to provide the facilities for in-depth study of music. The Local History and Archives Library is also located here and holds an extensive collection of primary source material on the theater: London (and some province) theater programs, playbills, and memorabilia from the 1800s to date. They do not, however, have the secondary source materials (the indexes, reference books, and periodicals); this collection is located at the Central Reference Library. The Victoria collection is alphabetized and arranged by theater; therefore, access to playbills and programs via the theater name.

THEATER RESEARCH IN GREAT BRITAIN

When I first started learning how to do research in England, one of my best discoveries was the important role of local public libraries as repositories of community theater history. All over England, the local libraries have been uniformly active in collecting materials about their local repertory theaters and the actors who played in their productions. Many of these collections are quite large and go back as far as the beginning of the library itself. Since the majority of Britain's great actors started in their home town repertory theater, be sure to take the time to contact the local library if you are researching an actor who may have started this way. Manchester, Bristol, Leeds, and Birmingham are only a few of many other cities where the public libraries have major theater collections that are available to researchers. My own research has benefited from research of this nature. A couple of years ago when I was looking for information about the Sheffield Repertory Theatre, a London theater librarian recommended that I contact the Sheffield public library. I did exactly that, with wonderful results since they had virtually everything I was looking for. Sylvia Pybus, Subject Librarian of the Local Studies Library at the Sheffield Central Library was most helpful to me. Through a series of phone calls and letters, she helped me determine what was available in her library and how my research could be done. She was even able to refer me to another helpful person, the Archivist for the Crucible Theatre, who had information useful to my research even though the Crucible had no connection with the theater I was researching. When I subsequently arrived in Sheffield, everything I needed was ready and waiting for me. Some of the material was far too fragile to be photocopied, but arrangements could be made to have it photographed. In addition, the Library had a historical photograph I needed and I was able to make arrangements to have a reproduction made of it too. But, I think that the one thing that will make my time there memorable (for them as well as me) was I spent the whole day feeding large British coins into the photocopy machine hour after hour, without a break. We all felt somewhat jubilant when I finished the job with just barely enough time to catch the last train back to London!

Because theater libraries are the only sources of large amounts of theater information, they are often asked to work on an integral basis with regard to the training courses provided by theater companies and acting schools. The Theatre Museum Library works with theater groups to provide support for educational services in the form of seminars and other programs for theater students.

Regretfully, at the time this book was going to press, two of the best theater libraries in Great Britain appear to be closing due to lack of funding. After years of financial problems, the British Theatre Association finally closed its doors and, with it, went one of the best theater libraries in the world. In addition, the highly respected Mander/Mitchenson Library can no longer sustain itself and has been unable to secure funding. I've left its entry in my book in the hope that a miracle will happen and/or that the collection will be acquired and moved intact to another institution. The British Theatre Association collection has been largely acquired by the Theatre Museum Library, which is in the process of integrating it into its collection. This makes the Theatre Museum Library the premier theater library in England and I recommend that anyone wanting to do research start there.

Theater Reference Research Resources

Amateur Theatre Yearbook. Annual. Platform Publications, P.O. Box 1, 30 Culver Rd., St. Albans, Herts, AL1 4ED.
> The yearbook is divided into geographical regions and lists amateur and community theaters, venues, available training, theater groups and organizations, publications, theater bookshops, suppliers, and any other information that may be available for the area.

American and British Theatrical Biography: a directory, by J. P. Wearing. Metuchen, NJ: Scarecrow Press, 1979. 1012 pp. ISBN 0-8108-1201-0, LC 78-31162.
> Arranged in alphabetical order by name of performer.

Artistes and Their Agents. Annual. See: page 438.

A Biographical Dictionary of Actors, Actresses, Musicians, Dancers, Managers & Other Stage Personnel In London, 1660-1800, by Philip H. Highfill, Kalman A. Burnim, and Edward A. Langhans. Carbondale, IL: Southern Illinois University. Volumes 1-12, 1973-1987. Future publications planned. LC 71-157068, ISBN 0809305186.
> One of the most valuable resources of early theater history. The set includes just about anyone associated with British theaters, opera houses, pleasure gardens, or other forms of public entertainment before 1800. Of immense value is the fact that lesser known people are included along with the famous. Entries vary in length from a short paragraph to several pages, with a number of good portraits.

Britain's Theatrical Periodicals, 1720-1967, by Carl J. Stratman. See: Chapter 6, page 173.

British Alternative Theatre Directory. See: *Directory of Playwrights, Directors, Designers.*

British Musical Theatre, by Kurt Ganzl. New York and London: Oxford University Press. 2 vols., 1986. LC 85-29705, ISBN 0-19-520509-X.

This set offers a virtually-complete review of British stage productions of musicals. Volume 1 covers 1865-1914, with most years given separate chapters. Coverage is provided for companies and productions throughout England. Each production listed has a plot summary, list of song titles, performance dates, and cast and technical credits. Volume 2 is arranged in the same way and covers 1915-1984. Appendices list printed music and recorded music available from the plays. Indexing is provided for names and show titles.

British Theatre Directory. See: *The Original British Theatre Directory.*

British Theatre Yearbook. Annual, 1989- . Edited by David Lemmon. Publisher: Croom Helm, Imperial House, 21-25 North St., Bromley, Kent BR1 1SD. Distributed in the United States by St. Martin's Press in New York. ISSN 1047-7101.

The series provides a yearly overview of British theater activities and events. It lists (with cast credits and photos) each London stage production for the year. In addition, it covers productions in the provinces and some of the larger touring companies. There are also several short essays which discuss current aspects of the theater world.

Contacts. See: *Spotlight Contacts,* page 444.

Creative Drama. Annual, 1949- . English Drama Association. Publication address: Stacey Publications, 1 Hawthorndene Rd., Hayes, Bromley, Kent BR2 7DX. Phone: 081-462 6461. ISSN 0011-0892.

Dictionary of the Theatre. Edited by David Pickering. London: Sphere Books. 556 p., 1988. LC 88-69046, ISBN 0747400199.

An alphabetical listing of performers, writers, plays, theatrical terms, theater buildings, touring companies, and other subjects. A quick reference resource.

Directory of Members, by The Directors Guild of Great Britain. Published irregularly, 1984- . 3d ed. is 1987. Address of the Guild: Lyndhurst Hall, Lyndhurst Rd., Hampstead, London NW3 5NG. Phone: 071- 431 1800. LC 84-43887.

The directory includes information about directors in television, film, theater, radio, and commercials. Information for each entry includes the director's name, area of direction, credits, address, and agent.

Directory of Playwrights, Directors, Designers. Biennial, 1979- . Eastbourne, East Sussex: J. Offord Publications. LC 85-2683, ISSN 0265-0932. Previous title: *British Alternative Theatre Directory* (1979-1987).

The directory is divided into listings for the professions noted in the title, with the largest number of entries for playwrights.

Directory of Theatre Resources: a guide to research collections and information services. Compiled by Diana Howard. Published under the auspices of two organizations: The Library Association, Information Services Group, *and* The Society for Theatre Research. 2d ed., 1986, 144p, LC 87-26809, ISBN 0 946347 08 5). The best way to obtain a copy is to order from The Publications Officer, Society for Theatre Research, c/o The Theatre Museum, 1e Tavistock St., London WC2E 7PA. The first edition was published in 1980 under the title *Directory of Theatre Research and Information Resources in the United Kingdom* by the Arts Council of Great Britain.

This is a highly recommended book for anyone planning to do theater research in Great Britain. Part 1, the major portion of the book, is a listing of collections of theater material in libraries, museums, and record offices throughout the country. Arrangement is by city and then by library. Part 2 lists theater societies and professional associations which provide information services, usually of a business or contact/contract nature for a dues-paying membership, but it may be of help to researchers. Ms. Howard is careful to make the point that most of these organizations have very small staffs and even fewer financial resources, and therefore may charge for information provided to non-members if they provide it at all. Although the book claims not to be a complete listing, nothing else comes close to providing the same information.

The DONMAR Reference Manual; for the theatre, film, video, and entertainment industries. Edited by Ian B. Albery and James Bishop. London: Donmar. 3d ed., 80 p., 1988. gb87-50758, ISBN 0951115316.

A directory of information of manufacturers, equipment, and services of interest to the theater industry. Regular features review new products and current theater literature and reference books.

Encyclopaedia of the Musical Theatre, by Stanley Green. New York: Dodd, Mead & Company, 1976. LC 76-21069. See: THEATER REFERENCE RESOURCES, page 179.

Contents includes the most prominent people, productions, and songs of the musical theater in New York and London up to 1976.

English Theatrical Literature, 1559-1900: a bibliography, incorporating Robert W. Lowe's *A Bibliographical Account of English Theatrical Literature* published in 1888. London: Society for Theatre Research. 486 p., 1970. LC 76-552584, ISBN 0854300007.

Originally published in 1888, and expanded in this edition to include American literature as well as British, the book is an annotated listing of rare early theatrical literature.

The Great Stage Stars, by Sheridan Morley. New York: Facts on File, 1986. (Illus., 484 p.) ISBN 0-8160-1401-9.

In-depth biographies of over 200 stars of the American and British stage.

London Musical Shows on Record, 1897-1976, by Brian Rust. Harrow: General Gramophone. 672 p., 1977. LC 78-307917, ISBN 0902740078.

A discography of recordings from the 1890s through 1975. Part 1 is a chronological listing of all London musicals presented on the London stage during the period noted, regardless of whether or not a recording was made. Part 2 lists shows, in alphabetical order, for which recordings were made. Both production information for the show and the recording are given. Part 3 lists performers and their recordings.

The London Stage, 1660-1800; a calendar of plays, entertainments and afterpieces, together with casts, box-receipts and contemporary comment; compiled from the playbills, newspapers, and theatrical diaries of the period. Carbondale, IL: Southern Illinois University Press. 5 parts in 11 volumes, 1960-1968. LC 60-6539. Part 1: *1660-1700;* Part 2: *1700-1729;* Part 3: *1729-1747;* Part 4: *1747-1776;* Part 5: *1776-1800.*

Each volume is chronological and covers each season of plays during that period. Cast and production credits accompany each play listing. Uniquely, all of the accompanying rare materials indicated in the subtitle add considerable color to the vision presented for each play. Two other works are designed to accompany this huge set. A companion work compiled by Emmett L. Avery and others contains critical introductions to each of the 5 parts of the main work and is titled *The London Stage; a critical introduction* (5 volumes, 1968, LC 76-2240). Each introduction provides commentary about the theater during the time period and provides an overview of the climate and social conditions in which it existed. A separate index to the set is published under the title *Index to the London Stage, 1660-1800* by Ben Ross Schneider (Southern Illinois University Press, 939 p., 1979, ISBN 0809309076). This index is a computerized listing of each name or play title appearing in the work, with reference to its location by date within the set.

The London Stage series, by J.P. Wearing. Metuchen, NJ: Scarecrow Press. *The London Stage, 1890-1899* (2 vols., 1976, LC 76-1825, ISBN 0-8108-0910-9); *The London Stage, 1900-1909* (2 vols., 1981, LC 80-28353, ISBN 0-8108-1403-X); *The London Stage, 1910-1919* (2 vols., 1982, LC 82-19190, ISBN 0-8108-1596-6); *The London Stage, 1920-1929* (3 vols., 1984, LC 84-10665, ISBN 0-8108-1715-2); *The London Stage, 1930-1939* (3 vols., 1990, LC 90-8883, ISBN 0-8108-2349-7).

A comprehensive historic set of reference volumes documenting the London theater and theater productions for the years noted. The work is noted for the detail it includes and the accuracy of its research.

London Theatre Index [year]. Annual, 1981- . Published by the London Theatre Record, 4 Cross Deep Gardens, Twickenham,

Middlesex. TW1 4QU. Phone: 081-892 6087. LC 83-11679, ISSN 0263-2322.

A yearly review of the London theater scene. It covers all of the shows, major and minor, and the people involved in their production. Indexed by play titles, actors, theaters. Lists agents. No photos, but it contains much of the same information as the defunct *Theatre Yearbook (London)* and is a good place to pick up where the past one left off.

London Theatres and Music Halls 1850-1950, by Diana Howard. London: Library Association. 291 p., 1970, reissued 1986. ISBN 0-85365-471-9.

This volume is a detailed historical study of theater buildings and music halls. It's divided into two parts: (1) A directory of theaters, music halls, and pleasure gardens; and (2) a guide to the literature and a directory of library collections about the subjects.

The Medieval Stage, by Edmund K. Chambers. London: Oxford University Press. 2 vols., 1903, 1978. ISBN 0198115121.

The authoritative reference work about this period. An in-depth coverage of the social and historical events surrounding the theater as well as a complete review of the types of drama that were popular then. Major scholars of the period have contributed to the work and long bibliographies are included.

The Original British Theatre Directory. Annual, 1972- . Richmond House Publishing Co., Ilford House, 133/135 Oxford St., London W1R 1TD. Phone: 071-437 9556. LC 89-18400, ISSN 0306-4107. Previous title: *British Theatre Directory* (1972-1988).

An annual listing all London theaters, municipal entertainment, production facilities, agents, publishers (books, periodicals, directories, bookstores), training and education facilities, and suppliers of services of use to the theater community.

The Oxford Companion to the Theatre. 4th ed. London and New York: Oxford University Press. 934 p., 1983. Reprinted with corrections, 1985. (First edition published in 1951) LC 83-235664, ISBN 0192115464.

Brief entries for people, plays, theaters, production companies, and special subjects. Coverage is international and starts at the earliest point of theater history. Older editions are also of value since recent editions are extensive revisions of the earlier ones. Newer editions include more information about the American theater and contemporary people of importance.

Performing Right Yearbook. Annual. London: Performing Right Society. See: page 536.

The Players' Library: the catalogue of the Library of the British Drama League, by the British Drama League. London: Faber and Faber. 1,115 p., 1950. LC 50-4789. *Supplements:* 1951, 1954, and 1956.
    A catalog of the library collection, including books and periodicals. A separate listing is provided for the League's collection of plays, with the date and publisher of first editions noted.

Spotlight Contacts. See: page 444.

"The Stage" Cyclopaedia; an alphabetical list of plays and other stage pieces of which any record can be found since the commencement of the English stage, together with descriptions, authors' names, dates and places of production, and other useful information, comprising in all nearly 50,000 plays, and extending over a period of upwards of 500 years. Compiled by Reginald Clarence. London: The Stage. 503 p., 1909. LC 10-9325.
    There isn't much left to say after you get through reading the title, but it's an impressive work that can be found in only the largest of theater research collections today. A microfilm version was reproduced in 1987 by Micrographics II in Charlottesville, VA. as part of their series: "Eighteenth Century sources for the Study of English Literature and Culture." (Reel number 728)

The Stage Yearbook. 1908-1969. No longer published. London: Carson and Comerford.
    This was one of the most valuable theater research resources around, and still is. All back volumes are most useful. It's a primary source of documentation for cast credits and other production information. It was a yearbook which listed all

theater productions, along with full cast and production credits. It also provided information regarding tours, festivals, repertory groups, and film and musical recording companies.

Theatre of the Fifties, by Sheila Wilson. London, Library Association. 64 p., 1963. (Library Association *Special Subject List,* no. 40) LC 65-69391.
   A small, but comprehensive, guide to conducting research about the theater in the 1950s. It provides a list of reference books, periodicals, and other materials helpful for that time period. A bibliography is also included.

Theatre World Annual (London); a pictorial review of West End productions with a record of plays and players. 1949/50-1966 (volumes 1-16). No longer published. London: Rockliff; New York: Macmillan.
   It was an excellent source of information and photos while it was published and is well worth purchasing if you can find a set. Material in the annual was selected from what was previously published during the year in *Theatre World* magazine and includes a substantial number of photographs from each play included as well as cast and production credits.

Western European Costume and Its Relation to the Theatre, by Iris Brooke. London: Harrap. 2 vols., 1939/40. Reprinted by Theatre Arts Books (New York) in 1964. LC 63-18334.
   Volume 1 covers the 13th century to the 17th century; Volume 2 covers the 17th century to the middle of the 19th century. The book illustrates and explains costume designs and fashions, along with the style and customs of the day.

Who's Who in the Theatre. 1912-1981 (volumes 1-17). London: Pitman; Detroit, MI: Gale. LC 12-22402. No longer published. Superseded by *Contemporary Theatre, Film, and Television.* See: page 196.

Theater Periodicals

ABTT News. 10/12 issues yearly, 1972-   . London: Association of British Theatre Technicians.

News and articles of interest to theater technicians. Employment opportunities, technical information on equipment, products, and services, and reviews of new literature. Reprints articles of interest from other publications. See Also: BRITISH THEATER ORGANIZATIONS, page 481.

Amateur Stage. Monthly, 1946- . Annual index by publisher. Address: P.O. Box 1, 30 Culver Rd., St. Albans, Herts, AL1 4ED. ISSN 0002-6867. Back volumes available on microform from UMI.
News and events of interest to the amateur stage community. Articles on theory, style, technical production techniques, and other topics. A listing of productions currently on stage and forthcoming around the country. Reviews of current shows and new literature.

British Theatrelog. Quarterly, 1978- . London: Associate British Centre of the International Theatre Institute. LC 82-20543, ISSN 0141-9056. Supersedes in part, *Theatrefacts.*

Cue; technical theatre review. Bimonthly, 1979- . Twynam Publishing, Kitemore, Faringdon, Oxfordshire SN7 8HR. LC 89-648376, ISSN 0144-6088. Indexed in: Current Technology Index (Previously: British Technology Index).
Articles on stage design, equipment, lighting, etc.; reviews of new books.

Drama; the quarterly theatre review. Quarterly, 1919- . London: British Theatre Association. LC 58-26806, ISSN 0012-5946. Now published separately from the BTA, the current address is: Cranbourn Mansions, Cranbourn St., London WC2H 7AG. Indexed in: BI, Arts & Humanities Citation Index, Book Review Index, Humanities Index, British Humanities Index. Back volumes available in microform from UMI.
Excellent articles on current stage plays and theater events in England, many high quality stage photos, and interviews with actors and other theater personnel. Uniquely, the publication reviews plays from throughout the British Isles, and as far away as Los Angeles, Canada, and Australia. Each issue contains ads for theater schools and courses of interest to aspiring stage actors. It also reviews new literature in the field.

Entertainment and Arts Management. Monthly, 1973- . Eastbourne, East Sussex: John Offord Publications. LC 86-15081, ISSN 0143-8980. Previous title: *Municipal Entertainment* (ISSN: 0140-976X).

Equity Journal. Quarterly, 1971- . London: British Actor's Equity Association. ISSN 0141-3147. Previous title: *Equity* (1971-77). It also absorbed and continued *Variety Artists Federation Newsletter.* See Also: British Actors Equity Association, page 500.

　　The journal for the members of the British association which represents actors and other performers in stage, screen, and television. It covers news and events, legislation, employment, union activities, contracts, and reviews new literature in all performing arts fields.

Gambit; an international drama quarterly. Quarterly, 1959-1989. Ceased publication with issue number 42/43. London: John Calder Publishers. Distributed in the United States by Riverrun Press (NY). LC 72-205445, ISSN 0016-4283.

　　Truly international in scope, it covered the theater in many countries. Back issues are good for historical research. Articles sometimes translate complete plays or provide long historical reviews of theater trends during a particular period. Playwrights receive considerable attention.

International Theatrelog. Quarterly, 1978- . London: Associate British Centre of the International Theatre Institute. LC 82-20643, ISSN 0141-9412. Incorporates *Theatrefacts.*

　　International in scope, each issue is a review, by country, of plays, revivals, festivals, and other theater events. About ten countries are covered, including both the East Coast and West Coast of the United States.

London Drama. Semiannual, 1973- . Stacey Publications, One Hawthorndene Road, Hayes, Bromley, Kent BR2 7DX. LC 86-15791. Previous title: *Broadsheet.*

　　This publication covers drama education in colleges and special schools for drama.

London Theatre Record. Fortnightly, 1981- . Cumulative indexes provided by the publisher. 4 Cross Deep Gardens, Twickenham, Middlesex, TW1 4QU England. LC 81-646222, ISSN 0261-5282.

Reproduces full reviews from major British newspapers and magazines (with the exception of the *Times*) of all current British stage productions. The emphasis is on the London stage, but other areas are covered too. The publication also serves as a source of current theater industry news regarding who's doing what and future plans for new productions.

Medieval English Theatre. Semiannual, 1979- . Lancaster, England: University of Lancaster, Department of English Language and Medieval Literature. LC 89-647264, ISSN 0143-3784. Indexed in MLA.

NTQ; New Theatre Quarterly. Quarterly, 1985- . Cambridge, England: Cambridge University Press. LC 85-643629, ISSN 0266-464X. Successor journal to: *Theatre Quarterly* (1971-1981).

Critical studies about modern drama and classical repertory, theory and practice, and educational programs.

Performing Right News. Irregular (3 or 4 issues yearly), 1954- . The Performing Right Society. See: page 536.

Plays and Players. Monthly, 1953- . London: Hansom Books. LC 75-647587, ISSN 0032-1559. Originally started as *The Play Pictorial* (1902-1939) and incorporated: *Theatre World* (1925-1965), and *Encore* (1954-1965) into its publication. Indexed in: Humanities Index.

One of the oldest periodicals which covers performers in radio, television, and film although the emphasis has been on the stage. It includes reviews from plays, playbills, and some photos. Profiles actors and their careers, often listing their stage credits. An excellent source of historical information. It also reviews new literature and makes an effort to cover the theater in other areas of England, New York, and parts of Europe.

Plays International. Monthly, 1985- . Address: F6 Greenwood Ct., Harlescott, Shrewsbury SY1 3TB. LC 86-36537, ISSN 0268-2028.

Reviews, interviews, and articles. International in scope with emphasis on Europe and the UK. Good reviews of London stage activities.

The Stage. See: *The Stage and Television Today.*

The Stage and Television Today. Weekly, 1880- . Stage House, 47 Bermondsey St., London SE1 3XT. Phone: 071-403 1818. ISSN: 0038-9099. Previous title: *The Stage* (1880-1959).

The longest running theater industry newspaper, starting as *The Stage* in 1880. Covers stage productions and industry news from all areas of the country. Excellent historical coverage of theater companies, productions, and actors in all provinces as well as in London. Some photos in older issues. Regretfully, there is no detailed index. As the title indicates, it now covers other areas of the British entertainment business. For example, the April 21, 1988 issue contained a section identified as "*The Stage's* annual supplement to country music."

Theatre Notebook; a journal of the history and technique of the British theatre. 3 issues/yearly, 1945- . London: Society for Theatre Research (c/o The Theatre Museum, 1 E. Tavistock St., London WC2E 7PA England. LC 88-1748, ISSN 0040-5523. Publisher index available for volumes 1-25 (1945-71). Indexed in: Humanities Index, MLA, Arts & Humanities Citation Index.

Well documented, scholarly articles about theater history throughout England. Reviews current literature.

Theatre Quarterly. Quarterly from 1971 - 1981. ISSN 0049-3600. Indexed in: Humanities Index, Book Review Index, others. No longer published. Superseded by *NTQ; New Theatre Quarterly.*

Theatre Research International. 3 issues yearly, 1958- . London: Oxford University Press (for the International Federation for Theatre Research). LC 76-641605, ISSN 0307-8833. Formed from two merged titles: *Theatre Research* (1958-1975) and *New Theatre Magazine* (1959-1975). Available on microform from UMI. Indexed in: Humanities Index, MLA, Historical Abstracts, Arts & Humanities Citation Index, Index to Book Reviews in the Humanities.

Scholarly approach to theater research, with carefully researched and documented articles about the theater in many smaller and third-world countries. Long reviews of current literature.

Theatre World. 1925-1965. Continued by *Plays and Players.*
The best theater research resource during the years it was published because of the large number of photographs it used of the plays it profiled. Each entry also included cast and production credits, opening dates, and the theater where it appeared. In addition, the magazine listed the plays and credits for a number of theater productions in and around the London area, news of the industry, and had brief articles about some of the actors.

Theatrefacts-Theatrelogs. Quarterly, 1974-1977. London: TQ Publications. Previous title: *Theatrefacts.* No longer published. Split into two new periodicals: *British Theatrelog* and *International Theatrelog.*

Theatrephile; popular theatre research. Irregular, 1983- . Theatrephile: 5 Dryden St., Covent Gardens, London WC2E 5BR. Phone: 071-240 2430. LC 84-646043, ISSN 0265-2609.
Articles highlight special theater collections in various libraries. Other articles are the result of considerable research itself and cover such diverse topics as the history of a particular historic theater building, performers from all ages, and music hall performances. Good bibliographies and illustrations (photos or drawings) often accompany the articles.

Theater Organizations

Association of British Theatre Technicians. 4 Pulteney St., London W1R 3DF. Phone: 071-434 3901. Publications: *ABTT News* (10/12 issues yearly, 1972-) and *Sightline* (Semiannual, 1967-).
The organization represents stage hands, technical experts, and other technicians in the theater and some other areas.

The British Theatre Association. Ceased to exist in 1990. Established in 1919 as The British Drama League. Publishes *Drama;* the quarterly theatre review. Presented the prestigious DRAMA AWARDS each year. Was heavily involved in presenting training and educational courses for theater professionals.

The Society for Theatre Research. Mail for the Society is currently received c/o The Theatre Museum, 1e Tavistock St., London WC2E 7PA.

The Spotlight. 7 Leicester Pl., London WC2H 7BP. Phone: 071-437 7631.

Not an organization per se, The Spotlight is the publisher of *Spotlight Casting Directory* and *Spotlight Contacts.* The organization also published information about child actors and a *New Actors and Actresses* series to highlight new talent. It offers two services: (1) the Enquiry & Records Service maintains current records on approximately 40,000 members of the profession; (2) an Advisory Service which provides information to clients about the acting credits of artists and provides audition facilities. It keeps extensive files and provides information about professionals in the British theater world, including directors, designers, and others in addition to actors. The main files, however, provide standard casting/career information on all British actors: their agents, current addresses when known, physical characteristics, special areas of work if applicable, and previous work. Files are constantly updated. A small number of internationally known people are included.

Theatre Information Group. Address: c/o Claire Hudson. The Theatre Museum, 1e Tavistock Street, London WC2E 7PA, England.

TIG is the UK affiliate of SIBMAS, the International Association of Libraries and Museums of the Performing Arts. Membership is made up of libraries, museums, drama schools, and those professionals working with information pertaining to the performing arts. The Group publishes an annual *Membership Directory* which lists the names, addresses, phone numbers, and staffs of participating institutions. The directory is a handy supplement to the Howard book mentioned previously because it contains current information. It can be purchased from the above address. If you write for information, be sure to enclose an SASE and two international postal coupons.

British Theater Research Facilities

Anyone interested in finding out where theater resources and collections are located throughout England should purchase, beg, borrow, or find some way to read a paperback book by Diana Howard (compiler) titled *Directory of Theatre Resources: a guide to research collections and information services.* (2d ed., 1986, 144p, ISBN 0 946347 08 5). See above for a detailed review.

The British Theatre Association Library

Editorial Note: The BTA went out of business by the end of 1990. The British Theatre Museum acquired most of the collection. The following description of the collection can serve as a guide to the collection that is currently being moved to the Theatre Museum Library.

The Main Reference Library has a large collection of approximately 125,000 volumes, which includes theater reference books (such as the *Spotlight* annual and *The Stage Yearbook*) and other publications vital to the study of theater history, biography, acting, stage design, costume, management, directing, funding, policy, and law. Excellent sets of out-of-print theater periodicals as well as current titles. Also has strong collection of newspaper clippings, including stage reviews and related articles from *The Times* back to 1901. Several other dailies and Sunday papers are now also clipped for relevant articles. Although the Library hasn't been able to systematically purchase them, it does have collections of theater programs and photographs acquired through donations. The Library has a number of special collections that have been donated by noted theater personnel. The theatrical library of William Archer (the eminent critic credited with bringing Ibsen to the London stage) consists of 1,500 volumes, playbills, letters, clippings, and memorabilia. The Library also has 144 volumes of *Lacey's* acting editions from the early 19th century, The Unity Theatre Archive, the Monumenta Scenica in 12 volumes, and prompt books from a wide range of productions. Lastly, it has a collection of over 56,000 play scripts and prompt scripts of British plays and theatre productions.

The Theatre Museum Library

Address: The Theatre Museum, 1 E Tavistock St., London WC2E 7PA.

Phone: 071-836 7891.

The Underground: The Museum is Located at Covent Garden and easily accessible by subway from the Covent Garden, Leicester Square, and Charing Cross stations.

Hours: Readers may use the Library by appointment Tuesday through Friday during the hours of 10:30 am-1:00 pm, 2:00 pm-4:30 pm.

Staff: Researchers may consult with a staff member by phone. Library staff members rotate responsibility for the public reference area on a daily basis. Claire Hudson is the Head of Library and Information Services.

Services: Limited photocopy service is available for a fee. The work must be done by the staff. Fees are charged for photographic services and reproduction rights.

General information: The Theatre Museum has been a department of the Victoria and Albert Museum since 1974, but its collections have a far longer history, many of them having been in the hands of private collectors before they were donated to the Museum. The Theatre Museum was opened as a separate museum at Covent Garden in 1987 as a response to public interest and demands for a separate museum. Because of Britain's interest in the theater and its importance to British culture, a separate museum was considered desirable.

The Collection: Theatre library materials were also moved from the main Victoria and Albert collection and a library was established at the new museum. Some of the materials designated for the collection (particularly material about theaters outside of London) are still in storage in other locations, but it is planned that the complete collection of research materials will soon be housed together in a building at another location, thus leaving the Covent Gardens building strictly for exhibition purposes.

The Library has a small reference/reading room with limited seating available for researchers. There is no open shelf access to the Library collection beyond the reference books in the reading room. The card catalog, also located there, offers author/subject access to the books in the stack collection. Because this library is very specialized, readers are encouraged to conduct as much of their general research as possible at a public or college library before approaching this one as a "library of last resort."

The Library has a number of books on the history of the theater and many of complete sets of current theater periodical titles as well as some which date back to the 18th century. Of special note is its large clipping collection with biographical files maintained on performers, and other files about popular and historically important subjects. There is also a large collection of photographs (black/white only) arranged by individual and production title. Readers should request a search of both if trying to locate photos of an actor in a particular production. A major part of the collection, as might be expected, covers London stage productions. These files are arranged by the name of the theater and then by year, followed by play title. Therefore, if you are looking for a particular production, it will be necessary to know the name of the theater where it was presented and the date of the production (the opening date is most often the one used). The Library staff can assist with this problem by consulting their in-house indexes. The boxes contain programs, press clippings, and photos (a project is currently underway to remove the photos and locate them with the rest of the photo collection). The Library also has an extensive collection of files about historical theater buildings which includes clippings, photos, postcards, and other materials. Readers should be prepared to supply the name of the town and the theater if they request a building file (for example: Sheffield, Playhouse). Files are kept on a wide variety of performing arts companies (Theatre, Dance, Opera, Circuses, and Puppet). A large special collection of annotated theater prompt books is also available for use in the Reading Room. The Library collects material on all aspects of the performing arts, including increasing amounts of information about popular music, as well as the more obscure areas (such as puppetry, magic, and the circus). This is a case where it is clearly important that researchers consult with a librarian prior to a visit so that materials from their collection can be assembled for use.

Special Collections: The Gabrielle Enthoven Theatre Collection was donated in 1924 and forms the basis of the Museum collection. It includes over a million playbills, programs, and other theater material dating from 1718. The Harry R. Beard Collection contains early French and Italian designs and engravings as well as other material dating back to the 18th and 19th centuries. Approximately 45 other special collections cover virtually every aspect of the performing arts and include photos from 1855, manuscripts and correspondence, sheet music, ballet material, tickets and tokens, and costumes and real objects.

Microfiche Collections: The microfiche collections include The Enthoven Collection of 19th Century Playbills from 75 London Theatres; The William Beaumont Morris Scrapbook Collection of six volumes relating to all aspects of the Diaghilev Ballet; the theater costume designs in the Victoria & Albert's Department of Prints and Drawings; and the V & A's collection of theater set designs. *No computer services.*

Garrick Club Library

Address: The Garrick Club, Garrick St., London WC2E 9AY.

Phone: (071) 836-1737.

The Underground: Leicester Square.

Hours: The Library is open to researchers BY APPOINT-MENT ONLY on Wednesdays, 10:00 am - 5:00 pm. Researchers should request permission to visit in writing and state the subject of their research. If the Library has some appropriate material and can accommodate the visit, an appointment will be scheduled. A small fee may be charged for the use of the collection. No photocopy facilities are available, but photographs can sometimes be made by arrangement. The club retains a photographer for this purpose.

General information: The Garrick Club was founded in the early 1800s and is a very traditional gentlemen's club with the library located on the top floor of a four story building. The walk up must be made on winding stairs along walls covered with beautifully framed old paintings of all shapes and sizes.

The Collection: A small library was established for the membership in 1831. Today, although the collection remains small by the usual library standards (it contains only about 7,500 volumes in two rooms), it is a most amazing collection of rare material that concentrates on British drama and the theater. Much of the material is late 18th and early 19th centuries, and includes letters, prints, playbills, playtexts, and theater programs, as well as books and pamphlets, that have been donated by Club members. One special collection is an original set (rows of carefully bound matching leather volumes) of rare Drury Lane (Covent Garden) playbills dating 1798-1853. The Henry Irving collection contains his personal correspondence and scrapbooks, photos and press clippings, and books about him. The C.B. Smith collection contains ten volumes of autographed letters to and from all of the major figures of the theater in the late 18th and early 19th centuries. The David Garrick collection also contains valuable letters, contracts, and clippings about Garrick and his family. Another donation is the set of prompt books of John Philip Kemble and the correspondence of Henry Kemble. The Evelyn Weeden collection contains two volumes of correspondence and press clippings. There are also a series of several volumes of costume account books and other theater records, and the minutes of the Theatre Royal, Drury Lane for most of the 19th century. The Library is proud of the iconographic collection, largely donated by Charles Matthews. The most import of the collection is five volumes of theatrical mezzotints. There are a number of photographs (some in albums) and postcards of early stage settings and actors. All together, there are several thousand theatrical engravings. A separate index and guide to the Club's theatrical paintings has been published. The rest of the collection is comprised of early editions of Shakespeare's plays or books about Shakespeare, biographies, general books on the theater, and a small number of 19th-century periodicals. The Library has a complete set of *The Era* (1858-1939) and *The Stage* (1957 to date).

The Raymond Mander and Joe Mitchenson Theatre Collection

Editorial Note: It appears that this private library collection has also gone out of business as of the middle of 1991. At this time, no one is sure what will happen to the collection. In the hope that it will remain together as a collection and be acquired by a suitable institution, the following description of the collection is being left in this book.

Address (as of July, 1990): The Mansion, Beckenham Place Park, Beckenham, Kent BR3 2BP. At the time of this writing, the Collection has serious financial problems and may move to another location or merge with another institution sometime in the future. Therefore, any researcher should contact the Collection well before making plans to use their materials.

Directions: Take the train just south of London to Beckenham. Once there, it's a moderate walk or short cab ride to the Mansion in the center of the Park.

Visitors: Only serious researchers are accepted. Write or call ahead to define your research needs. If it's determined that the Collection has the information you need, and it's not available anywhere else, an appointment will be made for your visit. Because of its reputation as an important archive for illustrations and other visual materials, the Library gets a number of researchers from the media, writers, publishers, and set designers. You may also find an occasional person working on a family history. They will respond to correspondence, but you should include return postage.

The Stacks: The shelves are not open to visitors. The staff will collect the resources you need and have them waiting for you when you arrive. Other materials can be requested and received at the time of your visit if necessary.

Services: Limited photocopy service is available; all copying must be done by a staff member.

The Collection: It is now a public trust, but was originally made up of the lifetime private collections of Raymond Mander and Joe Mitchenson. The two men spent many years of active interest in British theater and authored a number of books about the subject. Although Mr. Mander has died, Joe Mitchenson is still living and frequently can be found at the Collection. He is one of the most knowledgeable authorities about theater history in England and wonderful to talk with because he witnessed most of the productions since the 1930s in person.

The Collection is recognized as one of the most extensive in the country and includes materials from all areas of Great Britain, with the emphasis on London productions. The part of the library directly related to theater history is physically arranged by geographical area: Central London, Outer London, and the Districts. Following that, the materials are arranged by the name of the theater with the files containing historical materials about the theater, the building, and the playbills and other materials (photos, programmes, clippings, etc.) for all of its productions arranged in chronological order. There are also a number of posters. It has files for both the Bailey and Old Vic theatres, and there is a file on famous Hamlets. In addition, it has files on actors and actresses going back to the 17th and 18th centuries, dramatists, composers and conductors, singers, instrumentalists, and just about anyone who made a mark in the theater during the past 200 years.

There's a collection of Royal Variety performances, files on opera companies, wartime entertainment, circuses, bands, pleasure gardens, ballets, ventriloquists and conjurers, and many other subjects. Rare photos and engravings of people and costumes make up another part of the collection. One special collection is made up of over 20,000 postcards with scenes from plays or first night openings. The Collection is also blessed with a number of real objects from the theater, including costumes and props.

Besides the primary materials noted above, the Collection has historical sets of theater reference books and periodicals, including *London Theatre Record, The Stage Yearbook,* and *Play Pictorial Magazine.* It has a rare copy of *"The Stage" Cyclopedia* (1909, London: The Stage). Many pressbooks have come to the Collection as a result of private donations from actors and actresses.

Libraries Outside of London

Bodleian Library at Oxford University:
The John Johnson Collection of Printed Ephemera

Address: Bodleian Library, Oxford OX1 3BG

Phone: Oxford (0865) 244675.

Visitors : Visitors *must* be recommended for admission to the Bodleian Library by someone in a responsible position with credentials which can be verified. There is a special application form for this purpose which can be obtained by writing to the Admissions Officer of the Library. Once the application is submitted, the information is verified and the applicant notified of the decision. It is assumed that the applicant is seeking materials not available elsewhere and can list those materials he or she wishes to use during the visit. Needless to say, you should take care of this well in advance of a planned visit and have all of the paperwork completed before you leave home.

Publications: The John Johnson Collection: catalogue of an exhibition. Oxford: Bodleian Library. 87 p., illus., 1971. Also, a helpful dissertation is *Walter N. H. Harding and the Harding Drama Collection at the Bodleian Library, Oxford,* by Helene Elizabeth Solheim (University of Washington, 1985).

The stacks: The stacks are closed. There is only enough staff and space in the reading area to accommodate three visitors at a time. Visitors will need to discuss their needs with a staff member before their visit. A staff member will then collect the materials from the Collection and have them ready at the time of the appointment.

The Collection: The Bodleian is truly a historic library, having been established about 1320. Its first printed catalog was issued in 1605 and it is an official Depository Library of British Government publications. As in other British libraries, there is no detailed subject access. The Library is in the process of automating its collection, but the work done to date is available only to the staff. While there are many theater materials scattered throughout the main Bodleian Library Collection, most of the John Johnson Collection relates to theater history and is located separately. This special library was the private collection of Mr. Johnson, who was in charge of the Oxford Press from 1925 to 1946. The Collection was donated to the Bodleian in 1968 by the Press. The Collection is mainly stored in archival boxes and a detailed subject listing is printed as a guide to the Collection. Files include actors and actresses; individual authors and playwrights; broadsides; cigarette cards (with actors pictured on them); the cinema; circuses; clubs; concerts and concert bills; dance and dance programs; entertainers; fairs and festivals; London play places; magic; miniature theater; music and musicians; playbills; postcards; programmes; Shakespeare; song sheets; ballads; television; theater; tickets; and other topics.

FILM RESEARCH IN GREAT BRITAIN

Film Reference Resources

BFI Film and Television Yearbook. Annual, 1983- . London: British Film Institute. LC 84-37601, ISBN (1988-89) 0-85170-217-1.

The *Yearbook* serves as a general review of British film and television industry activities during the year as well as a report for the BFI and its divisions. The BFI reports cover a detailed financial report, restoration activities, membership activities, BFI projects with other organizations, new acquisitions, and reports from its divisions. The general industry section provides summaries of the major stories and events for the year in British film and television; a listing of British-made and financed feature films, USA productions based in Britain, and television films over 73 minutes in length; a list of all films over 40 minutes which were released commercially in Britain during the year; and film and television awards for the year. A directory provides names, addresses, phone numbers, and key staff names for archives and libraries, bookstores, production companies, associations and organizations, television stations and film companies, theaters, publishers, press contacts, and other services related to the industry.

British Film Actors' Credits, 1895-1987, by Scott Palmer. Metuchen, NJ: Scarecrow. 935 p., 1988. LC 87-31098, ISBN: 0-89950-316-0.
  Arranged alphabetically by actor, the book covers both the silent screen as well as modern film, the lesser known as well as the famous British actors. Each entry gives brief biographical information and a list of film credits.

The British Film Catalog; 1895-1985: a reference guide, by Denis Gifford. New York: Facts on File. Unpaged [1,152 p.], 1986. LC 86-6281, ISBN 0-8160-1554-6. Previously issued as: *British Film Catalogue, 1895-1970: a guide to entertainment films.* London: David & Charles 967 p., 1973. ISBN 0-7153-5572-4.
  The book is a catalog of information about all theatrical British films produced during the years noted. Arrangement of film titles is chronological (by year, followed by month of initial release or first showing). Each entry includes title, a brief plot summary, running time, production information, and cast credits. Entries have been given sequential index numbers, with an alphabetical index referencing that number so the title can be found in the body of the work.

British Film Fund Agency *Annual Report.* Annual, 1958-   . St. Martin's House, 16 St. Martin's-le-Grand, London EC1A 4EP England. ISSN 0068-2004.

British National Film & Video Catalogue. Annual, 1963-
Quarterly updates. London: British Film Institute. LC 86-648210, ISSN 0266-805X. Previous title: *British National Film Catalog* (1963-1983, ISSN 0007-1552). Volume 1-21 issued under previous title; volume 22 to date under current title.
  Complete bibliographic and production information for all films made and/or released in Great Britain. In addition to theatrical films, the index includes training and educational films, documentaries, independent productions, and television programs. Arranged by fiction or nonfiction categories. An alphabetical

title index is provided, as is a subject index. A directory of distributors accompanies each issue.

The Illustrated Directory of Film Character Actors, by David Quinlan. London: B.T. Batsford. 325 p., 1985. LC 88-180391, ISBN 0713444819. Published in the United States under the title: *The Illustrated Encyclopedia of Movie Character Actors.*
The book is a collection of biographies, photos, and filmographies of some of the screen's most respected character actors.

The Illustrated Directory of Film Stars, by David Quinlan. London: B.T. Batsford. 497 p., 1981. LC 82-111159. ISBN 0-7134-3891-6.
Arranged alphabetically by actor, the book includes photos, brief personal information about each person included, and a filmography (chronologically by release date).

The Illustrated Who's Who in British Films, by Denis Gifford. London: B.T. Batsford. 334 p., 1978. LC 79-310535, ISBN 0-7134-1434-0.
Arrangement is alphabetical by name of actor or director. Brief biographical facts are included, followed by a fairly comprehensive filmography (year and title).

International Film Guide. See: *Variety International Film Guide.*

International Index to Film Periodicals. Monthly, 1972- . Annual index volume by author, subject, and director. International Federation of Film Archives (F.I.A.F.). 90-94 Shaftesbury Ave., London W1V 7DH. New York: R.R. Bowker. LC 72-1964, ISSN 0000-0388.
Originally a card file service, then offered on microfiche. An index to over 100 film magazines from around the world. Access is by personal name, title, and subject.

Kemps International Film and Television Year Book. Annual, 1956- . Kemps Group, Publisher. Address: 1-5 Bath St., London EC1V 9QA England. Phone: 071-253 4761. New York: R. R. Bowker. LC 85-10947, ISSN 0075-5427. Previous titles: *Kemp's International Film & Television Directory* and *Kemps Film and Television Year Book International* (ISSN:0075-5427).

The volume covers the film and television industries in Great Britain and provides directory listings for agents, companies, products and services. A good source for current information. In addition, the volume also covers the industries by country, also listing production companies and relevant organizations.

Researcher's Guide to British Film & Television Collections. Edited by Elizabeth Oliver. London: British Universities Film & Video Council. New Rev. ed. [2nd ed.]. 176 p., 1985. ISBN 0901299405. A well-written and concise overview of film and television research collections in England. The guide covers national archives and large public libraries, regional collections, libraries and archives of television companies, production and stock shot libraries, special collections, and reference sources useful to the researcher. Each entry provides addresses, phone numbers, contact staff, visitor policies, an overview of the research collection, a brief history, and what access the visitor can expect to have to the collection. The book has an excellent review of the BBC Libraries, even though it must also tell the reader that the public does not have access to the facilities. Everyone planning to conduct extensive film and television research in England should have a copy of this book. The book ends with a bibliography of articles about British film and television and a listing of British and American film journals.

Screen International Film and TV Yearbook. Annual, 1947-   . King Publications. Kingscreen House, 6-7 Great Chapel St., Soho, London W1V 4BR England. Phone: 071-734 9452. LC 84-647269. Previous titles: *International Film and TV Yearbook, British Film and TV Yearbook* (1945-1982).
   An annual review of the film and television industries in over 30 countries. In addition, the Yearbook lists a number of international awards presented for the year, a listing of UK films produced during the year, UK yearly box office receipts, and an obituary section paying tribute to film and television people who died during the year.

Variety International Film Guide. Annual, 1964-   . Andre Deutsch, 34-35 Newman St., London W1P 3PD. (United States distributor Hollywood: Samuel French.). LC 90-14210. Previous title: *International Film Guide* (Tantivy Press, ISSN 0074-6053, 1964-1989).

The major portion of each Yearbook is an international review of film activity throughout the world, arranged alphabetically by country. Each section reviews the highlights of that country's film industry during the past year and includes the films produced during that time period. The annual also includes information for film festivals, film schools, libraries and archives, film bookshops and poster stores, provides a bibliography of book reviews, and a listing of current film journals.

A Who's Who of British Film Actors, by Scott Palmer. Metuchen, NJ: Scarecrow. See: page 326.

Film Periodicals

Afterimage. Irregular, 1970-   . London: Afterimage. ISSN 0261-4472. Indexed in: IITP.

A contemporary film magazine dealing with experimental films and independent filmmakers. Each issue usually has a special theme throughout.

Audio Visual. Monthly, 1946-   . Address: Mclarens, P.O. Box 109, Davis House, 66-77 High St., Croydon, Surrey CR9 1QH. LC 72-621437, ISSN 0305-2249. Previous titles: *16mm Film User* and *Film User.* Incorporated *Industrial Screen.* Indexed in MRD.

Geared toward educational institutions and teaching programs, the publication reviews new educational and corporate training videos. Reviews are full artistic and technical evaluations of the production. New equipment is also evaluated.

Critic. Critics' Guild. Weekly, 1950-   . 9 Compayne Gardens, London N.W. 6 England. ISSN: 0015-1203. Previous title: *Film Critics' Guild Bulletin.*

Equity Journal. Quarterly, 1971-   . London: British Actors Equity Association. ISSN: 0141-3147. Previous title: *Equity.* Incorporates: *Variety Artists Federation Newspaper.* See Also: page 500.

Covers news of interest to members: employment, legislation, proposed future productions, and other topics in the theatre, film, television, radio, and live performance areas.

Film. Monthly, 1954- . London: British Federation of Film Societies, 21 Stephen St., London W1P 1PL. Phone: 071-437 4355. LC 87-8514, ISSN 0015-1025. Available on microform. Available through UMI document delivery service. Indexed in: FLI, ICFR, MRD.

A monthly newsletter covering the activities and scheduled screenings of films by member film societies.

Film Dope. Irregular, 1972- . Address: 45 Lupton St., London NW5 2HS. LC 86-10262, ISSN 0305-1706. Indexed in FLI, IIFP.

Each issue contains a selection of film and television industry personnel (actors, directors, screenwriters, etc.) for which an overview is prepared containing biographical information, major career achievements, and a filmography.

Film Review. Monthly, 1951- . Spotlight Publications. Greater London House, Hampstead Road, London NW1 7QZ England. Previous title: *ABC Film Review* (ISSN: 0001-0413).

Reviews new films, recordings of film music, and new literature. Has a section for collectors to buy, sell, or trade anything related to films and actors.

Filmlog; index of feature film production and casting in Britain. Monthly. P.O. Box 789, London SW6 4EF England.

Provides information about film openings for actors.

Films and Filming. Monthly, 1954- . Address: Plus Publications, 248 High St., Croydon, Surrey CR0 1NF England. Phone 081-681 7817. LC 59-52240, ISSN 0015167X. Incorporated: *Focus on Film.* Indexed in: FLI, ICFR, IIFP, and IITP.

News, reviews of the latest films and videos, and interviews with major British film people. Feature articles about current topics, book and video reviews. Emphasis is on current activities. Publishes a list of films currently in production. Some coverage of film music and upcoming meetings or events.

Films on Screen and Video. Monthly, 1981- . Address: Ocean Publications, 22-24 Buckingham Palace Rd., London SW1W 9SA. LC 84-646242.

Newsletter of current activities in the film industry. Includes on-location and post-production work. Reviews newly released books and film products; reviews soundtrack recordings.

Framework; a film journal. Quarterly, 1975- . Paul Willemen, Publisher. 40A Topsfield Parade, London N8 8QA England. LC 81-645735, ISSN 0306-7661. Indexed in: FLI, IIFP, IITP, MRD.

A magazine for educators, film students, and historians. Contains articles on film theory, history, and criticism. Reviews books, periodicals, and new film products. Identifies upcoming festivals.

Historical Journal of Film, Radio, and Television. 3 issues yearly, 1980- . Carfax Publishing Co. (for the International Association for Audio-Visual Media in Historical Research and Education). Address: P.O. Box 25, Abington, Oxfordshire OX14 3UE. LC 81-642007, ISSN 0143-9685. Indexed in: FLI, IITP, MRD, Historical Abstracts, Arts & Humanities Citation Index.

An intellectual journal which emphasizes the role of the various forms of media (film, television, and radio) in influencing politics, culture, and history.

Image Technology; Journal of the BKSTS. Monthly, 1919- . British Kinematograph Sound and Television Society. Address: 547-549 Victoria House, Vernon Pl., London WC1B 4DJ. Phone: 071-242 8400. LC 87-640025, ISSN 0950-2114. Previous titles: *British Kinematographic Society Proceedings, BKSTS Journal* and *British Kinematography.* Indexed in: *British Technology,* and *Science Abstracts.* Reprints of articles available from UMI. See also: ORGANIZATIONS.

Periodical covering the technical aspects of film, television, and video production. Reviews new equipment in the audio and visual industries.

Monthly Film Bulletin. Monthly, 1934- . British Film Institute. LC 47-42975, ISSN 0027-0407. Indexed in: FLI, FRA,

IIFP, IITP, MRD. Sent to membership of BFI. Available on microform.

Articles about the film industry in Great Britain and the people in it. Provides extensive reviews of British releases and full production credits for the titles reviewed.

Movie. Quarterly, 1962- . Address: Cameron, 2a Roman Way, London N7 8XG. Phone: 071-609 4019/4010. LC 80-1607, ISSN 0027-268X. Indexed in: FLI, ICFR, MRD, and British Humanities Index.

Photoplay Movies & Video. Monthly, 1950- . Address: Argus Specialist Publications, P.O. Box 35, Wolsey House, Wolsey Rd., Hemel Hempstead, Herts HP2 4SS. LC 86-15526. Indexed in: FLI. Previous titles: *Films Illustrated* and *Photoplay Film and TV Scene.*

An illustrated monthly which publishes articles and interviews about actors and reviews the latest releases.

Screen (Incorporating Screen Education). Quarterly, 1959- . The Society for Education in Film and Television. 29 Old Compton St., London W1V 5PL. Phone: 071-734 5455. LC 83-11537, ISSN 0036-9543. Incorporated: *Screen Education.* Previous titles: *Society of Film Teachers Bulletin, Film Teacher,* and *Screen Education.* Indexed in: BI, FLI, ICFR, IIFP, IITP, MRD.

Interesting articles about film history worldwide.

Screen Digest. Monthly, 1971- . Annual index by publisher. Address: Screen Digest, Ltd., 37 Gower St., London WC1E 6HH. Phone: 071-580 2842. LC 87-16284. Indexed in: IITP.

Concise, brief articles about the latest news in the film, television, cable, broadcasting and media industries. Business oriented, with financial and technical developments an important part of each issue.

Screen International. Weekly, 1907- . King Publications. Kingscreen House, 6-7 Great Chapel St., Soho, London W1V 4BR LC 76-643629, ISSN 0307-4617. Previous titles: *Daily Cinema, Today's Cinema, Screen International and Cinema TV Today, Kinematograph Weekly,* and *Cinema TV Today.* The company also publishes a yearbook with a similar title.

News of the film and television industries, with additional coverage of videos. Weekly statistics of box office receipts. Also covers the industries on a worldwide basis, reviews new film releases and reports on filming in Great Britain.

Sight and Sound; the international film quarterly. Quarterly, 1932-   . Yearly index. London: British Film Institute. LC 41-396, ISSN 0037-4806. Indexed in: FLI, FRA, ICFR, IIFP, IITP, MRD. *British Humanities Index, Humanities Index, Art Index, Arts and Humanities Citation Index, Book Review Index.* Available on microform. See also: FILM RESEARCH FACILITIES.
     Excellent coverage of current film trends and events in England. Latest news concerning the industry, long interviews with actors and directors, and critical articles on film theory and practice. The magazine also provides long overviews of current cinema in other countries, with an emphasis on Europe. Thoughtful reviews of new films, both mainstream and independent.

Videodisc Newsletter. British Universities Film and Video Council. 3 issues yearly, 1983-   . ISSN: 0264-6358. Address: 55 Greek St., London W1V 5LR. See also: ORGANIZATIONS.

British Film Organizations

Association of Independent Producers. 17 Great Pulteney St., London WR1 3DG. Phone: 071-434-0181.

British Academy of Film and Television Arts. 195 Piccadilly, London W1V 9LG. Phone: 071-734-0022.

British Actors Equity Association. 8 Harley St., London W1N 2AB. Phone: 071-637 9311 and 636 6367. Publications: *Equity Journal* (1971-). The organization has incorporated the Variety Artists Federation and their publication, *Variety Artists Federation Newsletter.*

British Broadcasting Corporation. Television Centre, Wood Lane, London W12. Phone: 081-743 8000.

British Federation of Film Societies. London. Publications: *Film* (Monthly, 1954- .)

British Film Fund Agency. St. Martin's House, 16 St. Martin's-le-Grand, London EC1A 4EP England.

British Film Institute. See: pages 502-508.

British Film & Television Producers' Association. See: page 523.

British Kinematograph Sound and Television Society. 547-549 Victoria House, Vernon Pl., London, WC1B 4DJ. Phone: 071-242-8400.

British Society of Cinematographers. c/o Tree Tops, 11 Croft Road, Chalfont St. Peter, Gerrards Cross, Bucks SL9 9AE. Phone: 0753 888052.

British Universities Film and Video Council. 55 Greek St., London W1V 5LR England. Publications: *BUFVC Catalogue* of over 6500 audio visual materials suitable for use in higher education, *The Researcher's Guide to British Film & Television Collections*, *The Researcher's Guide to British Newsreels*, *British University Film News* (Indexed in: MRD), and *Videodisc Newsletter* (ISSN 0264-6358) which is a user's guide to new technology.
   The Council was established in 1948 by and for university teachers, but now includes all education levels. The purpose of the organization is to encourage the use, study, and production of audiovisual media, materials and techniques for teaching and research in higher education. Membership is open to educational institutions.

Broadcasting and Entertainment Trades Alliance. 181-185 Wardour St., London W1V 3AA. Phone: 071-439-7585.

Central Casting Ltd. 162-170 Wardour St., London W1V 3AT. Phone: 071-437 1881. Licensed by the Department of Employment to provide jobs for actors.

Directors Guild of Great Britain. Lyndhurst Hall, Lyndhurst Rd., London NW3 5NG. Phone: 071-431 1800.

The Entertainment Agents' Association Ltd. 403 Collingwood House, Dolphin Sq., London SW1V 3NE. Phone: 071-834 0515.

The Personal Managers' Association. Address: c/o The Secretary, Redfern House, Woodside Hill, Chalfont St. Peter, Bucks SL9 9TF. Represents the personal managers of artists, directors, writers, and other public figures.

Royal Television Society. Address: Tavistock House East, Tavistock Square, London WC1H 9HR. Phone: 071-387 1970.

Society of Authors Broadcasting (a subsidiary of The Society of Authors). Address: 84 Drayton Gardens, London SW10 9SB. Phone: 081-363 6642. Represents film, television and radio writers.

Variety Club of Great Britain. Address: 32 Welbeck St., London W1M 7PG.

The Writers Guild of Great Britain. Address: 430 Edgward Road, London W2 1EH. Phone: 071-723 8074.

British Film Research Facilities

British Film Institute

Address: 21 Stephen St., London W1P 1PL.

Phone: 071-255 1444

Publications: BFI Film and Television Yearbook (1983-   . Previously published as their *Annual Report* from 1932 until 1982), *BFI News* (Bimonthly, 1972-), *Monthly Film Bulletin* (Monthly, 1934-   ., ISSN: 0027-0407) and *N.F.T. National Film Theatre* (1957-   ., a monthly schedule of film showings at the NFT in London), and *Sight & Sound* (Quarterly, 1932-).

British Film Institute Title Index. London: British Film Institute. 2nd rev. ed., 1975. *Supplements* 1978, 1980. By subscription to World Microforms, London.

British Film Institute Personality and General Subject Index . Main collection. 1975. *Supplement.* 1973. London: British Film Institute. Microfiche. By subscription to World Microforms, 62 Green's Grove, London NW8 6ER.

British National Film & Video Catalogue, 1963- . The British Film Institute Library. See: page 493-494.

Catalogue of the Book Library of the British Film Institute. Boston: G.K. Hall. 3 vols., 1975.

National Film Archive Catalogue. 4 Parts. Published from 1960-1980. Three of the volumes identify the silent films in the collection; the fourth volume lists non-fiction films.

TV Documentation; a guide to BFI Library Services resources. London: BFI. Illus., 67 p., 1985. ISBN: 0-85170-181-7.
    The book provides detailed information about television re-search resources in two BFI departments: (1) the Library, and (2) Stills, Posters, and Designs. Most of the book covers the library collection of books, periodicals, indexing services and other reference resources, clipping files, and special collections. The clear instructions about how to use various collections of the library and how to do research are most helpful. The Stills, Posters, and Designs Division holdings are discussed and rules are presented for accessing the collection. If you plan to visit the BFI for any research purposes, this would be an excellent publication to study beforehand.

Visitor arrangements: Non-BFI members must pay a fee for a pass to use the Library, BFI members receive the privilege as part of the membership. If you plan on spending more than one day there, it costs less to join.
    Visitors should contact any department of the BFI before

their visit in order to receive the best service. Appointments to view films at the National Film Archive must sometimes be made weeks ahead of time, depending on how intensive the equipment use has become. Although you are not required to contact the Library before you come, you would be wise to do so if you plan to work on a complicated research project. In addition, they have only so much seating space and it is wise to be sure you will be guaranteed one. They were filled up every day I was there.

The Library. The BFI probably has the most user-friendly library in Great Britain, and that's because it may be the only library in the country funded sufficiently to provide enough staff to help patrons and to do what it takes to develop computer services.

The Library collection consists of reference resources, books, about 1,600 periodical titles from around the world, newspaper clipping files, scripts, program and press publicity materials, and other materials. The Library officially started collecting television information in 1961, so its early material is not as extensive in this area as it is about film. However, acquisition activities in both areas are about equal today. The periodical collection contains back historical files of ceased publications as well as current titles.

The BFI Library is unique in that it has maintained an in-house indexing service for many years. The staff has continually indexed, in considerable detail, the majority of film and television periodicals they receive, television program journals (like *The Listener*), millions of newspaper clippings, film festival programs, publicity packages from production companies, press materials received from many industry sources, and just about anything else they have received. Of particular interest to researchers is the fact that indexing is done for selected subjects, titles of film and television productions, personal names (personalities), and other topics. Indexing of television was started in 1975, long after the film files were begun, so limited indexing exists for TV before that date. The main card catalog is divided into five areas: author, title, subject, personalities, and title (films, tv programs).

Press clippings (collected from newspapers and magazines) go back to the 1930s and are sorted into three categories: personalities, program reviews, and subjects. They are then indexed, microfilmed (in fiche format) and filed under the heading selected.

The comprehensive indexing allows the Library to maintain thousands of files in its Personality collection, mostly on well known actors and film industry notables. However, it is also possible to find something on many lesser known people throughout film history. Some of the bibliographies of the more recognizable names are quite extensive and the articles cited go beyond their personal life and film or TV work. Articles about Orson Welles, for example, referred to his radio and stage credits.

It is possible to conduct some BBC television research at the BFI. They have a set of *BBC Handbooks* from 1928 forward, the *BBC TV Drama Index* (1936-1975), the *Granada TV Drama Index* (1957-1974), and almost a full set of duplicate BBC program publicity materials for recent years. The *BBC Program Index* (for radio and television) is divided into 4 parts: (1) Title Index (listing all titles by which a program might be known); (2) Main Index; (3) Contributor Index (names of people who made a significant contribution to a program); and (4) a Subject Index of nearly 3,000 terms. Better consult with the library staff about how to use it before you start, because there are some unique features to it. For example, you need to be aware of two quirks: the Contributor Index rarely includes the performers who appeared on a program, leaning instead toward the authors, interviewees, producers, and even the music composers. And the Subject Index does not invert personal names, so people are indexed by their first names instead of their surnames. The index covers all domestic programs, but not overseas broadcasts.

An extensive script collection for film and television programs (including series); both published and unpublished works (story lines, rehearsal or camera scripts, post-production scripts, etc.) are collected. The scripts that have been published are cataloged and treated like other published books. The unpublished are handled differently, depending on their value and whether or not they are part of a special collection; they are, however, still available to researchers.

Other special collections have been received from production companies and individual people. These collections contain annotated scripts, scrapbooks, personal correspondence, business papers (including contracts), and working production materials from particular films or tv shows. All of this material is indexed in great detail. Publicity packages, press releases, production schedules, announcements, and other film company and television station releases are received regularly and handled according to the type of material.

The Library also has spent the past several years transferring its files, indexes, and card catalog to its own database. The **SIFT** database (Summary of Information on Film and Television) has been compiled from data collected by the BFI since 1934. This includes the Library collection, the films in the National Film Archive, and the stills and other visuals in the Stills department. As a result, the following information can be found online:

(1) More than 300,000 films, television programs, and videos. The amount of information varies for each entry, but will probably include the release date, production and cast credits, plot summary, and running time. The more comprehensive entries will also have additional release information, references to other BFI collections which also have information about the film, and a bibliography of periodical articles.

(2) Data files on approximately one million people, with bibliographies on approximately 60,000 of them.

(3) Data on approximately 30,000 film and television organizations, with brief bibliographies for about 11,000 of them and current contact addresses for 15,000.

(4) Data on 4,000 events, such as festivals and award programs. Some bibliographies will be available.

The main access on the system is by title or elements in the title entry; authors and personal names may be retrieved under certain circumstances. Subject access is limited, but full availability is planned for the future. The system allows the user to assemble references on each topic from all collections within the BFI into one complete search.

The National Film Archive: The Archive was established in 1935 with the responsibility for acquiring, documenting, and maintaining a national repository of British films. In 1961, this mission was officially expanded to include television programs. This collection is now over 100,000 titles strong, and is fully indexed and will appear on the Library SIFT automated database. Acquisition and restoration priority is given to British films. It also carries out an extensive restoration program and provides research facilities for public visitors from around the world. The films themselves are stored at their storage facility, the Getty Conservation Centre at Berkhamsted, and must be delivered to the London Archive for viewing.

Viewing Services: The NFA provides viewing facilities for researchers to view the film collection. Inquiries should be made weeks ahead of time as they are often fully booked, especially during the summer months.

The Stills, Posters, and Designs Department: The largest part of the department by far is the collection of over three million film and television stills and half a million color slides (transparencies). The collection can be accessed via a card file in their reading room and also appears on SIFT, the Library's new automated database. Most stills were acquired through personal gifts, donations from production companies, and the receipt of publicity materials. Many of the stills packages for specific films include location photos as well as publicity photos. In addition, the department has nearly 20,000 portrait photographs of personalities and other related subjects (awards, general studio shots, social events, etc.). The largest growth in recent years has come from the increased acquisition of stills and publicity materials of television programs.

Since 1984 the BBC has regularly deposited sets of publicity photos of their programs with the agreement that the BFI would act as a point of viewing access for the public. Anyone wishing to purchase or obtain permission to use the photos is then referred to BBC to complete the transaction.

Visitor arrangements: Visitors should call for an appointment and to discuss their needs. If at all possible, any research that needs to be done should be completed before you approach the BFI. Requests can be handled by mail. Research services are available (for a fee). In addition, the department will supply copies of photos in their collection for approved projects, which includes research needs, publishers, film and television production companies, and other professional activities. Copyright clearance must be obtained from the original owner and is the responsibility of the client.

For a profile of services and facilities of the British Broadcasting Corporation (BBC), See: pages 517-519.

TELEVISION AND RADIO RESEARCH IN GREAT BRITAIN

Books, Annuals, Directories and Other Sources

Annual Review of BBC Broadcasting Research Findings. Annual, 1974- . BBC Broadcasting Research Department, Broadcasting House, London: W1A 1AA.

Studies and statistics about British television viewers and their viewing habits and/or patterns. Each annual has a compilation of the research conducted during the previous year.

BBC Annual Report and Handbook. Annual, 1928- . London:BBC. 35 Marylebone High St., London W1M 4AA. ISSN 0068-1377.

BBC Drama Index 1936-1975. London: Chadwyck Healey. 1976. Available on microfiche.

An index to BBC-produced television drama programming. Arranged chronologically by title. Information for each program includes title, author, production and cast credits, and broadcast dates.

Blue Book of British Broadcasting. Annual, 1974- . Tellex Monitors, Ltd., 47 Gray's Inn Rd, London WC1X 8PR. 15th ed., 548 p.,1989. ISBN 0950616702.
Includes BBC, IBA, and other companies involved in British broadcasting. A directory of important people, companies, organizations, and services for the year. Lists programs produced during the year.

BBC. *British Broadcasting, 1922-1972; a select bibliography.* London: British Broadcasting Corporation. 49 p., 1972. A brief list of historical books and periodical articles tracing the history of broadcasting.

Broadcast Production Guide. Annual. London: International Thomson Publishing, 100 Avenue Rd., London NW3 3TP. Phone 071-935 6611.
A directory of local production services for British television, video, and recording industries. Directory information for: audio equipment, artists' agents, cable industry personnel, film and TV distribution companies, stock libraries, film and video production facilities, music publishers, record companies, script writers, trade associations, and professional publications.

Broadcast Yearbook and Diary. Annual, 1961- . International Thomson Publishing, Ltd., 100 Avenue Rd., London NW3 3TP.
Reviews important events of the year and summarizes activities. A directory section provides information about organizations, stations and station personnel, related industry services, and production companies that supply programming. Educational programs for industry personnel, important conferences, and festivals are also listed.

Broadcasting in the United Kingdom, by Barrie MacDonald. Mansell Publishing. Address: Artillery House, Artillery Row, London SW1P 1RT. 266 p, 1988. LC 88-23392, ISBN 0-7201-1962-6.

The definitive research guide to British television and radio broadcasting. Starts out with a history of broadcasting, explains the legal and structural organization of the industry, and provides statistics and current information that serve to help the reader understand the changes that will be taking place over the next few years. The book also provides directory information about professional associations and trade organizations, coverage of useful reference sources and periodicals, a list of libraries and archives, and advice on how to do research in the field. Highly recommended for anyone working in British broadcasting research.

Cable and Satellite Europe Yearbook. Annual, 1985-   . London: 21st Century Publishing. LC 88-21166.

A relatively new publication designed to meet the information needs about the fast-growing cable and satellite industries in England and Europe. Organized into sections by country, each chapter leads off with a general article which reviews activities of the year and then provides detailed directory information for industry companies and organizations, people, regulatory bodies, and related services of interest for that country.

Commonwealth Broadcasting Association Handbook. Biennial, 1976-   . Commonwealth Broadcasting Association. Broadcasting House, London W1A 1AA.

Communications Abstracts. Quarterly, 1978-   . Sage Publications. See: pages 369-370.

Directory of International Broadcasting. Annual, 1978-   . Address: B.S.O. Publications, 3-5 St. John St., London EC1M 4AE. Phone: 071-253 7174. ISSN 0262-9771.

Provides worldwide directory information regarding associations and organizations, broadcasting systems, manufacturers of equipment, suppliers of services, and other information useful to the industry.

Factfile; The IBA's reference book for independent broadcasting [1988-1989]. Annual, 1988-   . Independent Broadcasting Authority, 70 Brompton Rd., London SW3 1EY. Alternate title: *IBA Factfile.*

This publication provides information previously available in the Reference section of the IBA *Yearbook of Independent Broadcasting,* which ceased publication in 1987. It includes a brief overview of IBA and a complete listing of IBA companies (brief description of ITV and ILR stations give yearly highlights, main personnel, addresses, phone numbers) that provide independent television and radio service throughout the British isles.

Granada TV Drama Index [1957-1974]. Granada Television, Granada Television Centre, Manchester M60 9EA. Microfiche, 1979.

Provides a nearly complete index to BBC and ITV television drama programming in Britain for 1957-1974. The most comprehensive listing of British television programs available. Arranged alphabetically by title, each entry provides author, cast and production credits, and broadcast dates.

Halliwell's Television Companion, by Leslie Halliwell and Philip Purser. London: Grafton Books. 3d ed., 941 p., illus., 1986. ISBN: 0-246-12838-0. The first edition in 1979 was published under the title *Halliwell's Teleguide.*

The book is a combination dictionary/biographical directory which mixes together in one alphabet information about television personalities, series, specials, and even some terms and phrases.

IBA Technical Review. Irregular, 1972- . Independent Broadcasting Authority, 70 Brompton Rd., London SW3 1EY. LC 86-837, ISSN 0308-423X.

Independent Broadcasting Authority Annual Report and Accounts. Annual, 1954- . Distributed by: H.M.S.O., London. ISSN 0309-0175. See also: Television.

Independent Production Handbook. Irregular, 1982- . Association of Independent Producers. Address: 17-18 Great Pulteney St., London W1R 3DG. LC 83-22326.

A combined membership directory, list of film and television companies, and other relevant information about film and television productions for the year.

International Index to Television Periodicals. Biennial, 1979- . International Federation of Film Archives (F.I.A.F.). Address: 90-94 Shaftesbury Ave., London W1V 7DH. ISSN 0143-5663. See: pages 374-375.

International Television Guide. See: *Variety International Television Guide*.

The ITV Encyclopedia of Adventure, by Dave Rogers. Boxtree, 36 Tavistock St., London WC2E 7PB. 593 p., 1988. ISBN 1-85283-217-7.
Detailed information about over 200 of the most popular British-produced television series screened on independent television (the ITV Network) from the 1950s to date. Arranged by series title, each entry includes a complete list of all episodes, cast, production credits, air dates, and plot synopses.

Professional Promotion Media Directory. Semiannual, 1984- . Professional Books, Ltd., 46 Milton Trading Estate, Abingdon, Oxon OX14 4SY. Phone: (0235) 834821. ISSN 0267-5528.

Professional TV & Radio Media Directory. Semiannual, 1982- . Professional Books, Ltd. Previous title: *Information on TV Directory* (ISSN 0263-9874). Also combines two former titles: *TV Directory* and *Radio Directory*.
Directory of the industries in England, with emphasis on important people in each organization, amateurs and professionals at the local level, support organizations of interest to the industry, production facilities, services and equipment vendors.

Professional Video International Yearbook. Annual, 1977- . Link House Magazine, Ltd., Link House, Dingwall Ave., Croydon 2TA. Phone: 081-686 2599. ISSN 0266-2256. Previous title: *International Video Yearbook* (ISSN: 0261-1910).
An international resource directory of people, services, and equipment in the broadcasting industry.

Radio Research: a Comprehensive Guide, 1975-1985; a survey conducted by the radio academy and funded by the IBA. London: BBC Data Publications. 1986. ISBN 0-946358-30-3.

The book was designed to review the state of radio production and broadcasting in Great Britain and Europe today. The introduction itself is a comprehensive essay on how to do radio research and very much worth reading if you can find a copy.

Television and Radio. Annual, 1963-88. Ceased publication. London: Independent Broadcasting Authority. ISSN 0262-6470. See: ORGANIZATIONS. Previous titles: *Guide to Independent Television and Independent Local Radio* and *ITV Guide to Independent Television* (ISSN: 0536-2121).

Even though it's no longer published, the back volumes of this publication are an excellent source of statistics and historical information if you can find them.

Variety International Television Guide. Annual, 1983- . London: Andre Deusch. U.S. distributor: Hollywood: Samuel French.

International coverage of the television business, including names and addresses of industry personnel and organizations, a review of programming, and current literature.

Who's Who On Television. Edited by Eddie Pedder. Independent Television Books, Ltd. 247 Tottenham Ct. Road, London W1P 0AU. 3d ed. 272 p., 1985. LC 88-133135, ISBN 0907965318.

An illustrated guide to 1,000 best known faces on British television. Each entry includes a brief biography and a photo.

Television and Radio Periodicals

Airwaves. Quarterly, 1974- . Independent Broadcasting Authority. Address: 70 Brompton Rd., London, SW3 1EY. Phone: 071-584 71011. LC 85-641936, ISSN 0267-3789. Previous title: *Independent Broadcasting* (ISSN 0305-6104). Indexed in: International Index to Television Periodicals.

Articles about trends in TV and radio programming, IBA member station news, announcements of IBA awards, and other news of interest to the industry and general public.

Ariel. Weekly, 1936- . London: BBC. 35 Marylebone High St.,
London. W1M 4AA England. Weekly in-house newsletter. ISSN
0004-1335. Indexed in Arts & Humanities Citation Index.

Broadcast. Weekly, 1973- . International Thomson Publishing.
23-29 Emerald St., London, WC1N 3QJ. ISSN: 0040-2788.
Includes a monthly supplement titled *Invision,* which reviews and
evaluates new equipment and technology in the industry. Previous
title: *Television Mail.* Indexed in: IIFP, IITP.
　Industry news magazine for the television, radio, and broadcasting industries.

Cablevision News. 3 issues yearly, 1973- . Cable Television
Association of Great Britain, 295 Regent St., London, W1R 7YA.
Previous title: Relay Association Journal.

C 4 (Channel Four Television). 3 times yearly, 1982- . Press
Information, The Press Office, 60 Charlotte St., London W1P
2AX. Phone: 071-927 8888. Weekly listing of Channel 4 programming. Articles on performers, new series, and important programs
of the week.

Combroad. Commonwealth Broadcasting Association. Quarterly,
1967- . Broadcasting House, London, W1A 1AA. LC 77-646923,
ISSN 0951-0826. Previous title: *Commonwealth Broadcasting
Conference* (1967-1974) and *Association Newsletter and Who's
Who.* Indexed in: Communication Abstracts.

Independent Broadcasting. Quarterly, 1974- . London: Independent Broadcasting Authority (IBA).

The Listener. Weekly, 1929- . Annual index. BBC, 35 Marylebone High St., London W1M 4AA. Phone 071-927 4950. ISSN
0024-4392. Indexed in: IIFP, IITP, BHI.
　A guide to BBC television and radio programming emphasizing
upcoming arts programs and specials. Articles about the programs, broadcasting issues; reviews of new films, television
programs, radio broadcasts, and new books. Feature articles are
often transcripts of BBC television and/or radio discussion about

important issues of the day. Heavy use of photos, both color and black and white.

Radio Times. Weekly, 1923- . British Broadcasting Company, 35 Marylebone High St., London W1M 4AA. LC 34-4877, ISSN 0033-8060. A title which briefly accompanied the main title: *The Radio Supplement.* Indexed in: IITP, *Children's Literature Abstracts.*

BBC's weekly complete guide to television and radio programming on their stations. The publication began when only radio programs existed; when television started, the program listings were added to this publication. Includes program schedules, articles on performers and important programs of the week.

Royal Television Society Bulletin. Monthly. See: page 502.

Stage and Television Today. See: page 480.

Television. Bimonthly, 1928- . London: Royal Television Society. LC 85-647402, ISSN: 0308-454X. See also: ORGANIZATIONS. Indexed in: IITP, *British Technology Index, Engineering Index,* and *Science Abstracts.* Previous titles: *Royal Television Society Journal* and *Television Society Journal.*

The oldest television journal for professionals in the industry.

Television; servicing, construction, color, developments. Monthly, 1934- . IPC Magazines, Ltd., Specialist & Leisure Group. King's Reach Tower, Stamford St., London SE1 9LS. Phone 071-261 5000. ISSN 0032-647X. Previous title: *Practical Television.* Indexed in *Science Abstracts* and *Pinpointer.* Articles are technical in nature.

Television and Video Production. Monthly, 1984- . McLaren Publishers, Ltd., P.O. Box 109, Scarbrook Rd., Croydon, Surrey CR9 1QH. Phone 10-688 7788. ISSN 0266-7460.

Monthly publication about television and radio in England.

Televisual. Monthly, 1982- . London: Communications Press. LC 88-640142. Previous title: *Corporate Video.*

TV Times. Weekly, 1955-   . Independent Television Publications, 247 Tottenham Court Rd., London W1P 0AU. ISSN 0039-8624.
England's weekly guide to independent television programming (all non-BBC stations). In addition to listings, it also publishes interviews, general articles, and profiles.

TV World; international business magazine for television. 10 issues yearly, 1977-   . Alain Charles Publishing, Ltd., 27 Wilfred St., London SW1E 6PR. ISSN: 0142-7466. Indexed in: IIFP.

Video Today. Monthly, 1980-   . Argus Specialist Publications, Ltd., P.O. Box 35, Wolsey House, Wolsey Rd., Hemel Hempstead, Herts, HP2 4SS. Phone: 0442 41221.

Video World. Monthly, 1979-   . Address: Galaxy Publications, Ltd., Box 312, Witham, Essex CM8 3SZ.

Which Video? Monthly, 1981-   . Argus Specialist Publications. 1 Golden Sq., London W1.
International equipment, product, and tape guide. Reviews new video releases in all formats.

Television and Radio Organizations

At the present time, two organizations run the world of British broadcasting (both television and radio), the BBC and the IBA. Although this has been true since the start of broadcasting in England, the British government has plans underway to change the structure to permit private corporations to take over much of the broadcasting activities as soon as the laws can be changed and a bidding process created. These anticipated changes are largely designed in response to the overall European common market goals for 1992. The only sure thing these days is that Europe 1992 will change things for the BBC and IBA as well as for the rest of British broadcasting. What the changes will be, no one can tell yet. Therefore, the situation as it exists today is described in the following pages.

British Broadcasting Corporation (BBC)

The BBC was established by the British government in 1922 to operate radio stations and expanded to television production in the early 1930s. The BBC today is broken up into several large corporations, with each handling a specific area. None of its research libraries are open for public use; in fact, there are very few actual points of contact for the general public to deal with the BBC in any way, with the exception of sales outlets for commercial products. This is a shame, since the BBC probably owns the largest and most valuable historical collection of news film, recorded sound, radio broadcasts, and television programs in the world. Even with all of the programs they discarded along the way, an almost unimagined volume of programs still exist in their archives.

As a bit of insight, I had the opportunity to deal with several BBC offices recently and found the people unfailingly polite, nice, and as helpful as they could be. However, I also thought the bureaucracy was the most stringent I've ever encountered. It took an incredible amount of patience to accomplish the work that needed to be done. The only advice I can give you is to make your contacts, practice stoic (but polite) perseverance, don't expect things to happen quickly, and don't give up. One friend of mine who runs a video production and distribution company had the same experience each time she dealt with the BBC to use some of their film in her productions. After months of phone calls and correspondence, and long periods of silence, the film usually appeared unannounced in the mail after she had given up all hope.

In order to identify and control their huge collection of archive materials, and provide effective research facilities for their thousands of staff members, the BBC has a number of specialized libraries in London; a network of libraries around the country serve as archives for locally-produced programs and research centers for regional BBC staffs. They are all restricted to BBC staff use, although a rare guest is allowed in under special circumstances. The libraries house BBC television film from 1948 to date; newsreel footage and radio news broadcasts; stock shot footage; locally produced radio programs; a large script collection for both radio and television programs; sound recordings of all types (including sound effects); several music libraries; a separate library for drama scripts; several libraries for program stills and other types of photos; and millions of press clippings about every subject imaginable (filed by country, local place, biographies, or subject). These clipping files are heavily used by their news staff because they cover decades of information from all of the British daily and Sunday newspapers. The news information libraries also clip international newspapers and a number of periodicals. Their London-based radio reference library is open to BBC staff 24 hours a day and emphasizes the performing arts and public personalities; one of the earliest clippings in the files is a 1919 article on T. E. Lawrence.

In addition, there are a number of special indexes that have been developed in-house: there are subject indexes to the clipping files; the film and drama materials; an index to radio programming from 1945 to date; radio scripts from 1922 forward; film and theater reviews worldwide; an index to the "Stage" magazine; biographical information; news events; and many other subjects. As a related service, they also develop detailed chronologies about important ongoing events, usually of a news nature.

The British Universities Film & Video Council's *Researcher's Guide to British Film & Television Collections* has an excellent review of BBC libraries and their collections. It is noted, however, that access is limited to internal staff use only and outside inquiries should be addressed to BBC Enterprises and not to the individual library. The BBC itself has a frequently updated *Guide to BBC Libraries & Information Services,* but it is not distributed publicly.

The following are other useful publications for BBC materials:

BBC Publications: *Annual Review of BBC Broadcasting Research Findings* (Annual, 1974-   ).

BBC. *Central Music Library. Catalogues.* 9 volumes, 1965/67. Each of the nine volumes covers a specific type of music, both vocal and instrumental, that is available in the vast BBC archives. Most of the cataloged material are compositions owned by BBC and either used on its programs or suitable for future use.

Even though the public may not have access to the BBC libraries, there is a way to get some research services from the BBC and perhaps even be allowed into a library. The point of contact for researchers is the BBC Data Enquiry Services, which was created in 1981 to provide access on a commercial basis.

BBC Data Enquiry Service

Address: Room 7, 1 Portland Pl., London W1A 1AA.

Phone: 071-637 0398.

Services offered: This is a fee-based research service that utilizes the immense BBC library research collections, in-house indexes, and commercial databases. Once you contact the service, a staff member will be assigned to work on your project and communicate directly with you regarding your project. They will do any type of project you want from creating bibliographies and in-depth research to checking quotes for providing biographical information on someone you expect to meet socially or professionally.

Costs: The work can be contracted on an hourly basis or by an annual subscription deposit account for a number of hours of work. Telephone calls, photocopying, and commercial online database searches are billed separately. Write for the prices.

Independent Broadcasting Authority (IBA)

Address: 70 Brompton Rd., London SW3 1EY.

Phone: 071-584-7011.

The IBA was originally founded as the Independent Television Authority (ITA) in 1954 and changed its name to the Independent Broadcasting Authority (IBA) in 1972 when it was also given authority for independent radio. IBA is a regulatory agency responsible for providing television and radio programming independent of, and in addition to, the BBC. While BBC is funded by license fees, independent television is funded by the sale of advertising in its programs. To accomplish this, ITA established ITV (Independent Television) in 1955 and ILR (Independent Local Radio) companies in 1972 to oversee and franchise independent stations. ITV has 15 regional companies that produce local television programs and share national programs; ILR has 46 radio stations that provide a variety of local programs, with more channels planned in the near future. IBA is responsible for selecting and contracting with the stations which provide the service, sets program standards and monitors as well as evaluates program content, controls advertising, and provides the technical staff and equipment which transmits the programs.

Publications: The IBA Annual Report & Accounts (Annual).

The Member contracting companies of IBA include:

(1) *Anglia Television, Ltd.* Address: Anglia House, Norwich, NR1 3JG. Phone: Norwich 0603 615151. Serves Eastern England.

(2) *Border Television.* Address: The Television Centre, Carlisle CA1 3NT. Phone: 0228 25101. Serves the border area of Scotland, the Isle of Man, and most of Cumbria.

(3) *Central Independent Television.* This station serves two regions, the East and West Midlands and maintains separate operations in each area. Address for the West: West Midlands, Central House, Broad St., Birmingham B1 2JP. Phone: 021 643 9898. Address

for the East: East Midlands Television Centre, Nottingham, NG7 2NA. Phone: 0602 863322.

(4) *Channel Television.* Address: The Television Centre, St. Helier, Jersey, Channel Islands. Phone: 0534 73999. Serves Jersey, Guernsey, and several smaller islands.

(5) *Grampian Television.* Address: Queen's Cross, Aberdeen AB9 2XJ Scotland. Phone: 0224 646464. Serves Northern Scotland.

(6) *Granada Television.* Address: Granada TV Centre, Manchester M60 9EA. Phone: 061-832 7211. Serves the North-West part of England.

(7) *HTV.* Address: The Television Centre, Culverhouse Cross, Cardiff, Wales CF5 6XJ. Phone: 0222 590590. Serves all of Wales and Avon as well as parts of Gloucestershire, Somerset, and Wiltshire.

(8) *London Weekend Television.* Address: South Bank Television Centre, London SE1 9LT. Phone: 071-261 3434. Provides weekend programming for London and the surrounding area.

(9) *Scottish Television.* Address: Cowcaddens, Glasgow G2 3PR Scotland. Phone: 041-332 9999. Serves Central Scotland.

(10) *Thames Television.* Address: Thames Television House, 306-316 Euston Rd., London NW1 3BB. Phone: 01-387 9494. Provides weekday programming for London and the surrounding area. Their sales subsidiary is: Thames International. Address: 149 Tottenham Court Rd., London W1P 9LL. Phone: 071-387 9494.

(11) *TSW (Television South-West).* Address: Derry's Cross, Plymouth, Devon PL1 2SP. Phone: 0752 663322. Serves the South-West of England (parts of

Somerset and Dorset, the Scilly Islands, Cornwall, and Devon).

(12) *TV-am*. Address: Breakfast Television Centre, Hawley Crescent, London NW1 8EF. Phone 071-267-4300. Broadcasts early morning programs throughout the UK between 6:00am - 9:00am daily.

(13) *TVS Television (Television South PLC)*. Address: Television Centre, Southampton SO9 5HZ. Phone: 0703 634211. Serves South and Southeast England.

(14) *Tyne Tees Television*. Address: The Television Centre, City Rd., Newcastle upon Tyne NE1 2AL. Phone 091-2610181. Serves the North and East areas of England.

(15) *Ulster Television*. Address: Havelock House, Ormeau Rd., Belfast BT7 1EB Northern Ireland. Phone: 0232 328122. Serves Northern Ireland.

(16) *Yorkshire Television*. Address: The Television Centre, Leeds LS3 1JS. Phone: 0532 438283. Serves the Yorkshire area.

Additional broadcast services are:

(1) *Channel Four Television*. 60 Charlotte St., London W1P 2AX. Phone: 071-631 4444. This company is a subsidiary of IBA, but is not a contractor.

(2) *Radio Telefis Eireann*. Address: Donnybrook, Dublin 4, Ireland. Phone: 081 693111. The national network of the Republic of Ireland.

(3) *Wales4 CYMRU-S4C*. Address: Welsh Fourth Channel Authority, Sophia Close, Cardiff, Wales CF19XY. Phone (0222) 43421. The network for Wales.

Other services include a satellite service which started broadcasts in August, 1989: *British Satellite Broadcasting (BSB)*. Address: 70 Brompton Rd., London SW3 1EY.

Phone: 071-581 1166. The service offers three channels (Galaxy, The Movie Channel, and NOW) to homes throughout England.

Independent Local Radio (ILR): The IBA organization responsible for providing independent local radio service throughout England. The first ILR station started in 1973 and ILR presently contracts with 46 independent radio stations, with additional franchises pending. The stations are required by law to provide a wide range of programming and most stations lean heavily on local-interest programs. A large portion of programs are live and/or aimed toward local or regional cultural events. For a complete listing of member stations (names, addresses, and phone numbers), see IBA's *Factfile.*

Broadcasting Associations and Organizations

Association of Independent Producers (AIP). Address: 17-18 Great Pulteney St., London W1R 3DG. Phone: 071-434 0181.
Founded in 1976, it currently represents nearly 1,000 film and television producers. It represents the interests of its membership to the government, broadcasting stations, and production companies. It also provides a wide range of educational courses and other membership services.

British Film and Television Producers' Association (BFTPA). Address: Paramount House, 162-170 Wardour St., London W1V 4LA. Phone: 071-437 7700. Founded in 1938. Previous name: Film Production Employers Association.
Represents the independent production industry in all areas of concern in film and television.

Independent Broadcasting Authority. See above.

Independent Programme Producers' Association (IPPA). Address: 50 Berwick St., London W1V 4RD. Phone: 071-439 7034. Trade association for Britain's independent television producers and production companies.

Independent Television Association. Knighton House, 56 Mortimer St., London W1N 8AN. Phone: 071-636-6866. Until 1988, the organizational name was: Independent Television Companies Association.

   The trade association exists to represent the television production companies (the ITV companies) appointed by the IBA to provide independent television programming. (See membership list under IBA.)

Independent Television News. Address: ITN House, 48 Wells St., London W1P 4DE. Phone: 071-637-2424.

   The company provides news programs for Channel 4, the Independent Television network, and other organizations.

The Radio Industry Council. Address: Landseer House, 19 Charing Cross Rd., London WC2H 0ES. Phone: 071-930 3206.

Radio Society of Great Britain. Address: Lambda House, Cranborne Rd., Potters Bar, Herts EN6 3JE. Phone: 0707 59015.

Royal Television Society. Tavistock House East, Tavistock Sq., London, WC1H 9HR England.

Television and Radio Research Facilities

BBC Data Enquiry Service (TV, film, radio, press cuttings) See: the profile of the BBC earlier in this chapter.

British Film Institute. See: the profile of the BFI earlier in this chapter.

Independent Broadcasting Authority Library

Address: 70 Brompton Rd., London SW3 1EY

Phone: 071-584 7011

The Underground: Knightsbridge.

Hours: 10:00 am to 5:30 pm weekdays. Open to visitors by appointment.

Visitor arrangements: The obligation of the Main Library at Brompton Road is to serve IBA staff, but it is open to serious researchers upon approval and acceptance. Requests may be made by letter or phone to the Library. However, the individual Libraries of the ITV stations are not open to the public; they are private production research libraries for the staffs of the companies. They do, however, have good historical collections of their company activities and can sometimes be approached with questions for information if all other sources are exhausted.

The Collection: The majority of books and periodicals deal with broadcasting, telecommunications, engineering, and other technical matters important to the management and development of television and radio facilities. Coverage is international and there are a number of historical titles. The Library has complete sets of ITV/ILR publications and annual reports, the *BBC Handbook* and *BBC Annual Report and Handbook* (1948-1987), and sets of *TV Times* and *Radio Times* from 1954 to date. A large collection of newspaper clippings dating from 1952 is arranged by subject and includes information about people, television series, press releases, publicity packages, and numerous other subjects.

Services: Limited photocopy services are available, subject to the copyright laws.

POPULAR MUSIC RESEARCH IN GREAT BRITAIN

The music industry in England is fascinating in that the country is influential on the international level well beyond what its geographical size and sales volume would normally justify. Other European countries have larger markets, but most new acts try to "break" in England as a means of reaching into the other markets.

Historically, radio has been important in developing the popularity of new acts as well as maintaining the success of established ones. Stations in England tend to play a variety of

music, not just a single format as is currently the norm in the
United States. Some do exist, however, as part of the
Independent Broadcasting Authority system. In fact, the
IBA just awarded a franchise for London's first jazz radio
station, London Jazz Radio.

BPI Yearbook. Annual, 1976-   . The British Phonographic Industry Limited, Roxburghe House, 273/287 Regent St., London W1R
7PB. Phone: 071-629 8642. ISSN 0142-7636.
   A complete review of the British recording industry that covers
   every format. Charts cover record, tape, CD, and cassette
   performance from every angle: sales, artists, regional airplay,
   income, awards, video sales, and foreign markets.

British Broadcasting Corporation (BBC). *Central Music Library.
Catalogues*. See section on the BBC, pages 517-519.

British Catalogue of Audio-visual materials; a subject catalogue of
audiovisual materials processed by the British Library. London:
British Library. Bibliographic Services. 481 p.,· 1979. LC 80-
498535, ISBN 0900220775. Updated by *Supplements*.

British Catalogue of Music. Semiannual, 1957-   . Annual cumulation. London: The British Library, Bibliographic Services Division. LC 58-2570, ISSN 0068-1407.
   A listing of new music acquired by the Library (from any source
   worldwide), new music published in Great Britain, and foreign
   music available in Great Britain through an agent. See Also: the
   description of the British Library.

British Federation of Music Festivals Yearbook. Annual, 1973-   .
Macclesfield, Cheshire: British Federation of Music Festivals.
ISSN 0309-8044.

British Music Yearbook. Annual, 1972-   . London: Rhinegold
Publishing. ISSN 0306-5928. Previous title: *Music Yearbook*.
Distributed in the United States by Schirmer Books/Macmillan
(New York). LC 75-649724, ISSN 0306-5928.

Includes information about all types of music, from opera to stage and television. Part 1 is a survey of music for the year and includes a variety of statistics; Part 2 contains directory information for businesses, professional organizations, and societies; Part 3 is a directory of professional services; Part 4 is a directory of performers and how they may be contacted; Part 5 lists festivals and competitions; Part 6 is directory of trade information (record companies, music and book publishers, periodicals, etc.); Part 7 lists libraries, museums, and educational facilities; and Part 8 lists music in places of worship.

The British Union Catalogue of Music Periodicals. Compiled by Anthony Hodges. London: The Library Association. 145 p., 1985. LC 85-168834, ISBN 0853655170.

The book lists a large number of British periodical titles, along with their starting dates and title changes. Following the basic bibliographic information, it lists libraries in Great Britain which have the title in their collection. Although it's not very comprehensive, the information is difficult to find anywhere else and this alone makes the book valuable.

The Catalogue of Printed Music in the British Library to 1980. Edited by Laureen Baillie and Robert Malchin. New York: Saur. 62 vols. 1981-1987. LC 81-151651, ISBN 0851579000.

A comprehensive historical listing of every piece of printed music that can be identified in the British Library. In addition to the Library's own catalog, a number of bibliographies, catalogues, and other historical materials were used to compile this work.

Gramophone, Spoken Word & Miscellaneous Catalogue. Annual, 1960- . Kenton, Middlesex: General Gramophone Publications. ISSN 0262-0812.

Annual list of recordings, in all formats, available in England.

Guide to Recording in the UK. Annual, 1981- . Rickmansworth, Middlesex: Association of Professional Recording Studios.

Directory of recording studios, equipment, and services for the industry. Lists industry personnel.

International Music & Opera Guide. Annual, 1977- . London: Tantivy Press. Distributed in the United States by Zoetrope (New York). LC 86-25643. Previous title: *International Music Guide* (LC 76-4626, 1977-1985).

International Who's Who in Music and Musicians' Directory. Triennial, 1935- . Cambridgeshire: Melrose Press. LC 76-641873, ISSN 0307-2894. Distributed in the United States by Gale Research Company. Previous title: *Who's Who in Music.*

Jazz in the Movies, by David Meeker. London: Talisman. New enlarged edition. 336 p., 1981. Reprinted by Da Capo Press (New York) in 1982. LC 81-17364, ISBN 0306761475.
    Alphabetical by film title, with a listing of the music titles and musicians in each film. The book also covers information on television films in which jazz was played or musicians appeared.

Jazz Records 1897-1942, by Brian Rust. Chigwell, Essex: Storyville Publications. 5th rev. and enl. edition. 2 vols., 1982. ISBN 0902391046.
    Arranged by name of the artist, this work lists over 30,000 early jazz and blues recordings (mostly 78 rpm) in Britain and the United States. Each entry has record label and number, musicians and/others involved with the recording, and recording session information if known.

Kemps International Music and Recording Industry Yearbook. Annual, 1965- . London: Kemps Group. Distributed in the United States by R. R. Bowker, New York. 20th ed., 1988. ISBN 0862591171.

Music in British Libraries; a directory of resources. Compiled and edited by Barbara Penney. London: Library Association. 3d ed., 452 p., 1981. LC 81-212170, ISBN 0-85365-981-8.
    A review of the music collections of over 700 libraries throughout Great Britain. Notes about each indicate services available, number of staff, and any special collections the library may hold. The book provides good coverage of the BBC music libraries, although the public does not have access to the collections.

Music Master Catalogue. Annual, 1974- . Monthly updates. Sussex: John Humphries Publishing, Ltd. LC 83-643234. Previous title: *Music Master* (ISSN:0308-9347). This publication incorporates two other titles: *Singles Master* and *Record Prices.*
  A catalog of records that are in print. Arranged in several sections: Artist, singles (by title), and albums (by title). Record labels and record numbers are given for each recording.

Music Master Labels List. Annual, 1980- . Hastings, Sussex: John Humphries Publishing. 6th ed., 1985.

Music Master. Annual, 1981- . Hastings, Sussex: John Humphries Publishing. LC 83-643234.

Music Week Directory. Annual, 1976- . London: Music World. LC 88-10851, ISSN 0267-3290. Previous title: *Music and Video Week Directory* (ISSN 0264-3383), *Music Week Industry Year Book,* and *Music and Video Week Yearbook.*
  A comprehensive guide to the music industry in Great Britain.

Music World Year Book. Annual, 1981- . Watford, Herts: Music Trade Association. LC 85-646138. Previous title: *Music World Directory.*

PRS Yearbook. Annual, 1977- . London: Performing Right Society. Alternate Title: *Performing Right Yearbook.* LC 88-649997, ISSN 0309-0884.
  The yearbook covers all areas of the performing arts and gives a variety of useful statistics for the year. One example: a breakdown of royalties paid to the Society by the various areas of the entertainment field for distribution to its members. See Also: page 536.

Professional Register of Artists. Annual, 1976- . London: Incorporated Society of Musicians. A directory for working members of the society (composers, performers, conductors).

Showcall. Annual, 1973- . London: Carson and Comerford. See: pages 443-444.

The White Book: the international production directory. ISSN 0265-8224, ISBN (1988): 0-947569-04-9. Subtitle reads: the international production directory to the entertainment, leisure, record, concert, film, video, conference and exhibition industries.

British Music Periodicals

BASCA News. Quarterly, 1979- . London: British Academy of Songwriters, Composers & Authors. ISSN: 0144-9621. See Also: page 535.

Blues & Soul. Biweekly, 1966- . Napfielf Publishers, 153 Praed St., London W2 1RL. LC 84-647873. Previous titles: *Black Music & Jazz Review* and *Black Music.*
  Articles, interviews, and historical pieces cover all types of Black music, with an emphasis on jazz. Also covered are such genres as reggae, soul, African music, and others. Publishes both British and American music charts. Reviews singles, albums, and new literature.

Blues Unlimited. Quarterly, 1963- . London: BU Publications. LC 88-662988, ISSN 0006-5153. Indexed in: MLA, Jazz Index.

Composer: magazine of the British Music Information Centre. 3 issues yearly, 1944- . London: BMIC. LC 86-13065, ISSN 0010-4337. This title supersedes the Guild's *Bulletin.* Indexed in: British Humanities Index, MI.
  Articles about contemporary music, news and new acquisitions of the Centre, and reviews of performances, new recordings, and recent books.

Contact: a journal of contemporary music. 3 issues yearly, 1971-. Philip Martin Music Books, 22 Huntington Rd., York YO3 7RL. LC 81-642085, ISSN 0308-5066.
  While the journal is academic in nature and covers more classical than pop music, it still approaches modern topics and styles that reflect all music. Reviews new books, some periodical articles, written music, and recordings.

Country and Western Roundabout. Quarterly, 1962- . c/o R.F. Benson, Editor, 21 Roseacres, Takeley, Dunmow, Essex. ISSN 0011-0094.

Country Music People. Monthly, 1970- . London: Country Music Press. LC 75-647509, ISSN: 0591-2237.

Country Music Roundup. Monthly, 1977- . Upper Precinct, Lincoln: Country Music Roundup Publishing Company. ISSN 0140-5721.

Folk Music Journal. Annual, 1965- . London: English Folk Dance and Song Society, 2 Regents Park Rd., London NW1 7AY. Phone: 071-485 2205. LC 86-9346, ISSN 0531-9684. Available on microform and through the document delivery service of UMI. Supersedes: *Journal of the English Folk Dance and Song Society* (1932-1964). Indexed in: British Humanities Index, MI, MLA, Arts & Humanities Citation Index.

Folk Roots. Monthly, 1979- . London: Southern Rag, Ltd. LC 86-640070.

Footnote; the magazine for New Orleans jazz. Bimonthly, 1969-89. Royston, Herts: Footnote. LC 75-648872, ISSN 0308-1990. Indexed in: MI, Jazz Index.

Gramophone. Monthly, 1923- . General Gramophone Publications, 177-179 Kenton Rd., Harrow, Middlesex HA3 0HA. Phone: 081-907 4476. LC 85-649842, ISSN 0017-310X. Incorporates: *Cassettes & Cartridges.* Indexed in: MI.
  Reviews new recordings in all musical areas as well as audio releases. Also reviews new literature, equipment, and some videos.

Guitar International. Monthly, 1972- . Mere, Wiltshire: Musical New Services, Ltd. LC 87-648698. Previous title: *Guitar* (LC 74-642359).
  Covers the world of performing and playing for all areas of guitar music. Discusses writing, technique and style, performing, new equipment, and personalities. Interviews with notable guitarists; reviews of new record releases, live performances, and literature.

Hi-Fi News and Record Review. Monthly, 1956- . Croydon: Link House Magazines. LC 82-5232, ISSN 0142-6230. Incorporates: *Audio Record Review.* Previous title: *Hi Fi News.* Available on microform from UMI. Indexed in: British Technology Index.
Covers pop, classical, and jazz music as well as various equipment products.

Hi-fi For Pleasure. Monthly, 1973- . Spotlight Publications: Morgan Grampian Group, 40 Long Acre, London WC2E 9JT. Phone: 071-836 1522.
Reviews of new equipment, buying guide, and reviews of new equipment, systems, services, and products. Good coverage of the CD industry developments.

International Musician and Recording World. Monthly, 1975- . London: Cover Publications. LC 76-645865, ISSN 0307-1472.
Historical articles, current topics, interviews, and profiles of genres and performers. Geared toward industry personnel and includes regular features regarding studio activity, equipment, trade news and events, and new developments. Reviews new recordings, books, and some performances.

Jazz Journal International. Monthly, 1948- . London: Jazz Journal Ltd. LC 77-643205, ISSN 0140-2285. Previous titles: *Jazz Journal and Jazz and Blues* (1974-1977) and *Jazz Journal* (1959-1973). Current title started in 1977. Available on microform and through document delivery service from UMI. Indexed in: MI, Jazz Index.
Includes interviews, historical articles, reviews of records and performances, plus news of the jazz world.

Melody Maker. Weekly, 1926- . London: IPC Magazines. Address: 1 Throwley Way, Sutton SM1 4QQ. Phone: 081-643-8040. LC 51-2576, ISSN 0025-9012. Available on microform from UMI. Indexed in: MI, Jazz Index.
Newspaper format covering the recording, live performance, and radio areas of the music industry. Articles about the latest news, industry issues, personnel changes, legislation, and activities of importance. Reviews latest releases. Has weekly popularity charts for many music formats and genres. Similar to *Billboard,* with

coverage limited to Great Britain. An excellent source of historical information and statistics concerning British popular music and performers.

Music & Musicians International. Monthly, 1952- . London: Orpheus Publications. LC 88-33002, ISSN 0952-2697. Previous title: *Music and Musicians* (1952-1980) and *Music & Musicians* (1981-1987). Incorporates another title: *Records and Recordings.* Provides own index to its record and book reviews. Is also indexed in: British Humanities Index.

An all-encompassing review of popular music, with an emphasis on the musicians and bands/orchestras that play everything from jazz to Sousa. Maintains a calendar of festivals schedules, news, social events. Reviews books, concerts and festivals, recordings, and equipment.

Music Business; musical instrument retailers and allied trade.Colchester: Feedback Publications. Monthly, 1986- . ISSN: 0269-0292.

Music Review. Quarterly, 1940- . Cambridge, Black Bear Press. LC 56-29749, ISSN: 0027-4445. Available on microform from UMI. Indexed in: British Humanities Index, Humanities Index, Arts & Humanities Citation Index, Music Index, RILM Abstracts of Music Literature.

Leans heavily toward classical, but does include some popular music.

Music Week. Weekly, 1959- . London: Spotlight Publications. ISSN: 0265-1548. Previous titles: *Music and Video Week* and *Record Retailer.*

Covers industry news for the music and recording industries. See Also: *Music Week Directory* for their annual.

Music World. Monthly, 1913- . Published for the Music Trades Association by Turret-Wheatland, Pen House, Penn Place, Rickmansworth, Herts WD3 1SN. Phone: 0923-777000. LC 82-643326. Previous titles: *Music Trades International* and *Pianomaker* (the 1913 original title). The current title started in 1979.

Industry magazine for businesses dealing with musical instruments. Articles evaluate new instruments, report on products and services, and review business conferences.

Musical Times. Monthly, 1844- . London: Novello and Company. LC 54-525, ISSN: 0027-4666. Available on microform and document delivery service of UMI. Indexed in: British Humanities Index, Arts & Humanities Citation Index, Music Index, RILM Abstracts of Music Literature.

New Hi-Fi Sound. Bimonthly, 1976- . Haymarket Magazines, 10-12 The Causeway, Teddington, Middlesex TW11 0JE. LC 84-641952. Previous titles: *Popular Hi-fi & Sound* (itself formed from *Popular Hi-Fi* and *Hi-Fi Sound*).

New Musical Express. Weekly, 1952- . London: IPC Magazines. ISSN 0028-6362.

Overtures; the magazine devoted to the musical on stage and record. Bimonthly, 1980- . Wembley, Middlesex: Overtures.

Popular Music. 3 issues yearly, 1981- . Cambridge and New York: Cambridge University Press. LC 82-645331, ISSN: 0261-1430. Indexed in: Music Index.
   A scholarly and well documented approach to all areas of popular music, including TV, video, and film music. Emphasis is on British and American music, but some attention is given to other countries. Recent issues have covered country music videos, television theme recordings, jazz in the ghetto, the music of Bob Dylan, and the popular music of various countries. Bibliographies accompany most articles. Extensive reviews of the latest literature of the field.

Popular Video. Monthly, 1980- . London: M & V Publications. ISSN: 0261-4200. Previous title: *Music and Video* (ISSN: 0144-7114).

PRS News. Semiannual, 1954- . The Performing Right Society, 29/33 Berners St., London W1P 4AA. Phone: 071-580 5844. ISSN 0309-0019. Previous titles: *Performing Right* (1954-1976) and

Performing Right News (1976-1988). See also: Performing Right Society, page 536.

R M. (Record Mirror). Weekly, 1954- . London: Spotlight Publications. LC 86-640743. Previous titles: *Record Mirror* (1979-1985), *Record Mirror & Pop Star,* and *Superpop.* Current title started in 1985.

Sound Scrutiny; a quarterly journal reviewing sound discs and cassettes for librarians and library users. Quarterly, 1983- . Ealing College of Higher Education, School of Library and Information Studies. LC 86-10933, ISSN 0264-0996.
   Reviews of new sound recordings in all formats, well-researched discographies, and reviews of new literature. Previous title: *Cassette Scrutiny.*

Tempo; a quarterly review of modern music. Quarterly, 1939- . Boosey and Hawkes Music Publishers, 295 Regent St., London W1R 6JH. Phone: 071-580 2060. LC 51-36700, ISSN: 0040-2982. Indexed in: British Humanities Index, Music Index, RILM Abstracts of Music Literature.
   Covers all areas of modern British music and reviews books and periodicals, recordings, composers. It's one of the older British music publications and has been included for many years in several major indexing sources.

What Hi-fi? Monthly, 1971- . Haymarket Publishing, 38-42 Hampton Rd., Teddington, Middlesex TW11 0JE. Phone: 081-977 8787. Previous title: *Popular Hi-Fi.* New equipment evaluations, buying guides, answers to technical questions.

Which Compact Disc & Hi-Fi for Pleasure. Monthly. London: Spotlight Publications.
   News and reviews of the latest CD releases and equipment.

British Music Organizations

British Academy of Songwriters, Composers & Authors (BASCA). Address: 34 Hanway St., London W1P 9DE. Phone: 071-436 2261. Publications: *BASCA News* (Quarterly, 1979-).

British Music Society. 100 Castle Rd., Chatham, Kent ME4 5HX. Phone: 0634 49939. Publishes an *Annual* and provides some research assistance and advice to members.

Composers' Guild of Great Britain. Address: 10 Stratford Pl., London W1N 9AE. Phone: 071-499 4795.

Confederation of Entertainment Unions. Address: 60-62 Clapham Rd., London SW9 0JJ.

Country Music Association (London Office of the American organization). 52 Haymarket St., Suite 3, London SW1Y 4RP. Phone: 071-930 2445.

Musician's Union. Address: 60-62 Clapham Rd., London SW9 0JJ. Phone: 071-582 5566.

The Performing Right Society. Address: 29-33 Berners St., London W1P 4AA. Phone: 071-580 5544. Represents authors, composers, and publishers of music. Publishes a newsletter for members (*PRS News,* irregular) and a yearbook (*Performing Right Yearbook,* annual; ISSN: 0309-0884).

Phonographic Performance Ltd. Address: Ganton House, 14-22 Ganton St., London W1V 1LB. Phone: 071-437 0311. A British recording industry company to license public performances and sound recordings.

Music Research Facilities

The libraries listed below were selected because they had something more to offer than just a general music collection. They are either depository libraries for the British government or have rare, special collections which contribute to the history of British music. For the most part, music collections in British libraries are so small that you will need to go to a depository library in order to find a collection of any size. If you need a more in-depth overview of British music research facilities, *Music In British Libraries* by Barbara Penney is an effective place to start.

British Institute of Recorded Sound

Address: 29 Exhibition Rd., London SW7.

Phone: 071-589 6603/4

Hours: 10:30 am to 6:00 pm weekdays; closed during lunch.

Visitor Arrangements: Open to the public without restriction. However, visitors would be wise to call ahead of time to reserve listening equipment.

The Collection: Books, periodicals, recordings, tapes. Special collections of classical music, some oral histories, and live recordings of theater performances made at the several British theaters. It also has a substantial collection of sounds and sound effects.

The British Library. Music Library

Address: Great Russell St., London WC1B 3DG.

Phone: 071-636 1544

Hours: Varying daily hours, Monday through Saturday.

Publications: The British Catalogue of Music. In addition, there are small pamphlets and catalogues available at the Library which provide details about some of the special music collections.

Visitor arrangements: See the main section about the British Library earlier in this chapter. Researchers must meet the requirements stated there.

The Collection: The British Library is the Copyright depository for all British music and, as such, contains one of the largest and historically valuable collections in the world. As with other subject areas, the researcher must be aware that he or she will need to go to different parts of the Library.

Many rare items must be used in the North Library, which is reserved for rare materials. General books must be used in the Main Reading Room. The Music Library concentrates on musical scores for all types of music, studies in music theory, and is the location of several large special collections on different types of British music. Most books, printed music, and music manuscripts can be read here. The Department of Manuscripts includes correspondence, some manuscripts, and other original materials important to the study of British music history.

Cambridge University

Address: University Library, Music Department, West Rd., Cambridge CB3 9DR.

Phone: 0223 61441.

Hours: Daily, except during special periods. Check ahead of time to be sure of the hours.

Visitor arrangements: By appointment, at the approval of the Librarian.

The Collection: The Library is a Copyright Library and therefore has a large general collection of music materials. The basic collection is comprised of books, periodicals, recordings, and scores. It has a number of early music scores and some music literature dating back to the 16th century.

Music Information Centre

Address: 10 Stratford Pl., London W1N 9AE.

Phone: 071-499 8567

Hours: 10:00 am - 5:00 pm, weekdays.

Visitor arrangements: By appointment.

The Collection: A small highly specialized collection concentrating on 20th-Century British music, especially contemporary composers. Materials include books, printed music, scores, manuscripts.

National Discography, The Sound Recordings Information Bureau

Address: Elgar House, 41 Streatham High Rd., London SW16 1ER.

National Library of Scotland

Address: National Library of Scotland, Music Room, George IV Bridge, Edinburgh EH1 IEW Scotland.

Phone: 031 226 4531

Hours: Monday through Friday, Saturday morning. Call ahead to verify hours.

Publications: Music in the National Library of Scotland. The Library also has several catalogues available that list parts of their manuscript collections.

Visitor requirements: Visitors may register in person at the time of their visit, which does not have to be approved ahead of time. However, as always, it would probably be to your benefit to contact the staff ahead of time since the staff is small and the reading room facilities limited.

The Collection: This is a Copyright Library and therefore includes a great deal of music published in Britain during the 19th and 20th centuries. The Collection is made up of books, periodicals, printed music, recordings, tapes, microforms, and some voice recordings. All parts of the Collection are available for reference only, but some photocopy services are available. As might be expected, a major emphasis of the Collection is on Scottish music. The Library has several major collections on particular areas of Scottish music, with some of the collections hundreds of volumes in size and containing correspondence, rare manuscripts, and original scores. Some of the materials are described in published catalogues.

The National Library of Wales

Address: The National Library of Wales, Aberystwyth, Dyfed SY23 3BU Wales

Phone: 0970 3816

Hours: 9:30 am - 6:00pm weekdays, Saturday morning.

Visitor requirements: Applications must be submitted and approved by the librarian. This can conceivably be accomplished in person at the time of your visit, but you might want to inquire ahead of time.

The Collection: A Copyright depository library. The Library has a small number of books and periodicals about music in general, but its strength is in a substantial collection of information about Welsh music. This includes printed music, information about Welsh composers, and a historical collection of 19th-century Welsh music.

National Sound Archives (The British Library)

See the section about the British Library in BRITISH REFERENCE RESOURCES.

Oxford University, The Bodleian Library

Address: Bodleian Library, Oxford OX1 3BG

Phone: 0865 44675

Hours: Weekdays and Saturday mornings.

Visitor requirements: The Library has a strict application process. The requirements are the same as those listed for the theater collection discussed earlier in this chapter.

The Collection: A Copyright depository library since the 1800s. Published music is arranged chronologically by year, and then by title. The Library has a large number of boxed sheet music collections that are in the process of being cataloged. The most important of these collections is the Walter N. H. Harding Collection of Sheet Music. Of special value are music hall songs, 18th-century music, songbooks, and vocal scores from musicals. The Collection also includes an extensive number of American popular songs from the 1930s to date. Any American music copyrighted in England will be in this Collection. Depending on the collection, the music will be arranged in various ways: broad subject area, composers, musical shows, and even by size.

INDEX

ABOUT THE AUTHOR

BARBARA PRUETT is a librarian, researcher, and writer who currently resides in Washington, D.C. She has a B.S. from Indiana University and a Master's in Librarianship from California State University at San Jose. In the early 1970s she was head of the Information/Research Center for Cesar Chavez's United Farm Workers before taking a position as head of Catholic University of America's Social Sciences Library. She has been active in the library profession for many years and has served two terms on the Council of the American Library Association and worked on a number of committees. Today she divides her time between being a library director for a special library on international trade and writing about subjects in the entertainment industry. She indicates a preference for the country music field and is the author of *Marty Robbins: Fast Cars and Country Music* (Scarecrow Press, 1990).